The Age of Commodity

The Age of Commodity

Water Privatization in Southern Africa

Edited by

David A. McDonald
and
Greg Ruiters

London • Sterling, VA

First published by Earthscan in the UK and USA in 2005

Copyright © David A. McDonald and Greg Ruiters, 2005

All rights reserved

ISBN: 1-84407-134-0 paperback
       1-84407-135-9 hardback

Typesetting by JS Typesetting, Porthcawl, Mid Glamorgan
Printed and bound in the UK by Cromwell Press Ltd, Trowbridge
Cover design by Danny Gillespie

For a full list of publications please contact:

Earthscan
8–12 Camden High Street
London, NW1 0JH, UK
Tel: +44 (0)20 7387 8558
Fax: +44 (0)20 7387 8998
Email: earthinfo@earthscan.co.uk
Web: **www.earthscan.co.uk**

22883 Quicksilver Drive, Sterling, VA 20166-2012, USA

Earthscan is an imprint of James and James (Science Publishers) Ltd and publishes in association with the International Institute for Environment and Development

A catalogue record for this book is available from the British Library

Library of Congress Cataloging-in-Publication Data

McDonald, David A. (David Alexander)
    The age of commodity : water privatization in Southern Africa / David A. McDonald and Greg Ruiters.
    p. cm.
    Includes bibliographical references and index.
    ISBN 1-84407-134-0 (pbk.) – ISBN 1-84407-135-9 (hardback)
    1. Water utilities—Africa, Southern. 2. Water-supply—Economic aspects—Africa, Southern. 3. Privatization—Africa, Southern. I. Ruiters, Greg, 1959– II. Title.

HD4465.A356M38 2005
363.6′1–dc22

                                                                                              2004022851

Printed on elemental chlorine-free paper

Contents

List of Figures, Tables and Boxes	vii
About the Contributors	ix
Acknowledgements	xi
List of Acronyms and Abbreviations	xii

Introduction: From Public to Private (to Public Again?)   1
David A. McDonald and Greg Ruiters

PART 1 THEORY AND PRACTICE

1 **Theorizing Water Privatization in Southern Africa**   13
   David A. McDonald and Greg Ruiters

2 **The New Water Architecture of SADC**   43
   Larry A. Swatuk

3 **The Constitutional Implications of Commercializing Water in South Africa**   59
   Sean Flynn and Danwood Mzikenge Chirwa

4 **Turning Off the Taps on the GATS**   77
   Karl Flecker and Tony Clarke

PART 2 CASE STUDIES IN SOUTH AFRICA

5 **Entrenching Inequalities: The Impact of Corporatization on Water Injustices in Pretoria**   99
   Peter McInnes

Box 1 *South African Water Caucus (SAWC) Resolution on Water and Trade Adopted August 2003*   118

6 **Managing the Poor by Remote Control: Johannesburg's Experiments with Prepaid Water Meters**   120
   Ebrahim Harvey

Box 2 *Resolution on Prepaid Meters by South African Municipal Workers' Union (Samwu)*   128

7   Public Money, Private Failure: Testing the Limits of Market Based
    Solutions for Water Delivery in Nelspruit   130
    Laïla Smith, Amanda Gillett, Shauna Mottiar and Fiona White

8   The Political Economy of Public–Private Contracts: Urban Water
    in Two Eastern Cape Towns   148
    Greg Ruiters

Box 3 *Declaration of the Coalition Against Water Privatisation (South Africa)* 166

9   The Murky Waters of Second Wave Neoliberalism:
    Corporatization as a Service Delivery Model in Cape Town   168
    Laïla Smith

Box 4 *Western Cape Anti-Eviction Co-ordinating Committee (South Africa),
      Press Statement*   188

10 'Free Water' as Commodity: The Paradoxes of Durban's Water
    Service Transformations   189
    Alex Loftus

Box 5 *The Phiri Water Wars of 2003*   204

11 The Rise and Fall of Water Privatization in Rural South Africa:
    A Critical Evaluation of the ANC's First Term of Office, 1994–1999   206
    Stephen Greenberg

PART 3 CASE STUDIES IN THE REGION

12 Stillborn in Harare: Attempts to Privatize Water in a City in
    Crisis   225
    Rekopantswe Mate

13 'There is *Still* No Alternative': The Beginnings of Water
    Privatization in Lusaka   240
    Karen Cocq

14 Water Privatization in Namibia: Creating a New Apartheid?   258
    Labour Resource and Research Institute (LaRRI)

Box 6 *Draft Manifesto Against Water Privatization in Namibia*   273

15 The New Face of Conditionalities: The World Bank and Water
    Privatization in Ghana   275
    Rudolf Nsorwine Amenga-Etego and Sara Grusky

Box 7 *The Accra Declaration on the Right to Water*   291

Index   293

List of Figures, Tables and Boxes

FIGURES

5.1	Tshwane households by income range	102
5.2	Average annual daily demand sold per area per day, year ending June 2001	103
5.3	Monthly household water consumption by tariff block in Pretoria and Mamelodi (July 2002–June 2003)	104
5.4	Tshwane household water tariff (2003–2004)	109
5.5	Tshwane's household tariff compared with Cape Town and Johannesburg (2003–2004)	111
7.1	Location of Mpumalanga Province in South Africa	131
7.2	Map of (renamed) Mbombela Municipality	137
9.1	Monthly consumption of 60 kl of water in Cape Town and Tygerberg (1997–2002)	175
9.2	Monthly consumption of 10 kl of water in Cape Town and Tygerberg (1997–2002)	176
9.3	Total water cutoffs in the Cape Town and Tygerberg administrations (1991–2001)	181
9.4	Water cutoffs per 1000 customers billed in Tygerberg (1999–2001)	182
13.1	Water bills for different consumption levels under NWASCO tariff structure	249

TABLES

1.1	Different forms of water services 'privatization'	16
2.1	SADC states' access to clean water and sanitation	44
2.2	International river basins shared between SADC states	49
4.1	GATS rules: current and under negotiation	81
5.1	Existing water service level summary	102
7.1	Monthly household income by locality and percentage of population in the Nelspruit TLC	132
7.2	Unemployment rates by locality in the Nelspruit TLC	133
7.3	Water tariffs in Nelspruit	142
9.1	Water tariff schedule for 2002/03	176
10.1	Charges in rand/kl of water consumed as of July 2003	192

11.1	Number and percentage of non-urban African households with selected water supply, 1996–1999	209
11.2	Percentage of African non-urban households paying for water, 1995–1999	214
11.3	Distance non-urban African household residents have to go to fetch water, 1996–1999	216
11.4	Per capita consumption on various water supply projects	217
11.5	Non-functioning schemes	217
12.1	Harare's sources of water and their net capacities	228
13.1	Severn-Trent's recommended 'rising banded tariff'	252

Boxes

15.1	Water sector reform conditions in IMF and World Bank loans to Ghana	282
15.2	Major consultant firms commissioned on Ghana water privatization	287

About the Contributors

Rudolf Nsorwine Amenga-Etego is a lawyer, farmer and activist. He is a member of the governing council of the Foundation for Security and Development in Africa, executive director of the Foundation for Grassroots Initiatives in Africa and national campaign coordinator of the Coalition Against the Privatization of Water in Ghana. He is also the Goldman prize recipient for 2004.

Danwood Mzikenge Chirwa is a lecturer in law at the University of Cape Town. He has published widely in the field of human rights and has practised law in Malawi.

Tony Clarke has been a civil society observer, writer and activist on international trade issues for over 30 years. He is founder and director of the Polaris Institute in Canada and co-author of several books on trade, water privatization and anti-corporate globalization activism.

Karen Cocq is completing a Master's degree in geography at Queen's University in Canada.

Karl Flecker is the education coordinator with the Polaris Institute. The Institute has been working with public sector unions and civil society in a number of countries, including South Africa, to better understand the implications of the WTO's GATS agreement.

Sean Flynn is an associate at Spiegel & McDiarmid in Washington, DC, and founder/director of the Institute on Law and Development. He was a clerk for Chief Justice Arthur Chaskalson in South Africa and a lecturer in constitutional law at the University of Witwaterstrand, Johannesburg.

Amanda Gillett holds a Master's degree in public and development management from the University of the Witwatersrand, Johannesburg. She is currently a programme manager with the Australian Agency for International Development (AusAID) in Pretoria.

Stephen Greenberg works in the rural NGO sector in South Africa as a researcher, writer and policy analyst. He has a Master's degree from the Department of Geography and Environmental Studies at the University of Witwatersrand.

Sara Grusky is an academic and midwife who now works with Public Citizen's 'Water for All' campaign, defending the rights of communities to clean and affordable water.

Ebrahim Harvey is a former journalist and recently completed a Master's degree at the University of the Witwatersrand on the Johannesburg water contract.

The Labour Resource and Research Institute (LaRRI) is a labour-based organization based in Windhoek, Namibia, which carries out education and research programmes on labour and development issues in Southern Africa. It is also a founding member of the African Labour Research Network (ALRN).

Alex Loftus is completing a DPhil in the School of Geography and the Environment at Oxford University looking at the political ecology of struggles for water in Durban.

Rekopantswe Mate is a lecturer in the Department of Sociology at the University of Zimbabwe. Her research focuses on development issues.

Peter McInnes is completing a Master's degree in sociology at the University of Witwatersrand on social mobilization, municipal services and the South African Bill of Rights.

David A. McDonald is director of Development Studies at Queen's University in Canada and co-director of the Municipal Services Project.

Shauna Mottiar is based in Durban as a researcher for the Centre for Policy Studies. She is a PhD candidate at the University of the Witwatersrand conducting research on democratic consolidation.

Greg Ruiters is senior lecturer in Political and International Studies at Rhodes University, South Africa, and co-director of the Municipal Services Project.

Laïla Smith is director of research and evaluation for the Contract Management Unit for the City of Johannesburg, and is responsible for monitoring Johannesburg Water.

Larry A. Swatuk is associate professor and head of the Natural Resource Policy, Institutions and Law Research Unit at the University of Botswana's Harry Oppenheimer Okavango Research Centre, Maun, Botswana.

Fiona White is a PhD candidate at the University of London working on civil society and social movements.

Acknowledgements

We would like to thank all of the contributors to this book for their commitment to rigorous and critical research. We also want to thank our colleagues in the Municipal Services Project (MSP) for their assistance and support in the production of this book and for their ongoing dedication to related research topics: Moses Cloete, Hameda Deedat, Mthetho Xali, Rebecca Pointer, Emma Harvey, Ntswaki Moreane, John Pape, Leonard Gentle, Melanie Samson, Roger Ronnie, Jeff Rudin, David Hemson, Godfrey Musaka, Rene Loewenson, Morna Ballentyne and Jane Stinson. Special mention is due to Patrick Bond for his initiation of the regional research and his insights into privatization debates in general, as well to Liane Greeff of the Environmental Monitoring Group for first getting us to think about a collection on water privatization in the region.

Meagan Freer and Christina Decarie spent many hours copy-editing material and we are grateful for their detailed work. Rob West from Earthscan has been an enthusiastic, professional and patient supporter. Maj Fiil-Flynn provided the photographs on the front and back covers of the book.

Funding for research and publication came in large part from the International Development Research Centre of Canada (IDRC). We are particularly grateful to Christina Zarovsky and Jean-Michel Labatut of the IDRC for their ongoing support of the Municipal Services Project (www.queensu.ca/msp).

This book is dedicated to all those in Southern Africa struggling for a more just and sustainable water future, be they public sector unions, social movements, non-governmental organizations, government officials or academics, and the innumerable informal groups and individuals who resist commodification on a daily basis as part of their everyday lives. It is with the latter that the ultimate site of anti-privatization struggle resides.

List of Acronyms and Abbreviations

ADB	African Development Bank
AFD	French Development Agency
AIDC	Alternative Information and Development Centre
ANC	African National Congress
APF	Anti-Privatisation Forum
BLA	Black Local Authority
BOOT	Build, Own, Operate and Transfer
BOTT	Build, Operate, Train and Transfer
BWB	Berliner Wasser Betriebe
CAP	Coalition Against the Privatization [of Water in Ghana]
CAPC	Central African Power Corporation
CAS	country assistance strategy
CEO	Corporate Europe Observatory
CESCR	Committee on Economic, Social and Cultural Rights
CGA	Central Governance Agency
CIDA	Canadian International Development Agency
CMA	Cape Metropolitan Area
CMC	Cape Metropolitan Council
CMU	Compliance Monitoring Unit
Cosatu	Congress of South African Trade Unions
CSO	Central Statistical Office
CTMM	Council of Tshwane Metropolitan Municipality
CUB	Citizen Utility Board
CUPE	Canadian Union of Public Employees
CWSA	Community Water and Sanitation Agency
CWSS	Community Water Supply and Sanitation
DBSA	Development Bank of South Africa
DC	district councils
DDA	Doha Development Agenda
DFID	Department for International Development
DPLG	Department of Provincial and Local Government
DRC	Democratic Republic of the Congo
DRC	Democratic Resettlement Community
DTF	Devolution Trust Fund
DTI	Department of Trade and Industry
DWAF	Department of Water Affairs and Forestry

DWD	Department of Water Development
EIB	European Investment Bank
Eminwa	Environmentally Sound Management of Inland Waters
ERT	External Review Team
ESAP	Economic Structural Adjustment Programme
ESF	European Services Forum
eTWS	eThekwini Water Services
EU	European Union
FFTUZ	Federation of Free Trade Unions of Zambia
FOEI	Friends of the Earth International
GATS	General Agreement on Trade in Services
GATT	General Agreement on Tariffs and Trade
GEAR	Growth, Employment and Redistribution
GNUC	Greater Nelspruit Utility Company
GOG	Government of Ghana
GOZ	Government of Zimbabwe
GTZ	Gesellschaft für Technische Zusammenarbeit
GWCL	Ghana Water Company, Ltd
GWP	Global Water Partnership
GWSC	Ghana Water and Sewerage Corporation
HCC	Harare City Council
HD	high density
HIPC	Heavily Indebted Poor Country Initiative
HSRC	Human Sciences Research Council
HWASA	Harare Water and Sewerage Authority
ICIJ	International Consortium of Investigative Journalists
IDRC	International Development Research Centre
IFIs	international financial institutions
Imatu	Independent Municipal and Allied Trade Union
IMF	International Monetary Fund
IPRSP	Interim Poverty Reduction Strategy Paper
IS	institutional strengthening
ISODEC	Integrated Social Development Center
ISPR	institutional strengthening and priority rehabilitation
IUCN	World Conservation Union
IWRM	integrated water resource management
JSN	Japan Services Network
JW	Johannesburg Water
KCM	Konkola Copper Mines
LACs	local action committees
LaRRI	Labour Resource and Research Institute
LOTIS	Liberalization of Trade in Services
LWSC	Lusaka Water and Sewerage Company
MAI	Multilateral Agreement on Investment
MAWRD	Ministry of Agriculture, Water and Rural Development
MFNP	Ministry of Finance and National Planning

MIIU	Municipal Infrastructure Investment Unit
MLGH	Ministry of Local Government and Housing
MLGNH&PW	Ministry of Local Government, National Housing and Public Works
MMD	Movement for Multiparty Democracy
MRR&WD	Ministry of Rural Resources and Water Development
MSP	municipal service partnerships
MTEF	Medium Term Expenditure Framework
Nepad	New Partnership for Africa's Development
NERP	New Economic Recovery Programme
NGO	nongovernmental organization
NPM	New Public Manager
NPMSS	Northern Pretoria Municipal Sub-Structure
NWASCO	National Water Supply and Sanitation Council
NWRMR	Namibia Water Resources Management Review
O&M	operating and management
OECD	Organization for Economic Cooperation and Development
OED	Operations Evaluation Department
PAC	Pan African Congress
PAZ	Privatization Authority of Zimbabwe
PCU	Programme Coordination Unit
PDG	Palmer Development Group
PIU	Project Implementation Unit
PPIAF	Public–Private Infrastructure Advisory Facility
PPM	prepaid meter
PPP	public–private partnership
PR	priority rehabilitation
PRSP	Poverty Reduction Strategy Paper
PSI	private sector investment
PSI	Public Services International
PSIRU	Public Services International Research Unit
PSP	private sector participation
PSP	private sector partnership
PSRP	Public Sector Reform Programme
PURC	Public Utility Regulatory Commission
PWC	PriceWaterhouseCoopers
RDC	rural district councils
RDP	Reconstruction and Development Programme
RDSN	Rural Development Services Network
RSS	Rural Support Services
SADC	Southern African Development Community
SAIRR	Southern African Institute of Race Relations
Samwu	South African Municipal Workers' Union
SAPP	Southern African Power Pool
SAPRI	Structural Adjustment Policy Review Initiative
SAPRIN	Structural Adjustment Policy Review Initiative Network
SAPs	structural adjustment policies

SAUR	Société d'Aménagement Urbain et Rural
SAWC	South African Water Caucus
SEATINI	Southern and Eastern African Trade, Information and Negotiations Institute
SELCo	Southern Electricity Company
SIDA	Swedish International Development Agency
SOEGC	State-Owned Enterprises Governance Council
SPC	special purpose company
SSA	Statistics South Africa
SWA	South West Africa
SWAPO	South West African People's Organization
TLC	Transnational Local Council
TNI	Transnational Institute
TUC	Trade Union Congress
UAW	unaccounted-for water
UN	United Nations
UNCED	United Nations Conference on Environment and Development
UNDP	United Nations Development Programme
UNEP	United Nations Environment Programme
UNESCO	United Nations Educational Scientific and Cultural Organization
UNI	Union Network International
UNIP	United National Independence Party
USCSI	United States Coalition of Service Industries
VAT	value-added tax
WASCO	Water and Sanitation Committee
WASP	Water Supply and Sanitation Policy
WDM	water demand management
WEDC	Water, Engineering and Development Centre
WES	water environment and sanitation
WINGOC	Windhoek Goreangab Operating Company
WNLA	Witwatersrand Native Labour Association
WRMS	Water Resources Management Strategy
WSCM	World Services Coalition Mission
WSDP	Water Services Development Plan
WSRS	Water Sector Restructuring Secretariat
WSSA	Water Services South Africa
WSSCC	Water Supply and Sanitation Collaborative Council
WSSD	World Summit on Sustainable Development
WTO	World Trade Organization
WWC	World Water Council
Zacplan	Zambezi River Action Plan
ZCTU	Zambia Congress of Trade Unions
ZIMPREST	Zimbabwe Program for Economic Transformation
ZINWA	Zimbabwe National Water Authority
ZRA	Zambezi River Authority
Zulawu	Zambia United Local Authorities Workers Union

Introduction: From Public to Private (to Public Again?)

David A. McDonald and Greg Ruiters

Water privatization – broadly defined for the purposes of this book – is an international phenomenon, occurring in such disparate places as England, China, Argentina, the Philippines and South Africa, and involving global institutions such as the World Bank and the United Nations.

Although the contexts, technologies and strategies for water privatization are different from one site to another, the debates tend to polarize in remarkably similar ways.

Those in favour of privatization argue that governments are corrupt, unaccountable, unimaginative and financially strapped, and unable to expand and upgrade water services on their own in a reliable and cost-effective manner. The private sector and its operating principles, they argue, must be a central component of water delivery strategies.

Opponents of privatization argue that private companies are only interested in the bottom line, charging the poor more than they can afford to pay (and cutting them off when they cannot pay), laying off workers or paying them less for the same work, cutting corners to save costs, creating health and safety risks for the public, and 'redlining' some low income communities altogether. It is also argued that private companies use bribes and corruption to obtain contracts, or simply 'low-ball' bids to get their foot in the door and then rapidly raise rates once entrenched.

It is not the purpose of this introductory chapter to discuss the merits and demerits of these arguments, however. The chapters in the book expand on these debates in much greater detail. What we want to emphasize here is the fact that these debates are taking place and that they are of critical importance. If, as both pro- and anti-privatization advocates tell us, 'water is life', then questions of who owns and operates water services – and who makes decisions about water pricing and investments – are central to people's lives and livelihoods. With over 1 billion people worldwide lacking access to potable water, more than 2 billion without access to sanitation, and some 2 million deaths a year from easily preventable diarrhoea-related illnesses, there is also a terrible urgency to the debate.

This book examines these debates in the Southern African context. We do not attempt to provide a full spectrum of opinions, however. The material here is uniformly critical of water privatization. This is not for lack of pro-privatization literature or pro-privatization researchers in the region. Just the opposite. There has been such a continuous deluge of pro-privatization writing and policymaking in Southern Africa over the past ten years (some of it academic but much of it based in consultancy reports for governments and donors, as well as in popular media articles) that a collection of material presenting a critical perspective is required to add better balance to the debate.

Having said that, the authors in this collection are not monolithic in the positions they take. Some are less critical than others of privatization and some see a potential role for the private sector in water services. Our aim has simply been to provide critically minded research that is academically sound, providing theoretically grounded and methodologically rigorous accounts of the dynamics of water privatization in the Southern African context, drawing on international literature and experience. It is up to the readers to formulate their own opinions on this critically important public policy matter.

Nor is it just water that we are ultimately interested in. The same basic debates are taking place in other service sectors such as electricity, waste management, transportation, health care and education, all of which are affected by the same neoliberal fiscal and political reforms affecting water. There are lessons to be learned from water for these other sectors and vice versa.

Defining Privatization

One of the most important aspects of the privatization debate is the definition of the term itself. We therefore dedicate the first section of Chapter 1 to a detailed discussion of the different variants of private sector involvement in water services. Readers may find it useful to read this chapter before other parts of the book to better understand what we mean by a 'broad definition' of privatization and why defining these terms is so important.

In brief, we use the term to refer to non-state actors involved in water delivery (including NGOs and community organizations) where the transfer of ownership and/or decision making responsibility to private interests occurs (in part or in total). This definition is adopted partly because privatization, in the strict sense of the word, refers only to the outright sale (divestiture) of state assets. Although this was the system of water privatization employed in the UK in the 1980s, there have been no major water service divestments of this kind anywhere else in the world since that time. Subsequent private sector participation in water has followed the so-called 'French model' which involves 'public–private partnerships' (PPPs) whereby the state continues to own the assets and is involved in the monitoring and decision making of the service delivery, but the actual operations and planning of water services are undertaken by the private entity.

We argue vigorously that these PPPs must also be seen as a form of privatization: a transfer of ownership and/or control that changes the operational calculus of a service from 'public good' to 'private profit', alters the underlying managerial ethos of water service organizations, and changes the nature of political relationships between citizens and the state. The term privatization is something of a misnomer in this regard, but given its widespread use in popular discourse, and the fact that the underlying premises and objectives of PPPs are much the same as divestiture, we have opted to use the word in this book.

We have, however, expanded the terminology to include 'commercialization', a process that refers to the more general pattern of running water services 'like a business' and that can be implemented without any private sector involvement at all. The 'corporatization' of water services – the creation of independent business units financially and managerially ringfenced from all other sectors in a municipality – has become the most popular form of introducing private sector principles into the water sector in Southern Africa and is often seen as a first step towards more explicit forms of private sector involvement. With corporatization, outsourcing of various functions such as meter reading and debt collection to private firms has also started to appear.

Underlying all of this activity, we argue, are the broad forces of commodification: the transformation of all social relations to economic relations, subsumed by the logic of the market and reduced to the crude calculus of profit. Water – while not necessarily the easiest of things to commodify – has come under increasing commodity pressure in Southern Africa to conform to the economic models of cost analysis and cost recovery and to the necessity of lowest cost production. All capitalist societies are susceptible to these pressures and all feel the pressure of international capital eager to tap into cheap water supplies and/or capitalize on the demand for this essential good. Hence the title of this book: *The Age of Commodity*.

This broad definition of privatization, and the identification of the commercializing and commodifying forces that underpin it, allow us to make arguments in this book that are not conceptually available to liberal analysts. The first is the extent to which privatization has been taking place in the region. Liberal academics, policymakers and media pundits – particularly in South Africa – have argued that there has been very little privatization taking place in the region/country. But these analysts fail to take into account the principles of commercialization that drive 'new public management' in the form of corporatization. It is these more complex and slippery forms of privatization that we grapple with in this book.

This broader definition of privatization also allows us – indeed forces us – to ask bigger questions about the motivations of capital and the sustainability of capitalism more generally (more on this below). With water central to the production *and* consumption of capital, and its control critical to the expansion of capitalism in the region, water commodification must be seen as part of a larger recolonization effort on the part of national and international capital seeking new consumer markets, new social relations and new production potentials/investments. Water privatization must be seen as a microcosm of these broad, macro-transformations.

STRUCTURE OF THE BOOK

The book is divided into three sections. The first – Theory and Practice – looks at the key ideological, legislative and constitutional issues shaping the water privatization debate in the region. Chapter 1, as noted above, deals with the definitional and conceptual parameters of privatization, but also outlines the extent to which water privatization has manifested itself in concrete terms in the region. Chapter 2 provides an overview of the 'new water architecture' of the Southern African Development Community (SADC), with a focus on the legislative developments that have lent themselves to increasing water privatization/commercialization.

Chapter 3 explores South Africa's much-vaunted, post-apartheid Constitution and examines the legal implications of water commercialization. The authors argue that there are numerous areas where commercialization creates constitutional tensions and some areas where there may already be constitutional violations (e.g. water cutoffs and prepaid water meters). Although South Africa is the focus of this chapter, the analysis has ramifications for legal debates in other parts of the region and elsewhere in the world.

Chapter 4 has a similar international resonance, looking at the impact of the World Trade Organization's General Agreement on Trade in Services (GATS) and how it affects water services in the region. Although the GATS has come under heavy attack from academics, policymakers and activists in other parts of the world for several years now (most notably since 1999 at the World Trade Organization (WTO) protests in Seattle) it is only recently that labour groups and other nongovernmental organizations in Southern Africa have begun to look seriously at the GATS agreements and ongoing GATS negotiations. Flecker and Clarke – two leading international analysts of this trade agreement – describe the mechanisms of GATS and how it may affect water services and water privatization in South(ern) Africa.

Part 2 of the book is a series of case studies of water commercialization and privatization in South Africa. The reason for the large number of South African case studies is that this is where water privatization/commercialization is most advanced in the region and where it has been most actively promoted (and resisted).

The case studies of South Africa offered here have been selected because they provide broad geographic and demographic coverage and/or because they have particular political or policy relevance (e.g. prepaid water meters, free basic water). They have also been selected because they highlight a useful range of important privatization themes with relevance to global water privatization debates: for example, corporatization, water cutoffs, corruption and donor conditionalities.

Chapter 5 examines efforts to corporatize water services in Tshwane (formerly Pretoria) and looks at the social and economic inequities that this transformation would entail if fully implemented (and already has to some extent). Chapter 6 looks at the increasingly popular use of prepaid water meters in South Africa, in this case in the city of Johannesburg. Touted by government and private sector providers alike as a pro-poor technological development which helps the poor better budget their water use, it is argued that these devices are intended primarily as a form of 'remote control' over consumers who cannot otherwise afford to pay for the water they need.

Chapter 7 looks at the 30-year concession in the city of Nelspruit, the first long-term water concession signed in South Africa with a private service provider and one that was seen at the time as a flagship for future public–private partnerships in the country. Beset by problems from its inception, and heavily criticized by labour and community groups ever since, it is not clear if the concession will survive its first ten years of operation. Smith et al tell the complex story of its pitfalls and shortcomings.

Chapter 8 reviews the experiences of two towns in the Eastern Cape province – Queenstown and Fort Beaufort – the first municipalities in the country to undergo water privatization (in the early 1990s). It discusses the impact of private service delivery in these towns, the nature of private contracts and concerns with regulating a massive multinational corporation.

Corporatization is again the central theme in Chapter 9, which examines ongoing efforts to corporatize water services in the city of Cape Town. Although the city has introduced some of the most progressive water tariff reforms in the country, and has been moderately successful in expanding water networks into township areas, the underlying commercialization of the water sector has served to undermine many of these potential gains; water cutoffs, household evictions and other forms of market based water regulation have negatively affected tens of thousands of households.

Durban is the subject of Chapter 10. As the first city to introduce 'free water' in South Africa (in the late 1990s) its managers and politicians have received considerable national and international praise. This chapter explores the facts and myths of this policy initiative and argues that much of the potentially progressive nature of free water has been subsumed by the larger water commodification trend in the city, with free water little more than an (insufficient) link to a larger commodification chain; price hikes and water restrictions for the poor are a more telling aspect of the Durban 'miracle'.

The final South African study, Chapter 11, looks at the experience with rural water privatization during the African National Congress's (ANC's) first term of office from 1995 to 1999. Great emphasis was placed on Build, Operate, Train and Transfer (BOTT) schemes at that time, with negative outcomes for rural households – typically the poorest and most under-serviced in the country. Greenberg discusses the reasons for these failures and the lessons to be learned for the future.

Part 3 provides several case studies of water privatization in other countries in the region. These are not as numerous as we had originally hoped (several chapters did not materialize) but this dearth of information is also due to the fact that concrete efforts to privatize/commercialize water in other SADC states are not as advanced as they are in South Africa (with some important exceptions such as Mozambique, which has experienced widespread privatization of water under the auspices of World Bank-imposed structural adjustment programmes). Nevertheless, it is hoped that the chapters provided here – and the broader conceptual material provided in Part 1 – will offer readers a sense of the politico-economic dynamics contributing to further water privatization/commercialization in the region.

Chapter 12 is a study of efforts to privatize water in Harare, Zimbabwe, during a period of severe political and economic crisis and illustrates the lengths to which donors, neoliberal policymakers, development banks and private companies will go to commercialize water services. Although water remains in public hands in Harare, it is clear that the situation is volatile and the city could indeed see some form of private sector involvement in water delivery in the future (as it has in other essential services such as waste management).

The focus of Chapter 13 is Lusaka, Zambia, where water also remains in public hands, but is being run increasingly like a private business and may well see more direct private sector involvement in the near future. This chapter again reveals the impact of neoliberal shifts on water management policy, as well as the aggressive manner in which private firms insinuate themselves into key decision making fora.

Chapter 14 looks at the corporatization and privatization of water in Namibia, a relatively recent shift that has spread quickly to affect virtually every municipality in the country due to the centralized nature of bulk water supply and pricing. A water stressed country at the best of times, poor Namibians are now finding themselves cut off from water supplies because they cannot afford to pay massive increases in water bills, or they are simply cutting themselves off because they cannot afford to buy water credits for their prepaid meters.

Chapter 15 steps outside the region for a look at the situation in Ghana. Although Ghana is not a SADC country, it was felt that its experience with water privatization is of sufficient interest to other parts of the continent to merit its inclusion. The conditionalities applied by the World Bank and the collaborationist nature of successive governments in trying to force through privatization measures speak to the need for vigilance in these terms in Southern Africa proper. So too are there lessons to be learned from resistance to water privatization amongst civil society organizations and labour groups in Ghana, with some links already having been established between anti-privatization groups in that country and other parts of the continent.

Which brings us to the question of resistance more generally. While there is a literature on the nascent and rapidly growing anti-privatization, anti-commodification movement in South(ern) Africa, we have opted – largely for space reasons – to restrict ourselves here to short statements from organizations in the region who are explicitly opposed to the privatization of water. A total of seven groups are represented (Anti-Privatisation Forum, South African Water Caucus, South African Municipal Workers' Union, Anti-Eviction Campaign, Coalition Against Water Privatization, Ada/Gui Senior Citizens and Destitute

Children's Association, and the National Coalition Against the Privatization of Water in Ghana). These brief 'statements', 'manifestos' and 'press releases' are placed between chapters in the book, generally where they have some direct relevance to the preceding text.

There is also considerable reference to anti-privatization movements in the text of the case studies and in the conceptual chapters of the book, providing what we hope will be a good sense of the scope, scale and character of the anti-privatization resistance movement in the region.

ALTERNATIVES TO PRIVATIZATION

We conclude this Introduction with a brief discussion of alternatives to privatization. We had originally planned for a full chapter on this topic to demonstrate (particularly for those who believe that 'there is no alternative' to privatization) the extent to which alternatives are being thought about and practised in the region and elsewhere. We opted in the end to leave this material to future publications, partly due to space limitations but more importantly because we felt that a single chapter would not do justice to what is necessarily a complex and nuanced literature and set of institutional and ideological practices. We can, however, provide a rough outline of the kinds of alternatives that are being thought about and researched to offer some indication of our thinking in this regard and to point to the rich potential for non-privatized water delivery.

Let us start by saying that we are not arguing that public ownership and management is inherently good or that the status quo with public water service is necessarily where we want to be. There are many examples of poorly run public water services in Southern Africa and elsewhere and we are as keen to see these systems change as advocates of privatization are. The task in our minds, however, is to translate public services into more effective, accountable operations that promote and defend public interests and social development. There are short-term and long-term measures and reforms that must be considered, but the former should as far as possible aim at promoting long-term shifts in the way we produce water, in social attitudes to water and in the way we use it (including ecologically rational land use planning and housing design). These considerations apply to domestic, industrial and agricultural uses as well as the supply chain (e.g. addressing the building of dams and expensive, environmentally damaging water transport systems).

In the short to medium term there are a number of reforms that can be put in place in Southern Africa that would make a significant difference to public water services and would help to stem (and reverse, we hope) the tide of water privatization/commercialization. The first, and most important, of these is a set of changes aimed at softening the current neoliberal inequalities in water delivery to better achieve the 'public good' aspects of water services: no prepaid meters for poor households; increased amounts of free water; better regulation of tariff structures so that they do not penalize the poor; and improved levels of infrastructure.

A second priority is increased public funding from national governments and international donors (without the conditionalities of private sector intervention) for improving the efficiency of water systems and access. These monies are desperately needed by cash-strapped municipalities (the level of government increasingly responsible for all aspects of water planning and operations in Southern Africa), which are finding themselves with enormous service delivery mandates but insufficient resources to follow through with their directives.

Funding for human and capital resources, infrastructure development and ongoing maintenance and operating costs to avoid onerous cost recovery policies for the poor is critical. But so too is funding for training of public employees and for workshops and resources to create more effective public services and keep them in public hands. The South African government spends millions of rands every year on workshops and consultants that tell municipal politicians and bureaucrats how to develop public–private partnerships (e.g. the Municipal Infrastructure Investment Unit (MIIU), which was started with funding from USAID) but has no programmatic or institutional equivalent tasked with promoting public sector alternatives.

To be fair, there have been some initiatives in South Africa to create 'public–public partnerships' (PUPs) in water delivery (e.g. Odi and Harrismith) which have met with some success, but these have been plagued by underfunding from higher levels of government and have failed to spark wider reforms. Nevertheless, PUPs in water services have been receiving increasing international attention, with a focus on creating partnerships between different levels of government, between governments at the same level, and between governments and public sector unions and communities. Private sector involvement is explicitly excluded from these agreements for the most part, with the objective of creating public sector capacity and making the public sector more transparent, more efficient, more responsive and more accountable. Although still in formative stages, the PUPs initiative is one that deserves more attention and resources in Southern African water services.

So too does participatory budgeting in Southern Africa. Experience with participatory budgeting in other parts of the world – most notably in Latin America and parts of India – has been enormously successful in rejuvenating public service budgets, refocusing public spending on the most needy sectors, and reinvigorating public support and commitment for publicly owned and operated services.

The trend in Southern Africa towards ringfenced business units that operate autonomously from other state and community institutions runs counter to these developments. Ringfencing needs to be replaced by more holistic, intersectoral management systems. Not only has this ringfencing led to narrow, market driven forms of cost recovery, it has created inefficient, near-sighted planning and operational patterns whereby water managers are unaware of planning and operations in related services such as waste management, stormwater drainage or health services, leading to potentially serious health concerns (the cholera outbreaks in South Africa since 2001 are a good example).

In the long term, there is a need to shift away from market approaches to society and nature more generally. There is a clear danger that privatization and commodification will cement old-style apartheid and class geographies and further reinforce discriminatory aspects of infrastructure distribution that characterized colonialism and apartheid in the region, making a meaningful transition to a more egalitarian social structure unlikely.

Alternatives need to consider whether the dominant image of water as money and money as a currency of social relations and nature is adequate. Instead of commodifying nature, then, what other feasible forms of valuing might we explore? Many of the new social movements demand that resources be defined socially in order to be used more equitably and produced under more humane and dignified conditions. The redistribution question (who gets what) also needs to become the production/procedural question (who produces what, for whom and why). Changing the distribution of public goods so that the needy merely get 'lifeline supplies' does not challenge either the roots of injustice or questions of decision making and powerlessness, and may simply reinforce the latter.

Finally, long-term water service alternatives must confront the artificial 'scarcity' problematic inherited from standard economics and the Malthusian catastrophism that informs mainstream water discourses and which has conveniently served as a rationale for water privatization and commodification.

These long-term reforms are clearly a long way off in the current regional and international ideological climate of neoliberalism, but progressive debates over water privatization must address these longer-term challenges and objectives. It is hoped that this book will contribute to a better understanding of the current pitfalls of water privatization and commercialization in Southern Africa and help point the way to new, more sustainable, forms of water production and consumption.

Part 1

Theory and Practice

Chapter 1

Theorizing Water Privatization in Southern Africa

David A. McDonald and Greg Ruiters

Water promises to be to the 21st century what oil was to the 20th century: the precious commodity that determines the wealth of nations (Fortune Magazine 15 May 2000).

That smooth-faced gentleman, tickling Commodity, Commodity, the bias of the world (Shakespeare, from King John).

What is water privatization, to what extent is it taking place in Southern Africa and why is it happening? These are the central questions we ask in this chapter, along with a brief discussion of growing opposition to water privatization in the region. In answering these questions we hope to provide a conceptual framework for the empirical sections of this book and lay the ground for a critical theoretical perspective on the driving forces of privatization.

One of the biggest conceptual hurdles in this debate, particularly for first-time observers, is the definition of the term. We therefore start with this question of definition and argue that privatization must be seen as a social intensification of capitalism and a shift in state–society relationships, rather than a mere collection of particular corporations taking over, or partnering in, water delivery. We look at the growing emphasis on public–private partnerships (PPPs) but also at the larger trend towards the commercialization of water, and how these concepts relate to one another. The conceptual apparatus used to pull this discussion together is that of commodification – a process integral to capitalist expansion and central to the marketization of all aspects of life, water included.

We then examine the extent to which water has actually been privatized/commercialized in the region – legislatively and in practice – followed by a discussion of who is promoting it and why. The central argument here is that water marketization is both widespread and influential and is being driven primarily by the structural demands of local and international capital and the continuing fiscal crisis of the state.

But this is a partial transformation – one that has been uneven across space and time in the region and one that continues to be riddled with legislative, discursive and practical tensions. Nevertheless, the trend is clearly towards increasing privatization and commercialization, particularly in the form of public sector corporatization where publicly owned and operated water systems are managed like private businesses, leading to harsh cost recovery measures such as repossessing houses, water cutoffs, prepaid meters and drip-valves that restrict water supply to the poor; all of which have spurred widespread civil insurgency and citizen disengagement.

What Is Water Privatization?

In its narrowest sense, privatization happens when the state sells its assets to a private company, along with all of the maintenance, planning and operational responsibilities that these assets entail. Over the past 30 years states have divested themselves of airlines, railroads, telephone services, health facilities and other services, thereby unlocking a new phase of capitalist expansion and innovation. Divestiture, as this form of privatization is formally known, was the model of water privatization adopted in the UK under Margaret Thatcher in the late 1980s, with entire water systems (from water collection, to reticulation, to sewage treatment) being sold to private firms (Ernst 1994; Schofield and Shaol 1997; Bakker 2003). Monitoring and regulatory oversight in this model of privatization remain a responsibility of the state, however, or a parastatal regulatory body.

The privatization of water services in other parts of the world does not generally follow the UK model though. Most municipal privatization schemes today do not involve any transfer of state assets, focusing instead on the transfer of operational and managerial functions to private companies (e.g. meter reading, personnel management, strategic planning, maintenance). Infrastructure and equipment typically remain in public hands – or are transferred back to public ownership after a specified period – and there may be joint responsibilities between the state and a private firm in managing operational functions. This model is used across the world by leading water and construction firms such as Suez and Vivendi who operate this way in over 12,000 towns and cities (Goubert 1986; Hanke 1987; Lorrain 1991; Kerf 1998).

More properly known as 'private sector partnerships' (PSPs) or, as will be used in this book, 'public–private partnerships' (PPPs), these institutional arrangements are nevertheless a form of privatization. There is a clear transfer of crucial decision making responsibilities from the public to the private sector and an effective transfer of power over assets to a private company, with qualitatively and quantitatively different rules and regulations guiding the decisions that are made and how citizens are able to access information. This broader definition of privatization is also accepted by leading international agencies such as the World Bank, the World Health Organization, the Water Supply and Sanitation Collaborative Council and various United Nations-related agencies who have actively promoted PPPs in water services in the South, such as the United Nations Development Programme, UN-HABITAT and UNICEF (see, for example, World Bank 1994, 1997, 2003; Lorrain and Stoker 1997; Kerf 1998; UNDP-World Bank 1998; WHO and UNICEF 2000).

It is also important to note that PPPs can range from small operations, such as one-person contractors who repair pipes in an informal urban settlement, to a large multinational company hired to manage the provision of bulk water and sanitation for an entire city. The size and types of contract can vary as well, from short-term, fee-for-service contracts, to 30-year licences. Although large water service multinationals like Suez, Vivendi, RWE Thames, and Bechtel tend to attract the most attention when it comes to water privatization debates, small firms and 'entrepreneurs' represent a large part of the privatization thrust, with these micro-enterprise deals often going unnoticed by the public. This smaller, 'creeping' form of privatization is as much a topic of interest in this book as the large multinational efforts to take over entire water systems.

Less easy to classify are forms of water privatization that involve the downloading of service responsibilities to individuals, communities and nongovernmental organizations (e.g. the digging of pit latrines or the repairing of water pumps by a community group). Represented in the neoliberal literature as 'active citizenship' (Burrows and Loader 1994) and 'community empowerment' – a counter to welfare dependency (Wolch and Dear 1989) – this transfer of water service decision making and responsibility also constitutes a move from the public (i.e. the state) to the private (in this case an individual or community). Although not necessarily acting with the same institutional or economic incentives and frameworks as a private company, the transfer of decision making power to individuals and communities nevertheless constitutes an abdication of responsibilities on the part of the state.

Table 1.1 provides a typology of privatization arrangements. Most water service agreements are hybrids of these categories, of course, tailored to suit the specific situation of individual governments and companies, but it should be clear from the table that all water privatization schemes involve some form of public and private sector participation.

Privatization, in other words, is not an either/or situation (*either* the state owns and runs a service *or* the private/community sector does). Water privatization must be seen as a continuum of public and private mixes, with varying degrees of involvement and exposure to risks by the two sectors (see Starr 1988). It is a conceptual and political mistake to pose the market (private) and the state (public) as binary opposites on this issue.

Moreover, as Bakker (2003, pp4, 36) has argued in the case of the UK, even the outright divestiture of state assets can, ironically, mean greater state involvement in water services, prompting her to employ the term 're-regulation' rather than 'deregulation' with regard to legislative changes that allow for greater private sector involvement in water services: 'a process in which the state has reconfigured its role, and in some instances expanded its powers and administrative reach . . . the state does not necessarily withdraw, but rather changes the nature of its interaction with citizens and corporations'.

The term privatization is therefore used in this book as a generic expression for a range of private sector involvements in service delivery rather than a single state of being. This is done in part because the term privatization is widely recognized in popular discourse (as opposed to 'public–private partnerships')

Table 1.1 *Different forms of water services 'privatization'*

Full divestiture	Divestiture refers to a situation where a water and/or sanitation utility has been fully privatized. Ownership of the utility rests with the private operator. The private operator is responsible for operation and maintenance, investments and tariff collection. The private utilities operate under the supervision of an independent public regulatory authority.
Service contract	This is the least risky of all partnership types. The public authority retains responsibility for operation and maintenance of the service, but specific components of the service (for example operating water treatment works or billing) are contracted out to the private sector. Service contracts usually have a duration of one to two years, due to the fact that the problems they address may be unique and short-lived. The local authority does not relinquish any managerial functions.
Management contract	The management contractor operates and maintains the service or parts of the service and may also undertake to reshape the system. The public authority monitors the private agent, but remains responsible for new investment. Management contracts tend to cover a time-span of two to ten years.
Lease or affermage	The lessor rents the facility from the public authority, which transfers complete managerial responsibility for operating and maintaining the system to a private company. Such contracts generally have a duration in excess of ten years. The contract specifies reporting requirements and service standards. Payments are split into fixed and volume-related amounts. (*Affermage* is the French term for 'farming out'.)
Concession	In this investment-linked contract the concessionaire has overall responsibility for the services, including operation, maintenance, and management as well as capital investments during the concession period. The concessionaire is also responsible for tariff collection and 'customer management'. The ownership of fixed assets is assigned to the local authority at the end of the contract. The contract, usually signed after competitive bidding, covers a period of 25 to 30 years. Regulation is by contract.
BOOT	Build, Own, Operate and Transfer contracts are generally used to construct new parts of a service system such as water treatment plants, dams and wastewater treatment plants, but can also be used for small water developments as well. The private operator builds the plant and assumes responsibility for operation and maintenance. After a

Table 1.1 *Different forms of water services 'privatization' (continued)*

	predetermined time the facility is transferred to the public authority. The length of a BOOT contract is typically 25 years.
Community/NGO provision	Community and nongovernmental organization (NGO) provision – an often neglected form of privatization – involves the transfer of some or all of the responsibility for water provision to the end user or a not-for-profit intermediary body. This is particularly common in low income, urban settlements in the South where local governments have asked community members and community organizations to supplement weak or nonexistent water and sanitation facilities/resources with their own labour (e.g. digging wells, laying or repairing pipes). Women tend to carry the burden of this form of privatization. NGOs play a key role as well, often taking on management and water allocation responsibilities.

and in part because it highlights the fact that assets and/or decision making responsibilities have passed from public to private hands.

But we cannot limit our discussion of privatization to direct private sector participation and control. Equally important is the question of private sector operating principles and mechanisms. The 'commercialization' of water services in the formally designated public sector is critical to our understanding of water delivery reforms in Southern Africa. This next section describes commercialization (and its most common institutional variant, 'corporatization') and discusses its links – mechanically and conceptually – to privatization.

THE COMMERCIALIZATION/CORPORATIZATION OF WATER

The commercialization of water refers to a process by which market mechanisms and market practices are introduced into the operational decision making of a water service: for example, profit maximization, cost recovery, competitive bidding, cost-benefit analysis, performance targeted salaries, ringfenced decision making, demand-driven investments, etc. (Stoker 1989; Pendleton and Winterton 1993; Dunsire 1999; Leys 2001; Olcay-Unver et al 2003). This is in opposition to the more traditional public sector operating principles of integrated planning, (cross) subsidization, supply-driven decision making, equity orientation and so on (keeping in mind that there are no ideal or absolute types here; i.e. commercial principles and more traditional public sector management principles can run concurrently, to varying degrees).

The most popular institutional form of commercialization in Southern Africa has been corporatization, where water services are ringfenced into stand-alone 'business units' owned and operated by the (local) state but run on market principles. Corporatization involves two major organizational shifts. The first entails financial ringfencing, whereby all resources *directly* involved in the delivery of a service are separated from all other service functions (e.g. personnel in water are separated out for accounting purposes from personnel in waste management and are not allowed to do work for the other unit). Where resources are shared by more than one department (e.g. information technology, vehicles) the ringfenced entity pays the other unit a full-cost fee for the use of those resources (see Shirley 1999; PWC 1999; PDG 2001; Whincop 2003; Bollier 2003).

The purpose of this financial ringfencing is to create a transparent form of accounting where all costs and revenues related to the service can be identified, along with any subsidies in and out of the ringfenced unit. This is intended to reveal the real costs/surpluses of running a service and allows managers to identify areas of financial loss/gain that may have otherwise been hidden in the intricate accounting systems and cross-subsidization mechanisms of an integrated service delivery scheme with centralized accounting. Financial ringfencing also creates an opportunity to introduce financially driven performance targets for managers (i.e. managers are rewarded for meeting loss/profit targets). This approach introduces market based salaries for managers with the aim of attracting 'world class' executives who are expected to pay their way by ensuring that the bottom line is positive.

The second aspect of corporatization is managerial ringfencing: the creation of separate business units managed by appointed officials operating at arms length from the municipal authority. Elected officials still set standards and service delivery goals for a corporatized service unit, as well as monitor and evaluate its activities, but the daily management and long-term planning of the unit are done by the ringfenced management team.

What is the link between corporatization and privatization? First and foremost is the change in management ethos with a focus on a narrow and increasingly short-term financial bottom line. So complete can this shift in management culture be that water systems which are fully owned and operated by the state (i.e. considered to be fully 'public') can be more commercial than their 'privatized' counterparts, with managers aggressively promoting and enforcing cost recovery and other market principles (see, for example, the chapters on Cape Town and Durban in this volume).

Second, corporatization often promotes outsourcing as an operating strategy and discreet form of cost-cutting. A competitive operating environment, in turn, requires deregulating (or re-regulating) monopolistic control of the service and allowing multiple service providers to compete with the ringfenced unit to provide a particular service at cost-effective prices (e.g. meter reading). The removal of subsidies, for instance, forces state-owned enterprises to compete for finance on an equal basis with private firms or other corporatized entities within and across municipalities. In some cases, the corporatized entity may have to compete with a private firm for the management of an entire water system.

Third, corporatization can act as a gateway for direct private sector investment, ownership or control by making public water services more attractive to the private sector. Private companies, after all, are not interested in buying into services with intricate and/or hidden cross-subsidization structures, inflexible and politically integrated decision making procedures, or anti-market management cultures. Water systems that have been delineated from other service functions with clearly defined costs and revenue structures, with some form of managerial autonomy, and with market-oriented managers are much more likely to attract interest from private firms.

Not all corporatization efforts are mere preparation for bigger privatization plans, but this is a real – and growing – motivation for municipalities that are adopting the corporatization model. As one senior manager interviewed in Cape Town about that city's plans to corporatize its water services remarked (McDonald and Smith 2002, p32):

> *Lyonnaise des Eaux has come knocking on my door on two occasions. These French water companies have become too powerful to resist. The takeover is inevitable. I want to run our services like solid business units to make sure that we negotiate from a position of strength when it does happen.*

Commercialization therefore paves the way for private sector involvement in water services and/or creates publicly owned and operated water systems that behave, for all intents and purposes, like a private sector water provider, mimicking business discourses and practices and serving to 'hollow out' the state (Stoker 1989; Clarke and Newman 1997; Dunsire 1999; Taylor-Gooby 2000).

Tying all of this together are the underlying processes of water commodification. Only when water is treated as a commodity can it be effectively commercialized and, eventually, privatized. It is at this politico-economic juncture that we see the full significance of water's commercialized and privatized transformation emerge: water stripped of its image as an abundant, nature-provided good for public benefit, to water as a scarce, monetized entity subject to the same laws and principles of the market as shoes, lampshades or computers.

Only by examining these processes of commodification can we go beyond the narrow institutional and operational definitions of privatization and commercialization described above and more fully appreciate the transformative effects of treating water as a private good. Privatization and commercialization must be seen as part of this wider process of intensified and extensified capitalism.

WATER COMMODIFICATION

We start by examining neoclassical definitions of commodity and commodification, partly because these definitions have been so influential and dominate public discourse on the topic but also because they are now being used to justify privatization and commercialization in the water sector.

A commodity, in neoclassical economic terms, is anything that can be bought and sold in the marketplace in exchange for another commodity or for money.

'Commodification', therefore, is any act, practice or policy that promotes or treats a good or service as an article of commerce to be bought, sold, or traded through market transactions (Watts 1999; Brown 2003; Williams and Windebank 2003). According to neoclassical theory, to be commodified, a good or service must have the characteristics of a 'private good': it must be rival in its consumption (i.e. one person's consumption of that good denies consumption by another person: for example, a chocolate bar) and it must be excludable (people can be denied access if they do not pay: for example, admission to a movie). Private goods can therefore be priced for individual consumption and respond well to market signals.

'Public goods' on the other hand resist commodification because they are non-excludable (i.e. people cannot be prevented from using a good or service because they did not pay for it: for example, clean air) and non-rival (i.e. consumption by one person does not diminish the amount available for the next person: for example, street lighting). According to neoclassical theory public goods and services are unlikely to be provided by a private firm under market conditions because they are prone to 'free riders', making it too risky for a private firm to invest in producing them.

Water, in neoclassical theory, lies between these two poles, being neither a pure private good nor a pure public good (sometimes referred to in the neoclassical literature as a 'merit good'; Neutze 1997). Merit goods and services are things that would almost certainly be underprovided if left solely to market forces (e.g. education for the poor). In the case of water, if there were no public sector provision it is likely that there would be some private sector providers offering water services to those who could afford them (as was the case in Britain, for example, in the 1800s). But since private firms only take into account their own costs and benefits it is unlikely that a socially optimal level of water services would be provided to all.

The response of some economists to this dilemma has been to argue that the state should encourage private firms to produce more of a particular public good (e.g. by subsidizing its production) or that the state should provide the good or service itself. Neoclassical theory would therefore argue that water, as a quasi-commodity, only partially responsive to market forces, would be underprovided from a public goods point of view if left entirely to market forces.

But since the late 1970s this notion of water as a merit good has increasingly come under attack by neoliberals who argue that water provision must be seen as a private good like any other: responsive to market indicators; flexible in its demand; and rival and excludable in its consumption. *The Economist* has gone so far as to call water the 'first commodity', arguing that it is 'a tradable commodity like coal and oil and timber . . . and should be treated as such'. 'Only by accepting that water is a tradable commodity', it argues, 'will sensible decisions be possible' (*The Economist* 1992).

Herein lies the key analytical twist in neoliberal writing on water privatization and commercialization. Not only is it argued to be theoretically sound to regard water as a private good, it is deemed an economic, social and environmental imperative to treat it this way. Subsidizing water as a public/merit good, or having the state provide water without competitive pressures, leads to inefficient and unaccountable water provision, undermining its public good characteristics through waste, unresponsive behaviours and corruption. Treating water as a private good, on the other hand, creates efficient and accountable water delivery systems and therefore more desirable public good outcomes (Hanke and Walters 1987; Bauman et al 1998).

The policy upshot of this line of argument is that the privatization and commercialization of water is deemed both acceptable and necessary. To do anything else would be irresponsible. And hence the basis for a newly emerging moral discourse on water privatization that argues that market competition and commercialization in the water sector is a 'pro-poor' policy choice (see, for example, Foster and Aranjo 2001; Estache et al 2002).[1]

To avoid this analytical trap we must see the commodification of goods and services historically (in the *longue durée*), as part of a larger, dynamic process of change, one that is unique to capitalism and central to an understanding of capital accumulation and the contradictions within a market economy. We also need to situate the state and class struggles within shifting state–market mixes.

Marx based his critique of capitalism on this very point, arguing that the commodity and its transformation through a system of wage labour is at the heart of the capitalist mode of production: 'Our investigation must therefore begin with the analysis of a commodity' (Marx 1978, pp302–303). For Marx, a good's exchangeability is not predetermined by characteristics inherent in the physicality of that good or service, but by the value imparted to it in the production process, determined by the labour necessary to produce it, and expressed in the form of money, as price. Although all things have a 'use value' – the qualitatively defined characteristics that differentiate something from other goods or services and may differentiate it from itself across time and space – this use value is transformed to 'exchange value' in the exchange process, a strictly quantitative measurement that differentiates goods by their monetary worth alone, as determined by the market. Thus water, with its qualitatively different use values (e.g. religious practice, aesthetic beauty, recreational enjoyment, physiological necessity) becomes a homogenized, quantitatively differentiated commodity in the exchange process, valued only by its price.

Commodification entails the transformation of relationships, formerly untouched by commerce, into commercial relationships. Under capitalism, many goods and services which previously had no market value or were self-provided within households have been brought into the market fold and mass production. New commodities are created with the expansion of markets to new geographic areas and new sectors that may not yet have been marketized, while a deepening of commodification is accomplished through the deregulation of exchange mechanisms, allowing further penetration of market principles into under-marketized spheres.

Capital, as Kovel (2002, p42) argues, sees 'each boundary/barrier as a site for commodity formation' but this process is not always consciously pursued since some opportunities arise perversely. Examples of this are the business of cleaning up pollution or making drugs to fight the effects of overeating and new diseases unleashed by ecological decay. Bottled water is another good example: a response to the (perceived) contamination and unreliability of (public) municipal water supplies. The wide range of services that now make up the 'service sector' – from bereavement and psychological services to private security firms to child-care to fast food – attests to capital's 'reckless addiction' to growth and its uncontrollability (Meszaros 1998; Kovel 2002, p44). Firms compete with each other to get faster and newer services and gadgets to the ever receptive, ideal consumer. New 'needs' are invented as a necessary business strategy.

Water is currently experiencing all of these commoditizing pressures. It is being commodified for the first time in some places (mostly rural areas of Africa and Asia) and having its commodification intensified through de(re)regulation in others.

Some goods and services lend themselves to deeper and faster commodification than others, however. Water, despite what *The Economist* says, is not a particularly easy good/service to commodify. As Bakker (2003, pp33, 89) argues, water is an 'uncooperative commodity' due to its biophysical characteristics: expensive to transport and requiring large, lumpy capital investments lending itself to 'natural monopoly'. It is these characteristics, she argues, that have created so many un-commodity-like problems in the British water privatization experience.

There can also be political and cultural differences across countries/regions that affect what gets commodified, where things are commodified and the rate at which commodification takes place. 'Cultures of resistance' and tensions inherent in the shift to commodification can slow the commodification process down and make it uneven (Williams 2002; Williams and Windebank 2003). Thus, although there are powerful pressures to commodify (Harvey 1990, 2003) commodification is not necessarily a linear or inevitable process.

Nevertheless, we have seen a steady expansion of market relations and commodification around the world over the past few centuries, with remarkable acceleration in the past few decades. Commodification may not be complete, and it may not be inescapable, but 'the reality of capitalism is that ever more of social life is mediated through and by the market' (Watts 1999, p312).

Water is no exception. Its commoditization may be slow in some places, and uneven geographically, but the underlying pressures of commodification remain, with far-reaching transformative effects.

What are these transformative effects? There are at least two that are particularly relevant to water. The first is that the social rationale for its production is submerged by a focus on exchange value, with 'public good' service ethics and a commitment to professional values overrun by the necessity of turning a profit/surplus. Second, there is a rationalization of service delivery along industrial lines – the 'Taylorization' of services – whereby service activities are cut into increasingly smaller, stand-alone functions, with less skilled tasks being conducted by less skilled and cheaper workers and more skilled tasks being increasingly automated. The result is the creation of 'cost centers', with discrete service functions coming under the same product cycle pressures as hard goods such as computers or washing machines (Leys 2001, pp84–95).

We see the effects of this commodification in water services in the dissection of tasks into smaller and smaller pieces, separated from other water activities and analysed for efficiency improvements (e.g. meter reading, pipe repairs), mechanization (e.g. prepaid meters), outsourcing and possible downloading (e.g. do-it-yourself sanitation systems dug by low income communities).

Here we see corporatization as the logic of commodification par excellence: the compartmentalization of all hitherto integrated service functions into stand-alone, cost recovery units; the homogenization of measurement and reward structures; and the increasingly narrow focus on a financial bottom line. Corporatization may not be the same as privatization in the narrow, ownership sense described at the outset of this chapter, but it does serve to embed market logics into all aspects of the decision making process about water production and distribution, and results in many of the same outcomes.

Based on this we can say that water commodification has had a profound effect on water services in Southern Africa. The majority of water services in the region may still be in public hands – therefore allowing liberal analysts to argue that water has not been privatized in the region[2] – but the reality is that virtually all water systems in Southern Africa have been fundamentally transformed by the (growing) pressures of commodification, as evidenced by the increasing number of public–private partnerships and the running of public water services like a private business.

There are several lessons to be drawn from this line of argument. First, goods and services are not inherently 'public' or 'private' according to some innate set of physical characteristics (as neoclassical theorists would have us believe). The commodification of a good or service is a socially and historically constructed phenomenon that cannot be understood outside of its relationship to a given set of social relations of production.

Second, commodification is not – as some critics earnestly but mistakenly infer – simply an act of attaching a price to a good or service that used to be provided for free. Commodification is a systemic and comprehensive transformation of our material lives; price is merely its external appearance.

Third, to call for the 'decommodification' of water – as many anti-privatization critics do by arguing that water should be provided for free – is to call for nothing less than the rupturing of the social relations that contributed to its commodification in the first place, a radical (and commendable) idea but one that is sometimes unintended by its proponents.

The last, and most important point for the purposes of this chapter, is that commodification is the driver of privatization, commercialization and corporatization. It is, ultimately, the process that facilitates a transfer of ownership and control of resources from public to private hands. At the very least, commodification creates the conditions for goods and services to be captured by the logic of the market, with all of the concomitant inequities and multi-tiered standards that go with this. These are the cascading effects of commodification and they are inherent in all capitalist economies.

Nevertheless, we must distinguish between different institutional forms of water marketization and acknowledge that ownership of assets does matter. In other words, a publicly owned, corporatized water system is different from a privately owned water system, if not in the fundamentals of its practice then at least in terms of the potential public control over its operation. But we cannot ignore the fact that the commodification process slowly erodes the differences. Whether, and how long, public water services in Southern Africa can resist these broader commodification pressures, and stay in public hands, remains to be seen.

Privatization and Commercialization in Practice

To what extent, then, has water actually been privatized and commercialized in Southern Africa? We begin with a look at legislative developments that have served to promote privatization and commercialization and then discuss the extent to which water services have been privatized/commercialized in institutional terms. The overall picture is one of widespread and rapidly expanding marketization, with legislation, international trade agreements, multinational corporations and other pro-market forces poised to deepen the commercialization trend.

Legislative developments

Swatuk (Chapter 2, this volume) reviews some of the major policy changes that have taken place in in SADC countries in the past decade, including cross-border, SADC-based protocols. Other chapters in this book look at country-specific legislative and constitutional developments. We will not, therefore, provide a detailed overview of these matters here.

What must be highlighted, however, is the almost universal liberalization of the water sector in the region. The Water Services Act of 1997 in South Africa, the Namwater Act in Namibia in 1997, the Namibian Water Resources Management Bill of 2001, the Urban Councils Act in Zimbabwe in 1995, the Water Supply and Sanitation Act of 1997 in Zambia, the Water Services Corporation Act of 1992 in Swaziland, and the creation of the Water Supply Investment and Assets Fund and the Council for the Regulation of Water Supply in Mozambique in 1998 – to name but a few – all open the door to private sector investment and/ or increased commercialization (for a discussion of constitutional developments related to water privatization see Flynn and Chirwa, Chapter 3, this volume; also see Stein 2002).

Nor is it just water services that are being targeted. Other municipal services such as electricity, waste management, housing, community health care, libraries and abattoirs have come under privatization pressures across the region since the 1980s (Kerf and Smith 1996; Bond 2000; Qotole et al 2001; Samson 2003). So, too, has there been pressure to privatize other service sectors such as health care and education (Bennell 1996; Kayizzi-Mugerwa 2003; Sy 2003) as well as state-owned enterprises in telecommunications, media, transportation (roads, airports, ports), steel, gas, mining, agriculture and manufacturing (Solomon and van Schalkwyk 1995; Deme 1997; Affulo 1999; Leblanc-Wohrer 2001; *The Economist* 2003).

That water should be part of this broad privatization trend should come as no surprise, especially given its integral place in the market cycle and the enormous attention paid to water privatization by donor agencies and international financial institutions (more on this below). Legislation that explicitly *prevents* private sector involvement or commercialization in the water sector would be an anomaly, and we are not aware of any SADC country that has attempted to do this.

Nevertheless, this is a policy transformation in progress. Legislation has certainly pried open the privatization door in the region but there are often conflicting policy messages, and there is reluctance on the part of some senior policymakers – at least at a rhetorical level – to be seen to be too strongly pro-privatization.

Post-apartheid South Africa is illustrative of this partial legislative shift. After decades of arguing for the nationalization of key sectors of the economy[3] the African National Congress (ANC) abruptly moved towards a market-friendly policy position in the early 1990s, with the 'new South African Government committed to open markets and privatization', according to the US Trade and Development Agency (*Trade and Export News*, 25 July 1997; see also O'Meara 1996, Marais 1998 and Bond 1999 for a critical review of this ideological transition).

The ANC signalled its legislative commitment to water commercialization and privatization shortly after coming to office in 1994 with the adoption of the Water Services Policy in November of that year, stating that 'the Department [of Water Affairs and Forestry (DWAF)] will consider proposals for the private sector to provide services where these may be in the public interest and where this approach is supported by the community concerned' (RSA 1994, p15). This was not the first piece of legislation to allow water privatization in South Africa, however – the apartheid government had introduced broad-based legislation in the late 1980s allowing for privatization and deregulation of services (Heymans 1991) – but it was the first legally binding statement from the ANC that post-apartheid water delivery was going to be private sector friendly. This legislation was followed by the Water Services Act of 1997 and the National Water Act of 1998, as well as several acts related to local government (e.g. the Municipal Services Act of 2000) that further clarified and entrenched the opportunities for private sector involvement in water services delivery.

New, post-apartheid legislation has also entrenched the shift to corporatization with the sanctioning of stand-alone corporations to run water services and with an increasing emphasis on cost recovery and fiscal ringfencing. Take, for example, the directive in the Municipal Systems Act (RSA 2000a, s74.2.d) – omnibus legislation that deals with municipal services throughout the country – that service delivery should be as 'cost reflexive' as possible. In the *White Paper on Water Supply and Sanitation* (RSA 1994, p19) it is argued that 'government may subsidise the cost of construction of basic minimum services but not the operating, maintenance or replacement costs'. The subsequent *National Sanitation Policy White Paper* (RSA 1996, p4) states that: 'Sanitation systems must be sustainable. This means . . . payment by the user is essential'. The *White Paper on Water Policy* (RSA 1997, p4) argues that in order to 'promote the efficient use of water, the policy will be to charge users for the full financial costs of providing access to water, including infrastructure development and catchment management activities'.

The ANC has tempered its position on *full* cost recovery through the use of indigency clauses, progressive block tariffs and, most recently, the introduction of 'free water' for an initial block of consumption (6 kilolitres (kl) per household per month, based on 25 l per person per day for a household of eight), but the extent to which these equity measures have been implemented, how equitable they are and whether they have had a significant impact on quality of life remain a matter of heated debate in the country (McDonald and Pape 2002).

The South African government has attempted to alleviate the privatization concerns of its labour union allies – notably the Congress of South African Trade Unions (Cosatu) – by signing a National Framework Agreement in 1998 which stated that the public sector was the 'preferred service provider' for essential services such as water and sanitation. This commitment was reiterated in the ANC's local government election manifesto in 2000. President Mbeki has also made appearances at Cosatu and South African Communist Party meetings stating that he was committed to public sector reform, and has made similar points in all of his State of the Nation Addresses, as he did in February 2001: 'We have decided that this year the government itself, in all its spheres, and the public sector as a whole, must make a decisive and integrated contribution toward meeting the economic challenges the country faces'.

None of these commitments is legally binding, however. It is the Municipal Systems Act that determines the scope for private sector involvement in water services, and this Act fails to use the term 'preferred provider' altogether. In fact, the most relevant section of the Act (Chapter 8, Part 2) places the public sector on equal footing with alternative service delivery options, including public–private partnerships and outright divestiture. Although a municipality must 'first assess . . . internal mechanisms' when evaluating service delivery options, it may, at the same time, 'explore the possibility of providing the service through an external mechanism' (RSA 2000a, pp72–74). The promises made in the National Framework Agreement to keep the public sector as the 'preferred provider' are effectively trumped, in legal terms, by this binding legislation.

Further commitment to privatization/commercialization is found in the Department of Local and Provincial Government's *White Paper on Municipal Service Partnerships* (the ANC's term for PPPs). Released in early 2000, the paper attempts to clarify the government's position on 'preferred options' but succeeds merely in downgrading the public option to one that is no more important than private sector initiatives:

While the Government is committed to facilitating the use of MSP [municipal service partnerships] arrangements, this does not mean that MSPs are the preferred option for improving service delivery. It is rather that MSPs should enjoy equal status among a range of possible service delivery options available to municipal councils (RSA 2000b, p14).

Mike Muller, the long-standing Director General of the Department of Water Affairs (DWAF) in South Africa, exemplifies this policy 'schizophrenia' in a paper presented to an international conference in 2002. Speaking of the 'vexed role of the private sector in water service provision', he criticizes the 'aggressive push by international water and financial interests for private engagement' in the South, but falls short of rejecting privatization. Rather:

there is a vital role for private expertise and resources in providing water services... If we do not want to give credibility to those who describe private sector engagement as neo-imperialist expansion... we must demonstrate that it is the product of rational institutional decisions designed to achieve public objectives... This is not irrational optimism. There are good reasons to believe that we are at a juncture at which new approaches are possible (Muller 2002, pp6–7).

South Africa is also a signatory to a number of important international agreements that promote privatization (as are many other SADC states). The General Agreement on Trade in Services (GATS) is the most problematic in this regard (see Flecker and Clarke, Chapter 4, this volume) but there are other agreements that bind South Africa to a pro-privatization orientation: for example, the market-friendly Johannesburg Plan of Implementation adopted at the World Summit on Sustainable Development (WSSD) in 2002 with its focus on 'partnerships for development'. These 'partnerships' include communities, nongovernmental organizations (NGOs) and other public sector bodies, but the emphasis is on private sector involvement, as indicated in Section X.99 of the Plan. Countries should:

Complement and support the Doha Ministerial Declaration [on GATS] and the Monterrey Consensus [on development finance] by undertaking further action at the national, regional and international levels, including through public/private partnerships, to enhance the benefits, in particular for developing countries as well as for countries with economies in transition, of trade liberalization.

Existing privatizations

How has this legislation played itself out in concrete, implementational terms? There has been a considerable amount of actual water privatization and commercialization in the region, particularly in South Africa where there has been widespread experimentation with outsourcing and PPPs (e.g. management contracts, BOOTs (Build, Own, Operate and Transfer), etc.). Notably, there has been no outright divestiture of water systems to private companies along the lines of the UK ('We will not sell our public water services infrastructure to the private sector', was South Africa's Water Minister Ronnie Kasrils' emphatic statement on this point to a conference on water privatization in 2003),[4] but there are private water firms operating in various capacities in virtually every country in the region (Bayliss 2002).

Most of the large water multinationals have offices in the region and many have large service contracts. Vivendi (operating as Veolia Environnement) has offices in South Africa and Mauritius. SAUR (operating as Siza Water in its contract in Dolphin Coast) has an office in South Africa (and was involved in a long-term concession in Mozambique until it pulled out in December 2001). Biwater has offices in Tanzania, Angola, Zimbabwe, Zambia, South Africa, Mauritius and Seychelles and operates the Nelspruit concession (see Smith et al, Chapter 7, this volume). Suez has offices in South Africa and manages the water supplies of more than 5 million people in the Eastern Cape and Johannesburg (see Ruiters, Chapter 8, and also Harvey, Chapter 6, this volume). RWE Thames Water has an office in South Africa as well, and although it does not have a contract in the region at the moment the company's website states that it has 'been working to identify a suitable area within South Africa for a pilot project to build on [our] work providing water supplies to deprived communities'.[5] There are smaller multinationals operating in the region as well, such as Aguas de Portugal, which has contracts in Mozambique and Angola.

There are also joint ventures with local firms, 'empowerment' initiatives such as in Nelspruit where black empowerment group Sivukile is a minor partner in the Biwater-led management consortium running that concession. Many medium and small local firms are engaged in outsourcing, with contracts for meter reading, pipe laying, water testing, water cutoffs and so on, being commonplace.[6]

This small-scale contracting out would appear to make up a sizeable portion of the privatization taking place in the region. It is impossible to say with certainty what portion of water services is being provided by private suppliers in this way because of the difficulty of collecting data from so many different sources and because of the piecemeal way in which this small-scale privatization takes place, but outsourcing to local contractors is widespread in Southern Africa, as it is in other parts of the world (Donahue 1989; Lorrain and Stoker 1997), and appears to be on the increase as municipalities are forced by political and economic pressures to cut costs (via the downloading of service responsibilities without adequate fiscal transfers to support them).

But, as discussed earlier, the institutional arrangement is not necessarily as important as the ethos and principles that drive service delivery. As water in the region becomes increasingly corporatized so too does the 'privateness' of the service. As the chapters in this book on Johannesburg, Durban, Cape Town, Pretoria (Tshwane) and Namibia illustrate, the corporatization of water services has resulted in a de facto privatization of water supplies; cost recovery, water cutoffs, outsourcing and two-tiered water systems have become the order of the day. Many of these so-called 'public' utilities are in fact more 'private' than systems run by multinational companies in terms of their aggressive orientation to cost recovery in particular. It is cold comfort, then, to hear former Minister of Water Affairs for South Africa, Ronnie Kasrils, claim that 'the vast majority (97 per cent) of water services providers are expected to remain in the hands of public utilities' in South Africa.[7]

Many corporatized entities in the region also behave like private multi-nationals outside of their home country. South Africa's parastatal electricity provider (Eskom) and Durban's bulk water supplier (Umgeni Water) are cases in point: both are engaged in private contracts to run services in other parts of the continent (Umgeni in Nigeria and Eskom in Uganda). Rand Water, the ringfenced bulk water supplier in the Johannesburg area, is also expanding into private ventures outside the country: in Jordan with the DISI-Mudawarra water conveyance scheme as well as with smaller projects in several African countries, the largest of which is the 'PSP Urban Water Management Contract' in Ghana. Recent legislative changes in South Africa facilitate this expansionist push by making it easier for water boards to be involved in water schemes elsewhere in the world (with a particular focus on Africa, as per the emphasis in the New Partnership for Africa's Development (Nepad) priorities).

Nor can we forget the involvement of NGOs and community organizations in water delivery in the region (also a form of 'privatization' as in our discussion above). Mvula Trust in South Africa is the largest single player in this respect, with a national office in Johannesburg, nine regional offices and a full-time staff of over 100 (see www.mvula.co.za), but there are dozens of other local and international NGOs active in the water sector in the region, involved in everything from financing water schemes to operating water services to involvement in policymaking.

Community based water management is more localized and tends to involve voluntary labour in small-scale water systems (see Greenberg, Chapter 11, this volume), but these initiatives do involve the transfer of public sector decision making authority to private individuals and communities, fragmenting planning and service implementation, undermining public sector labour unions and contributing to the Taylorization of services by downloading less skilled tasks to a voluntary workforce (see Leys' (2001, p90) discussion of the role that 'do-it-yourself' labour plays in the commercialization process).

On the whole, the Southern African experience with privatization is typical of the new global trend towards a multiplicity of public–private partnerships, outsourcing and corporatization. Although the bulk of water services in the region are still (and may continue to stay) in 'public' hands the region is poised for further marketization of water services, not less.

Why Is It Happening?

The question of why water privatization and commercialization is taking place is a hotly contested one. Neoliberal analysts have argued that privatization occurs because states fail: state officials are rent-seeking, inefficient, unaccountable, inflexible and unimaginative. Privatization is seen as a rational and pro-poor policy choice, obvious to anyone willing to look at the track record of public versus private sector water delivery: 'Privatization really works', says the World Bank (2000, p5). 'Consumers are not bothered about economic philosophy – they just want better service at lower prices'.

Hodge (2000, pp35–46), in his review of the privatization literature, identifies five core theories that have been used to explain the privatization phenomenon (internationally and across all sectors): public choice theory, agency theory, transaction cost analysis, new public management and property rights theory. Although different in their individual foci all have at their core the belief that people respond best to market incentives and that market based systems are inherently more efficient and more transparent than traditional public sector arrangements. '[W]e have witnessed a renewed cultural enthusiasm for private enterprise', he argues, spurred on by 'a deficit-induced imperative to limit government spending' (Hodge 2000, p35).

We argue, by contrast, that the privatization of public services has not happened because it has been inspired by some renewed sense of cultural enthusiasm for the market, but rather that it has become a necessity imposed on the state by economic circumstances (Meszaros 1998; Swyngedouw et al 2002, p128): reduced public borrowing; cutting of state spending; liberalization; and the opening up of new economic fields for intensified capital accumulation.

It is possible to trace this shift historically. As economies and the construction of new dams shrank in the 1970s, competition for opportunities in the water sector intensified. This happened at the same time as the state, under fiscal pressure, could no longer keep up spending levels on new infrastructure or in maintaining the old. The privatization of downstream activities – traditionally done by the state – offered new business options, and even if these were risky, contracts could be designed to make them less so. For the water and engineering-construction industry, privatization was seen as a way to absorb idle productive capacity and excess commodities (see Harvey 1982, p329).

The strongest states have now made privatization and opening up markets to their companies a condition of foreign aid. When the US bailed out Mexico in 1994 one of the conditions for the loan was more rapid privatization; that is, Mexico had to absorb even more exports of US capital (Moody 1997). Similar conditionalities are being applied by the US to Iraq; a US$680 billion contract was awarded to American-owned Bechtel in 2003 for service delivery management and upgrades in that country.

Privatization forms part of a frenzied 'process of concentration and consolidation, leading to an oligopolistic economic structure of water utility companies on a world scale' (Swyngedouw et al 2002, p134). According to a comprehensive study of water multinationals by Yaron and Rycroft (1999), between 1994 and 1998 there were 139 water-related mergers and acquisitions, with a total market value of nearly £10 billion. The rate of mergers and acquisitions exploded in 1999 with what were then the largest mergers in history, including the acquisition of US Filter, valued at over US$6 billion, by Vivendi.

Although only in its infancy, the private water sector in the United States generates more than US$80 billion a year in revenue, four times the sales of Microsoft Corporation.

Nowhere in the mainstream literature on privatization is there recognition of the argument that privatization and commercialization are a response to the pressures of an ever-expanding marketization of social relations under capitalism. Nor is there any discussion in mainstream debates of the radical thesis that capitalists must constantly seek new geographic and sectoral areas of investment as a response to capital overaccumulation, or that capitalists are constantly forced to (re)create the physical means of production through the creation (and destruction) of built environments that facilitate market expansion. 'Privatization', argues David Harvey (2003, pp149–50), 'has, in recent years, opened up vast fields for overaccumulated capital to seize upon. . . The neo-liberal project of privatization of everything makes a lot of sense as one way to solve the problem'.

For global capital seeking new areas to commodify, and new sectors in which to invest overaccumulated capital, the water sector (and health and education and other service sectors) provides an enticing opportunity. Worth an estimated US$1 trillion in annual revenue (with only 5–10 per cent of the global water sector currently 'privatized'), it is little wonder that water has attracted so much attention from private capital. As a non-substitutable good with low elasticity of demand, and with the potential for rapid growth through network expansion, population increases and the creation of boutique products such as bottled water (now the second largest bottled beverage by sales in the US and growing rapidly internationally), water offers many advantages to oligarchic capital in particular.

The downside for capital is that the water market in many emerging economies has lost some of its sheen as private firms realize the risks of nonpayment in poor communities and the difficulties and expenses of building water service infrastructure in informal urban settlements and remote rural areas. Witness Suez's recent withdrawal from its much-celebrated 25-year concession contract in Manila and the fact that it is also considering withdrawing from its concession in Buenos Aires. In January 2003 Suez management issued a press statement saying that the company would have a 'reduction of exposure to emerging countries by more than one-third as measured by capital employed [and would instead be] focused on the most profitable and recurrent activities within the global businesses'.

This diminished enthusiasm would appear to be true of Southern Africa as well, as illustrated by SAUR's withdrawal from its concession in Maputo and problems with its concession in Dolphin Coast, South Africa (Hemson and Batidzirai 2002), but it does not mean that large multinationals or local capital are beating a hasty retreat from the water market. The current strategy would appear to be one of switching to shorter-term investments (e.g. Suez's five-year management contract in Johannesburg), more selective geographic coverage (focusing on commercially viable regions/neighbourhoods), and leveraging additional government/funder subsidies and state guarantees to operate in commercially risky areas (see Hall 2003). The fact that so many international water companies still have offices in the region is testament to this (revised) profit optimism.

WHO IS PROMOTING PRIVATIZATION?

Not surprisingly, some of the biggest boosters of water privatization in the region are the private companies themselves. These 'water giants' have spent considerable time and effort trying to secure PPP opportunities. From 'knocking on doors' in Cape Town to flying bureaucrats to visit water concessions in other countries[8] to hosting workshops and producing glossy brochures to sponsoring pro-privatization research, the large private water firms have been actively seeking contracts in the region since at least 1986 when a French delegation first came to South Africa (at the height of apartheid's horrors) to meet with government officials (Ruiters, Chapter 8, this volume).

But it is not just the international water companies that stand to gain. Consultancy firms such as PriceWaterhouseCoopers and KPMG have been active in promoting privatization efforts in the region, often acting as consultants to local governments investigating their service delivery options (see, for example, McDonald and Smith 2004). These same firms are also part of large pro-privatization consortia in Europe and the US lobbying for the expansion and acceleration of GATS (see Flecker and Clarke, Chapter 4, this volume).

Local firms have also been promoters of privatization. National and local chambers of commerce have been actively lobbying local governments in South Africa to privatize services, for example, because they are perceived to reduce tax burdens and/or offer contract opportunities for local entrepreneurs. Empowerment companies have been particularly supportive of this trend, as beneficiaries of affirmative action contracts, especially for small and micro-enterprise businesses.

Another set of privatization promoters are the international financial institutions, most notably the World Bank, which has been active in the region for decades and is arguably the single most influential body in the world promoting water privatization. Bond (2000) has documented the role of the World Bank in promoting the privatization of water and other essential services in South Africa in detail, from its first Mission Teams in the early 1990s to its ongoing use of conferences and policy support to win the 'hearts and minds' of policymakers. Similar efforts have been made by World Bank officials in other parts of the region (see the discussions of Namibia and Ghana, Chapters 14 and 15, this volume, and Mozambique, Zandamela 2001). Other development banks have been active promoters of privatization as well, such as the Development Bank of Southern Africa and the European Investment Bank (on the latter see Mate, Chapter 12, this volume).

Most recently these development banks have been heavily criticized for attaching conditionalities to their lending, with direct and indirect pressures to commercialize and/or privatize water services. The experiences of Ghana and

Zimbabwe are described in this volume but there are other SADC countries (and beyond) not discussed here that have been effectively forced to privatize water and other essential services by the World Bank and the International Monetary Fund (Grusky 2001; Zandamela 2001; ICIJ 2003).

The World Bank has also teamed up with the United Nations Development Programme (UNDP) to create the Urban Management Programme (now situated within UN-HABITAT) which promotes private sector involvement in services. The UNDP has, in turn, established the Public–Private Partnerships for the Urban Environment programme, with an office in Namibia, mandated to 'introduce the PPP idea into ongoing environmental and local governance programmes'.[9]

Bilateral development agencies have also been a factor. USAID, for example, sponsored the formation of the Municipal Infrastructure Investment Unit (MIIU) in South Africa in 1997, with the stated mission of 'encourag[ing] and optimis[ing] private sector investment in local authority services' (www.miiu.org.za/mission.html). Activities involve 'assistance to local authorities in the process of hiring private sector consultants and the management of contracts with the private sector' and 'developing project proposals involving private sector investment', including 'contracting out of the management of ongoing services; concessions to operate the local authority's assets over a defined period; contracts requiring the private sector to Design, Build, Finance and Operate assets to deliver services for the local authority; privatization of assets and services'. The MIIU has provided advice and funding to dozens of municipalities in the country, including the controversial 30-year concession to run the water and sanitation systems in Nelspruit and the five-year management contract in Johannesburg.

Britain's aid agency, the Department for International Development (DFID), has been actively promoting PPPs and private investment in the water sector in the region as well, through its Infrastructure and Urban Development Department. DIFD's total expenditure on water-related projects was £87 million in 2001–2002, about half of which is channelled through pro-privatization multilateral institutions such as the World Bank (*Hansard* 2004). DFID has also hired what George Monbiot calls the 'ultra-right wing' Adam Smith Institute to act as a consultant on privatization, tasked with 'telling countries like South Africa how to flog off the family silver' (*Guardian*, 6 January 2004). Monbiot goes on to point out that DFID spent £56 million on assisting the government of Zambia to privatize its copper mines in 2003 but 'just £700,000 on improving nutrition' in the country, and that in Ghana, '[DFID] made its aid payments for upgrading the water system conditional on partial privatization'.

Germany's aid agency, GTZ, has been active in the promotion of water commercialization (see LaRRI, Chapter 14, this volume, for a discussion of its role in Namibia), as has the Canadian International Development Agency (CIDA); the latter spent Can$4.2 million in 2003:

> *to develop public–private partnership training programs that will be taught in local institutions throughout the region. In Southern Africa, public–*

private partnerships are an important part of encouraging foreign investment in the region and promoting greater social and economic equity (CIDA 2002).

Most, if not all, donor agencies operating in the region are supporting PPP efforts, either directly through bilateral funding or indirectly through support for multilateral agencies such as the World Bank or pro-privatization coalitions such as the World Water Council.

National and local governments and individual politicians and bureaucrats have been active promoters of privatization as well. The legislative developments outlined above provide a formal indication of this ideological orientation at the national level but there are less formal expressions of this hegemony in the way of speeches, attendances at pro-privatization conferences and openings of privately run water systems. No less an authority than Nelson Mandela has publicly endorsed prepaid water and electricity meters and the creation of public–private partnerships, going so far as to say that 'privatisation is the fundamental policy of our government' (as quoted in Pilger 1998, p606).

Local governments, as the 'hands and feet' of service delivery, play a critical ideological and implementational role here. With decentralization a defining feature of most political systems in the region, local governments are increasingly choosing some form of commercialization/privatization. National legislative frameworks and/or fiscal squeezes often force local governments to opt for commercialization/privatization, but it is evident that local politicians and bureaucrats (not to mention local chambers of commerce and small-scale entrepreneurs) are also ideologically committed to the marketization of water services (for a detailed discussion of Cape Town see McDonald and Smith 2004).

Local authorities are also active promoters of commercialization, often working to convince their colleagues in other municipalities that water commercialization is the best policy choice, and organizing regular pro-commercialization workshops and conferences. Take, for example, the South African Prepayment Week conference that took place in June 2004 sponsored by City Power (the corporatized electricity provider in Johannesburg) with the assistance of officials from other municipalities in South Africa and parastatal organizations (e.g. City of Cape Town, electricity provider Eskom), which was designed to promote prepayment water and electricity systems to improve cost recovery.

Local NGOs have been active promoters of privatization in the region too – such as Mvula Trust in South Africa – but there are large international organizations that must be considered here as well. The World Water Council (WWC) – the self-proclaimed 'International Water Policy Think Tank' – is an umbrella organization that develops pro-privatization policy directions for water resources management, and advises on policy matters for decision making bodies. Organizations involved in founding the Council include the World Bank, the United Nations Development Programme (UNDP), the United Nations Educational Scientific and Cultural Organization (UNESCO), the World Conservation Union (IUCN) and the Water Supply and Sanitation Collaborative Council (WSSCC). Members include the South African Department of Water Affairs and Forestry, the Zambezi River Authority, the SADC Water Coordinating Unit and the National Water Directorate in Mozambique. The WWC's sister organization, Global Water Partnership (GWP), with many of the same founding members and the same pro-privatization orientation, has partnerships with Angola, Botswana, Democratic Republic of Congo, Lesotho, Malawi, Mozambique, Namibia, South Africa, Swaziland, Tanzania, Zambia and Zimbabwe.

Finally, there is the role of the media. Although no systematic study of the media's attitude towards (water) privatization has been conducted in the region, a regular monthly compilation of English-language print media in Southern Africa by the Municipal Services Project since mid-2000 suggests an overall newspaper bias towards privatization.[10] Pro-privatization positions are particularly strong in the financial press, not surprisingly, but these attitudes appear to dominate the print media as a whole. Newspaper articles that are critical of privatization do exist but these tend to be opinion pieces (op-eds) written by activists and academics rather than coverage by regular columnists.

What critical coverage there is appears to be almost entirely in the South African press (where the privatization debate is the most public and the most hotly contested). Critical media coverage of privatization in the rest of the region is almost nonexistent, with articles on the subject tending to be uncritical, matter-of-factly or outright supportive in their reportage of the commercialization trend.

Opposition to Privatization

Opposing this juggernaut of pro-privatization supporters in Southern Africa is a loose but growing network of local and international NGOs and community groups, academics and labour unions. There is a rapidly growing literature on these social/labour movements in South and Southern Africa, much of which deals with the explicitly anti-privatization focus of many of these groups (Desai 2002; Bramble and Barchiesi 2003; Desai and Pithouse 2003; Greenberg 2004). Some of this opposition is discussed in the case study chapters of this book and in the boxed inserts between some of the chapters that outline the positions of some of the most prominent anti-privatization organizations (namely, the South African Coalition Against Water Privatization, the Anti-Privatisation Forum, the Anti-Eviction Campaign, the South African Water Caucus, the South African Municipal Workers' Union, and the Ghana National Coalition Against the Privatization of Water).

We do not have the space here to discuss this anti-privatization phenomenon in detail or to engage in the growing debates over the strengths and/or weaknesses of this anti-privatization movement. Our aim is simply to point out that there is opposition to water privatization/commercialization in the region and it is increasingly linked across countries and around the world. In South Africa, this opposition comes primarily from the community groups mentioned above and others such as the Concerned Citizens Forum in Durban (formed in 1997 with Fatima Meer, former ANC stalwart and biographer of Nelson Mandela), most of which are concentrated in larger urban areas.

Union resistance has been strong at times as well, but has been muted by the strong ties between the ANC and Cosatu, the largest trade union federation in the country. Nevertheless, Cosatu has staged several countrywide strikes, drawing several million workers off the job, to protest against the privatization of services. The South African Municipal Workers' Union (Samwu) – a Cosatu member – has been the most vocal in its anti-privatization stance and has, as a result, found its relations with Cosatu and the ANC leadership severely strained at times.

Nongovernmental organizations such as the Environmental Monitoring Group, Earthlife Africa, Alternative Information and Development Centre (AIDC) and SEATINI (in Zimbabwe) have been important here as well, organizing workshops, conducting research and coordinating regional meetings and networks to resist privatization (e.g. through the formation of the Southern African Peoples Solidarity Network), sometimes in collaboration with progressive academics and research groups (e.g. International Labour Research and Information Group (South Africa), Labour Resource and Research Institute (Namibia)).

There are relatively few anti-privatization groups operating outside of South Africa, however, a reflection, no doubt, of the financial and organizational constraints that all nongovernmental and community based organizations in the region face, let alone groups that are explicitly anti-neoliberal. Nevertheless, there is a nascent anti-privatization movement growing in other SADC states (e.g. Zimbabwe Anti-Privatization Forum, The Justice, Peace and Development Centre (Zambia)) and in other parts of the continent that have linked up to the regional debates (e.g. the Ghana National Coalition Against the Privatization of Water).

It is important to also consider international support for anti-privatization initiatives in Southern Africa. Public Services International (PSI) – a public sector union confederation representing approximately 20 million public sector workers around the world – has an office in Johannesburg and has been active in anti-privatization debates in the region, as has its research wing, the PSI Research Unit (PSIRU). Other international organizations directly engaged in anti-privatization debates in the region include: Public Citizen; 50 Years Is Enough; Polaris Institute; Council of Canadians; Canadian Union of Public Employees; ATTAC; and Focus on the Global South.

Interestingly, international media coverage of water privatization and commercialization has been more critical on average outside of Southern Africa than it has been within the region, with newspapers such as the *New York Times*, the *London Observer* and the *Washington Post* running large feature articles critical of privatization initiatives in South Africa. News magazines such as *The Ecologist* and *Mother Jones* have provided equally critical coverage, as have National Public Radio in the United States, the Canadian Broadcasting Corporation (radio and television) and other print and electronic media in Europe, Asia and Australia; the International Consortium of Investigative Journalists have compiled a comprehensive critique of water privatization in South Africa (and other parts of the world) in both radio and book format (ICIJ 2003). 'Indie' media coverage of anti-privatization debates and struggles in the region has been strong as well.

Concrete successes for these anti-privatization groups have been admittedly few, but anti-privatization pressures have arguably been instrumental in the development of some (potentially) progressive policy initiatives (e.g. the 'free water' policy in South Africa) and have been hugely successful at slowing down the rate of service cutoffs and household evictions due to nonpayment of bills, partly through the mobilization of massive community resistance and partly because of clandestine efforts to 'illegally' reconnect homes that have had their water or electricity cut off. It can also be argued that public awareness of the dangers of privatization and commercialization has increased through the actions of these organizations – at least in South Africa where a highly politicized populace is alert to debates over social and economic justice issues.

Nevertheless, privatization debates in the region remain very much a David and Goliath battle, with the World Bank, the IMF, bilateral funding agencies, regional development banks, the vast majority of politicians and bureaucrats, and the neoliberal press and mainstream academia lined up to promote privatization/commercialization on one side, against a determined, but largely dispersed and underfunded network of anti-privatization groups and individuals on the other.

Whether the anti-privatization movement can sustain itself in the face of this fierce and deep-pocketed neoliberal offensive – let alone be able to contribute constructively to the development of more public-oriented service policies – remains to be seen. Suffice it to say that it will be a difficult and lengthy site of struggle.

NOTES

1   The World Bank has a website dedicated to research on privatization and 'pro-poor' policy (http://rru.worldbank.org/PapersLinks/Results.aspx?topicids=3).
2   A good example here are comments made by the editor of the *Mail & Guardian* in Johannesburg, Ferial Haffejee, as follows:

> *There is a view among social movements and the intelligentsia linked to them that South Africa has undergone a massive exercise in water and electricity privatisation. It is plain wrong, yet is repeated over and over again – as if repeating it often enough will make it true. Only four of 284 municipalities – and relatively small ones at that – have contracted out the management of water. It may be four too many, but it is hardly the large-scale sell-off touted in the media. As for electricity supply – none, none of it has been privatised* (11 June 2004).

Haffajee fails to mention that about 5 million people are serviced by these 'privatized' systems. More importantly she fails to see contracting out or corporatization as being problematic, a trend that affects virtually every municipality in the country.

3   Recall the Freedom Charter of 1955:

> *The national wealth of our country, the heritage of South Africans, shall be restored to the people; The mineral wealth beneath the soil, the Banks and monopoly industry shall be transferred to the ownership of the people as a whole; All other industry and trade shall be controlled to assist the well-being of the people* (from the section entitled 'The People Shall Share in the Country's Wealth!').

4   From an address given to the African Investment Forum on the Involvement of the Private Sector in Water and Sanitation, held in Johannesburg on 7 April 2003. Quote taken from press release from DWAF on 8 April 2003.
5   See www.thames-water.com, accessed 30 April 2004.
6   Joe Modise, former Minister of National Defence in South Africa, was a Director of Unihold Business Solutions which won several controversial tenders for water cutoffs and municipal debt collection in Eastern Cape municipalities in 2000–2001.
7   From an address given to the African Investment Forum on the Involvement of the Private Sector in Water and Sanitation, held in Johannesburg on 7 April 2003. Quote taken from press release from DWAF on 8 April 2003.
8   The French government paid for two senior policymakers from Cape Town to visit French company water contracts in Latin America in 1997 (Loftus and McDonald 2001, p2).
9   www.undp.org/ppp, accessed 25 January 2004.
10 See www.queensu.ca/msp for an archive of these news articles.

REFERENCES

Afullo, T.J.O. (1999) 'Telecommunication and Information Infrastructures in the Botswana and SADC Development Strategy', Internet Research, vol 9, no 4, pp287–96
Bakker, K.J. (2003) *An Uncooperative Commodity: Privatizing Water in England and Wales*, Oxford University Press, Oxford
Bauman, D., Boland, J. and Hanemann, M. (1998) *Urban Water Demand Management*, McGraw Hill, New York
Bayliss, K. (2002) 'Water privatisation in SSA: Progress, problems and policy implications', paper presented at the Development Studies Association Annual Conference, University of Greenwich, 9 November
Bennell, P. (1996) 'Privatization, Choice and Competition: The World Bank's Reform Agenda for Vocational Education and Training in Sub-Saharan Africa', *Journal of International Development*, vol 8, no 3, pp467–87
Bollier, D. (2003) *Silent Theft: The Private Plunder of Our Common Wealth*, Routledge, London

Bond, P. (1999) *Elite Transition: From Apartheid to Neoliberalism in South Africa*, University of Natal Press, Durban
Bond, P. (2000) *Cities of Gold, Townships of Coal: Essays on South Africa's New Urban Crisis*, Africa World Press, Trenton, New Jersey
Bramble, T. and Barchiesi, F. (eds) (2003) *Rethinking the Labour Movement in the 'New South Africa'*, Ashgate, London
Brown, J.R. (2003) 'Understanding and Responding to the Commodification of Water', discussion paper, Amigos Bravos/Somos Vecinos, Commodification Project
Burrows, R. and Loader, B. (1994) *Towards a Post-fordist Welfare State?*, Routledge, London
CIDA (Canadian International Development Agency) (2002) 'Canada Supports Sustainable Development in Africa', press release (#2002-45), 31 August
Clarke, J. and Newman, J. (1997) *The Managerial State*, Sage, London
Deme, M.R. (1997) 'The Problems of Privatization: The Experience of Sub-Saharan African Countries', *International Review of Administrative Sciences*, no 63
Desai, A. (2002) *We Are the Poors: Community Struggles in Post-Apartheid South Africa*, Monthly Review Press, New York
Desai, A. and Pithouse, R. (2003) '"But we were thousands": Dispossession, Resistance, Repossession and Repression in Mandela Park', Centre for Civil Society Research Report no 9, University of Natal, Durban
Donahue, J. (1989) *The Privatization Decision*, Basic Books, New York
Dunsire, A. (1999) 'Then and Now: Public Administration, 1953–1999', *Political Studies*, vol 47, no 2, pp360–78
The Economist (1992) 'The First Commodity', 28 March, p11
The Economist (2003) 'Telecoms in South Africa: No Longer on Hold', 8 February
Ernst, J. (1994) *Whose Utility: The Social Impact of Public Utility Privatization and Regulation in Britain*, Open University Press, Buckingham
Estache, A., Woden, Q. and Foster, V. (2002) 'Accounting for Poverty in Infrastructure Reform: Learning from Latin America's Experience', World Bank Institute Development Study, World Bank, Washington, DC
Foster, V. and Aranjo, C. (2001) 'Does Infrastructure Reform Work for the Poor: A Case Study from Guatemala', background paper for Guatemala Poverty Assessment, World Bank, Washington, DC
Goubert, J.P. (1986) *The Conquest of Water*, Princeton University Press, Princeton, New Jersey
Greenberg, S. (2004) 'Post-Apartheid Development, Landlessness and the Reproduction of Exclusion in South Africa', Centre for Civil Society Research Report no 17, University of Natal, Durban
Grusky, S. (2001) 'Privatization Tidal Wave: IMF/Bank Water Policies and the Price Paid by the Poor', *Multinational Monitor*, no 22
Hall, D. (2003) 'Water multinationals in retreat: Suez withdraws investment', PSIRU Research Report, January, www.psiru.org/reports/2003-01-W-Suez.doc
Hanke, S. (ed) (1987) *Prospects for Privatisation*, Academy of Political Science, New York
Hanke, S. and Walters, S. (1987) 'Privatization and Natural Monopoly: The Case of Waterworks', *Privatization Review,* Spring, pp24–31
Hansard (2004) United Kingdom Parliamentary Transcripts, 4 May, www.parliament.the-stationery-office.co.uk/pa/cm200304/cmhansrd/cm040505/text/40505w31.htm
Harvey, D. (1982) *The Limits to Capital*, Chicago University Press, Chicago
Harvey, D. (1990) *The Condition of Post-Modernity*, Basil Blackwell, Oxford
Harvey, D. (2003) *The New Imperialism*, Oxford University Press, Oxford

Hemson, D. and Batidzirai, H. (2002) *Public Private Partnerships and the Poor: Dolphin Coast Water Concession*, Water, Engineering and Development Centre, Loughborough University, Leicestershire

Heymans, C. (1991) 'Privatization and Municipal Reform', in M. Swilling, R. Humphries and K. Shubane (eds) *Apartheid City in Transition*, Oxford University Press, Cape Town

Hodge, G.A. (2000) *Privatization: An International Review of Performance*, Westview Press, Boulder, Colorado

ICIJ (International Consortium of Investigative Journalists) (2003) *The Water Barons: How a Few Powerful Companies are Privatizing Your Water*, Centre for Public Integrity, Washington, DC

Kayizzi-Mugerwa, S. (ed) (2003) *Reforming Africa's Institutions: Ownership, Incentives and Capabilities*, United Nations World Institute for Development Economics Research, New York

Kerf, M. (ed) (1998) 'Concessions for Infrastructure: A Guide to their Design and Award', Technical Papers no 399, World Bank, Washington, DC

Kerf, M. and Smith, W. (1996) 'Privatizing Africa's Infrastructure: Promise and Challenge', Technical Paper no 337, World Bank, Washington, DC

Kovel, J. (2002) *The Enemy of Nature, The End of Capitalism or The End of the World?*, Zed Books, London

Leblanc-Wohrer, M. (ed) (2001) *Privatisation International Yearbook, 2001*, Thomson Financial, London

Leys, C. (2001) *Market-Driven Politics: Neoliberal Democracy and the Public Interest*, Verso, London

Loftus, A. and McDonald, D.A. (2001) 'Lessons from Argentina: The Buenos Aires Water Concession', Occasional Paper no 2, Municipal Services Project, Cape Town

Lorrain, D. (1991) 'Public Goods and Private Operators in France', in R. Batley and G. Stoker (eds) *Local Government in Europe: Trends and Developments*, Macmillan, London

Lorrain, D. and Stoker, G. (eds) (1997) *The Privatisation of Urban Services in Europe*, Pinter, London

McDonald, D.A. and Pape, J. (2002) *Cost Recovery and the Crisis of Service Delivery in South Africa*, Zed Books, London

McDonald, D.A. and Smith, L. (2002) 'Privatizing Cape Town: Service Delivery and Policy Reforms since 1996', Occasional Paper no 7, Municipal Services Project, Cape Town

McDonald, D.A. and Smith, L. (2004) 'Privatizing Cape Town: From Apartheid to Neoliberalism in the Mother City', *Urban Studies*, vol 41, no 8, pp1461–84

Marais, H. (1998) *Limits to Change: The Political Economy of Transition in South Africa*, Zed Books, London

Marx, K. (1978) 'Capital, Volume One', in Tucker, R.C. (ed) *The Marx–Engels Reader*, W.W. Norton and Company, New York

Meszaros, I. (1998) 'The Uncontrollability of Globalizing Capital', *Monthly Review*, vol 49, no 9

Moody, K. (1997) *Workers in a Lean World*, Verso, New York

Muller, M. (2002) 'Lessons from Johannesburg and Pointers for the Future', paper presented at Water 2003: What Should be Done Conference, October, London

Neutze, M. (1997) *Funding Urban Services*, Allen Unwin, St Leonards, Australia

Olcay-Unver, I.H., Gupta, R.K. and Kibaroglu, A. (eds) (2003) *Water Development and Poverty Reduction*, Kluwer Academic, London

O'Meara, D. (1996) *Forty Lost Years: The Apartheid State and the Politics of the National Party 1948–1994*, Ravan Press, Johannesburg
PDG (Palmer Development Group) and School of Governance (2001) *Corporatization of Municipal Water Service Providers Research Report*, Water Research Commission, Cape Town
Pendleton, A. and Winterton, J. (eds) (1993) *Public Enterprise in Transition: Industrial Relations in State and Privatized Corporations*, Routledge, New York
Pilger, J. (1998) *Hidden Agendas*, Vintage, London
PWC (PriceWaterhouseCoopers) (1999) *Corporatization Models for Water and Waste Water Directorates*, PWC, Cape Town
Qotole, M., Xali, M. and Barchiesi, F. (2001) 'The Commercialization of Waste Management in South Africa', Occasional Paper Series no 3, Municipal Services Project, Cape Town
RSA (Republic of South Africa) (1994) *White Paper on Water Supply and Sanitation*, Government Printer, Pretoria
RSA (Republic of South Africa) (1996) *White Paper on National Sanitation Policy*, Government Printer, Pretoria
RSA (Republic of South Africa) (1997) *White Paper on Water Policy*, Government Printers, Pretoria
RSA (Republic of South Africa) (2000a) *Local Government: Municipal Systems Act*, Government Printer, Pretoria
RSA (Republic of South Africa) (2000b) *White Paper on Municipal Service Partnerships*, Government Printer, Pretoria
Samson, M. (2003) *Dumping on Women: Gender and Privatisation of Waste Management*, Municipal Services Project and Samwu, Cape Town
Schofield, R. and Shaol, J. (1997) 'Regulating the Water Industry, Swimming Against the Tide or Going Through the Motions', *The Ecologist*, vol 27, no 1, January/February
Shirley, M.M. (1999) 'The Roles of Privatization versus Corporatization in State-Owned Enterprise Reform', *World Development*, vol 27, no 1, pp115–36
Solomon, M.H. and van Schalkwyk, J. (1995) 'Privatization in the Minerals Sector in South Africa', *Raw Materials Report*, vol 11, no 3
Starr, P. (1988) 'The Meaning of Privatization', *Yale Law and Policy Review*, no 6, pp6–41
Stein, R. (2002) 'Water Sector Reforms in Southern Africa: Some Case Studies', in A. Turton and R. Henwood (eds) *Hydropolitics in the Developing World: A Southern Africa Perspective*, African Water Issues Research Unit, Pretoria
Stoker, G. (1989) 'Local Government for a Post Fordist Society', in Stewart, J. and Stoker, G. (eds) *The Future of Local Government*, Macmillan, Basingstoke, UK
Swyngedouw, E., Kaika, M. and Castro, E. (2002) 'Urban Water: A Political-Ecology Perspective', *Built Environment*, vol 28, no 2, pp124–37
Sy, J.H. (2003) 'Partnership in Higher Education in Africa: Communications Implications beyond the 2000s', *African and Asian Studies*, vol 2, no 4, pp577–610
Taylor-Gooby, P. (2000) *Risk, Trust and Welfare*, Macmillan, Houndsmill, UK
UNDP–World Bank (1998) *Water and Sanitation Programme 1997–98 Report*, Water and Sanitation Programme, Washington, DC
Watts, M. (1999) 'Commodities', in Cloke, P., Crang, P. and Goodwin, M. (eds) *Introducing Human Geographies*, Arnold, London
Whincop, M.J. (ed) (2003) *From Bureaucracy to Business Enterprise: Legal and Policy Issues in the Transformation of Government Services*, Ashgate, Aldershot, UK
WHO and UNICEF (2000) *Global Water Supply and Sanitation Assessment: 2000 Report*, UNICEF, New York

Williams, C.C. (2002) 'A Critical Evaluation of the Commodification Thesis', *The Sociological Review*, vol 50, no 4, pp525–42

Williams, C.C. and Windebank, J. (2003) 'The Slow Advance and Uneven Penetration of Commodification', *International Journal of Urban and Regional Research*, vol 27, no 2, pp250–64

Wolch, J. and Dear, M. (eds) (1989) *The Power of Geography*, Unwin Hyman, Boston, Massachusetts

World Bank (1994) *World Development Report 1994: Infrastructure for Development*, Oxford University Press, New York

World Bank (1997) *World Development Report 1997: The State in a Changing World*, Oxford University Press, New York

World Bank (2000) 'Africa Region', Information Brief no 49, World Bank, Washington, DC

World Bank (2003) *World Development Report 2003: Sustainable Development in a Dynamic World: Transforming Institutions, Growth, and Quality of Life*, Oxford University Press, New York

Yaron, G. and Rycroft, N. (1999) *Suez Lyonnaise Des Eaux*, Polaris Institute and Council for Canadians, Ottawa

Zandamela, H. (2001) 'Lessons from Mozambique: The Maputo Water Concession', Report for the Municipal Services Project, unpublished research paper, available at www.queensu.ca/msp

Chapter 2

The New Water Architecture of SADC

Larry A. Swatuk

There is a new water architecture emerging in the Southern African Development Community (SADC). It is an architecture that takes its cue from both local conditions and global thinking and practice. It involves national reform processes that seek to rewrite outdated water acts, to articulate far-seeing water policies, and to restructure the management of the resource so that the natural watershed or catchment area becomes the unit of decision making rather than an artificial political boundary. This new architecture changes the institutional scale and stakeholders of water management and shows trends towards the privatization of water resource development. Cash-strapped SADC countries claim it is necessary to involve business in what are called public–private partnerships (PPPs).

In this chapter I examine the character of this new water architecture in the region. I start with an historical overview of water resources, locating current patterns of exploitation in the colonial and postcolonial context. I then turn to an examination of the various motivators behind the reform process, looking at national, regional and global influences, before concluding with a discussion of the new dimensions of a SADC water system.

HISTORICAL GEOGRAPHY OF WATER AND HUMAN SETTLEMENT

Water resources are highly unevenly distributed in Southern Africa. The region receives most of its water during the wet summer season (October–April) when rain arrives from the Indian Ocean. Most of this water, however, falls within 400 km of the east coast of the continent. In addition, drought and flood, sometimes occurring simultaneously, are normal regional events (Chenje and Johnson 1996, p2).

There has been a great deal of scholarly and policy-oriented discussion regarding the scarcity of freshwater resources in the region. This is true in a rather mechanical sense: given the regular increase in population and a static absolute amount of water, per capita availability will inevitably decline. However, it is imperative that we understand the socially constructed nature of freshwater resource scarcity vis-à-vis human needs, and the human impact on water availability (Van Koppen 2003, p1048).

Access to fresh, potable water and water based sanitation systems is less decided by facts of nature and more by the deep historical and social inequalities of the region (see UNDP et al 1998, pp16–37). National trends, as presented in Table 2.1, while a good indicator of the state of delivery in the region, mask the facts of intranational disparities. Moreover, there are rural/urban, gender, class and race aspects to inequalities of access, with poor, black females in rural areas, for example, being most likely to lack access to both potable water and adequate sanitation. From Table 2.1 it is apparent that Malawi, Mozambique, Swaziland and Zambia have the highest proportions of unserved populations. Lack of access to sanitation is, in most countries, more severe than lack of access to safe water.

Table 2.1 SADC states' access to clean water and sanitation

Country	Total population (millions)		Population growth rate (%)		% population without access to...	
	1999	2015	1975–1999	1990–2015	safe water 1990–1998	sanitation 1990–1998
Angola	12.8	20.8	3.0	3.1	32.0	—
Botswana	1.5	1.7	2.9	0.7	10.0	45.0
Lesotho	2.0	2.1	2.1	0.4	38.0	62.0
Malawi	11.0	15.7	3.1	2.2	53.0	97.0
Mozambique	17.9	23.5	2.3	1.7	54.0	66.0
Namibia	1.7	2.3	2.7	1.8	17.0	38.0
South Africa	42.8	44.6	2.1	0.3	13.0	13.0
Swaziland	0.9	1.0	2.9	0.7	50.0	41.0
Tanzania	34.3	49.3	3.1	2.3	34.0	14.0
Zambia	10.2	14.8	3.0	2.3	62.0	29.0
Zimbabwe	12.4	16.4	3.0	1.7	21.0	48.0
DRC	49.6	84.0	3.2	3.3	32.0	—

(—) = not available
Source: UNDP (2000, pp170–71; 2001, pp155–56)

Changing patterns and forms of human settlement also impact on the forms of use and styles of management of water resources. Settler style colonialism resulted in the creation of what Crosby (1986) calls 'neo-Europes'. Urban centres developed delivery systems based on the technologies imported from water-rich Europe. Typically, the lion's share of supplied water went to irrigated agriculture, with mines and industries also enjoying privileged access. This continues to be the case today, with irrigation commanding an average of 65–75 per cent of the region's exploited water resources (Pallett 1997).

However, the attempt to reproduce Europe in Africa also meant that indigenous food crops and farming methods were displaced by European ones, often resulting in the substitution of drought-resistant food crops with water-guzzling beverage crops and minimum tillage systems with soil eroding practices. Choices of settlement locations with no regard to water sources also created problems. Both Bulawayo and Harare, for example, were military sites. Johannesburg and Kimberley grew out of the mid-19th-century gold and diamond rushes. The site for Windhoek, chosen because of the presence of a spring, is an exception. Unlike precolonial patterns of human settlement, the colonial/settler impact has resulted in large populations congregating relatively far from adequate freshwater resources. In consequence, the region has a recent history of large-scale water transfer and storage schemes (Heyns 2003). This supply-oriented thinking remains dominant even today (Mwendera et al 2003).

All of these patterns of settlement and attendant problems are exaggerated in the context of apartheid social engineering, replicated to a large degree in Zimbabwe and Namibia, and to varying degrees in Botswana, Swaziland and Zambia: alienation of fertile land and the creation of plantation agriculture; forced removals of indigenous people and their relocation to arid homelands; the creation of ill-placed or non-serviced locations, which in the beginning were little more than dormitories for cheap labour.

Changing global structures of production have also exacerbated settlement problems in the region. Countries which had long supplied labour to the mines and farms of South Africa – recruited via Witwatersrand Native Labour Association (WNLA) – in recent years have seen the return of tens of thousands of these citizens, retrenched as the South African mining industry continues to restructure. Cities like Blantyre, Malawi, and Maseru, Lesotho, have increased numbers of newly unemployed and displaced people.

Taken together, what these facts reveal is water security for the few and insecurity for the many. The crisis of scarce water is socially constructed; its roots are historical, the result of deliberate actions taken in the service of settler and colonial interests. Its contemporary manifestations result from a combination of continuing elite privilege, shallow social and physical science, and the collective actions of millions of people responding logically to abiding conditions of poverty and underdevelopment.

The region's water resources cannot be discussed outside of these facts. Indeed, it is a mistake to think that managing water is an apolitical issue concerning choices of appropriate technology and strategies for sectorally specific human resource development. To the contrary, the region's water is merely a pool reflecting back to us the contradictory faces of unlimited privilege for the few and limitless poverty for the many. How then to better manage these resources?

REASONS FOR RECENT REFORM

Given the above historical and contemporary setting, the pressures for reform of the water sector come in many shapes and sizes, some with more influence and better organization than others. In this section I discuss motivators for reform from three perspectives: national, regional and global. The list provided is not exhaustive. It is meant to be indicative of the primary forces driving water resources management reforms.

National

In most SADC states, water resource use and management has long followed a colonial path of development, with various limited modifications after independence. This means that the infrastructure and socio-hydrology that has grown up around the resource has privileged white settlers in urban and rural settings, as well as settler and foreign capital in industry, mining and large-scale agriculture. During the colonial/apartheid periods there was a general neglect of the needs and concerns of indigenous people. In the South African case, present problems are worse than they might have been if, for example, water-borne sanitation systems, storm sewers and the like had been built along with the apartheid era's dramatic expansion of roads. But the intention of better road networks was apartheid control, not the satisfaction of basic human needs. The recent massive influxes of people into urban and peri-urban areas (and punitive cost recovery policies) have set the scene for health emergencies (such as epidemics of cholera) because of the absence of reticulated sewage systems.

In Angola and Mozambique, the departing Portuguese deliberately sabotaged infrastructure, for example, by pouring cement into drainpipes. During the long periods of civil war anything of value that could be removed and sold on the open market was, including ceramic bathroom fixtures and copper/lead piping in households and apartment buildings. Today in Beira, Mozambique, people buy water by the bucketful in markets set up outside high-rise buildings lacking basic infrastructure.

In all SADC countries, the independence period saw a dramatic expansion of activity surrounding the provision of basic needs, with a specific focus on the rural areas and the exploitation of groundwater resources. Not only did this create new layers of bureaucracy, it also cost the state a great deal of money. In some cases, this state-building exercise was complicated by South African destabilization of the region. Still today, the Beira and Tete corridors of Mozambique show the scars of war.

Generally speaking, surface water and groundwater have been treated as separate entities. Surface water is usually under the control of a central authority, such as the Department of Water Affairs, whose task it is to supply bulk raw and treated water to urban households and for commercial purposes. The department is usually also responsible for overall planning, for providing vision. Groundwater, on the other hand, has generally been treated as a private good (i.e. those with the capacity to extract it can do so without charge) although limits may be placed on the total abstractable amount. This policy has resulted in such oddities as Harare homeowners drawing water from boreholes to minimize their costs even though both ground and surface water are part of the same watershed. In the rural areas, water has been treated as an essential public service, so the focus here usually has been provision via borehole under the auspices of district councils (DC) or rural district councils (RDC).

This resource split also foreshadows the multiple players in the provision and administration of water including some or all of the following: river boards (usually an association of commercial farmers holding riparian rights or permits), RDC and DC, provincial administrations, national government through several ministries and related departments (agriculture, water, wildlife and tourism, land and mineral resources), city councils, and a wide variety of funding and servicing agencies (e.g. district development fund, agricultural extension services). Although these groups liaise with one another, it is inevitable that conflicts and sometimes conflicts of interest arise in the attempt to manage the resource. It would be wrong to suggest that an overall policy exists to smooth the decision making process. In a recent interview of a high ranking technocrat in Botswana's Ngamiland District Land Use Planning Unit, the question was asked, 'What role do you play in the making of water policy?' The response: 'Water policy? Do we have one?' (Swatuk and Rahm, forthcoming).

Lastly, policymakers throughout the region recognize that current allocations favour irrigated agriculture, mining and industry. This leads to waste due to inefficient use and high state subsidies (in some cases, the water is free), widespread pollution due to the inability to police the ways in which (toxic) waste is disposed, and a decline in the overall quality and quantity of the resource due to agro-industrial practices, particularly for downstream users.

Thus, to summarize the pressures for water reform at national level we may borrow from the Government of Zimbabwe's Water Resources Management Strategy document (Government of Zimbabwe 2000, pp7–8) wherein nine factors are identified:

1   continuing inequities of use and access;
2   too many actors/institutions and too little coordination;
3   increasing competition for a scarce and finite resource;
4   generally poor water resources;
5   declining quality of that limited resource;
6   lack of state-generated finance to adequately run the sector;
7   lack of a common policy/benchmark by which to judge actions in the sector;
8   a narrow band of stakeholder involvement in the sector;
9   recurrent drought on a large scale.

Regional

By region I mean that group of states constituting the SADC, which for the purposes of this chapter excludes Mauritius and the Seychelles and deals only with the continental land based members. Regarding pressures for reform at this level, I will mention only three: the potential for integrated, regional development; the contrast between a well-watered north and a poorly watered south; and the fact of shared watercourses.

In terms of regionally centred development, the post-apartheid era has seen a proliferation of activities geared to exploit the complementarities of the region's resources, wherein water is regarded as a factor of production (Swatuk and Vale 2000). Emblematic of this new regionalism is the push towards an integrated energy network linking the hydropower (real and potential) of the north to the coal-based thermal power of the south. Driving this enterprise is the Southern African Power Pool (SAPP) led most conspicuously by the South African energy giant Eskom (Horvei 1998; Swatuk 2000).

Water is central in a variety of other regional development initiatives: for example, the attempt to sell Southern Africa as a global tourist destination of choice (nonconsumptive use), and to manufacture or trade upon already existing subregional complementarities in the form of growth corridors (Beira, Maputo, Trans-Kalahari) and cross-border initiatives (transfrontier parks) that combine consumptive and nonconsumptive forms of water resource use. Numerous SADC protocols (on trade, energy, tourism, water resources, labour) seek to legislate regularities that will build around these activities.

Related to these initiatives is the fact that the bulk of the region's water resources are found in the north, whereas most of its people and industrial development are found further south, particularly in South Africa. South Africa's growing demand for water has led policymakers there to consider a number of international inter-basin transfer schemes. The Lesotho Highlands Water Project (Phase I) is already operational and remains highly controversial (Pottinger 1996; Bond and Ruiters 2001). Interstate and institutional discussions have been under way for some time regarding the possibility of drawing water from the Zambezi River (via the Matabeleland water transfer project, contested but under construction) and possibly the Congo River further north. Some observers consider the Democratic Republic of Congo's (DRC) inclusion in the SADC to have been spurred by the future promise of that country's vast natural resources, not the least of which is water (Swatuk 1997).

Lastly, the SADC region is characterized by numerous international river basins. One of the consequences of settler colonial policy was that rivers became convenient means for demarcating borders, so what were once the life sustaining arteries of regional settlement became the life threatening loci of potential water wars today (see Swatuk and Vale 1999 for details).

As can be seen in Table 2.2, there are at least 15 international watercourses in the SADC region. Usage of these waterways has, historically, proceeded along the lines of either unilateral exploitation of the resource within national boundaries or exploitation based on a bilateral or multilateral agreement signed by the basin states. Usually these agreements have been single issue oriented: that is, regarding water transfer, storage and use by agriculture (an irrigation scheme), industry (hydropower) or primary consumption (an urban population). Until very recently there has been little attempt to rationalize or coordinate the impacts of these many and various agreements either within a specific basin or in terms of broader regional sensibilities.

In the 1980s, however, this all began to change. If one were to attempt to pinpoint a defining moment in progressive approaches to regional cooperation

Table 2.2 *International river basins shared between SADC states*

Basin	Basin states	Special features
Buzi	Mozambique, Zimbabwe	Two small hydropower installations in Mozambique; one of the dams used for irrigation
Cuneme	Angola, Namibia	Potential hydropower of 2400 MW; four dams in Angola; one in Namibia controversial because of impact on indigenous people (at Epupa gorge)
Cuvelai	Angola, Namibia	Low and erratic run-off; 40 dams built to provide water for agriculture, livestock, and about 50% of Namibia's people; inter-basin transfer from Cuneme to Cuvelai
Incomati/ Nkomati	Mozambique, South Africa, Swaziland	Twenty-two large dams in catchment with two more in progress; several international operating agreements; clear indications that natural flows in dry season greatly reduced through abstractions
Limpopo	Botswana, Mozambique, South Africa, Zimbabwe	Four dams in Botswana, one in Mozambique, 26 in South Africa, nine in Zimbabwe; transfrontier national park planned in basin
Maputo/ Pongola	Mozambique, South Africa, Swaziland	Five dams in South Africa, four in Swaziland, one in Mozambique; important water source for population of southern Mozambique; much flow diverted by South Africa and Swaziland
Nata	Botswana, Zimbabwe	Partly ephemeral; considered to be of little international significance
Okavango	Angola, Botswana, Namibia	Endorheic river system designated a World Heritage site; planned off-take near Runde to bring water to Windhoek; draft catchment management plan recently completed; potential peace in Angola could lead to upstream development
Orange	Botswana, Lesotho, South Africa, Namibia	Most overdeveloped river in region with 24 large dams in South Africa, five in Namibia and two in Lesotho; numerous intra- and inter-basin transfers; location of controversial Lesotho Highlands Water Project
Pungwe	Mozambique, Zimbabwe	Off-take near headwaters in Nyanga National Park Mountain brings water to the Zimbabwean city of Mutare; sugar plantations, national park, city of Beira dependent on downstream flow
Rovuma	Malawi, Mozambique, Tanzania	No significant development made or planned but could gain in significance for Mozambique if Save/ Pungwe flows decreased in future

Table 2.2 *International river basins shared between SADC states (continued)*

Save	Mozambique, Zimbabwe	Osborne dam in Zimbabwe unused at present; sugar plantations in lowlands in Mozambique; provides 20% of Mozambique's surface water; supports highest density of rural Zimbabwe population; Chimanimani and Gonarezhou national parks in basin
Umbeluzi	Mozambique, Swaziland	Two dams in Swaziland, one in Mozambique
Zaire/ Congo	DRC, Angola, CAR, Cameroon, Tanzania, Zambia	Potential hydropower development at Inga Rapids with 34,000 cumecs at high flow; is main 'road' in DRC; potential 45,000 MW largest hydroelectric energy in world
Zambezi	Angola, Botswana, Malawi, Mozambique, Namibia, Tanzania, Zambia, Zimbabwe	Fourth largest river basin in Africa; supports 20 million people (30% of total population of basin countries); first UNEP Eminwa project led to Zacplan then SADC water protocol; two dams in Malawi, five in Zambia, 12 in Zimbabwe, one in Mozambique; numerous developments planned (more hydropower, inter-basin transfer pipelines, irrigated agriculture), some of controversial nature

Source: Adapted in part from Ohlsson (1995, pp55–57) and Conley (1996, pp24–55)

on shared water resources, it would be the 1985 United Nations Environment Program (UNEP)-led decision to use the Zambezi River as a pilot case in its Environmentally Sound Management of Inland Waters (Eminwa) project. Meetings attended by then SADC states were held in Nairobi (1985), Lusaka (1986) and Gaborone (1987), out of which was established Zacplan – the Zambezi River Action Plan – immediately designated a 'concerted action programme of SADC'.

It is significant that two defining moments in regional water resource management centred on the Zambezi River. In the late 1950s, the Kariba Dam was built in the hopes of providing the electricity requirements for the industrialization of the then federation of Rhodesia and Nyasaland. According to Moyo et al (1993, p326), 'with an area of 5250 km^2, it is Africa's largest reservoir, having a capacity of 180,000 million cubic metres'. In 1986, Zimbabwe and Zambia created the Zambezi River Authority (ZRA), a bilateral arrangement for the management of the waters and hydropower resources of the middle Zambezi. According to Chenje and Johnson (1996, p166): 'ZRA replaced and took over the properties of the old Central African Power Corporation [CAPC]'. Unlike Zacplan, however, the ZRA, like its CAPC predecessor, is centrally concerned with the management of water along a limited portion of river as a factor of production. Zacplan, on the other hand, seeks to manage the waters of the entire Zambezi River Basin in an integrated and sustainable way, including its environmental use. Thus, old and new approaches to water resources management coexist in a single basin, signalling the uneasy relationship that exists throughout the SADC region between old ideas of partial, exclusivist modernization and new ones of holistic, inclusive sustainable development.

Hoping to build on the latter, Zacplan became the template for the now well-known SADC 1995 protocol on shared watercourse systems. Revised and signed in August 2000 by all SADC member states except for the DRC, the protocol came into force in October 2000 following ratification by the required two-thirds of the member states. The revised SADC protocol aims, inter alia, to facilitate interstate cooperation for judicious and coordinated utilization of the region's shared water resources. The overall aim is to facilitate broad-based and sustainable socioeconomic development.[1]

Aside from the trend towards regional protocols, a number of specific initiatives have also emerged in the form of standing commissions, technical units and the like (e.g. the operational Okavango, Orange/Senqu, Limpopo and Cunene River Basin Commissions; the proposed Zambezi River Basin Commission).

Clearly, one of the great motivators for reform at the regional level comes from individual SADC state participation at UN and other international fora. Indeed, one could make the argument that most SADC state activity in the area of environmental resources management came in preparation for and following on from the United Nations Conference on Environment and Development (UNCED) meeting held at Rio de Janeiro in 1992. While SADC state interests in forging regional agreements on water and other natural resources management have local roots, the influence of international thinking and action should not be underestimated. To quote Van Koppen (2003, p1048): 'One can speak of a global movement for IWRM-based [integrated water resource management] water reform, in which African stakeholders take active part'.

Global

Global discourses – sustainable development, environmental security, development and peace, and the increasing linkage of economic development, tourism and conservation – are now firmly entrenched in virtually every policy document regarding natural resource use. For example, the South African Department of Water Affairs and Forestry *White Paper on a National Water Policy for South Africa* (DWAF 1997, p35) states that:

> *the quantity, quality and reliability of water required to maintain the ecological functions on which humans depend shall be reserved so that the human use of water does not individually or cumulatively compromise the long term sustainability of aquatic and associated ecosystems* (Principle 9).

Similarly, Chapter 7 of the Government of Zimbabwe's *Water Resources Management Strategy* (2000, pp57–66) is entitled 'A Fair Share for the Environment'.

With specific regard to water, the attempt to move towards 'demand management' – which involves working within the existing limitations of the found resource rather than augmenting supply, and towards consideration of water resources as part of a wider ecosystem through the promotion of integrated water resources management – reflects global thinking (e.g. the Dublin Principles, Agenda 21) as well as local realities.

Global worries regarding environmental security have filtered down to the regional level, particularly in the form of water wars (Ohlsson 1995; Hudson 1996). One of the claims motivating the regional water reform process is the following made by South Africa's Water Research Commission in 1994: 'South Africa will run out of water between 2020 and 2030 unless measures to combat the shortage are taken' (quoted in SAIRR 1994, p1). Pallett (1997, pp44–45) claims that Botswana, Malawi and Namibia exist in conditions of 'absolute water scarcity', while South Africa and Zimbabwe suffer 'water stress'. Despite a growing global consensus regarding the unlikelihood of water wars (even in Homer-Dixon 1999), these claims preface virtually all academic and policy writing on water and/or environmental security in the region.

The scientific measures supporting these truth claims are internationally derived. For example, European scholar Malin Falkenmark (1986) established the benchmarks for 'water stress' (more than 600 people per 'flow unit', equal to 1 million m^3) and 'absolute water scarcity' (more than 1000 people per 'flow unit'). According to this measure, in 1995 there were said to be 4257 people per flow unit in Botswana, 1500 in Malawi and about 1200 in Namibia. However, after reciting these facts, Pallett points out that these statistics are a crude measure which neither distinguishes between total run-off or available run-off, nor accounts for groundwater resources or water available from lakes; hence the clearly misleading figures for Botswana and Namibia, which derive most of their freshwater from groundwater sources, and for Malawi, whose major source of freshwater is Lake Malawi.

Moreover, a significant portion of Falkenmark's water allocation is given over to irrigation, yet the vast majority of food produced in both Southern Africa and the world uses 'green water' (rainwater that has been absorbed by plants), not extractions from surface and ground water supplies. Lastly, throughout Southern Africa the vast majority of freshwater – of the order of 70 per cent of all water used – is used by irrigators, most of whom are producing cash crops for export. If there is a freshwater shortage, should current allocations not be the subject of interrogation? Pallett (1997) suggests that, were better methods put into use, current levels of irrigated agricultural production in the region could be sustained while using one-sixth of the present amount of water. Why, then, are these things not being done?

These are rhetorical questions, of course. The point is to show how global narratives get imported into the SADC context and, without questioning, sometimes become the basis upon which future policy is made. The same might be said about privatization, as will be shown below.

Running like an undercurrent through both the sustainable development and environmental security discourses are key neoliberal assumptions which are also at the heart of recent Western thinking on the interrelationship between development and peace: that is, development involves social change which, if it is to result in peaceful societies, must rest upon open markets and liberal democratic forms of governance. Although contested in a wide variety of international forums, this perspective has gained the upper hand in mainstream approaches to environment and natural resources use and management. Duffield (2001, pp10–11) defines the 'liberal peace' in the following way:

> *The idea of* liberal peace ... *combines and conflates 'liberal' (as in contemporary liberal economic and political tenets) with 'peace' (the present policy predilection towards conflict resolution and societal reconstruction). It reflects the existing consensus that conflict in the South is best approached through a number of connected, ameliorative, harmonising and, especially, transformational measures.*

How these ideas translate into policy is most readily seen in the present directions being taken by donors in the SADC region. All major donor policies rely on (at least) the following five assumptions:

1 State-by-state structural adjustment programmes are a necessary part of regional economic growth and development.
2 Regionally integrative activities (e.g. in the areas of trade and transboundary natural resources management) build economies of scale and facilitate regional comparative advantage, so facilitating sustainable niche development.
3 Where possible, 'developmental' activities should cultivate 'smart-partnerships' between civil society actors in recipient countries and private enterprises in donor countries.
4 Recipient states should become facilitators rather than initiators of development. Hence, they should concentrate on creating and upholding regulatory frameworks wherein the private sector can pursue developmental activities which are self-defined.
5 All of these activities should be undertaken in the spirit of democratic participation, including transparent and accountable forms of decision making.

Like the need to locate the water reform process within the context of historical continuities, we must also consider the degree to which current global ideological trends determine both the regional process of reform and its likely outcome. With this in mind, let us now turn to the emerging architecture of water management in the SADC region.

THE EMERGING ARCHITECTURE

National water reforms are nested within a wide series of regional and global initiatives, many of which are interlinked. For South Africa's water policy-makers this is a good thing:

> *With the ending of apartheid, South Africa's water law review has not had to be conducted in isolation from the rest of the world as in the past. The problems confronted here are not unique. . . As a result, not only is there a large amount of international thought, policy and practice which can be recast to meet the specific conditions of South Africa but South Africa's own efforts to address water policy in a structured and principled way have attracted great interest* (DWAF 1997, p11).

In general, at the national level the new water architecture attempts to tie a shared vision based on equity, sustainability and efficiency to a system of delivery dependent on stakeholder involvement. In terms of institutions, the catchment itself is to be the unit of social organization and resource management. New water acts based on freshly minted water master plans are being put in place across the region. Zimbabwe has gone furthest in the reform process with a new water act, and catchment councils in place. South Africa, having enacted a number of new water laws, faces some difficulty in establishing new catchment authorities. The initial stipulation that stakeholders must themselves petition the Department of Water Affairs and Forestry to become a Catchment Management Authority has resulted in contrary applications often representing partial interests (e.g. white commerical farmers and Eskom versus emerging farmers in the Crocodile River basin) (Schreiner and Van Koppen 2002).

Debt distressed states such as Malawi, Mozambique, Tanzania and Zambia are moving ahead with donor orchestrated reforms (including privatized urban water delivery systems). Swaziland, a key riparian in several river basins, and heavily dependent on South Africa (for capital) and Mozambique (for cheap farm labour) is also moving ahead with the reform process. Namibia, too, is strongly committed to these reforms, working towards the establishment of catchment councils within its primarily ephemeral river systems. Botswana and Lesotho, whose rivers are all internationally shared watercourses, are active mostly in the area of transboundary river basin commissions.

In all cases, the stated objective is to make water resources management a sustainable, self-financing enterprise. Catchment councils/management authorities are to be empowered with the ability to collect payment in the form of fees for permits, levies for flowing and stored water, and penalties for a variety of offences, among other things. Development in the catchment is to be guided by a management plan developed by the council/authority. All stakeholders are to be party to these plans and onside regarding revenue generating practices and procedures. However, what we have seen is the way in which already empowered actors seek to dominate and control the institutional mechanisms or, in the case of some city councils, most mines, some large-scale farmers and almost all smallholders (who fear loss of access to the resource altogether), the new architecture has been deliberately ignored (Dube and Swatuk 2002).

Clearly there are contradictory forces at work. For example, the new water architecture claims to work towards a fairer and more sustainable allocation of resources. Yet, if catchment councils in particular, and the water sector in general, are to be self-financing, this means that each has a vested interest in the continuing and probably expanding sale of water for commercial use. This therefore means that councils are likely to favour those that can pay for water, that is, those who already know how to exploit the resource. As another example, all SADC national water authorities acknowledge that new supplies will continue to be tapped. Yet, they also claim that integrated water resource management requires working within the limits of the specific catchment. Creating new water requires not augmenting supply but restraining demand.

There are numerous approaches to demand management, some more progressive than others (Goldblatt et al 1999). But in almost every case, policy-makers prefer new supply to demand control. The reasons for this are fairly obvious: a dense web of private capital and public power, the former tied to profit and the latter to votes and the status quo, view supply as the far more lucrative option (Gumbo and Van der Zaag 2002).

Pricing Water: Whose Water Is It Anyway?

All SADC states now claim a central concern with water demand management (WDM) (Mwendera et al 2003). Thinking about WDM is being facilitated by a number of regional (e.g. SADC water sector) and regionally based (e.g. World Conservation Union (IUCN), UNDP, Global Water Partnership (GWP)) institutions, as well as donors (e.g. the Swedish International Development Agency (SIDA) through its support for the 'communicating the environment' programme and Water Research Fund for Southern Africa). WDM considerations are also clearly reflected in basin management plans, for example the draft Okavango River Basin Management Plan.

At the centre of WDM is pricing policy. Along the lines of the business dominated second World Water Forum at the Hague, SADC states now acknowledge that water must be treated as an economic good. As a scarce commodity, it should not be underpriced. SADC states differ in their pricing policies: for example, Botswana sets tariffs to reflect the costs of supply to different centres and users, and Zimbabwe sets what is called a national blend price. Most SADC states implement a rising block tariff, some with steeper blocks than others. In this way, heavier water users subsidize those who use less water. Most states also include a lifeline tariff where, for example, a certain amount of water may be provided free of charge by the state (say 25 l/day/person, as is the case in South Africa) or a minimal fee is charged (e.g. in Botswana where a family of eight with piped water in an urban setting using about 50 l/person/day would pay less than US$2.00/month in total).

In principle, SADC states are claiming commitment to water pricing policies geared to full cost recovery. Given that throughout the region the major users have historically had their water heavily subsidized, if paying for it at all, it remains to be seen how this will play out in practice. It also raises questions about new systems of delivery for those historically disadvantaged by the apartheid system: if new systems are built, who will pay the full cost?

Early evidence drawn from across the region suggests that the primary motivation for reform is external: that is, it emanates from the donor community which is firmly committed to neoliberal economic approaches to development in recipient states; hence the contradictory outcomes of policy implementation. While full cost recovery and management at the lowest appropriate level may reduce the economic burden on the central state in line with structural adjustment conditionalities, it raises endless contradictions and numerous conflicts at the level of the water point. Indeed, smallholder farmers in the Rufiji river basin in Tanzania are convinced that the reform process is designed to *decrease* their access to upstream water in order to ensure a more steady supply for the downstream Tanesco (the parastatal electricity supply company) hydropower plant. Debt distressed and human resource limited states like Malawi, Mozambique and Tanzania seem content to let the conflicts play themselves out at the local level (Kashaigili et al 2003; Madulu 2003; Mulwafu et al 2003).

Conclusion

Rain falls and water flows. It knows no borders. Yet we have inherited a series of lines on a map which tell us that some people have a (riparian) right to this water while others do not. Privatization further suballocates this resource with no guarantee of sustainable use, conservation, improved quality and the like.

According to Savenije (2002, p744), water is not just another economic good. While cost recovery is important, it should not blind us to the need for active state intervention to overcome the development deficit in the region. The question may be, cost recovery from whom? Saying that water is an economic good does not necessarily imply that a market price needs to be paid for it to make the allocation efficient. In fact, it does not mean that it should be paid for at all.

At minimum, deals made at regional, national, subnational and local levels must be transparent and those who make the deals must be held accountable. While pressures for public–private partnerships in the management of the region's water resources remain high, it is imperative that broader *public–public* partnerships be struck to ensure that privatization does not mean, as I fear it will come to mean, the state absolving itself of its developmental role.

Notes

1 See, for example, www.sardc.net/Editorial/Newsfeature/waterprotocol.htm

References

Bond, P. and Ruiters, G. (2001) 'Drought and Floods: Water Shortages and Surpluses in Post-Apartheid South Africa', draft manuscript

Chenje, M. and Johnson, P. (eds) (1996) *Water in Southern Africa*, African Books Collective, Oxford

Conley, A. (1996) 'A Synoptic View of Water Resources in Southern Africa', in H. Solomon (ed) *Sink or Swim? Water, Resource Security and State Co-operation*, IDP Monograph Series, no 6, Institute for Defence Policy, Pretoria

Crosby, A. (1986) *Ecological Imperialism: The Biological Expansion of Europe 900–1900*, Cambridge University Press, London and New York

Dube, D. and Swatuk, L. A. (2002) 'Stakeholder Participation in the New Water Management Approach: A Case Study of the Save Catchment, Zimbabwe', *Physics and Chemistry of the Earth*, vol 27, nos 11–22, pp867–74

Duffield, M. (2001) *Global Governance and the New Wars*, Zed Books, London

DWAF (Department of Water Affairs and Forestry) (1997) *White Paper on a National Water Policy for South Africa* (April), Government Printer, Pretoria

Falkenmark, M. (1986) 'Fresh Water: Time for a Modified Approach', *Ambio*, vol 15, no 4, pp194–200

Goldblatt, M., Ndamba, J., van der Merwe, B., Gomes, F., Haasbroek, B. and Arntzen, J. (1999) *Water Demand Management: Towards Developing Effective Strategies for Southern Africa*, IUCN, Gland, Switzerland

Government of Zimbabwe, Ministry of Rural Resources and Water Development (2000) 'Water Resources Management Strategy for Zimbabwe', Government Printer, Harare

Gumbo, B. and Van der Zaag, P. (2002) 'Water Losses and the Political Constraints to Water Demand Management: The Case of the City of Mutare, Zimbabwe', *Physics and Chemistry of the Earth*, vol 27, nos 11–22, pp805–14

Heyns, P. (2003) 'Water Resources Management in Southern Africa', in M. Nakayama (ed) *International Waters in Southern Africa*, UNU Press, Tokyo

Homer-Dixon, T. (1999) *Environment, Scarcity and Violence*, Princeton University Press, Princeton, New Jersey

Horvei, T. (1998) 'Powering the Region: South Africa and the Southern African Power Pool', in D. Simon (ed) *South Africa in Southern Africa: Reconfiguring the Region*, James Curry, London

Hudson, H. (1996) 'Water and Security in Southern Africa', in H. Solomon (ed) *Sink or Swim? Water, Resource Security and State Co-operation*, IDP Monograph Series no 6

Kashaigili, J.J., Kadigi, R., Sokile, C. and Mahoo, H. (2003) 'Constraints and Potential for Efficient Inter-sectoral Water Allocations in Tanzania', *Physics and Chemistry of the Earth*, vol 28, nos 20–7, pp839–52

Madulu, N.F. (2003) 'Linking Poverty Levels to Water Resource Use and Conflicts in Rural Tanzania', *Physics and Chemistry of the Earth*, vol 28, nos 20–27, pp911–18

Moyo, S., Sill, M. and O'Keefe, P. (1993) *The Southern African Environment*, Earthscan, London

Mulwafu, W., Chipeta, C., Chavula, G., Ferguson, A., Nkhoma, B.G. and Chilima, G. (2003) 'Water Demand Management in Malawi: Problems and Prospects for its Promotion', *Physics and Chemistry of the Earth*, vol 28, nos 20–27, pp787–96

Mwendera, E. J., Hazelton, D., Nkhuwa, D., Robinson, P., Tjijenda, K. and Chavula, G. (2003) 'Overcoming Constraints to the Implementation of Water Demand Management in Southern Africa', *Physics and Chemistry of the Earth*, vol 28, nos 20–27, pp761–78

Ohlsson, L. (1995) *Water and Security in Southern Africa*, Publications on Water Resources no 1, Department of Natural Resources and the Environment, Stockholm, Sweden

Pallett, J. (ed) (1997) *Sharing Water in Southern Africa*, Desert Research Foundation of Namibia, Windhoek, Namibia

Pottinger, L. (1996) 'The Environmental Impact of Large Dams', in Group for Environmental Monitoring (eds) *Record of Proceedings: Lesotho Highlands Water Workshop*, GEM, Johannesburg

SAIRR (South African Institute of Race Relations) (1994) *Annual Survey*, SAIRR, Johannesburg

Savenije, H.H. (2002) 'Why Water is Not an Ordinary Economic Good, or Why the Girl is Special', *Physics and Chemistry of the Earth*, vol 27, nos 11–22, pp741–44

Schreiner, B. and van Koppen, B. (2002) 'Catchment Management Agencies for Poverty Eradication in South Africa', *Physics and Chemistry of the Earth*, vol 27, nos 11–22, pp969–76

Swatuk, L.A. (1997) 'Tapping Congo's wealth', *African Agenda*, no 15, pp40–42

Swatuk, L.A. (2000) 'Power and Water: The Coming Order in Southern Africa', in Hettne, B., Inotai, A. and Sunkel, O. (eds) *The New Regionalism and the Future of Security and Development*, Macmillan, London, pp210–47

Swatuk, L.A. and Rahm, D. (2004) 'Integrating Policy, Disintegrating Practice: Water Resource Management in Botswana', *Physics and Chemistry of the Earth*, vol 2

Swatuk, L.A. and Vale, P. (1999) 'Why Democracy is Not Enough: Security and Development in Southern Africa in the 21st Century', *Alternatives*, vol 24, no 3, pp361–89

Swatuk, L.A. and Vale, P. (2000) *Swimming Upstream: Water and Discourses of Security, Security, Ecology and Community*, Working Paper Series no 2, CSAS, School of Government, University of Western Cape, Belleville, South Africa

UNDP (United Nations Development Project) (2000) *Human Development Report*, Oxford University Press, New York

UNDP (United Nations Development Project) (2001) *Human Development Report*, Oxford University Press, New York

UNDP (United Nations Development Project), SADC, SAPES (1998) *SADC Regional Human Development Report 1998*, SARIPS, Harare, Zimbabwe

Van Koppen, B. (2003) 'Water Reform in Sub-Saharan Africa: What is the Difference?', *Physics and Chemistry of the Earth*, vol 28, nos 20–27, pp1047–54

Chapter 3

The Constitutional Implications of Commercializing Water in South Africa

Sean Flynn and Danwood Mzikenge Chirwa

> *A society must seek to ensure that the basic necessities of life are provided to all if it is to be a society based on human dignity, freedom and equality* (Government of the Republic of South Africa v Grootboom 2000, para 44).

Commercialization of a municipal service occurs when the service is delivered according to rules and principles normally reserved for private commercial markets. As the chapters in this book attest, South Africa is increasingly involving the private sector in the delivery and management of services, and municipalities have adopted business models for water services, including the corporatization of various departments. On the one hand, such policies reflect a desire to improve administrative efficiencies and to maximize cost recovery (McDonald and Pape 2002). But private market mechanisms distribute goods and services based on willingness and ability to pay. This may conflict with the definition of access to basic services as core rights in the South African Constitution, with the implicit requirement that mechanisms for distribution recognize and uphold the underlying equality of membership in society (see Walzer 1984, p209).

This chapter explores the key constitutional implications of privatizing and commercializing water services. We begin with a short introduction to the right to water in the South African Bill of Rights. We then analyse four specific elements of commercialized water in South Africa: the decision to privatize or corporatize service provision; the imposition of full cost recovery pricing; the disconnection of services (including through prepaid meters); and the provision of a limited amount of free basic water.

An Introduction to the South African Right to Water

Alongside the right to have access to sufficient food, health care services and social security under section 27(1), the South African Constitution includes the right to have access to 'sufficient water'. In terms of section 27(2), the state is enjoined to take 'reasonable legislative and other measures, within its available resources, to achieve the progressive realisation' of this right. The recognition of the right, in turn, imposes certain duties on both state and non-state actors that may be enforced by courts.

The right to water: Duties of the state

Traditionally, human rights bind the state. Section 8(1) of the Constitution codifies this conventional principle by stipulating that the Bill of Rights 'applies to all law, and binds . . . all organs of state'. According to section 7 of the Constitution, the state is enjoined to 'respect, protect, promote and fulfil' the rights in the Bill of Rights. Each of these duties can be given more specific content with reference to international law, which courts 'must consider' in interpreting the South African Constitution (Section 39(1)(b); see also *S v Makwanyane* 1995, paras 36–37).

The negative duty to respect rights

The duty to respect rights is negative in nature: the state must refrain from unjustifiably interfering with the enjoyment of the right. The Constitutional Court recognized the potential for enforcement of social and economic rights against violations of the duty to respect in *Ex Parte Chairperson of the Constitutional Assembly: In re Certification of the Republic of South Africa* (1996). The Court (para 78) explained: '[a]t the very minimum, socio-economic rights can be negatively protected from improper invasion'.

De Waal et al (2001, p401) suggest that a prima facie violation of the duty to respect the right to water would exist, should a policy or practice have 'the effect of denying individuals their existing access to water'. International human rights norms suggest further that 'law or conduct leading to a decline rather than progressive improvement in living and housing conditions would be a violation of this negative aspect of the socio-economic rights and could be declared invalid' (see also Liebenberg 2003). Moreover, the United Nations Committee on Economic, Social and Cultural Rights (CESCR), which has jurisdiction over the interpretation and enforcement of the internationally recognized right to water, identified the following as examples of potential violations of the duty to respect the right to water (UN CESCR 2002, paras 21, 44):

- any practice or activity that denies or limits equal access to adequate water;
- unlawfully diminishing or polluting water;
- limiting access to, or destroying, water services and infrastructure as a punitive measure;
- arbitrary or unjustified disconnection or exclusion from water services or facilities;
- discriminatory or unaffordable increases in the price of water; or
- pollution and diminution of water resources affecting human health.

Positive duties and the Grootboom standard

Unlike the duty to respect the right to water, the duties to protect, promote and fulfil rights are 'positive' in nature because they require state action by legislative or other means. Positive duties with respect to the right to have access to sufficient water in the South African Constitution are specifically expressed in section 27(2). This requires the state to take 'reasonable legislative and other measures, within its available resources, to achieve the progressive realisation' of the right.

By defining specific positive obligations to take measures to progressively realize each socioeconomic right, the Constitution 'recognises that at the level of basic needs . . . profound inadequacies require state intervention' (Chaskalson 2000; see also Liebenberg and Pillay 2000, p16). In the landmark case of *Government of the Republic of South Africa* v *Grootboom* (2000), the Constitutional Court held that positive social and economic rights obligations are enforceable. The Court explained (para 41) that in any case challenging the failure of the state to take sufficient positive measures 'the real question will be whether the legislative and other measures taken by the state are reasonable'.

The reasonableness inquiry is composed of two main factors (as described by the court in *Grootboom*). First, the court discussed programmatic requirements that flow from the Constitution's system of cooperative government. It held that a reasonable programme 'must clearly allocate responsibilities and tasks to the different spheres of government and ensure that appropriate financial and human resources are available' (para 39). Legislation on its own is not enough. The plan will 'invariably have to be supported by appropriate, well-directed policies and programmes implemented by the executive' in each sphere (para 42).

Second, the court held that programmes for socioeconomic rights obligations must be 'balanced and flexible', including 'appropriate provision for attention to . . . crises and to short term, medium and long term needs' (para 43). It further held that a programme that 'excludes a significant segment of society', or that fails to respond to those 'whose needs are most urgent', cannot be reasonable (paras 43–44). A progressive programme, it held, must ensure that social and economic rights are 'made more accessible not only to a larger number of people but to a wider range of people as time progresses' (para 45).

Positive duties under international law

Under international human rights norms, the duty to protect the right to water 'requires State parties to prevent third parties from interfering in any way with the enjoyment of the right to water'. It requires the adoption of 'the necessary and effective legislative and other measures to restrain, for example, third parties from denying equal access to adequate water; and polluting and inequitably extracting from water resources, including natural sources, wells and other water distribution systems' (UN CESCR 2002, para 23).

The duty to protect also applies where water services are privatized (in the broad sense of the term, adopted in this book). According to the CESCR (2002, para 24), if water services are operated or controlled by third parties: 'States must prevent them from compromising equal, affordable, and physical access to sufficient, safe and acceptable water'. This must be done through an 'effective regulatory system . . . which includes independent monitoring, genuine public participation and imposition of penalties for non-compliance'.

The duty to promote the right to water under international law requires the state to provide sufficient information and educational programmes to enable people to realize the right. The CESCR has explained that the duty to promote the right to water includes obligations to promote access to information concerning the hygienic use of water, protection of water sources and methods to minimize waste of water. The duty to promote the right to water through water saving practices and provision of water saving technologies may be particularly important where poor citizens are restricted to a small amount of free water.

The duty to fulfil the right is the most expansive positive obligation under international human rights law, and is twofold: first, an obligation to facilitate better access to water for those with inadequate access; and second, an obligation to provide water to those who do not have the means to access sufficient water on their own.

Duties of private entities in relation to the right to water

The application of the South African Bill of Rights is not limited to state action. As section 8(2) states: 'A provision of the Bill of Rights binds a natural or a juristic person [i.e. a commercial enterprise] if, and to the extent that, it is applicable, taking into account the nature of the right and the nature of any duty imposed by the right'.

Some constitutional duties may apply directly to private entities. Section 9(4) provides that: 'No person may unfairly discriminate directly or indirectly against anyone' on any ground listed in subsection 2. The Promotion of Equality and Prevention of Unfair Discrimination Act, 2000, enacted to give effect to the right of equality and the prohibition of unfair discrimination, provides in section 24(2) that: 'All persons have a duty and responsibility to promote equality', and includes 'socio-economic status' as a prohibited grounds for unfair discrimination (section 1(xxvi)).

The Constitutional Court in *Grootboom* suggested that the duty to respect socioeconomic rights binds private actors. The Court (para 34) stated that section 26 places, 'at the very least, a negative obligation upon the state and all other entities and persons to desist from preventing or impairing the right to access to adequate housing'.

APPLYING THE BILL OF RIGHTS TO MUNICIPAL COMMERCIALIZATION POLICIES

From this general exposition of the duties in the Bill of Rights, we turn to its application to some specific commercialization policies being considered or implemented in South Africa. The basic conclusion of this section is that more attention should be given to human rights norms in the planning and evaluating of service delivery options and performance indicators, for example through integration of human rights impact statements into planning processes (see Hunt 2002).

The decision to privatize or corporatize

The role of human rights

Human rights law does not mandate that the state be the sole provider of basic services (Hunt 2002; Tsemo 2003). In *Grootboom* (para 35) the Constitutional Court recognized that 'it is not only the state who is responsible for the provision of houses, but other agents within our society, including individuals themselves, must be enabled by legislative and other measures to provide housing'. The Court similarly noted in both *Grootboom* and *Soobramoney* that the state has a wide margin of discretion regarding the choice of measures to implement socioeconomic rights.

Privatization or corporatization does not mean, however, that the state may delegate its human rights obligations to the private sector or a new entity. As discussed above, the state has duties to respect, protect, promote and fulfil human rights implemented through appropriate regulatory mechanisms. These obligations bind the state irrespective of privately or publicly provided services.

Human rights law stipulates that basic principles should be incorporated into planning, delivery and evaluation processes. We discuss these below.

Affordability and equity

Like any policy to progressively realize social and economic rights, a policy to privatize or corporatize water services must comply with the reasonableness test propounded by the Constitutional Court in *Grootboom*. The policy must be programmatically reasonable in its conception and implementation; it must also be substantively reasonable by making appropriate provision for water crises and short-, medium- and long-term needs and ultimately result in more accessibility for all segments of society.

The duty to respect the right to water and to promote greater access for all segments of society requires the state to ensure that pricing will not make water unaffordable, particularly for the poorest. For example, a decision to ringfence a service like water and cut all subsidies from other service areas may violate the duty to respect rights if it results in the new entity not having adequate resources to provide sufficient water to the poor. In addition, the state must ensure that efforts are made to equalize access to services and to adopt reasonable interim measures in the period while inequalities remain. Planning to actualize human rights norms must ensure that programmes to privatize or corporatize water services do not inhibit progress towards equalizing access to services.

Participation and regulation

Strong participatory norms apply to any decision to restructure basic service delivery. Section 33 of the Constitution requires that all administrative action be procedurally fair. Notice and hearings are required before a decision is taken to commercialize a public service. Section 4 of the Promotion of Administrative Justice Act calls for a public inquiry or another appropriate procedure in cases of administrative action that materially and adversely could affect the rights of the public.

Moreover, water delivery is a local government function, and municipalities are enjoined by section 152 'to encourage the involvement of communities and community organizations in the matters of local government'. Section 153 further requires that municipalities manage their administration, budgeting and planning processes 'to give priority to the basic needs of the community'.

Participatory norms apply *beyond* the initial decision making process to the operation of a public service provider. Section 195(2) makes it clear that the principles governing public administration, including requirements that 'the public must be encouraged to participate in policy-making' and that 'transparency must be fostered by providing the public with timely, accessible and accurate information', extend beyond 'every sphere of government' and all 'organs of state' to all 'public enterprises'. The term 'public enterprises' appears to envision circumstances when a public function is provided by a private entity through contract or otherwise. As described above, the duty to protect the right to water requires the state to prevent third parties from compromising equal, affordable access to sufficient water. Such protection must be ensured through independent monitoring, genuine public participation and imposition of penalties for non-compliance (UN CESCR 2002, para 24).

Institutional mechanisms for ensuring continued participation and accountability in planning and regulatory processes are diverse. In Brazil, a model of participatory planning has been implemented at local and national levels (Löwy 2000). In countries as diverse as the United States and Bolivia, millions of consumers are served by electricity, telephone or water cooperatives in which the customers themselves own the utility, receive all profit dividends and select its managers (World Bank 2002, National Cooperative Business Association 2004). Some corporatized utilities, such as in Sacramento, California, are governed by a board directly elected from special municipal utility districts (Sacramento Municipal Utility District 2003). Illinois and other states require utilities to invite customers to join voluntary Citizen Utility Boards (CUBs) that collect a small membership fee and use the resources to finance organizers, lawyers, economists, lobbyists and other staff to help utility customers intervene in regulatory, administrative and legislative processes concerning service delivery (Nader 2000). In the UK, an independent nondepartmental National Consumers Council is funded by the Department of Trade and Industry to advocate on behalf of ratepayers in regulatory and legislative proceedings and oversee public and private utilities (National Consumers Council 1998). The South African Constitution does not mandate that any of these particular institutional formations be adopted. But a plan to corporatize or privatize service delivery in a manner that does not ensure continued public participation and oversight may offend human rights and constitutional principles protecting public accountability.

Full cost recovery and tariffs

Access to water in South Africa is increasingly determined by consumer tariffs that seek to cover the full cost of the service. This cost includes the initial cost of installing the infrastructure (capital cost) and the expenses associated with operating and maintaining the infrastructure (marginal costs) (Bond et al 2003, p12). A range of policy and legislative measures supports the practice of cost recovery in South Africa. The *White Paper on Water Policy* adopted in 1997 explained that users would be charged for the full financial costs of providing access to water including infrastructure development and catchment management activities in order to 'promote the efficient use of water'. An earlier White Paper argued that it is 'not equitable for any community to expect not to have to pay for the recurring costs of their services' (DWAF 1994, p23). The Municipal Systems Act states that the delivery of municipal services should be 'cost reflexive'.

The constitutional implications of pricing policies must be analysed in the context of South Africa's history. White South Africans and the industrial sector benefited immensely from heavily subsidized municipal services during the apartheid era. White suburbs and the business sector continue to benefit from the racially skewed investment policies in the sense that the cost of installing the necessary water supply infrastructure has been written off to a large extent (McDonald and Pape 2002, pp20–22). By contrast, the black/poor majority benefited little from the former policies of subsidizing municipal services. The water infrastructure inherited by these communities from the apartheid regime is inadequate and in need of higher maintenance and upgrading costs. Consequently, charging each community the full cost of service delivery leads to higher rates in areas most disadvantaged by apartheid, perpetuating the effects of unfair discrimination in the past. Some prepaid meters in rural KwaZulu-Natal, for example, charge multiple times the price per litre of water as is charged in the previously advantaged suburbs of Richard's Bay (Cottle and Deedat 2002, p79).

As a counter-illustration, in *City Council of Pretoria* v *Walker* (1998, para 27), the Constitutional Court rejected a claim by a resident in a formerly white area that subsidized flat rates for disadvantaged areas violate the equality clause. The Court rejected 'the view that cross-subsidization is discriminatory and that levying of different rates for the same services is always unfair'. The Court explained that 'this view . . . looks to formal rather than substantive equality' (para 62). Substantive equality requires recognition that the legacy of apartheid's targeted development of white communities 'is all too obvious in many spheres, including in the provision of services and infrastructure for them in residential areas'. According to the Court, the ideals of equality would not be achieved if 'the consequences of those inequalities and disparities caused by discriminatory laws and practices in the past are not recognised and dealt with' (para 46). It held that the flat rate was permissible 'while phasing in equality in terms of facilities and resources, during a difficult period of transition' (para 27). The Court further opined that charging the same rate in disadvantaged areas 'could produce a highly inequitable result' because of the impact of apartheid policies on communities and individuals. 'The tariffs themselves may vary from user to user, depending on the type of user and the quality of service provided' (para 85).

The National Water Act of 1998 (section 5(1)) empowers the minister to establish 'from time to time, after public consultation, a pricing strategy that may differentiate among geographical areas, categories of water users or individual water users'. According to this section, the 'achievement of social equity is one of the considerations in setting differentiated charges'. Section 97(1)(c) of the Municipal Systems Act also authorizes lifeline tariffs for municipal services on the basis of indigence. With the exception of free water policies, discussed below, these provisions have not been implemented. There is no current national policy that ensures, for example, that areas disadvantaged by past discrimination pay lower rates than formerly white areas. In fact, ring-fencing policies have led to many disadvantaged areas, particularly poorer and rural areas, paying higher per unit costs.

Duties to subsidize the development of disadvantaged areas exist in comparative law. For example, after ending legal racial segregation in the US in the 1950s, a series of federal court decisions required local governments to prioritize the development of black communities that had been disadvantaged by deliberate discrimination. In the lead case, *Hawkins* v *Town of Shaw* (1971, 1292–93), it was held that municipalities were under a constitutional obligation to 'propose a program of improvements that will, within a reasonable time, remove the disparities that bear so heavily on the black citizens' of racially planned towns, taking as 'a most reasonable yardstick . . . the quality and quantity of municipal services provided in the white area of town'. Subsequent federal court injunctions impounded all available infrastructure investment resources and ordered that they be used for set schedules of investments in black areas before any non-emergency upgrading in white areas (*Johnson* v *City of Arcadia* 1978; *Dowdell* v *City of Apopka* 1983; Haar and Fessler 1986; Gillette 1987).

The CESCR adopted a substantive, redistributionist conception of equality with respect to service pricing. It stated that '[a]ny payment for water services must be based on the principle of equity, ensuring that these services . . . are affordable for all. Equity demands that poorer households should not be disproportionately burdened with water expenses as compared to richer households' (UN CESCR 2002, para 27).

With the introduction of free basic water in South Africa the progressive block tariffs approach charges higher volume users more than low volume users. The effectiveness, and constitutionality, of this tool is being compromised, however, by rating structures that rise steeply, and often discriminatorily (higher in poor areas), after the first free block (McDonald 2002, p28). Such practices may be challenged under the Constitution's right to water and equality clauses for imposing an unreasonable burden on the poorest consumers.

Disconnections and limitations of water service

With the implementation of full-cost recovery policies, providers are increasingly cutting or limiting services if consumers default. Since 1994, increasing numbers of households have been cut off; some have lost their homes, and others been blacklisted (Deedat et al 2001; Fiil-Flynn 2001; McDonald and Pape 2002). The use of trickle valves and other service limitation devices has become widespread as a way to limit household indebtedness. These practices, however, unduly limit people's ability to access necessary water, and therefore fail to meet the proportionality test in section 36 of the Constitution.

Section 4(3) of the Water Services Act, No 108 of 1997, prohibits denying any person 'access to basic water services for non-payment, where that person proves, to the satisfaction of the relevant water services authority, that he or she is unable to pay for basic services'. Regulation 3 of Government Notice R509 of 8 June 2001 defines the basic services level as 'a minimum quantity of potable water of 25 litres per person per day (ppd) or 6 kilolitres per household per month'. This amount is guaranteed for free to all households by national policy. As described in the section discussing the free water policy below, 25 l per person per day is *not* a sufficient amount of water to allow many people to live in a healthy environment and enjoy other constitutionally protected rights. Thus, even a limitation through a trickle valve or other device that permits continued consumption of 25 l ppd is a limit on the constitutional right to have access to sufficient water that must be justified under section 36 of the Constitution.

Banning service disconnections

Section 36(1) of the Constitution states:

> The rights in the Bill of Rights may be limited only in terms of law of general application to the extent that the limitation is reasonable and justifiable in an open and democratic society based on human dignity, equality and freedom, taking into account all relevant factors, including
>
> (a) the nature of the right;
> (b) the importance of the purpose of the limitation;
> (c) the nature and extent of the limitation;
> (d) the relation between the limitation and its purpose; and
> (e) less restrictive means to achieve the purpose.

The section 36 proportionality analysis requires 'more powerful' justification depending on the extent of the limitation (*S v Manamela and Another* 2000, para 69). Thus, a complete water cutoff, or limitation to a level below basic needs, may call for exacting scrutiny by a court.

Banning devices (flow limiters or prepaid meters) that limit water services as a means of credit control is not without precedent. The United Kingdom Water Services Act of 1999 prohibits all disconnection or limitation of water services to private dwelling houses, children's and residential care homes, prisons, educational institutions, hospitals and nursing homes, and premises occupied by emergency services. In advocating for the ban on disconnections, the UK National Consumers Council also noted that disconnection is not practised in Scotland and Northern Ireland: '[i]n cases of nonpayment, the companies can use normal civil methods of debt recovery' (National Consumers Council 1998, p7). The UK Department for Environment, Food and Rural Affairs (1999) noted that the ban on water limitations was passed because: 'No person should have to face the prospect of cutting down on essential water use – for washing, cooking and cleaning – because they cannot afford their bill'.

A similar ban on water limitations for credit control purposes may be possible under section 36 of the South African Constitution. Of particular relevance may be that 'less restrictive means' are available to government to promote cost and debt recovery. Debt collection through court processes that include adequate bankruptcy protection to prevent essential service deprivation to the poor exist.

Collateral and collective service deprivations

Some South African municipalities have implemented collateral disconnection policies. Collateral service deprivations refer to cutting one service because of arrears for another, for example, cutting electricity for water arrears. Collective service deprivations are different: these refer to cases where entire geographical areas are punished because some portion of the community failed to pay their accounts (Fiil-Flynn 2001).

No national legislation should authorize collective or collateral service deprivations, and ambiguous statutes must be interpreted to avoid limiting the rights of citizens (*S v Bhulwana* 1996, para 388).

In the case of *Hartzenberg and Others v Nelson Mandela Metropolitan* (2003), the court held that the Standard Electricity Supply By-law of the Province of the Cape of Good Hope (1987) and the Municipal Systems Act *do not* authorize the discontinuance of prepaid electricity by a municipality due to arrears on water accounts. If a collateral or collective disconnection proceeds without legal authorization, the practice is also unconstitutional under section 36 of the Constitution. In the US, courts have held that 'a public service corporation cannot refuse public services because the patron is in arrears with it on account of some collateral or independent transaction, not strictly connected with the particular physical service' (*Garner v City of Aurora* et al 1948, 302). The court in *Garner* held that the city could not authorize water cutoffs for failure to pay refuse charges, agreeing with the complainant that this is an 'unlawful and arbitrary power' (298). By similar reasoning, the disconnection of one service not strictly connected to a service for which there is nonpayment may violate the proportionality requirement in section 36. An arbitrary power cannot be reasonable (see *Pharmaceutical Manufacturers Association of SA* 2000).

Fair procedures and a hearing for disconnections

Any disconnection or limitation of a water service without a sufficient opportunity of the affected citizen to be heard at a meaningful time and in a meaningful manner may be unconstitutional. Section 33 of the Constitution states: 'Everyone has the right to administrative action that is lawful, reasonable and procedurally fair'. A requirement of procedural fairness may also come into play in the analysis of the nature and extent of a limitation under the section 36 proportionality enquiry.

The Promotion of Administrative Justice Act (2000, Section 3(1)), which gives effect to the rights in section 33 of the Constitution, requires administrative action that 'materially and adversely affects the rights or legitimate expectations of any person' to give a person adequate notice of the proposed action and rights to review or appeal and to request written reasons and a 'reasonable opportunity to make representations'. Section 4(3) of the Water Services Act 108 of 1997 contains parallel procedural requirements, providing that procedures for the limitation or discontinuance of water service must 'be fair and equitable' and 'provide for reasonable notice of intention to limit or discontinue water services and for an opportunity to make representations'.

The specific content of 'fair', 'reasonable' and 'equitable' procedures are left to determination on a case-by-case basis. Long-standing constitutional principles require more protective procedures to be put in place to guarantee against unjustified and arbitrary deprivations where the vital interests of the individual are at stake (*Mathews v Eldridge* 1976).

The highest standards for notifications require that the person subject to the impending action be personally informed and understand the nature of punitive action. The person also ought to be informed of his/her rights to contest the action. Some municipal by-laws require weak forms of notification before a service limitation. Section 9.c of Johannesburg Bylaws, for example, states that 'a final demand notice *may* be sent and *may* be hand delivered or posted, per mail, to the most recent recorded address of the consumer', implying that a service limitation may proceed in absence of actual notice to the affected individual (emphasis in the original). Such standards may be constitutionally unreasonable because they fail to require means that are proportional to the serious interest affected.

Regarding the content of notice, in *Residents of Bon Vista Mansions* v *Southern Metropolitan Local Council* (2002), Budlender expressed doubt that a standard notice, 'if it does not inform the consumer of his or her statutory rights to make representations, meets the requirements of the [Water Services] Act'. He explained: 'The right [to make representations] is not likely to have real meaning unless the service provider informs consumers of its existence, which it could easily do'. Similarly, in *Memphis Light, Gas and Water* v *Craft* (1978), the US Supreme Court held that a standard electricity cutoff notice including a statement of arrears and an information phone number was not sufficient to meet constitutional due process requirements. It held that a municipality must provide 'notice reasonably calculated to apprise respondents of the availability of an administrative procedure to consider their complaint of erroneous billing' (18). Under these standards, a notice may be insufficient where it does not fully tell the individual of all available means to dispute the action and all available appeals.

In matters of the form of representation, where the state seeks to limit a person's life, health or liberty in a substantial way, proportionality analysis may require a full hearing before an impartial adjudicator, with a heavy burden on the state to prove all relevant facts. Despite the gravity of the interest affected by water limitations, some South African by-laws extend only the opportunity to submit *written* representations (Johannesburg Bylaws, section 9.c). By contrast, the US Supreme Court has held that a full evidentiary hearing before an impartial adjudicator is required before termination of welfare grants that provide 'the very means by which to live' (*Goldberg* v *Kelly* 1970, 264). Limiting representations to written complaints may be unreasonable and inequitable in relation to the interest affected. Many poor people do not have sufficient writing ability to be able to effectively advocate on behalf of their interests in continued service. A more appropriate procedure may be offered by traditional debt collection processes in a court of law before an impartial adjudicator entrusted to uphold the constitution and its rights to have access to essential services.

Prepaid meters denying rights

The use of prepaid meters (PPMs) with automatic shut-off valves completely removes protections such as a hearing before a cutoff, and PPMs radically alter the relationship between the citizen and state. Any automatic shut-off device limits the right to water, which should be 'sufficient and *continuous*' for basic needs including drinking, sanitation, washing of clothes, food preparation and hygiene (UN CESCR 2002, para 12(a), emphasis added). A continuous flow of water is particularly important to cater to unforeseen and exceptional needs, such as responding to a fire or other emergency, sickness or increase in household size. Accordingly, the use of meters that automatically shut off after a certain amount of water is used or when the prepaid units are used up should be subject to the section 36 limitations analysis.

The use of PPMs conflicts with the Water Services Act, which requires 'reasonable notice' and 'an opportunity to make representations' prior to the restriction. In *R v Dir Gen* (1999), the Queen's Bench Division held that automatic shut-off valves in prepayment units in the UK violated similar procedural requirements contained in the 1991 Water Services Act (prior to the ban on water limitations to certain premises). The court held that the shut-off valves were illegal because they cut water supply without the required written notice or procedural protections for individuals who could not afford or who disputed their bills. The court rejected the argument that the consumers had waived their statutory protections by allowing the PPM to be installed in exchange for forgiveness of their arrears. The court concluded: 'where a water undertaker is fixed with the statutory responsibility of supply[ing] water to customers, it cannot abrogate that responsibility even in circumstances where the consumer has purported to accept a variation of the statutory procedures relating to disconnection'.

Under the conflicts of law provisions of the Constitution (section 146), the national procedures for disconnections in the Water Services Act prevail over provincial or local law where necessary for 'the promotion of equal opportunity or equal access to government services' or to establish norms and standards requiring uniformity across the nation. Thus, any local law conflicting with the procedural rights in the Water Services Act may be held to be *ultra vires*.

Any legislation authorizing automatic shut-off valves may be held to be an unreasonable limitation of the right to water under section 36. The purpose of prepaid meters is to 'enable consumers to take ownership of their water usage and to budget effectively' (Johannesburg Water 2003). The presumed benefits of prepaid meters are that consumers can more easily determine their water usage and can pay incrementally. Prepaid meters that allow individuals to monitor their water usage and pay on an incremental basis are available *without* automatic cutoff valves, and are used presently in the UK. Thus, there is a 'less restrictive means' to harness any potential benefits from a prepaid meter without limiting the right to water.

Free basic water services

With the state's duty to fulfil socioeconomic rights it must provide for those unable to afford access on their own (UN CESCR No 15, para 25). The free basic water policy announced in the December 2000 municipal elections represents an effort to progressively realize the right to sufficient water (Steytler et al 2003). The Department of Provincial and Local Government explains that the free water policy is based on 'a belief in the right of all South Africans to receive at least a common minimum standard of service, and the constitutional duty of all three spheres of government to ensure it'. In terms of the policy, every household is entitled to at least 6 kilolitres (kl) per month, or 25 l per person per day.

The Constitutional Court has rejected contentions that social and economic rights entail a 'minimum core' entitlement that is enforceable 'immediately upon demand' (*Grootboom* para 95). Its approach is rather to define the full scope of the right and then ask whether the state has adopted 'reasonable legislative and other measures, within its available resources, to achieve the progressive realisation' of that right (*Grootboom* paras 33, 94; see also *Soobramoney* v *Minister of Health, KwaZulu-Natal* 1998 para 11). As described above, the reasonableness inquiry primarily involves: (i) whether the programme clearly allocates responsibilities and is backed by appropriate implementation measures; and (ii) whether the programme is balanced and flexible, including provision for short-term needs and for those living in desperate and intolerable situations.

Under the *Grootboom* standards, it may be unconstitutional to implement the free water programme in a way that does not afford equal concern and respect for the poorest, including those living in poorer municipalities, rural areas or informal settlements. It has been reported that many of these areas are often neglected in service provision. Before the national programme was implemented, for example, rural areas in KwaZulu-Natal were required to pay for water at communal standpipes with a R50 connection fee while residents of Richard's Bay were guaranteed 6 kl of free water in their houses (Cottle and Deedat 2002). In some areas, free water is only provided to those with *formal* infrastructure, leaving many rural areas and informal settlements without any essential service provision (often in areas prone to cholera).

Moreover, the water charge after the first free block is punitive for poor households that require more than the 6 free kilolitres. All of these circumstances may raise constitutional questions under the *Grootboom* standard regarding whether programmes and tariffs are sufficiently balanced so as to provide for the neediest and those living in intolerable situations.

In the first instance, it may be necessary for courts to analyse whether 6 kl per household constitutes a 'sufficient' amount of water in terms of the Constitution. The second question is whether particularly high charges after the first block of free provision effectively prevent the poorest from accessing more than this amount. Thirdly, household sizes vary and larger, poor households are discriminated against when only 6 kl are provided free. Fourthly, municipalities assume that each site has one household, but many townships have multiple households on any single site. These issues may also arise in a limitation case if the government asserts that a trickle valve or other limitation device is permissible because it does not limit the right to have access to 'sufficient' water protected in section 27 of the Constitution.

The exact amount of water needed to enjoy all rights in the Constitution will vary depending on circumstances, including the region of the country one lives in, the type of water technology (including water-saving technology) a household has access to, whether water is needed for growing food, and so on. It has been reported that 25 l is an amount of water sufficient only for two toilet flushes per person per day (De Visser et al 2003, p43). A large amount of other evidence suggests that most households will be compromised in their ability to enjoy a healthy environment if limited to 25 l ppd:

- The World Health Organization estimates that access to 25 l ppd is a minimum to maintain life, but that enjoyment of a healthy life requires much more. The same study estimates that 50 l ppd is generally needed to reach a 'low' level of concern over health impacts and that 100 l ppd is the minimum needed for 'all basic personal and food hygiene', including laundry and bathing but not including water to grow food (Bartram and Howard 2003).
- Johannesburg Water estimates that '[a]n acceptable monthly household consumption for a working class region similar to Soweto with similar socio-economic conditions is 20kl [83 l ppd]' (Johannesburg Water 2003, p7).
- Wilson and Ramphele (1989) estimated that black townships in the Eastern Cape consumed an average of 80 l ppd while white households in nearby areas consumed between 200 and 300 l ppd.
- Recent research by the South African Municipal Workers' Union concluded that the amount of water needed to meet environmental health concerns is 63 to 110 l ppd, an estimate that does 'not include water used for subsistence gardening or the operation of small businesses – practices which are often essential for the survival of the poor' (Cosatu 2003).
- In the UK, per capita domestic water consumption for 1996/97 was 145–157 l a day; per capita daily domestic and small business consumption in 1995 was 162 l in Austria; 191 l in Sweden; 175 l in the Netherlands; and 237 l in Switzerland (National Consumers Council 1998).

These statistics suggest that a free basic water policy limited to 25 l ppd will not, in itself, ensure that every person has access to sufficient water, including those unable to provide themselves with the additional water they need. To meet constitutional concerns, more flexibility may be required to ensure that more people can access sufficient clean water by, for example, expanding the amount of free water available to the poor (see ANC 1994, section 2.6, calling for ensuring 20–30 l ppd in the 'short term').

CONCLUSION

This chapter has demonstrated that a rich constitutional and legislative framework exists in South Africa which, if used optimally, can help promote the voices and interests of the poor. Although there is no generally recognized duty on the state to be the sole provider of basic services, human rights law provides a framework for the ways basic services must be provided. Thus, where municipalities decide to use a private service provider, or to corporatize both the process of making the decision for new service provision arrangements and its implementation, they must comply with human rights duties, including those relating to participation, equitable pricing, progressive facilitation of access, and just rules and procedures regarding deprivations. Ultimately, defining and enforcing these legal rights is a political struggle requiring the active participation of the poor and allied organizations.

REFERENCES

ANC (African National Congress) (1994) *The Reconstruction and Development Programme*, Umyanyano Publications, Johannesburg

Bartram, J. and Howard, G. (2003) *Domestic Water Quantity, Service Level and Health*, World Health Organization, Geneva

Bond, P., Ruiters, G. and McDonald, D.A. (2003) 'Water Privatization in Southern Africa: The State of the Debate', *ESR Review*, vol 4, no 4, pp11–13

Chaskalson, A. (2000) 'The Third Bram Fischer Lecture: Human Dignity as a Foundational Value of our Constitutional Order', *South African Journal of Human Rights*, vol 16, p193

Cosatu (Congress of South African Trade Unions and the South African Municipal Workers' Union) (2003) 'Joint Submission by Cosatu and Samwu on the Draft White Paper on Water Services', presented to Department of Water Affairs and Forestry, Government of South Africa

Cottle, E. and Deedat, H. (2002) *The Cholera Outbreak*, Rural Development Services Network and International Labour and Research Information Group, Braamfontein and Woodstock, South Africa

Deedat, H., Pape, J. and Qotole, M. (2001) *Block Tariffs or Blocked Access? The Greater Hermanus Water Conservation Programme*, Municipal Services Project Occasional Paper Series, no 5, MSP, Cape Town

De Visser, J., Cottle, E. and Mettler, J. (2003) 'Realising the Right of Access to Water: Pipe Dream or Watershed?', *Law, Democracy and Development*, vol 7, no 1, p27

De Waal, J., Currie, I. and Erasmus, G. (2001) *The Bill of Rights Handbook*, Juta & Co, Johannesburg

Department for Environment, Food and Rural Affairs (UK) (1999) *Water Industry Act 1999: Delivering the Government's Objectives*, Defra, London

DWAF (Department of Water and Forestry Affairs) (1994) *White Paper on Water Supply and Sanitation Policy*, DWAF, Pretoria

Fiil-Flynn, M. (2001) *The Electricity Crisis in Soweto*, Occasional Paper no 4, Municipal Services Project, Cape Town

Gillette, C. (1987) 'Equality and Variety in the Delivery of Municipal Services', *Harvard Law Review*, vol 100, p946

Haar, C. and Fessler, D. (1986) *The Wrong Side of the Tracks: Revolutionary Rediscovery of the Common Law Tradition of Fairness in the Struggle Against Equality*, Simon and Schuster, New York

Hunt, P. (2002) 'The International Human Rights Treaty Obligations of States Parties in the Context of Service Provision', Submission to the *UN Committee on the Rights of the Child: The Private Sector as Service Provider and its Role in Implementing Child Rights*, Office of the High Commissioner for Human Rights, Geneva

Johannesburg Water (2003) 'Rapid progress with new water project for Soweto', www.johannesburgwater.co.za/specialprojects/specialprojects_gcinamanzi.html

Liebenberg, S. (2003) 'Socio-Economic Rights', in M. Chaskalson, J. Kentridge, J. Klaaren, G. Marcus, D. Spitz and S. Woolman (eds) *Constitutional Law of South Africa*, Juta & Co, Cape Town

Liebenberg, S. and Pillay, K. (eds) (2000) *Socio-Economic Rights in South Africa*, Socio-Economic Rights Project, Community Law Centre, Cape Town

Löwy, M. (2000) 'A "Red" Government in the South of Brazil', *Monthly Review*, vol 52, no 6

McDonald, D.A. (2002) 'The Theory and Practice of Cost Recovery in South Africa', in D. A. McDonald and J. Pape (eds) *Cost Recovery and the Crisis of Service Delivery in South Africa*, Zed Books, London

McDonald, D.A. and Pape, J. (eds) (2002) *Cost Recovery and the Crisis of Service Delivery in South Africa*, Zed Books, London

Nader, R. (2000) 'Democratic Revolution in an Age of Autocracy', in R. Nader (ed) *The Ralph Nader Reader*, Seven Stories Press, New York

National Consumers Council (UK) (1998) *Finding a Basis for Water Charges, Balancing Social, Economic and Environmental Needs*, PD 47/E2/98, NCC, London

National Cooperative Business Association (2004) 'About cooperatives', www.ncba.org/abcoop_util.cfm

Sacramento Municipal Utility District (2003) 'About SMUD', www.smud.org/about/index.html

Steytler, N., Mare, C. and Mettler, G. (2003) 'The Process of Privatizing Basic Services under the Municipal Systems Act', unpublished

Tsemo, S. (2003) 'Privatization of Basic Services, Democracy and Human Rights', *ESR Review*, vol 4, no 4, pp2–4

UN CESCR (United Nations Committee on Economic, Social and Cultural Rights) (2002) 'Substantive Issues Arising in the Implementation of the International Covenant on Economic, Social and Cultural Rights. General Comment No. 15. The right to water (arts. 11 and 12 of the International Covenant on Economic, Social and Cultural Rights)', E/C.12/2002/11

Walzer, M. (1984) 'Welfare, Membership and Need', in M. Sandel (ed) *Liberalism and its Critics*, New York University Press, New York, pp199–218

Wilson, F. and Ramphele, M. (1989) *Uprooting Poverty: The South African Challenge*, David Philips, Cape Town

World Bank (2002) *Bolivia Water Management: A Tale of Three Cities*, Precis no 222

COURT CASES

City Council of Pretoria v *Walker* 1998 (2) SA 363 (CC); 1998 (3) BCLR 257 (CC)

Dowdell v *City of Apopka*, 698 F.2d 1181 (11th Cir. 1983)

Ex Parte Chairperson of the Constitutional Assembly: In re Certification of the Republic of South Africa 1996 (4) SA 744; 1996 (10) BCLR 1253 (CC)

Garner v *City of Aurora* et al, 149 Neb. 295 (1948)

Goldberg v *Kelly*, 397 U.S. 254 (1970)

Government of the Republic of South Africa v *Grootboom* 2000 BCLR (11) 1169 (CC)

Hartzenberg and Others v *Nelson Mandela Metropolitan* (Despatch Administrative Unit), 2003 JOL 10625 (SE)

Hawkins v *Town of Shaw*, 437 F.2d 1286 (5th Cir. 1971)

Johnson v *City of Arcadia*, 450 F. Supp. 1363 (M.D. Fla. 1978)

Mathews v *Eldridge*, 424 U.S. 319, 335 (1976)

Memphis Light, Gas & Water Division v *Craft*, 436 U.S. 1, 22 (1978)

Minister of Health v *Treatment Action Campaign* 2002 (5) SA 721 (CC); 2002 (10) BCLR 1033 (CC)

Pharmaceutical Manufacturers Association of SA and another In re: the ex parte application of the President of the Republic of South Africa and others 2000 (2) SA 674 (CC); 2000 (3) BCLR 241 (CC)
R v Director General of Water Services, [1999] Env L.R. 114 (Q.B.D. 1998)
Residents of Bon Vista Mansions v Southern Metropolitan Local Council 2002 (6) BCLR 625 (W)
S v Bhulwana 1996 (1) SA 388 (CC); 1995 (12) BCLR 1579 (CC)
S v Makwanyane 1995 (3) SA 391 (CC)
S v Manamela and Another 2000 (3) SA 1 (CC); 2000 (5) BCLR 491 (CC)
Soobramoney v Minister of Health, KwaZulu-Natal 1998 (1) SA 765 (CC); 1997 (12) BCLR 1696 (CC)

Chapter 4

Turning Off the Taps on the GATS

Karl Flecker and Tony Clarke

Since January 2000, member states of the World Trade Organization (WTO) – including South Africa – have been steadily renegotiating a global trade and investment treaty called the General Agreement on Trade in Services (GATS). This trade agreement targets an extensive list of services for cross-border trade and investment and has direct and far-reaching consequences for water services in Southern Africa.

This chapter explains the history, politics and mechanisms of GATS and discusses its implications for water privatization in South Africa. It is a story that many people in South(ern) Africa are unaware of but which, like so many other international trade deals conducted largely behind closed doors, has direct implications for people's lives, especially the poor.

WHAT IS THE GATS?

The General Agreement on Trade in Services is the first (and currently the only[1]) set of multilateral rules governing international trade in services. Negotiated during the Uruguay Round of the General Agreement on Tariffs and Trade (GATT) – the forerunner to the WTO – the GATS was developed in response to the massive growth in the services economy over the past three decades (e.g. finance, communications, tourism, education, health care, water and sanitation, etc.) which now accounts for approximately 60 per cent of global output, 30 per cent of global employment and nearly 20 per cent of global trade (WTO 2003, p35).

As with other WTO trade agreements, the GATS binds all member states (currently 147 countries) to the rules and regulations agreed to. But unlike its predecessor, the GATT, the WTO is able to enforce these rules with its Dispute Settlement Unit, compelling member states to change their laws to conform to a WTO ruling or face sanctions and/or be forced to pay compensation to the winning country – giving the WTO unprecedented global governance powers (Clarke 2000, pp4–6; Sinclair 2001, pp1–2).

The GATS is designed to facilitate the liberalization of trade and foreign investment in services and to establish general rules and regulations that govern these relations. Article XIX.1 makes clear that the aim of this agreement is to 'progressively raise the level of liberalization'. As a multilateral agreement it is designed to create universal guidelines for trade and investment and to discourage more limited bilateral trade deals between two or a few countries (typical of pre-WTO trade negotiations) and to minimize exceptionalities. It is, in other words, a trade and investment instrument of global significance and global reach, intended to set the rules for service trade and investment into the future and to generate rapid growth and expansion of services internationally.

The legal text of the GATS is divided into two parts. The first part is the text of the actual Agreement, referred to as Articles and Annexes. This portion defines the scope of the agreement, provides definitions and articulates general obligations. These Articles and Annexes apply uniformly to all member states of the WTO. The second part is referred to as the Schedules of Specific Commitments undertaken by WTO members. Subject to negotiation and agreement with other member states, it is this section that details specific service sectors that will be open to cross-border trade and subject to GATS rules.

Because the GATS is an existing agreement that is currently being expanded, it is worth noting that specific GATS commitments to liberalize services within a country were made between WTO members during various negotiations between 1994 and 1999 (the WTO was officially created on 1 January 1995). These agreements, called 'protocols', were limited to only a few service areas such as financial services, basic telecommunications and maritime transport services.

The current GATS negotiations process, however, commits all member countries to comprehensively expand the number of services subject to global liberalization and at the same time agree to formulate new rules that will apply to the expanded agreement.

Where Is Water in the GATS?

Service sectors subject to the GATS coverage are identified between WTO members using a common classification system called the Central Products Classifications Code (CPC Code), which is kept by the United Nations Statistics Division. The Code organizes services into ten major headings:

1 agriculture, forestry and fishery products;
2 ores and minerals; electricity, gas and water;
3 food products, beverages and tobacco; textiles, apparel and leather products;
4 other transportable goods, except metal products, machinery and equipment;
5 metal products, machinery and equipment;
6 construction work and constructions land;
7 trade in services; hotel and restaurant services;
8 transport, storage and communication services;
9 business services, agricultural, mining and manufacturing services; and
10 community, social and personal services.

'Water' is included explicitly in the second category. However, the list of subcategories of these sectors includes thousands of services, and water services appear frequently. For example, a search of the CPC Code using water as a key word reveals hundreds of related classifications, from bottled water to dam construction. Subsets of the CPC Code also include water-related activities such as the collection, purification and distribution of water.

Other categorical headings, such as 'community, social and personal services', include sewage treatment – another way in which water services are accounted for in the GATS classification system. Hundreds more can be found when the system is searched by classification rather than simply using the index system. Shrybman (2001b, pp30–31) has shown that a search for 'water' in the WTO listings produces no fewer than 594 references.

This coding system is important because it illustrates how exposed water services are to liberalization under the GATS system and, equally importantly, why government negotiators must be highly conversant with the complex and redundant CPC codifications if they are to avoid inadvertently making commitments to service sectors in which water is a (sub)category – a mistake that is all to easy to make in the rarefied world of GATS negotiations.

WTO members are reviewing the utility of these CPC Codes, in part because of the reasons stated above, in part because the classification list was first established over a decade ago and does not fully reflect the reality of today's service economies, and in part because the GATS agreement states that it can cover any service offered in a country, not just the ones explicitly listed in classification documents.

Arising from these discussions, categories such as 'environmental services' have come into usage at the GATS negotiations table, with this cluster now covering a range of water-related services. The European Union (EU) has argued that 'environmental services' should include the 'collection of water' (WTO document database 2000; Gould and Joy 2002).

Researchers at the Centre for International Environmental Law and the Worldwide Fund for Nature have noted that these terminological discussions have created controversy in two other areas that are relevant to water. The first is energy services (although the current GATS classifications do not use a heading for 'energy services', WTO member countries are nonetheless identifying energy activities as targets for the GATS regime[2]). The production and distribution of energy services, be they hydroelectric power plants, dams or petrochemical fuel-based energy sources, all involve water and impact on water quality. The GATS implication is that trade in these energy services would be relevant to domestic water management and conservation policies. Second, WTO members have raised concerns with services incidental to manufacturing – again, a category that is used when countries make commitments or are requested to make commitments. Such services are governed by many domestic regulations, including those regulations regarding water takings and the discharge of pollutants. Such commercial activities are likely to be affected by the GATS regime (Tuerk and Holland 2003).

Water services are therefore embedded throughout the GATS agreement and are subject to a wide range of direct and indirect trade and investment reforms. Despite such far-reaching consequences for communities, only national governments can be parties to the GATS and its internal developments. Nonstate actors, nongovernmental organizations, community based groups, labour unions and private sector organizations are not allowed to participate directly, although governments can (and often do) act on behalf of specific sectors at WTO meetings. Many governments in fact give preferential consultations with corporate, rather than community, interests in the process of negotiating the GATS.

THE GATS RULE BOOK

International trade agreements developed under the WTO are complex and written in the intricate language of trade lawyers, bureaucrats and economists. This section strives to unpack some of the key rules of the GATS as they pertain to water. Trade agreements rely on a number of legally binding principles that obligate governments and which now can be enforced through a WTO dispute settlement body.

There are four core rules from existing trade and investment agreements that the GATS relies on:

1 Most Favoured Nation rule (MFN);
2 National Treatment rule (NT);
3 Domestic Regulation rule (DR); and
4 Market Access rule (MA).

The 1994 GATS mandated further negotiations of rules in three areas:

1 emergency safeguards, that is, developing rules that would provide temporary protection to domestic services suppliers facing global liberalization;
2 subsidies, that is, developing rules to constrain government's ability to fund the service sectors; and
3 procurement, that is, developing rules affecting how governments can purchase services for the direct use or benefit of governments.

These rule-making talks fall under the mandate of the Working Party on GATS Rules. There is no formal deadline for completing this work, and this rule making is interconnected with other WTO trade agreement negotiations.

Table 4.1 outlines some of the key existing GATS rules and new GATS rules under negotiation, with a comment on each rule's status and a brief explanation. Under the GATS, rules such as MFN are called general obligations, meaning they apply to WTO members and all service sectors, while rules like National Treatment are termed specific obligations which would apply to specific sectors and specific commitments that a country makes. A country may limit or set

Table 4.1 *GATS rules: current and under negotiation*

GATS article	Current status	Explanation
Most Favoured Nation (Article II)	Exists now. Applies to all services in all countries	Countries must give services and service suppliers from each country with which they trade 'no less favourable' treatment than they give to services and suppliers from any other foreign trading partner. This article prohibits governments from distinguishing between trading partners for social or political reasons (i.e. violating human rights) and has the practical effect of consolidating commercialization wherever it occurs. This rule runs throughout WTO agreements.
National Treatment (Article XVII)	Exists now. Applies only to services that countries have committed to. Countries are under pressure to commit more services to National Treatment coverage	A requirement that countries treat all foreign services and suppliers at least as favourably as they treat their domestic services and suppliers, effectively prohibiting governments from favouring domestic companies over foreign-based companies. In addition, government measures that have the effect of creating disadvantages for foreign service suppliers, even if that is not their intention, are not permitted. This rule runs throughout WTO agreements.
Domestic Regulation (Article VI)	Exists now. May apply to all services and countries	Member countries must prove to trade panels that their domestic regulations, policies, procedures, technical standards and qualification requirements are not 'unnecessary barriers to trade in services' and 'not more burdensome than necessary'
Market Access (Article XVI)	Exists now. Applies only to services that countries have committed to. Countries are under pressure to commit more services to Market Access coverage	This rule gives foreign service providers the right to establish operations in member countries and not be restricted by quantitative limits, such as number or size of operations. In addition, no type of legal entity delivering a service can be barred and no limiting percentages of foreign ownership can be applied.

Table 4.1 *GATS rules: current and under negotiation (continued)*

Government Procurement (Article XIII)	Under negotiation	This rule would restrict the ability of governments to apply 'non-trade measures' when making government procurement decisions (e.g. local purchasing criterion, residency requirements, or potentially even commitments to restorative equity or affirmative action practices).
Emergency Safeguards (Article X)	Under negotiation The initial three-year timeline beginning in 1995 for completion was not met	This rule would allow developing countries to delay the implementation of certain rules in order to protect their economies and citizens from excessive foreign competition.
Subsidies (Article XV)	Under negotiation National Treatment and Most Favoured Nation coverage applies to Subsidies	This rule would restrict the use of government subsidies in areas like public works, municipal services and social programmes. Combined with commercial presence provision articulated under modes of supply, this proposed rule could enable a service investor to not only compete for business against the domestic public sector but also for domestic public funding granted by governments to these service institutions.
Transparency (Article III)	Under negotiation	This rule would require all levels of governments within a member country to consult with corporations providing services before passing or changing any laws or regulations that could impact the service sector.

conditions when it is making specific commitments for service sectors: for example, limiting or exempting its national policies that grant water rights such as free water programmes, or regulations that promote water conservation or limit pollutant discharges into water bodies. However, it is critical that these limitations or conditions be specified in a country's schedule of commitments in order to be recognized. South Africa has made little use of the exemptions or limitation tools available and, therefore, has taken few concrete safeguard measures to try to protect its national polices or services related to water, sewage, refuse or sanitation services. South Africa has limited its commitments made under the environmental services category to apply only to consultancy services, but this may be challenged by other WTO members wanting broader access to water services.

GATS proponents argue that government's ability to chart its own course in service liberalization is also possible via the exemption of governmental measures clause (Article 1.3b), suggesting that government's ability to regulate is unimpeded by the GATS. GATS critics argue that this exemption is narrowly defined and therefore very limited in terms of use. Article 1.3b states that government measures are exempted only when the service supplied is 'in the exercise of governmental authority', which is defined as any service that is supplied neither on a commercial basis nor in competition with one or more services suppliers. Most countries' public services are often a mix of monopolized and competitive services, or involve the private sector explicitly, or are offered on a cost recovery basis, thus making it difficult to clearly identify an exempt service as defined in the governmental authority exemption clause (Barlow and Clarke 2002, p168; Sinclair and Grieshaber-Otto 2002, pp17–25).

Shrybman (2001a) also notes that the limitations of the GATS exemption for government measures that 'protect health, animal or plant life' are permitted only insofar as they are 'necessary'. The issue of who determines what is 'necessary' will not be dealt with here[3] but suffice it to say that the GATS text avoids importing protective environmental and public interest language from other multilateral agreements to exempt government measures that relate 'to the conservation of exhaustible natural resources', such as water.

Finally, the current GATS negotiations are seeking not only to expand the number of service sectors where GATS rules will apply, but also to have specific obligation rules apply across the board to all sectors and for all WTO/GATS signatory countries. Civil society organizations monitoring the GATS negotiations have argued that the negotiations process is aimed at getting developed countries to expose substantially more of their service sectors to market access and national treatment rules (Wesselius 2002, pp3–10; Gould and Joy 2002, pp10–19; Joy 2003, pp3–9; WSCM 2004).

The GATS 2000 negotiation process is also seeking to develop other rules governing global trade in services. Some examples are rules that will affect how government can procure or purchase services or rules related to governments subsidizing domestic service delivery. Another area is developing rules requiring governments to inform the service industry of any laws, policies or regulations it is considering that may affect the service industry sector.

The GATS is clearly a unique agreement. In the words of a former WTO Director General, it extends 'into areas never before recognized as trade policy' (Sinclair 2000, p4). No other WTO agreement comes close to the GATS in terms of its ambitions or complexity. The wide scope of the agreement, and the far-reaching powers of the GATS rules, backed up with binding enforcement mechanisms and the sanctioning powers of the WTO's dispute settlement mechanism, provide substantial evidence to support the European's Commissions contention that the GATS is 'first and foremost an instrument for the benefit of business' (Sinclair 2001, p4).

Corporate Lobbying for GATS

As noted above, services are the fastest growing sector in international trade and have enormous market potential, with the water sector alone estimated to be worth in the order of US$1 trillion a year. Service industry transnationals based in the US and EU dominate the service sector as a whole and they recognize the significant markets and economic potential that Southern countries' service markets represent. A multilateral trade and investment agreement like GATS that facilitates broad access to these markets is particularly attractive to transnational service industries.

Major lobby groups

To advance their interests, global service corporations have organized themselves into powerful continental lobby groups. These lobby groups have played an important role in the history and development of the GATS negotiations. The three major lobby groups are: the United States Coalition of Service Industries (USCSI, or CSI); the European Services Forum (ESF); and the Japan Services Network (JSN).

Each of these lobby groups involves powerful transnational corporations with extensive international interests in various service sectors. Research and activist groups such as Corporate Europe Observatory, Transnational Institute, Friends of the Earth International and the Polaris Institute have researched these industry lobby groups and exposed their considerable power to influence the design and development of the WTO trade and investment rules (FOEI and CEO 2003; Polaris Institute 2003).

The following sections provide an overview of some of the key corporate members of these lobby groups that are working actively to advance the GATS agreement. Note, in particular, the presence of water corporations in both the US and European cartels (Puscas 2002).

US Coalition of Service Industries (USCSI)

USCSI is composed of nearly 60 major corporations with vested interests in securing global markets for their service products, including: electronic entertainment and telecommunications giants AOL Time-Warner, AT&T and IBM; energy and water enterprises such as Haliburton and Vivendi Universal; financial houses such as Citigroup, Bank America and JP Morgan Chase; investment houses such as Goldman Sachs and General Electric Capital; health insurance companies such as CIGNA; management and consultant firms such as KPMG and PriceWaterhouseCoopers; and express delivery services such as United Parcel Service and Federal Express. Enron was also a prominent member of the CSI, but in the midst of its accounting scandal was removed from the USCSI website of members. It is unknown if this was because Enron did not pay its US$25,000 membership fee or if the Coalition wanted to distance itself from

Enron. Even so, Arthur Andersen, Enron's highly discredited accounting firm, remains in the Coalition.

European Services Forum (ESF)

ESF comprises 50 corporations providing for-profit services in several key sectors, including: major banking institutions such as Barclays plc and Commerzbank AG; telecommunications giants such as British Telecom, Telefonica and Deutsche Telekom AG; water giants such as Vivendi and Suez-Lyonnaise des Eaux; health insurance companies such as the AXA Group and CGNU (CGU + Norwich Union); privatization service agencies such as Arthur Andersen Consulting and PriceWaterhouseCoopers; publishing and entertainment conglomerates such as Bertelsmann; plus brand name operations such as Daimler-Chrysler Services and Marks & Spencer plc.

Japan Services Network (JSN)

JSN has a membership of approximately 60 Japanese companies with the CEO of the Mitsubishi Corporation heading the Network. The JSN was started in October 1999 by the Japan Federation of Economic Organizations (Keidanren) as Japan's chief extra-parliamentary negotiating and lobbying body for promotion of rapid liberalization of trade in services through the Services 2000 negotiations in the WTO.

Although each of these lobby groups has tremendous influence within the WTO/GATS processes, it is the US-based transnationals that played a pivotal role in hosting the Seattle WTO Ministerial in 1999; these are the self-acknowledged powerhouse behind the GATS negotiations process: 'Without the enormous pressure generated by the American financial services sector, particularly companies like American Express and Citicorp, there would have been no services agreement' (D. Hartridge, Director of Services Division, WTO, as quoted in Sinclair 2000, p22).

The current Director General of the WTO, Dr Supachai Panitchapakdi, publicly stated at the US Department of Commerce that the USCSI:

> *with its extensive global network and influences in the world . . . has successfully served to advance and secure the interests of its members, more importantly, in shaping US policies and promoting US interests within the international fora, thereby ensuring progressive global market liberalization* (Panitchapakdi 2002).

Of course, the US service industry groups are not acting alone. The EU is the lead player in imports and exports of commercial services and they too have influential corporate lobby groups pushing their own agenda. Research by European civil society groups revealed that corporate interests, specifically the financial services industry sector via a UK-based group called the Liberalization of Trade in Services (LOTIS) committee, have considerable influence in the GATS negotiations. This LOTIS committee is chaired by Andrew Buxton, former Chairman of Barclays Bank, which is itself a member of the ESF.

Buxton was asked by the EU Trade Commissioner in 1998 to replicate what he had previously done in the US: that is, to organize the EU services industry and recruit prominent chief executive officers who would 'act as a link between the Commission and a wide range of service industries as the WTO talks widened their horizons into other service industries'. Buxton took his task seriously, quickly establishing the ESF and populating it with more than 40 CEOs from various service industries, making it clear that his goal was 'to give the services sector a high public profile in the GATS 2000 negotiations'. In September 1999 a senior EU trade official, Robert Madelin, stated that the EU plan was to rely heavily on the network set up by Buxton: 'We are going to rely on it [the ESF] just as heavily as on member states' direct advice in trying to formulate our objectives' (Wesselius 2002).

The reliance between the EU Trade Department and the corporate services lobby group ran deep and ran silent. Corporate Europe Observatory – a European-based public policy research and campaign group – revealed that between 1999 and 2001 government working groups held numerous secret meetings with the LOTIS committee (FOEI and CEO 2003). Palast (2001) reported that government officials had gone so far as to share confidential government negotiating documents with service industry giants like PriceWaterhouseCoopers, Goldman Sachs, Morgan Stanley Dean Witter and Prudential Corporation, as well as inside information on the negotiating positions of the European community, the US and developing nations. Apparently these promoters of the GATS 2000 negotiations had reason to be secretive.

By scouring minutes of these meetings (minutes that were subsequently removed from the internet), Eric Wesselius (2002) of CEO found that on at least two occasions the LOTIS committee plotted to hire consulting firms and academics to provide arguments to counter critics of the GATS agenda. Minutes of these meetings note that 'the pro-GATS case was in fact vulnerable when the NGOs asked for proof of where the economic benefits of liberalization lay'.[4]

Barry Coates, Director of the World Development Movement, a UK-based citizen's organization that monitors the WTO and its impacts on development policy, said at the time of the discovery: 'Looking at these minutes, it was worse than we thought, [the WTO GATS proposals] are a stitch-up between corporate lobbyists and government' (Palast 2001).

The level of intimacy afforded to the service cartels like the ESF was also extended to specific service industry sectors, like the water corporations. Corporate Europe Observatory, using access to information legislation, unearthed documents which revealed that officials of the European Commission had met with and communicated regularly with representatives from various large water companies and that the requests put forth by the EU to the 109 countries as part of the 2002 GATS negotiations directly reflected the corporate interests of these water companies.

Water companies Suez, Vivendi, Aqua Mundo and Thames Water (which is the main water subsidiary of RWE) attended a meeting on 17 May 2002, in Brussels, with the European Commission and several representatives from other European companies to discuss water-related services in GATS. Following this meeting a questionnaire was sent to each of the water companies which made it clear that: 'One of the main objectives of the EU in the new round of negotiations is to achieve real and meaningful market access for European services providers for their exports of environmental services'. The document also asked the companies about obstacles they faced when trying to enter new markets.

Olivier Hoedeman of Corporate Europe Observatory reported that 'these documents reveal that the [European Commission] clearly identifies with the interests of the corporations when it designs its GATS negotiating goals. The Commission is using GATS to pursue the market expansion interests of large EU-based water corporations' (Politi 2003).

SOUTH AFRICA IN THE WTO

South Africa became a member of the WTO at the time of its official opening on 1 January 1995 but had already signed the GATS agreement on 15 April 1994, which was then ratified by the South African Parliament on 6 April 1995.

Riaz Tayob from the Southern and Eastern African Trade, Information and Negotiations Institute (SEATINI) points to critical dates that challenge the democratic legitimacy and public awareness of South Africa joining the GATS. Tayob notes that the first democratic election (27 April 1994) took place just days after South Africa signed on to the agreement and the government's detailed schedule of commitments were entered into less than a year after that election. In addition, given the level of detail required to join the WTO and the time required, it is likely that extensive negotiations preceded any definitive agreement on a democratic transition, namely the final Constitution of South Africa in 1996 (Tayob 2003).

It is reasonable, therefore, to suggest that South African citizens and democratically elected political representatives were not party to the WTO accession or the GATS commitments discussions in any meaningful sense. This lack of citizen involvement in GATS discussions continues.

Nevertheless, South Africa's Department of Trade and Industry (DTI) is supportive of the WTO, stating that South Africa supports the principle of a 'single undertaking through which the results of negotiations on all issues are adopted by all members in their entirety'. On the GATS negotiations, the department states:

> *In our view, services negotiations hold great potential for economic development, in terms of the growing direct contribution of services to the economy (GDP), its indirect contribution as an input into other sectors (manufacturing) and, generally, in improving overall economic efficiency and competitiveness.*[5]

DTI's support for the WTO received commendation from the outgoing WTO Director General, Michael Moore. After a secretive two-day visit to South Africa in February 2002, where Moore met with President Thabo Mbeki and Trade and Industry Minister Alec Erwin, Moore praised South Africa's decisive contribution to trade negotiations: 'South Africa has been punching above its weight... and Mr Erwin is a trusted and highly respected negotiator who has never changed his song' (*Business Day*, 12 February 2002).

If there is any doubt where the South African government stands in relation to the WTO liberalization agenda, one need only to examine its role at the Fourth WTO Ministerial held in Doha, Qatar, in 2002. It was there that a select six-country team was appointed in a behind-closed-doors process to act as 'friends' of the Chair at that ministerial meeting.

South Africa was one of these 'friends'. Martin Khor and colleagues from the Third World Network detailed in their report, *Six Days of Shame in Doha*, the story of big-power bullying and blatant use of influence and pressures applied by these 'friends' who implemented a 'well rehearsed coup d'état carried out with the WTO secretariat in charge' (Khor et al 2002). These 'friends' pulled the meeting back from the brink of failure and produced a last-minute agreement referred to as the Doha Development Agenda (DDA). South Africa's trade representatives clearly 'punched' well and with persuasive clarity.[6]

Also worth mentioning is the fact that Erwin has been moved to Minister of Public Enterprises since April 2004, seen as a signal by the financial press in South Africa as 'an attempt to get South Africa's derailed privatization and restructuring programme back on track... [by tapping into Erwin's] considerable negotiating skill, honed in years of tough trade talks with the EU, the US and the European Free Trade Association' (*Business Report*, 29 April 2004).

POTENTIAL IMPLICATIONS OF GATS FOR WATER SERVICES IN SOUTH AFRICA

We turn now to our main objective in this chapter: assessing the implications of GATS for South Africa's water services. However, because the GATS remains an unfinished project, with rules still being negotiated and categories of services still to be fully defined, the discussion here is necessarily speculative in nature. With that caveat, we outline below some possible GATS scenarios to illustrate the kinds of concern raised by this agreement for water services in South Africa.

We further preface these comments by reminding the reader that virtually all government measures related to water rights and management fall under the purview of Article 1 of the GATS which says that the agreement covers 'measures affecting the trade in services', where 'measures' is defined as *any* measure, 'whether in the form of a law, regulation, rule, procedure, decision, administrative actions, or any other form'. Moreover, the GATS covers 'measures *affecting* trade in services', with legal critics of the GATS pointing out that even if the measure in question has an incidental impact on trade, GATS rules would still apply: 'Not only does GATS cover governmental measures regulating trade in services, but also those measures designed to regulate production, protect the environment and ensure public health or consumer protection and which simultaneously affect trade in services' (Tuerk and Holland 2003, p24).

GATS scenarios

Given the all-encompassing coverage of the GATS it is possible to imagine several scenarios.

Scenario 1

A foreign service supplier, via its home base government, challenges South Africa's 'free water policy',[7] claiming that the investment, operation and maintenance requirements to provide 6 kilolitres (kl) of water per household per month for free constitute an 'unnecessary barrier to the trade in services and is more burdensome than necessary' to achieving their stated objectives, arguing that this water policy violates GATS Article VI:4.

In addition, a foreign service supplier, via its government, could cite the GATS Market Access obligations in Article XVI and argue that the GATS prevents a country from placing quantitative limits of any kind on service delivery. Extending the scenario, should the South African government decide to expand its free water programme towards the promised medium term levels of 50 l per person per day or introduce dramatically steeper block tariff structures to better cross-subsidize water for the poor and/or better promote conservation, under the proposed GATS rules on 'transparency' the South African government would be required to consult with the industry sector first, with private firms conceivably resisting any tariff changes that might negatively affect their profit margins. Once informed of a proposed policy change, a foreign service provider could then call upon its home government to challenge the contemplated measure as an 'unnecessary barrier to trade' and argue that the new policy constitutes a violation of the Domestic Regulation disciplines, the Most Favoured Nation and National Treatment clauses, and/or the Market Access rules as defined by the GATS regime.

Furthermore, GATS rules could affect the South African government's ability to direct private sector service water operators to fulfil economic empowerment initiatives such as local hiring, equity procurement and ensuring equitable access to water to low income communities. As Sinclair and Grieshaber-Otto (2002, pp52–58) point out, there is nothing like the Market Access rule in any other international commercial treaties. The rule prohibits governments from placing restrictions on the number of service suppliers or operations, the value of service transactions, the number of persons that may be employed in a sector and, significantly, the types of legal entity through which suppliers may supply a service.

Scenario 2

A foreign service supplier, via its home base government, challenges the South African government's National Water Act and the National Water Resource Strategy's community based management framework. These subnational levels of government fall under the GATS jurisdiction and it is therefore conceivable that a community based resource management approach may conflict with a water corporation's plans to extract water. This conflict could change the perceived conditions of competition, creating an 'unnecessary barrier to trade' and being 'more burdensome than necessary'.

Scenario 3

A foreign service provider, via its home base government, challenges the Department of Water Affairs and Forestry's (DWAF) licensing requirements or technical regulations or standards or qualification requirements for personnel, citing specific measures, standards or requirements as 'more burdensome than necessary' and an 'unnecessary barrier to trade'.

Each of these scenarios illustrates the kinds of risk to government policy posed by the GATS. A more detailed examination of the legal and technical intricacies of these sorts of scenarios has been undertaken by the Center for Environmental Law and Worldwide Fund for Nature utilizing a comparative framework of GATS implications by looking at water management policies, water rights, licences, qualifications, quantitative limits and pollution control measures from South Africa, India, the EU, Australia and Brazil (Tuerk and Holland 2003). It is worth highlighting the paper's main conclusions, as they raise important concerns for water policymakers. Areas identified for potential conflict with the GATS and domestic water policies are:

- The GATS has the power to affect policies that regulate the granting of water rights.
- The GATS Market Access rules prohibit policies that aim to avoid overexploitation of water resources by placing quantitative limits on the resource.
- The GATS rules can create legal insecurity for quantitative policies governing water takings related to economic activities that can impact on the operations of service suppliers.
- The GATS Domestic Regulations rules may limit regulators' capacity to establish and verify professional qualifications.
- The GATS Domestic Regulations rules may constrain countries' abilities to use licences, permits or technical regulations that are intended to protect and preserve water.
- The GATS Domestic Regulations may constrain countries' abilities to include environmental considerations in the determination of financial aspects of concession contracts in the water sector.

- The GATS Domestic Regulations may constrain countries' abilities to require licence holders to conduct sustainability impact assessments and the requisite documentation.
- The GATS rules may be used to undermine or eliminate government measures that strive to preserve water by regulating use and ownership of lands with springs.
- The GATS Domestic Regulations rules negotiations mandate and National Treatment obligations may constrain regulatory powers of countries across all services.

Is the South African government aware of these dangers? Yes and no, it would seem. While the Department of Trade and Industry continues to 'punch above its weight' by aggressively pursuing and expanding the WTO agenda, it would appear that the DWAF has some major reservations. Mike Muller, the Director General of DWAF, has gone so far as to urge 'OECD countries and their companies, preferably both, to call for water services to be taken off the table in the GATS and related trade negotiations' (Muller 2002, p6). But DWAF has, at the same time, been expanding the opportunities for private sector intervention in the water sector in the country (as other chapters in this book amply attest to) and there is no formal DWAF policy on the GATS. Where the South African government officially stands on water and the GATS is impossible to determine.

TURNING OFF THE TAPS ON THE GATS

Despite the havoc that the GATS could wreak on sustainable and equitable service delivery in South Africa and despite the South African government's neutral (at best) and bullish (at worst) position on trade and investment liberalization within the WTO more generally, there is resistance to these initiatives in South Africa. Although knowledge about the GATS amongst labour unions, nongovernmental agencies and community organizations is limited, it is growing and becoming part of a larger international awareness and struggle against these corporate-driven trade and investment schemes.

Citizens around the world are demanding to know what role their governments are taking in WTO/GATS negotiations. People want to know what services are being put on the trading table and are beginning to ask who these transnational service corporations are and what their track record is.

The resistance to the GATS has taken on many forms. At the local government level many community based politicians are worried about the democratic deficit that marks WTO negotiations. The GATS affects all levels of administration, from the national to the local, yet local authorities are not included in the negotiation process. The GATS jeopardizes many of the fundamental principles of federalism and curtails the scope of municipal governments to follow an independent policy on public services.

In response, local governments, often at the urging of their citizenry, are passing 'No-GATS' resolutions en masse. In Canada, over 70 municipalities and the National Federation of Canadian Municipalities have passed resolutions expressing concern about the GATS negotiations, many explicitly demanding that the federal government proceeds no further (Gould 2002). Similarly, resistance is taking place amongst local governmental authorities in the UK and Switzerland. In France, more than 150 municipalities have declared themselves GATS-free areas.

Strategic interventions

'Turning off the taps on the GATS' will require additional strategic interventions by labour and community groups. There are five possible interventions to consider, with specific reference to South(ern) Africa.

Demand full public disclosure

The secrecy of WTO negotiations continues to be a major weakness. Since the Seattle Ministerial meetings in 1999 the WTO has attempted to ensure more transparency in its operations. But looks and substance are two different things. As the EU GATS documents leaked in 2002 demonstrate there is still a long way to go before a transparent system is in place. Unions and community organizations in South Africa must continue to press the DTI to release the complete 'requests' and 'offers' made and received for access to public service sectors along with the calls for removal of laws and regulations in South Africa that service corporations find 'burdensome'. A systematic filing of Access to Information petitions for public disclosure of key documents may be in order.

Expose domestic regulatory conflicts

Through the GATS, economically powerful countries, on behalf of their corporate clients, are negotiating new rules in cross-border trade-in-services which trample on the jurisdiction of subnational governments. Article VI of the GATS already contains specific measures to be used to ratchet down unwanted laws, policies and programmes. As noted earlier, a 'necessity test' may be added, compelling governments to *prove* that certain laws and regulations are necessary and do not pose a threat to the GATS rules. A strategy designed to expose the conflict between federal government, on the one hand, and regional/local governments, on the other, regarding their authority over issues like water, health care, education and social services under the GATS is needed. The South African parliamentary committees responsible for local and provincial government services are critically important to lobby in this respect.

International 'monkey wrenching'

Information about 'requests' being made during GATS negotiations provides opportunities for playing the positions/demands of one set of national government negotiators against another. This was one of the tactics that was successfully used to derail the Multilateral Agreement on Investment (MAI) negotiations. Consider, for example, the fact that EU countries are demanding access to water services in developing countries but are not reciprocating with liberalization in other key areas of interest to developing economies (e.g. agriculture). Creative action strategies can be developed with allies in other countries to throw 'monkey wrenches' into the negotiating process by stirring up public debate on specific issues that dramatize contradictions and expose the violations of national laws and customs of another country.

Community non-compliance

The fact that global rules are being negotiated by national governments, which will have a direct effect on the jurisdiction and responsibilities of local governments and municipalities, without their consent, raises the prospect of local governments and communities exercising non-compliance. If, for example, new GATS rules are negotiated and implemented which could potentially have a negative effect on community health care, education, water, waste management, postal or social services, a municipal government which had not given its consent could decide not to comply with the GATS rules. A campaign could be mounted in selected communities across the country encouraging local governments to establish special task forces or standing committees to do an assessment of the potential impacts of the GATS regime on community public services, an assessment of the assets of community based public services that already exist in their jurisdictions, plus develop and recommend corresponding actions of non-compliance that might be undertaken.

Targeted corporate campaigns

The for-profit service corporations that are the driving forces behind the new GATS rules could also become potential targets for campaigns in South Africa. Although governments must remain the prime target in the fight for public services, it is crucial that strategic priority be put on confronting the real power that is driving the agenda for privatization. The water corporations and their supply lines – from the companies that make the prepaid meters to the workers to the managers making decisions about laying standpipes – must increasingly and strategically become the focus of resistance campaigns. In the case of water services, unions and social movements in several countries have already begun to identify Vivendi and Suez as common targets for mounting global action campaigns (Clarke 2002).

CONCLUSION

In the end, all of this could be moot if the current GATS negotiations continue to falter. The negotiations timelines set by the Third Ministerial in 1999 dictated that WTO member countries submit requests indicating their interest for access to other service markets by the end of June 2002, including requests for changes or clarifications of other countries' domestic regulations that were considered impediments to trade in services. Only 30 or so country requests were filed by the deadline, 90 per cent of which came from developed countries. Countries receiving requests were to reply with their offers or commitments by 31 March 2003, but very few offers were received in time.

As of April 2004, barely 30 per cent of WTO member countries had put forward their initial offers for liberalizing services. WTO members attending the April 2004 Council on Services meetings in Geneva were disappointed with the results of the ongoing request–offer phase of the services negotiations. While developed countries focused their criticism on the low number of offers, most developing countries stressed that the quality of the offers made was unsatisfactory (*Bridges Weekly Trade News Digest* 2004).

Hamid Mamdouh, WTO Director of the Trade in Services Division, admitted in a briefing to NGOs on 27 March 2004, that the WTO 'need[s] offers from another 54 countries, mainly developing countries, along with a commitment to improve existing offers, if there is to be real momentum on the GATS front'. He went on to suggest that a GATS agreement was unlikely to be realized by January 2005 and at best might only be realized by 2007.

Given the stalled status of the GATS and the WTO agenda in general, trade officials are hurriedly trying to piece together a so-called 'framework agreement'. The goal is to forge an agreement by July 2004 that will contain sufficient commitments on agriculture to propel things forward and generate new momentum on the GATS front. WTO officials are using any opportunity available to challenge the growing perception that trade negotiations are stalling.

But given the enormous resources behind the GATS and the WTO, and the high stakes at play for aggressive multinational firms in the service sector, it is unlikely that the GATS will go away any time soon. As one WTO delegate remarked after a series of GATS meetings, 'like the aftermath of a nuclear attack, it seems that only the GATS and the cockroaches have the capacity to survive' (*Bridges Weekly Trade News Digest* 2003).

The GATS may not be the only threat to increased water privatization and commercialization in South Africa, but it looms large on the horizon. South African labour, community and nongovernmental organizations, as well as government authorities at all levels and in all sectors, must acknowledge and address the concerns raised by the GATS expansionist agenda.

NOTES

1 Because the promoters of GATS are now finding it difficult to create the comprehensive deal on trade in services, there are efforts under way to establish GATS-like rules, or 'guidelines', in other international bodies such as the Organization for Economic Cooperation and Development (OECD) and UNESCO, using GATS language. Nevertheless GATS remains the only omnibus agreement on these matters.

2   See the leaked EU requests of over 100 countries in which energy services are targeted (www.polarisinstitute.org).
3   In the WTO, determining whether government regulations are 'necessary' or not vis-à-vis trade agreements may be decided by something called the 'necessity test'. For example, licensing laws, professional standards and apprenticeship programmes would be scrutinized against the criterion of a critical trade focused question: Are these laws, standards or programmes 'more burdensome than necessary to ensure the quality of service?' (Article VI 4b). Gregory Palast, a UK investigative journalist, has reported that the task of this scrutiny could fall to an international agency with veto power over all WTO member countries' parliamentary and regulatory bodies. Wesselius (2002) and Palast (2001) have uncovered a number of internal memos from inside the WTO and between a 'group of captains of London finance that call themselves the British Invisibles' indicating that GATS proponents are prepared to have national laws and regulations struck down if they are 'more burdensome than necessary' to business. Conscious of the criticism that GATS rules threaten public interest, the WTO Secretariat has suggested in an internal memo that trade agreements adopt an 'efficiency principle'. Relying on marketplace efficiencies has the advantage, claims the WTO Working Group in the memo, that 'it may be politically more acceptable to countries to accept international obligations which give primacy to economic efficiency'.
4   The revealing minutes have since been reposted at www.gatswatch.org/LOTIS/2337.html
5   Quote taken from a DTI paper entitled 'Notes on South Africa's Approach to the WTO and key elements of a Negotiating Position', dated December 2000. The paper was downloaded in May 2003 from www.dti.gov.za/07-itedd/downloads/sa_wto_approach_and_elements.pdf, but as of April 2004 it has been removed from DTI's website.
6   Although speculative, it is interesting to note that in late January 2004 Alec Erwin was described by the Foreign Affairs journal as 'a favourite to become the next director general of the WTO'. DTI staff have denied this possibility (Pressly 2004).
7   Since December 2000, the South African government has been slowly implementing this policy in municipalities. Although not formally legislated, and still unevenly applied across the country, the 'free water policy', as it is called, has nevertheless been introduced widely in the country.

REFERENCES

Barlow, M. and Clarke, T. (2002) *Blue Gold: The Battle against Corporate Theft of the World's Water*, Stoddart, Toronto

Bridges Weekly Trade News Digest (2003) 'GATS: Business As Usual Despite Cancun Failure', *Digest* vol 7, no 33

Bridges Weekly Trade News Digest (2004) 'WTO Services Council: Members Find Offers Disappointing', vol 8, no 13

Clarke, T. (2000) 'By What Authority!' pamphlet, Polaris Institute and the International Forum on Globalization, Ottawa

Clarke, T. (2002) 'Stop the GATS Attack – A Strategic Planning Guide', Polaris Institute, Ottawa

FOEI and CEO (Friends of the Earth International and Corporate Europe Observatory) (2003) *Business Rules: Who Pays the Price?*, FOIE, Mexico and Uruguay

Gould, E. (2002) 'The Good and the Bad News for Local Governments', fact sheet, Council of Canadians, Ottawa, Canada

Gould, E. and Joy, C. (2002) *In Whose Service: The Threat Posed by the GATS to Economic Development in the South*, GATS Briefing Series, World Development Movement, London

Joy, C. (2003) *GATS: From Doha to Cancun*, GATS Briefing Series, World Development Movement, London

Khor, M., Hormeku, T. and Reddy, M. (2002) *Six Days of Shame in Doha*, African Briefing Paper, Third World Network, Bangkok, Thailand

Muller, M. (2002) 'Lessons from Johannesburg and Pointers for the Future', paper presented at *Water 2003: What Should Be Done*, London, 11 November, www-dwaf.gov.za/Communications/Departmental%20Speeches/

Palast, G. (2001) 'The WTO's Hidden Agenda', *The Guardian*, 9 November

Panitchapakdi, S. (2002) Keynote address, US Business–Government Dialogue, Washington, DC, February

Polaris Institute (2003) *Global Water Grab: How Corporations Are Planning to Take Control of Local Water Services*, Polaris Institute, Ottawa

Politi, D. (2003) *Privatizing Water: What the European Commission Doesn't Want You to Know*, Center for Public Integrity, Washington, DC

Pressly, D (2004) 'Erwin Tipped for the Top WTO Post', *Business Day*, 30 January

Puscas, D. (2002) *Enron Style Corporate Crime and Privatisation: A Look at the US Coalition of Service Industries*, Polaris Institute, Ottawa

Shrybman, S. (2001a) *WTO: A Citizen's Guide*, Canadian Centre for Policy Alternatives and J Lorimer & Company, Toronto

Shrybman, S. (2001b) *The GATS and Water: An Assessment of the Impact of Services Disciplines on Public Policy and Law Concerning Water*, Council of Canadians, Ottawa

Sinclair, S. (2000) *GATS: How the WTO's New 'Services' Negotiations Threaten Democracy*, Canadian Centre for Policy Alternatives, Ottawa

Sinclair, S. (2001) 'The GATS, Democratic Governance and Public Interest Regulation', paper presented at the *Royal Society of Canada Symposium on the WTO*, Ottawa, 17 November

Sinclair, S. and Grieshaber-Otto, J. (2002) *Facing the Facts: A Guide to the GATS Debate*, Canadian Centre for Policy Alternatives, Ottawa

Tayob, R. (2003) 'South Africa – EU request analysis', draft report for Southern and Eastern African Trade, Information and Negotiations Institute (SEATINI), Harare, Zimbabwe, 4 October

Tuerk, E. and Holland, R. (2003) *GATS, Water and the Environment: Implications of the GATS for Water Resources*, World Wildlife Fund for Nature, Gland, Switzerland

Wesselius, E. (2002) *Behind GATS 2000: Corporate Power at Work*, TNI Publications, Amsterdam

WSCM (World Services Coalition Mission) (2004) *WSCM Minutes*, 22 March, Geneva

WTO (World Trade Organization) (2003) *Understanding the WTO*, WTO, Geneva

WTO Document database (2000) EC Environmental Services, document code: S/CSS/W38, December, www.wto.org

Part 2

Case Studies in South Africa

Chapter 5

Entrenching Inequalities: The Impact of Corporatization on Water Injustices in Pretoria

Peter McInnes

This chapter focuses on the provision of water and sanitation services in the newly incorporated Council of Tshwane Metropolitan Municipality (CTMM – formerly known as Pretoria, hereafter referred to as Tshwane). The provision of water and sanitation services in Tshwane provides insight into the tensions and contradictions that have resulted from the commercialization of these services, and in particular the growing trend towards 'corporatization'.

I explore the dual character of national policies on water provision in this case study by comparing, on the one hand, the aggressive cost recovery and service cutoff practices of South African municipalities, and, on the other hand, a language of rights, social equity and ostensibly positive policies such as progressive block tariffs, free basic services and indigent policies (McDonald 2002, p21). It is the purpose of this chapter to assess the relative influence of these contradictory policies on the delivery of water services in Tshwane.

The most prominent manifestation of the government's commitment to the constitutionally enshrined right to water is the Department of Water Affairs and Forestry's (DWAF) Free Basic Water policy. The policy, which was announced at the end of 2000, requires local governments to provide free basic water to households (6 kilolitres (kl) per household per month). In Tshwane, free basic water is available to all residents regardless of income. However, the first 6 kl are charged at a rate of R4.50 per kilolitre and then 'visibly rebated' on the bill so the account holder is made aware of the fact that the free water they receive has an actual production cost.

The issue of arrears on water bills also starkly demonstrates the tension between aggressive cost recovery and more progressive policies. Both the municipality and the media place great emphasis on recovering the massive arrears debt despite the seeming impossibility of low income consumers' being able to afford their current services bills (*Pretoria News* 2002). Many households have municipal services arrears (including electricity, water and waste removal), with some as high as R80,000 (interview, Themba Ncalo, May 10, 2002). In June 2003 the average services and rates debt in the Tshwane townships of

Atteridgeville, Saulsville and Mamelodi was in the vicinity of R20,000 (CTMM 2003a, Annexure 1). Total household debt for all services in Tshwane in June 2003 was approximately R1 billion (CTMM 2003a). Some lucky households who have been able to register as indigent have had their arrears cancelled but many soon fall into arrears again, unable to keep up payment on their current water accounts.

In a city in which the Water Services Development Plan notes that 35 per cent of all households in townships survive on less than 1000 rand a month (CTMM 2002a, p42) the Mayor, Father Smangaliso Mkhatshwa, talks of the need to reverse the 'culture of non-payment' and to introduce 'stricter credit control measures' (Mkhatshwa 2002). But while the focus of the local media and the mayor is on household debt in the townships, business arrears amounted to some R300 million for the same period (CTMM 2003a).

Key to the emergence of the arrears crisis in Tshwane has been the desire, heavily influenced by national policy, to charge prices which reflect the full cost of water and sanitation services to households with only minimal cross-subsidization from rich to poor consumers. The evidence presented in this chapter will demonstrate that the free basic water supplies as currently delivered by Tshwane are inadequate to address this affordability problem for low income households and do not meet the basic water needs of residents.

The current plan is to corporatize, or ringfence, water and sanitation services in Tshwane (CTMM 2002b). This restructuring, while making revenue collection and spending arguably more accountable, will limit the ability of essential services such as water to be cross-subsidized either from the general rates base or from electricity revenues.

One of the key drivers in this restructuring of water services is the need for municipalities such as Tshwane to finance upgrades of existing infrastructure as well as address backlogs in townships with limited municipal revenue sources (CTMM 2003b, p39). Although grants from national government to support service extension have increased modestly of late, since 1994 these intergovernmental transfers have been woefully inadequate in assisting municipalities with their service backlogs (McDonald 2002, p23). In the 2001–2002 Tshwane budget, for example, national and provincial grants and subsidies amounted to a minuscule 2.07 per cent of all operating income (CTMM 2002e, p19). The model adopted by Tshwane to corporatize its water services ostensibly delivers the potential for increased revenue to finance operations and provides, perhaps more importantly, a politically saleable option for water restructuring, in contrast to other more controversial forms of privatization. The key to this political saleability is the retention of ownership and management control within the public sector. However, as this chapter will discuss, one of the key goals of corporatization is the adoption of private sector management practices.

The implications of corporatization are far-reaching. If a sustained surplus can be generated from these services it could justify increased involvement of private capital in either the management or delivery of the services. This scenario has in the short and long term significant implications for the welfare of Tshwane's 967 water and sanitation employees (employment figures, National Treasury 2003, p216) as well as the communities they service. In the short term there is the potential for job losses through outsourcing of various service provision components in an attempt to drive down labour costs. There may also be increasing conflict in townships as households suffer from high water prices and credit control practices that increasingly reflect commercial rather than public imperatives.

A Profile of Tshwane Metropolitan Municipality

While this chapter looks at the whole of Tshwane the detailed data on water consumption patterns and water cutoffs and restrictions is drawn primarily from those areas contained in the old City Council of Pretoria. Information from other councils incorporated into Tshwane was, in 2002 when the majority of research for this study was undertaken, not available. As a result the newly integrated councils are not fully represented in terms of the more detailed discussion of water consumption and service cutoffs and restrictions. A further reason for this omission is that retail water supply in parts of Tshwane, such as Odi magisterial district in the northern part of the municipality, are managed by contracts with external service providers such as Rand Water and Magalies Water. Those interested in more information on Odi and its experiments with public–private partnerships in water delivery should consult Pape (2001).

The current Tshwane metropolitan municipality is made up of 14 councils amalgamated as part of the national municipality demarcation process. This structure was formally ushered in with the municipal elections of December 2000. The area covered by Tshwane is almost 60 km wide and 70 km long. It includes areas such as Centurion, Crocodile River, Pretoria, Akasia, Soshanguve, Mabopane, Winterveld, Temba and Hammanskraal. The first integrated budget of the city was approved on 18 June 2001.

In 2001 there were a total of 252,905 households in formally recognized urban areas connected to water services with primarily full service connections in the home (CTMM 2002a, p42). There were a further 152,200 informal households connected to water services. Informal households' land tenure is not formally recognized by the municipality. There are plans to upgrade many of these areas to full water services. Where these communities cannot be upgraded in situ they will be moved. The total number of consumers, including households, businesses and farms, in 2001 was 430,900 (CTMM 2002a, p42).

According to information available from the 2001 census, detailed in Figure 5.1, approximately 32 per cent, or one in three of Tshwane's households, live on less than R800 a month. Many households live in extreme poverty with one in five households living on less than R400 a month.

Table 5.1 provides a picture of considerable unmet need in terms of water services. About 25 per cent of households or approximately 700,000 people in Tshwane fall below the minimum standards for water services under the Water Services Act; that is, a standpipe within 200 m of the household.[1] On the positive side close to 70 per cent of households have access to water on site, either within the house (65 per cent) or through a yard tap (5 per cent).[2]

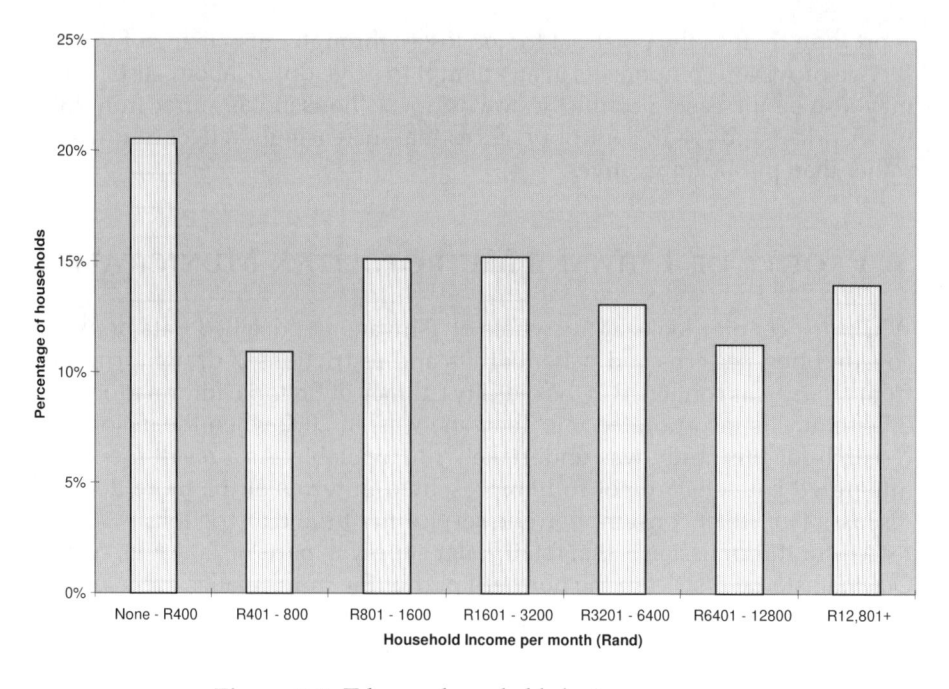

Figure 5.1 *Tshwane households by income range*

Source: Ghana 2001

Table 5.1 *Existing water service level summary*

Current service levels	Households		Total	
Service type	Informal	Formal	Units	%
No service	13,039		13,039	3
Tank(er)	47,142		47,142	11
Standpipe 500 m	52,183		52,183	12
Standpipe 200 m	22,822		22,822	5
Yard tap	14,794	278,800	295,844	69
Full service	2250			
Total	152,230	278,800	431,030	

Source: CTMM 2002a, p46

TSHWANE'S WATER CONSUMPTION PATTERNS

Water consumption patterns amongst those with in-house connections also demonstrate deeply unequal patterns of water service. The Pretoria district is a good example. Making up a small proportion of Tshwane's total population, Pretoria accounts for 56 per cent of all consumption. If Centurion, an industrial and predominantly high-income residential area, is included, that figure

AADD sold per area (437 Ml/d)

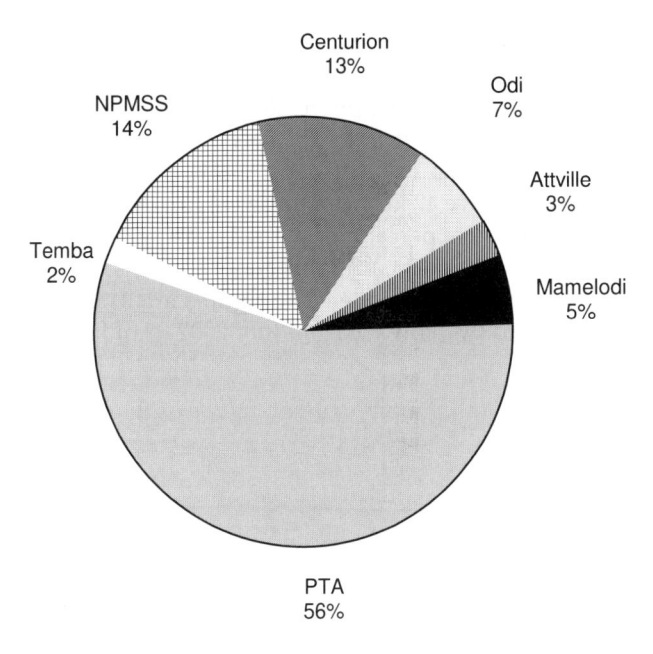

- Centurion 13%
- Odi 7%
- NPMSS 14%
- Attville 3%
- Temba 2%
- Mamelodi 5%
- PTA 56%

Figure 5.2 *Average annual daily demand sold per area per day, year ending June 2001 (1 megalitre (Ml) = 1000 kl)*

Source: CTMM 2002a, p63

increases to 69 per cent (see Figure 5.2), despite the fact that they make up only 44 per cent of all consumers in Tshwane (CTMM 2002a, p42).

The bulk of water consumption within Tshwane boundaries is by domestic households (55 per cent) but as the previous paragraph demonstrates the bulk of the water sold is consumed in the formerly white residential areas. Large businesses also consume a lot, 30 per cent of daily volumes (CTMM 2002a, p62), while they make up less than 0.6 per cent of actual consumers. Business consumers represent a possible source of revenue with which to ensure sufficient supplies of affordable water to low income communities through cross-subsidization. Tshwane has, however, failed to adequately exploit this potential source of revenue, as this chapter will demonstrate further below. (Figure 5.2, it should be noted, represents only the water sold. Some 24 per cent of all water in Tshwane is lost through leaky pipes, illegal connections and inaccurate and faulty meters.)

Comparing household water consumption in Pretoria and Mamelodi provides a more detailed picture of the inequalities in water consumption between the 110,000 mainly affluent households of Pretoria (largely white) and the 30,000 mainly poor households of Mamelodi (largely black). It is important to note that this data may give a skewed picture of water consumption by households who receive full water services. If data were included from the newly incorporated northern areas of Odi, Temba and, to a lesser extent, Northern Pretoria Municipal Sub-Structure (NPMSS), where poverty is generally greater, the differences would most likely be starker.

The introduction of a new, stepped water tariff in July 2001 enables us to track high consumption more accurately by specifying total household monthly consumption in seven blocks, or tariff steps: 0–6 kl, 6–12 kl, 13–18 kl, 18–24 kl, 24–30 kl, 30–42 kl and above 42 kl. From these we can determine what percentage of households, and what percentage of total consumption, falls within each block. This enables the identification, in general terms, of those areas that consume excessive amounts of water. The figures are drawn from the latest available data provided by Tshwane from July 2002 until June 2003.

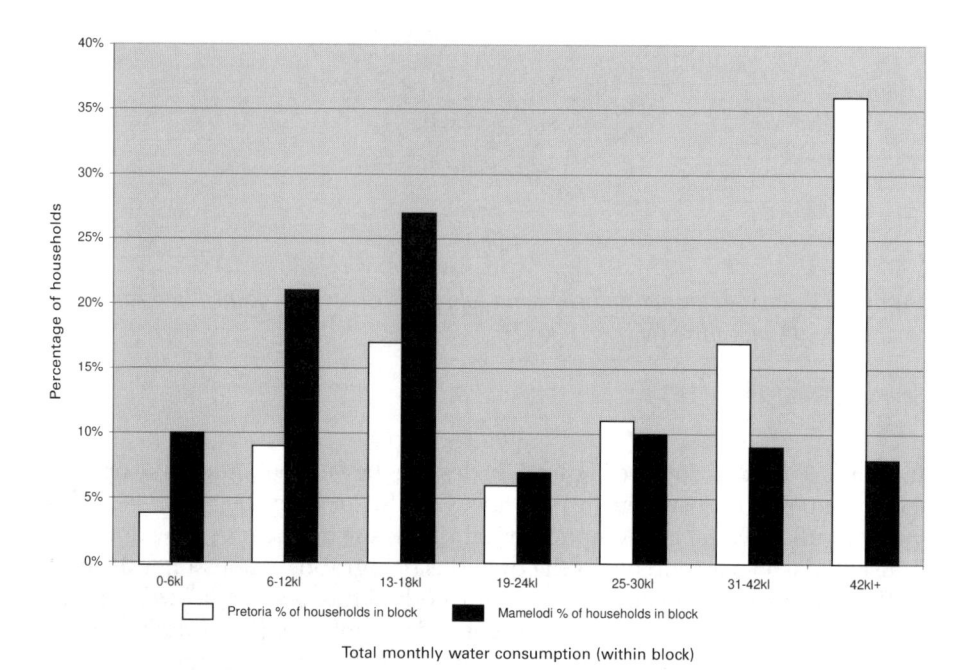

Figure 5.3 *Monthly household water consumption by tariff block in Pretoria and Mamelodi (July 2002–June 2003)*

Source: Graph constructed from raw data supplied by CTMM

Figure 5.3 shows a stark class/race divide, with 36 per cent of all households in Pretoria using more than 42 kl of water per month compared with 8 per cent of households in Mamelodi. Average total consumption by Pretoria households in the 42 kl+ tariff block was a phenomenal 84 kl. By contrast, 58 per cent of all households in Mamelodi consume less than 18 kl of water per month.

Also noteworthy is that fact that only 10 per cent of households in Mamelodi consume less than 6 kl of water per month, raising questions about the adequacy of 6 kl per household as the basis of the free water policy of national government.

What is corporatization?

Corporatization is a model adopted in recent years by some developed and developing countries as a way of restructuring government trading services such as water or electricity in order to increase their efficiency. A recent publication by the World Panel on Financing Water Infrastructure, a pro-privatization group chaired by Michel Camdessus, the former Managing Director of the IMF, argued that water providers should create ringfenced units that create 'separate accounts [from other service sectors], some managerial, commercial and financial autonomy, and clear and consistent objectives set by governments, municipalities or users'. Governments that fail to adopt this approach create 'widespread inefficiency and waste ... coupled with arbitrary political interference' (Winpenny 2003, pp9–10). The reforms adopted by Tshwane broadly follow this mantra without overtly privatizing the water service provider.

When a service provider is corporatized the ownership and management is retained in the public sector but it is ringfenced financially and managerially from other services. Ringfencing separates all financial and human resources directly involved in the delivery of a particular service from all other functions of, in this case, the municipality. Where services were previously shared the full cost of providing that service is now paid to the other department. This structure clearly identifies all costs and revenues related to the services, and the real costs and surpluses of running a service are identified (see McDonald and Ruiters, Chapter 1, this volume, for a more detailed description of corporatization).

Financial ringfencing is accompanied by managerial ringfencing. Managers of the corporatized service providers operate at arm's length from the elected officials of the municipality. The elected officials set standards and service delivery goals and monitor and evaluate the activities of the corporatized service unit. However, the ringfenced management team does the long-term and daily planning of the corporatized service unit. Managers can focus narrowly on the technical and financial concerns of their particular sector with less day-to-day political interference from elected officials. In some cases other municipal departments such as those dealing with the provision of welfare services will also have conflicting agendas that will be less likely to get a hearing from a corporatized entity.

As a result, assessment of managerial performance can be dramatically changed. Financially driven performance targets can be introduced for managers for meeting surplus/loss targets. In this way remuneration of senior managers can be linked to the level of surplus provided to the municipality. Such performance based pay can create dangerous incentives with managers focusing on surplus targets while ignoring important broader social welfare objectives.

Corporatization can only be fully understood by reference to the public sector organizational values that corporatization aims to transform. Traditionally, government-run essential service providers behaved in ways that reflected the complex character of their particular services. In providing water and other essential services to the community, governments had a full range of social, economic and environmental objectives to meet (Ranald 1996, p94). In certain circumstances, though not necessarily all cases, social values, such as equity, clearly predominated over values such as economic efficiency. This was particularly so in the water sector. One way this was reflected at the ground level in many developed countries was through pricing water to households based on property values rather than on how much a household consumed. In this way water was priced roughly according to your ability to pay and not necessarily on the basis of how much the household used.

Commercial services providers are less concerned with social or environmental values and focus more narrowly on financial objectives such as maximizing profitability, increasing share price levels and increasing market share, to name just a few. Some of these objectives are clearly not relevant for a corporatized water services provider, as it remains wholly within the public sector. However, because the managerial techniques and performance measures are adopted from the private sector these narrow financial goals can easily predominate. It is this model that is being adopted by Tswhane.

The corporatization of water services in Tshwane

The Manager of Strategic Planning and Services in Tshwane, Mr Frans Mouton, stated in April 2002 that four main options were being explored in the restructuring of water services in Tshwane (interviews, Frans Mouton, 30 April and 10 May 2002). These included:

- maintaining the status quo and leaving the responsibility for delivering water as an internal department of Tshwane Municipality;
- corporatization or ringfencing based on the model adopted in Durban Metro with the creation of Durban Water and Waste;
- a short-term management concession where management is contracted out, such as in Johannesburg; and
- full privatization, or the Nelspruit model, with an open tender where the water service provider is contracted out to a private corporation such as Biwater or Suez.

However, after discussing this last option, Mouton stated 'we are not even considering that [full privatization] as an option'(interview, Frans Mouton, 30 April 2002). In what became the Water Services Development Plan (WSDP) for Tshwane, it was proposed that 'the best mechanism is for the provider to be structured into an Autonomous Ringfenced Municipal Business Unit',[3] where that is taken to mean '[t]he establishment of a corporate entity of a legal person/

institution operating under the ownership and control of the municipality' (CTMM 2002a, p91).

There appears to have been little or no public debate on this decision to corporatize water services. Nor was there any explanation in the WSDP as to why corporatization was the chosen model. The WSDP simply notes that this decision was based on assessments carried out in line with sections 76 and 77 of the Municipal Systems Act 32 of 2000. Mr Mouton noted briefly that corporatization was 'an easy option because you have very little labour problems as trade unions are very against privatization'.

The WSDP's proposal to create a Municipal Business Unit was accepted by Tshwane Council in late 2002 but had been discussed well before this time. In an internal discussion document sent by Dr T. E. Thoahlane, the Municipal Manager, to senior officers in Tshwane on 6 February 2002, entitled 'The Path to Building an Internationally Acclaimed African City', the case for corporatization was put forcibly:

> [F]ar too many services/functions/departments depend entirely on the rates base which is not sustainable. Income generating services/departments are made to compete on the same level as non-trading services/departments and the income is then swallowed in this big 'black hole' called the income budget. In the process nobody is held accountable for this income or whether the income generated is optimal and how one could improve on the revenue streams. This also negatively impacts on the said trading service to effectively utilize the income generated to expand and improve its service delivery and infrastructure provision (CTMM 2002b, p2).

The WSDP furthers the case, arguing that 'Tshwane is fundamentally locked into the old paradigm that the public sector is sole provider of all goods and services and that more bureaucratic rules and red tape as well as cumbersome policies and procedures is the answer' (CTMM 2002a, 91). The WSDP authors go on to argue:

> Tshwane needs to build a new institution, which will empower the public servant to do more with less and to find a creative balance and to combine the ethics, values and business principles of hard-core managerialism, the New Public Manager (NPM), performance management and the ethics and values of the public sector (CTMM 2002a, p91).

What is the context in which the 'hard-core managerialism' and the 'ethics and values' of the public sector will be balanced? Firstly there are the 'constitutional obligations and other mandates' but immediately contrasted with this is the need to 'survive in this globalized and competitive environment'.

The question is, can public sector values, which ideally view service provision more holistically by placing a greater emphasis on water's social and environmental attributes, survive in what appears to be a fight for survival – the consequence of the ruthless competition imposed by increasingly globalized economies? In this Darwinian environment some argue that the only option left for local governments is to aggressively engage in the competition on the terms set by dominant local government players in the international marketplace (Ballard and Schewella 2000).

Impacts of corporatization

While corporatization is not yet finalized in Tshwane it is possible to highlight its key features and forecast its potential impacts. The preparatory work for corporatization can be seen in the new tariff structure introduced in mid-2001, increased water cutoffs and water restrictions due to a growing emphasis on recovering debts, and the introduction of an indigent policy. Each of these factors will be explored in terms of its impact on the core principle of equity and the need to address the unequal water consumption patterns outlined above.

It should also be noted that increased outsourcing and consequent job losses will probably increase once corporatization is finalized as has been the case with corporatization initiatives in other parts of South Africa and other countries. These developments will, no doubt, be justified on the basis of controlling costs and maximizing the business unit's surplus.

Unequal water tariffs

If managed properly, block tariffs allow for redistribution of water resources from wealthier to poorer areas through targeted cross-subsidization. Tshwane's tariff structure fails to do this and is unlikely to improve under a corporatized system.

The current tariff structure was implemented on 1 August 2001, and was formulated in response to the national government's commitment to providing free basic water. This tariff structure is shown in Figure 5.4, reflecting 2003–2004 charges and the seven-step system. The most striking aspect of this tariff structure is its flat gradient. After the third block there is only a 23c increase over the next four blocks. Most of the cross-subsidization burden for the zero-rated first block therefore falls on the third and fourth blocks, which means that low income households that consume between 6 and 18 kl of water per month (50 per cent of Mamelodi households, as in indicated in Figure 5.3) bear the heaviest burden of all, particularly when one takes into consideration the cost of water as a percentage of household income. Once a low income household consumes more than 6 kl of water in a month it is hit with a steep price hike that effectively nullifies any household savings incurred with the free block. Even the fiscally conservative National Treasury (2003, p222), using Tshwane's tariff to illustrate its point, raised a note of caution here, arguing that 'there is some evidence to suggest that poor households using more than 6 Kl per month are adversely affected by the steep increases in tariffs after the free 6 Kl'.

The objectives of the new tariff structure, as articulated by the Tswhane Water Tariff Work Group, are as follows (CTMM 2001a, p2):

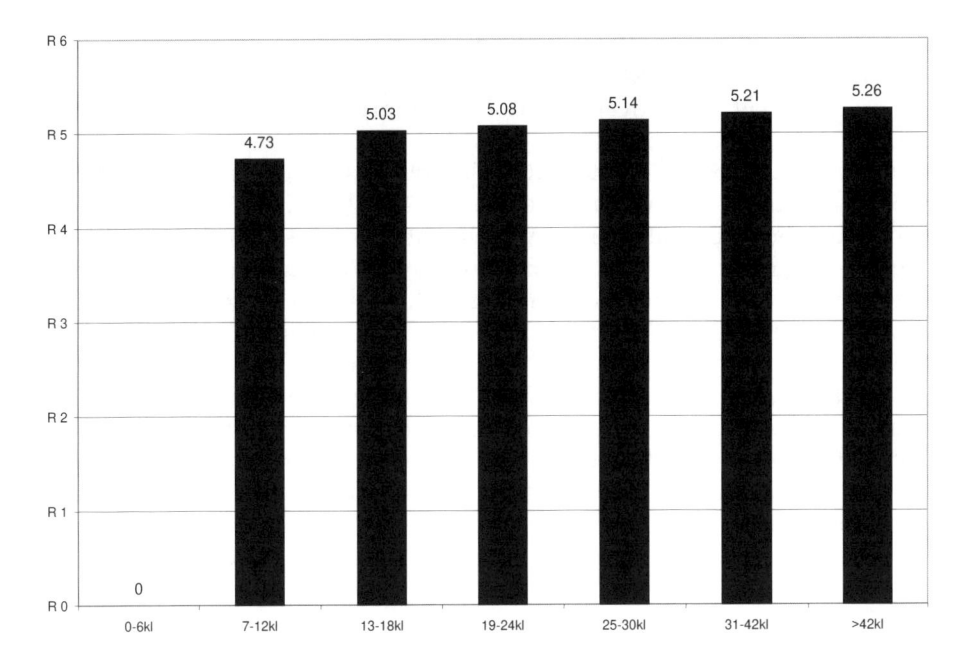

Figure 5.4 *Tshwane household water tariff, rand per kl, VAT not included (2003–2004)*

Source: www.tshwane.gov.za/munserv/munserv.htm

- ensure financial sustainability through the recovering of all cost, with possible surplus;
- be administratively easy to implement and understand;
- be fair, accountable and transparent to all consumers; and
- promote water conservation and the efficient use of water.

The first principle places the tariff firmly within the ANC government's neoliberal cost recovery paradigm. (A review of the proposed tariffs in 2001 by a Department of Water Affairs and Forestry consultant praised the structure as 'ensuring that all consumers face a water price that reflects the cost of supply' (DWAF 2001, p6).) But even within this paradigm there is room for more egalitarian policy interventions through the implementation of a more progressive, *sharply rising* block tariff. Yet this potential for cross-subsidization is barely exploited.

The requirement that the tariff be fair to all consumers has clearly not been met and would appear to also violate the provincial Gauteng Water Services Forum recommendations that domestic household tariffs should be guided by the following principles (CTMM 2001a, p2):

- zero-rated first block to ensure basic water services (6 kl per household per month) to all;
- subsidized second block to cover at least operational and maintenance cost;

- full cost recovery on the third block to cover operational, maintenance, capital and depreciation and overhead cost; and
- progressively bigger cross-subsidization from the fourth and higher blocks.

The document goes on to state that the last block 'should be set at a level that would deter unnecessary high water use' (CTMM 2001a, p4), thereby trying to promote water conservation. However, the flat structure of Tshwane's tariffs do the opposite, evidenced by the enormous amounts of water consumed in high income areas. Indeed, water consumption in the top block has *increased* between August 2001 and May 2003 while price increases over the same time in this block have been negligible in real terms.

The twisted logic of Tshwane's tariffs is captured in a quote by the Divisional Manager of Water and Sanitation, Andre Lochner, writing in the CTTM's newsletter in June 2001. Lochner argued that the tariff policy provided a 'financially viable strategy that would be fair and show no bias toward any consumer':

> *The fairness of this strategy is firstly centred around the fact that all households will receive 6000 litres (6kl) of water free each month. Secondly, all consumers who use more than the free amount will be paying more, whether they are rich or poor.* Rich consumers will not be subsidizing poor consumers; rather consumers who have a high consumption, even if they are poor ... will pay more (CTMM 2001b, emphasis added).

Lochner's objective, it appears, is to minimize the impact of new tariffs on wealthier households. In effect this treats both poor and rich households in exactly the same way despite their different circumstances, and affirms the old cliché that there is nothing more unequal than treating the unequal in an equal manner! Lochner makes no distinction between poor households with many members who have a justifiable need for high water consumption and wealthy, double-income, no kids households with low water consumption.

Meanwhile, the role of businesses and industrial consumers as a source of cross-subsidies to finance new infrastructure and lower tariffs for poor households is not mentioned at all. In many countries this type of cross-subsidy has been an important part of financing household water services. In Australia, for example, before the introduction of neoliberal water reforms in the 1990s the cross-subsidies between different customer classes were marked. Commercial and industrial users paid considerably more per kilolitre for water than households did. An Australian Industry Commission study in 1992 found that in 1990–1991 the average commercial establishment paid 15 times more for its water than the average household (cited in Shadwick 2002, p16). To the extent that businesses and industrial users are mentioned in Tshwane's tariff policy at all, it is with reference to special procedures that enable *reduced tariffs* for the purposes of local economic development (CTMM 2001a, p3).

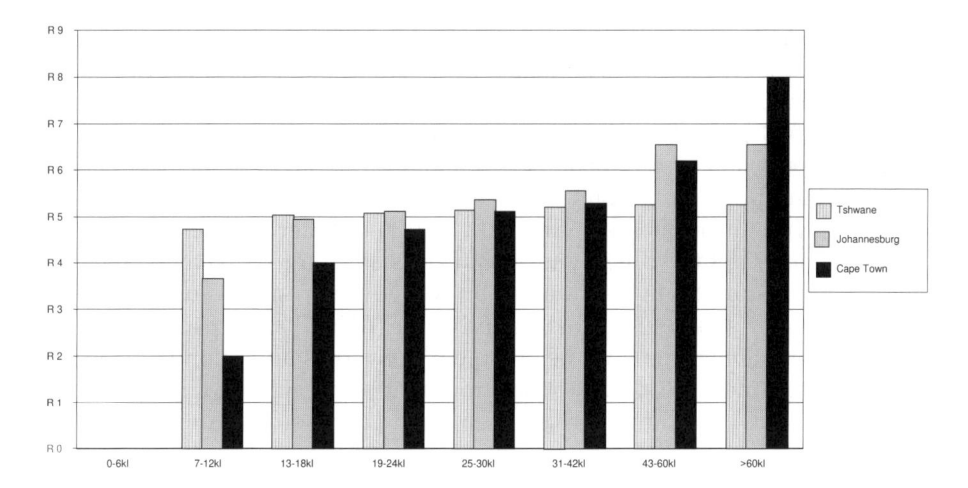

Figure 5.5 *Tshwane's household tariff compared with Cape Town and Johannesburg, rand per kilolitre (2003–2004)*

Sources: www.johannesburgwater.co.za/finance/finance_tarrif.html,
www.capetown.gov.za/budget/tariff_gw_frameset.asp,
www.tshwane.gov.za/munserv/munserv.htm

Finally, Tshwane's household tariff is much less progressive than Johannesburg and Cape Town's household tariffs (see Figure 5.5). Cape Town and Johannesburg's step structures differ slightly from Tshwane's so they have been adjusted somewhat for comparative purposes but the discrepancies are clear. Notably Tshwane's second block is 50 per cent more expensive than the same block in Cape Town, while its last tariff block is 34 per cent lower than Cape Town's.

Despite the essentially regressive nature of these tariffs, upper-income residents in Tshwane can still become quite irate at the suggestion that they should subsidize low income households. The media in Pretoria is not above fanning these flames of indignation either, with the *Pretoria News* (2002) arguing in an editorial entitled 'Go out and fetch what's owed' that:

> law abiding citizens who diligently pay their dues are going to be squeezed for more money to help keep the city running while the thousands who refuse to pay are secure in the knowledge that no steps will be taken against them. It is outrageous that the council still does not know what it should be doing to force people to pay for services.

Cutoffs and restrictions

A corporatized water service provider, if it is to be sustainable, must maintain a surplus. To do so it must be able to restrict or cut services in order to enforce payment from households. The user-pays mentality in domestic water supply is a comparatively recent phenomenon in the world and in South Africa.

The World Bank advocates three basic methods to achieve cost recovery (Kerf et al 1998, p30): disconnection in the case of nonpayment; installing hard-to-tamper-with and prepayment meters; and promoting self-policing amongst the user community. In Tshwane all three methods have been used to encourage payment, with an emphasis on the first two. Rand Water's[4] experiments with prepayment meters were highly successful in establishing high payment levels but water consumption was found to be very low as residents utilized other available water sources such as groundwater (DWAF 2001, p4). The use of prepayment water meters has been largely shelved as an option in Tshwane despite their undoubted advantages to water service providers including guaranteed payment and, through the practice of self-disconnection, the avoidance of the political opprobrium of provider initiated disconnection (Drakeford 1998, p593). The main reason given for this was the lack of a continuous supply to poor households of the electricity required to run the meters (interview, J.C.J. Eicker, 7 May 2002). Each unit is also expensive. But given Johannesburg and Cape Town's recent attempts to trial prepayment water meters (see Harvey, Chapter 6, this volume) there may yet be an attempt to introduce them in Tshwane.

Disconnection has also been used as a debt control mechanism. In the Atteridgeville, Mamelodi and Pretoria area in October and November 1999 there were 5559 disconnections for nonpayment and only 296 reconnections in the same period. Between April and July 2000 there were another 1017 disconnections of water and only 202 reconnections (raw data supplied by Alta Du Plessis, CTMM).

Tshwane began seriously exploring other options to full disconnection that merely restricted water flow, somewhere around the end of 2000. This policy shift appeared to be in response to community resistance to cutoffs as well as the need to comply with national government's free basic water policy (interview, Themba Ncalo, 10 May 2002). Tshwane's Credit Control Policy section 3.11.1 states: 'Water supply to defaulting private household debtors will not be completely discontinued, but rather be limited for health reasons. Other types of debtors who are in default and whose water supply is involved, will be completely deprived of the service'.

By April 2001, 12,591 push button taps had been installed.[5] Push button taps are placed next to the water meter requiring household members to leave the house or yard to get access to water. They require downward pressure for them to work and only provide a small amount of water at low pressure. It was estimated that using a push button tap took upwards of an hour to fill a 5-l container (interview, Themba Ncalo, 10 May 2002). In May 2001 the roll-out of push button taps was halted temporarily, again, after community resistance. The taps were widely perceived to be degrading and humiliating to those forced to use them and were suspended after pressure from the council (interview, J.C.J. Eicker, 7 May 2002). In August 2001 push button taps were abandoned entirely and replaced by mechanical restrictors that limit the flow of water. The water supply is available inside the dwelling thereby avoiding the shame and serious inconvenience of push button taps. This option enables a maximum of 600 l a day or 18 kl per month, but the flow rate is set at 12 kl per month for nonpaying customers (interview, Johan Ulrich, 24 April 2002).

In the six months after the introduction of the free basic water policy in August 2001 water restrictions were placed on 13,731 households. In the first six months of 2003 water restrictions averaged 5485 per month or 32,910 households (CTMM 2003a, p3).

It is unlikely in the short term that Tshwane will return to its policy of full disconnection. Nonetheless, there are still bureaucrats pushing for full cutoffs as a more effective form of financial management, as evidenced in the following quote from the Tshwane credit control division: 'Credit control and debt collection have not reached a satisfactory level of effectiveness, due to private households water supply only being reduced and not completely cut, compared to the case with non-households' (CTMM 2002c, p1).

The large arrears burden and the threat of a protracted rates and service payment boycott is seen by credit ratings agencies as the key threat to Tshwane's credit rating (CTTM 2001d). A positive risk rating from credit rating agencies is necessary to fund further infrastructure development, a point made all the more critical with the recent reintroduction of a municipal bonds market in South Africa.

Council documents on the arrears problems often see the harshest of strategies as being the most effective in dealing with the arrears issue. Thus, commenting on a positive 7.5 per cent increase in payment patterns in the three months ending April 2001, a report to the Mayoral Committee from the Credit Control Division notes: 'This is in contrast to the previously reported negative trend and is ascribed to increased summonsing action. Should the municipal manager be in a position to empower evictions again, the payment rate can improve further' (CTTM 2001c).

The fact that Tshwane has now outsourced its debt collection services for debt of over 90 days may create additional pressures for harsher cost recovery (CTMM 2003b).

Indigent policies

Under the Municipal Systems Act 2000, Section 97, municipalities are required to develop a credit control and debt collection policy which must provide for 'indigent debtors' in a manner 'that is consistent with its rates and tariff policies'. Council approved Tshwane's indigent policy on 6 September 2001 (CTMM 2001e). It was updated in August 2002 with a small but significant change: instead of suspending debt with the hope that the arrears might somehow be repaid, registrants had their debt cancelled.

Indigent policies are favoured by international financial institutions over cross-subsidization through the tariff system due to their transparency: it is easier to identify how money used to ameliorate the negative impact of market based pricing is being spent. As a result, indigent policies often form part of the key policy platform of a water sector privatization programme as they attempt to deal with the problem of affordability for low income communities for full cost recovery pricing of water services (WSSCC 1999, p27).

Indigent policies have a number of problems though (Elson 2002, p91). Firstly, they are relatively expensive to administer, a criticism levelled at Tshwane's previous indigent policy (DWAF 2001, p4). In order to address this concern the council outsourced the screening of applicants to ward councillors in early 2002 as a way of reducing the cost of the programme. Secondly, by targeting specific groups indigent policies run the risk of stigmatizing the poor by providing onerous, demeaning and often difficult to understand criteria that have to be fulfilled before entitlements are granted. Public officials, and in this case councillors, may exercise such discretion that the claimant has few if any rights. The professional assessment section of the application form for registration as an indigent in Tshwane contains, for example, a section where the councillor or public official has to make an 'Assessment of lifestyle'. Thirdly, in an attempt to limit demands on the fiscus, indigent policies can become too narrowly targeted, denying access to worthy recipients that fall just outside the income criteria.

For registration as an indigent account holders must prove that their household earns less than R1400 per month, that they do not own another house, and that the municipal value of their home does not exceed R388,000. Successful applicants need to be assessed every 12 months. Once registered, indigent households are charged a low cost housing tariff for waste collection (R18.90) and receive a 25 per cent reduction on sanitation and property assessment levy charges. This reduction was reduced from an initial 50 per cent (interview, Joyce Msiza, 15 April 2002). Despite this the reduced tariffs are still too high for many indigent households and indigent arrears in June 2003 stood at R15.3 million, only 10 months after all debts were cancelled (CTMM 2003a).

Indigents are also given prepaid electricity meters, which have a 10 per cent surcharge over electricity charged by regular credit meters. At the time this was justified on the basis that the surcharge could assist with the interest charges on the suspended debt. But the electricity surcharge gives the clear impression that indigents are being punished for being poor.

In mid-2003 there were 27,000 registered indigents in Tshwane (CTMM 2003b, p30). Tshwane household income data suggested that upwards of 188,000 households could potentially be registered as they earn less than R800 a month, with 47 per cent of households earning less than R1600 a month (Census 2001, see Figure 5.1). Indigent registration clearly falls well below possible demand.

Possible reasons for this may include confusion over formal credit control policies which offer benefits for debt repayment, but *only* if 60 per cent of the household's arrears are paid off up front. But because this facility is only available to account holders who earn less than R2400 a month, it is simply unaffordable to many. It is also possible that the benefits of being declared indigent are outweighed by the considerable inconvenience, personal intrusiveness and complexity of being registered, or that administrators are simply unable to cope with the demand.

CONCLUSION

The commitment to full cost recovery in water and sanitation services in South Africa conflicts with the government's commitment to 'a better life for all'. The extent to which government fails to provide basic services, or provides them at a cost that demands services be cut or significantly underprovided, will have the effect of delegitimizing their rule. If these socioeconomic rights are denied, the spirit of reciprocity that characterized the difficult, but internationally acclaimed, transition to the new South Africa, is threatened.

Crucial to any solution to the problems of affordability of water services for low income households is the need to abandon the fiscally conservative, cost recovery mentality which sees only narrow profit and loss criteria as a way of measuring success. The proposed corporatization of water services in Tshwane makes such abandonment extremely unlikely and heralds a potential intensification of full cost recovery strategies.

Nonetheless, achievable short-term goals to lift some of the burden from low income households can be adopted in Tshwane and must include the following:

- adequate levels of free basic water (at least 50 l per capita per day instead of the current 25 l);
- a reduction in the price per kilolitre for domestic household consumption in the blocks immediately after the first free block;
- a significant increase in the final tariff block for wealthy domestic households to assist financing of greater assistance for low income households;
- increased and rising business tariffs to assist financing to low income households; and
- a more generous indigent policy with less onerous, intrusive and restrictive criteria.

NOTES

1. This figure was from raw data provided by Mr J. Cattanach, collected to determine the extent of backlog in water and sanitation services delivery in Gauteng Province (GDDPLG 2001).
2. Data from Census 2001 suggests a lower figure of 13 per cent of households below the minimum service standard with 80 per cent of households having access to water on site either within the house (49 per cent) or through a yard tap (31 per cent). This chapter assumes that the municipal data is more accurate.
3. In the final draft this was changed to 'Autonomous Municipal Entity'.
4. Rand Water is South Africa's bulk water supplier but in peri-urban areas in Tshwane was involved in retail supply of water.
5. The following information is pieced together from interviews with Tshwane Council Officers and ASCORA, Councilor Themba Ncalo and Council Documents including a 'Water Pilot Project: Background Document'.

References

Ballard, H. and Schewella, E. (2000) 'The Impact of Globalisation on Local Government in South Africa', *Development Southern Africa*, vol 17, no 5, pp737–49, December

Census (2001) from Municipal Demarcation Board, Municipal Profiles 2003 www.demarcation.org.za/municiprofiles2003/index.asp

CTMM (Council of Tshwane Metropolitan Municipality) (2001a) 'Implementation of a Uniform Tariff Structure and Policy for Potable Water in the City of Tshwane Metropolitan Municipality Area', WE 8/1/P, mimeo

CTMM (Council of Tshwane Metropolitan Municipality) (2001b) 'Tshwane to Run with New Uniform Water Tariff Structure', *CTMM Newsletter*, 1:3, June

CTMM (Council of Tshwane Metropolitan Municipality) (2001c) Finance Division CT: Arrears and sundry accounts (Cut offs and legal processes) levels of debtors in arrears: April 2001, Report of the Mayoral Committee, 24 July 2001 at 435

CTMM (Council of Tshwane Metropolitan Municipality) (2001d) Finance Division: Credit rating of the city of Tshwane Metropolitan Municipality, Report of the Mayoral Committee, 24 July 2001 at 456

CTMM (Council of Tshwane Metropolitan Municipality) (2001e) Finance Division: policy for the indigent, ST B2/1 Council resolutions 6/9/2001 and 29/08/2002

CTMM (Council of Tshwane Metropolitan Municipality) (2002a) Water Services Development Plan, Final Draft (For Approval) June

CTMM (Council of Tshwane Metropolitan Municipality) (2002b) 'The Path to Building an Internationally Acclaimed African City: Framework for the City of Tshwane's Strategy to Ensure Global Competitiveness and a Sustainable Growth', internal discussion document, dated 30 January 2002

CTMM (Council of Tshwane Metropolitan Municipality) (2002c) Levels of Debtors in Arrears: August 2001–February 2002, Portfolio Committee, Ref No. ST – B18/2, 4/3/2002

CTMM (Council of Tshwane Metropolitan Municipality) (2002d) Budget 2002–2003

CTMM (Council of Tshwane Metropolitan Municipality) (2002e) The City of Tshwane *Metropolitan Municipality Annual Report* 2000/2002

CTMM (Council of Tshwane Metropolitan Municipality) (2003a) State of Debtors in Arrears, Portfolio Committee, Finance and Audit, Ref No: ST – B18/2, 20 August

CTMM (Council of Tshwane Metropolitan Municipality) (2003b) 'Mid-term Report December 2000–June 2003', www.tshwane.gov.za/munserv, 21 January 2004

DWAF (Department of Water Affairs and Forestry) (2001) *Free Basic Water Implementation Strategy, Case Study: Tshwane Metropolitan Council*, Palmer Development Group, Cape Town

Drakeford, M. (1998) 'Water Regulation and Pre-payment Meters', *Journal of Law and Society*, vol 25, no 4, pp588–602, December

Elson, D. (2002) 'For an Emancipatory Socio-Economics', *New Agenda*, vol 5, first quarter 2002

GDDPLG (2001) *Business Plan for the Elimination of the Backlog in Water and Sanitation Services in the Gauteng Province*, Government Printer, Pretoria, 30 November

Kerf, M., Gray R., Irwin, T., Levesque, C. and Taylor, R. (1998) *Concessions for Infrastructure: A Guide to Their Design and Award*, World Bank Technical Paper No 399, Washington, DC

McDonald, D.A. (2002) 'The Theory and Practice of Cost Recovery in South Africa', in D.A. McDonald and J. Pape (eds) *Cost Recovery and the Crisis of Service Delivery in South Africa*, Zed Books, London

Mkhatshwa, Mayor Father Smangaliso (2002) 'State of the City Address', edited version in *Pretoria News*, 28 February

National Treasury (Republic of South Africa) (2003) 'Intergovernmental Fiscal Review 2003', www.treasury.gov.za

Pape, J. (2001) *Poised to Succeed or Set Up to Fail? A Case Study of South Africa's First Public-Public Partnership in Water Delivery*, Occasional Papers No 1, Municipal Services Project, Cape Town

Pretoria News (2002) Editorial 'Go out and fetch what's owed', no 1, 9 May

Ranald, P. (1996) 'Redefinition of the Public Sector: Serving Citizens or Customers?', in A. Farrer and J. Inglis (eds) *Keeping it Together: State and Civil Society in Australia*, Pluto Press, London

Shadwick, M. (2002) *A Viable and Sustainable Water Industry*, National Competition Council Staff Discussion Paper, AusInfo, Canberra

WSSCC (Water Supply and Sanitation Collaborative Council) (1999) *Vision 21: A Shared Vision for Hygiene, Sanitation and Water Supply*, Johannesburg

Winpenny, J. (2003) 'Financing Water for All: Report of the World Panel on Financing Water Infrastructure', www.gwpforum.org/gwp/library/FinPan/Rep.MainRep.pdf

INTERVIEWS

Councilor Themba Ncalo, Attridgeville and Saulsville Concerned Residents Association (ASCORA), 10 May 2002, ASCORA offices, Pretoria city

Mr J. Cattanach, Chief Engineer, Gauteng Provincial Government, Corner House, Johannesburg, 23 March 2002

Mr Frans Mouton, Manager, Strategic Planning and Regulation, CTMM, 30 April 2002 and 10 May 2002 (by email)

Mr J.C.J. Eicker, Manager Credit Control, CTMM, 7 May 2002, City Treasury, Pretoria

Mrs Joyce Msiza, Acting Director Developmental Social Welfare Services, CTMM, 15 April 2002 (by phone)

Mr Johan Ulrich, CTMM, 24 April 2002 (by phone)

Box 1 *South African Water Caucus (SAWC) Resolution on Water and Trade Adopted August 2003*

The South African Water Caucus (SAWC) notes with concern the negative impact of the private sector, in particular the large corporations, on water resources and water service delivery, and the role of the World Trade Organization (WTO) in this regard.

The WTO's General Agreement on Trade in Services (GATS) is designed to further open up the water sector to large corporate interests. GATS will exacerbate the crisis of delivery of water services. It will lead to further privatization, more unscrupulous corporations, the introduction of prepayment meters and more cutoffs, attachments of property and evictions. It will compromise government support to the poor and sound the death knell for the possibility of introducing free basic water. In so doing, it will flout the constitutional right to water.

The new issues pushed by the North in Doha, Qatar, including investment, competition and government procurement, further open the doors for the large corporations. The Agreement on Agricultural together with GATS undermine community food security and small-scale farming.

The WTO policies are being imposed after years of other damaging policies, notably the World Bank and International Monetary Fund (IMF) structural adjustment programmes and self-imposed structural adjustment in the form of GEAR and Nepad.

The interlinkage of all these institutions and policies creates a context in which the corporations are all-powerful. They dominate governments and people and have free reign to introduce further change for the worse.

The SAWC notes with particular concern the approach of the Ministry of Trade and Industry in driving a pro-corporate agenda and gambling with our services, our rights, our health and our lives. The Ministry fails to consult on these critical issues and keeps information behind closed doors.

The government approach facilitates the expansion of South African business into the continent and allows them to profit at the expense of people of the continent. South African parastatals such as Eskom and water utilities have moved into the continent as private companies for profit.

The SAWC insists that our rights to water are respected, that the constitutional provisions on water are upheld and that rights to natural and traditional water sources are protected.

As such, the SAWC rejects the privatization of water in all its forms, whether it be the sale of assets; lease agreements; delegated management; public–private partnerships; Build, Operate, Train and Transfer schemes (BOTT) or any other form.

The SAWC says:

Private sector out of water!
Water out of GATS!
No to the new issues!
No to the WTO, GEAR and Nepad!

The SAWC argues for the decommodification of water. The public sector should carry out its responsibility as implementer at the level of water resources, water distribution and water service delivery. Government should work with communities to introduce public works and other programmes to repair and extend community infrastructure.

> The water industry should not be for profit. Any surplus raised by the industry should be used for the further extension of water services. Corporations that damage the environment and pollute water resources must be made to repair the damage done and compensate people negatively affected.
>
> The SAWC insists that government should respect the rights of all in South Africa to water and to the information needed to protect those rights.
>
> The SAWC supports the Phantsi WTO! platform and is part of the campaign to mobilize people against the WTO and government's active promotion of the institution.
>
> Phantsi WTO!
>
> Water for all!

Chapter 6

Managing the Poor by Remote Control: Johannesburg's Experiments with Prepaid Water Meters

Ebrahim Harvey

> *I support prepaid meters because it will bring about an understanding of the costs of water, since we are living a lie. People say that water comes from God. It may be true but God does not pay for the pipes. We need to change the mindset. We need to educate people about the costs and that as citizens we have rights and responsibilities* (interview with Brian Hlongwa, political head for water on the Johannesburg Mayoral Committee).

Since 1994 much has changed in the forms of administering municipal services to the black townships of South Africa. Commercialization and prepaid meters (PPMs) in particular are changing the relationships between consumers and the state. In Johannesburg, South Africa's largest city, a new politics of consumption is arising based on the idea that market relationships embodied in prepayment for services are empowering and educating poor consumers into modern forms of rationality. This chapter seeks to vigorously rebut this conception of water service delivery.

I start with a brief conceptual overview of the consumption politics associated with prepaid meters, with specific reference to the British experience. A case study of Johannesburg follows, looking at prepaid water services in two of Johannesburg's largest township areas, Orange Farm and Soweto. The chapter concludes with a discussion of current battles around prepaid water meters between residents of Johannesburg and Johannesburg Water (JW), the corporatized entity that runs the city's water and sanitation services.

The shift to prepayment metering provides a striking example of the reshaping of social relations of consumption and the new political technologies for managing the poor since the African National Congress (ANC) took power in 1994. On the one hand, prepayment meters allow utilities to avoid the high transaction costs of dealing with the problems of late payment, debt and disconnection typically associated with low income users; on the other hand it shifts the burden of managing difficult household reproduction problems firmly on to the 'sovereign' consumer.

Prepaid Water as a Remote Political Technology

The prepaid water meter has become particularly popular among municipalities with large numbers of poor people. From an administrative and financial point of view, managing the poor costs the municipality less since there are no meter readings, no billing statements, and no arrears or credit controls. Yet, as Marvin and Guy (1997, p34) argue, prepaid meters are more than cost saving devices; they are a new political technology for managing the poor. They make three central arguments to support their argument. First, remote technological management shifts responsibility for water use to customers who must now communicate with the meter, charge it and disconnect themselves from the water network when they cannot afford to pay. Second, prepayment effectively closes direct relations by mediating all contracts through the meter. And third, prepaid technologies allow water companies to disengage from high transaction costs with poor and low income consumers (e.g. debt collection). Mark Drakeford (1998, p595) takes this further: 'The development of pre-payment meters allows disconnections to be socially privatized. The devices allow the obligations placed upon powerful companies to be circumvented and the consequences transferred into the private lives of the least powerful individuals'.

There are two other important economic-political advantages that these meters have for private water companies, manufacturers and local government: PPMs provide a steady and reliable revenue stream, and they help evade politically explosive public water cutoffs. The cutoffs are invisible with PPMs since they occur silently, inside the homes of the poor.

Direct and Hidden Costs to the Consumer

For the consumer, 'the connection between pre-payment purchase, debt and hardship is indisputable' (Drakeford 1998, p596). Unlike households on credit meters, the prepaying home needs hard cash, leaving it with less flexibility than those on normal meters. Furthermore, the household may have to buy recharge vouchers or coupons in particular denominations, reducing payment flexibility. The household also has to invest time and travel costs into the purchasing of prepaid coupons whereas homes on credit meters simply pay their utility bills at their convenience. Outlets selling prepaid coupons can be far from where people stay and generally have limited opening hours, which can mean that a household cannot get water until they reopen. Thus, prepaid meters transfer costs from the service provider to the consumer.

Without water, households with prepaid meters may be forced to take shortcuts or beg, borrow or steal water. A survey in England showed that:

> *273 of the 1,027 households with pre-payment devices went without water for 24 hours or more. Figures from one company, Severn Trent, suggested that 49 per cent of customers in the trial had been without a water supply*

after running out of emergency credit. Of those cut off for more than seven hours 28 per cent borrowed money, 18 per cent stored water with the attendant public health risks, while 13 per cent went without water altogether (Drakeford 1998, p598).

In the end, Liverpool Council in the UK decided to reject the installation of prepaid meters, leading to a lengthy court battle won by the municipalities and consumers who opposed these devices. The municipalities were concerned about the health hazards resulting from cutoffs. Eventually, the UK government outlawed prepaid water meters altogether; the Water Industry Act of 1999 banned any form of disconnection or limitation of water for nonpayment, including prepaid meters and trickle valves.

JOHANNESBURG WATER AND PREPAID METERS IN SOUTH AFRICA

Johannesburg Water is an outcome of the 'iGoli 2002 Plan', which the city developed in 1999 to deal with its financial and organizational crises. The purpose of the plan, according to its architects, was to radically change the Metropolitan Council's overall organizational form. The council believed that 'although the crisis manifests itself as a financial crisis, this was symptomatic of a deep underlying organisational crisis. Investigations of the reasons for the crisis revealed them to be embedded in a range of fragmented and dysfunctional systems' (City of Johannesburg 2001, p32). Only by separating out various departments into independent ringfenced units, driven by hard budget constraints, would performance improve. Corporatization also 'offered greater autonomy and flexibility to the management of the service to introduce commercial management practices to the delivery system'. As Anthony Still, the council's transition manager for water and sanitation noted, 'we are losing R130 million from people who are in the system but are not paying for their services' (Mothibeli 2000).

The economic logic of corporatized water was that 'payment levels and revenues will increase with improved management'. The council teamed up with the French multinational water company Suez, signing a five-year management contract in 2001, arguing that:

they [Suez] bring experience of similar turnaround challenges in cities around the world. They will bring impetus, focus and experienced management. Bringing in a private partner will not only improve the rate of revenue collection but will also improve the quality of service delivery which is good news for consumers (Mothibeli 2000).

As an arm's-length utility, it was argued that JW would be removed from political interference and political modes of decision making deemed inefficient by neoliberal policymakers. Commercial objectives and market principles would thus encourage a depoliticized service. This, in short, is why prepaid water meters have been introduced in poor communities in South Africa and around the world; 'prepayment water technology has potential for substantial growth' according to the Water Research Commission (2003).

Prepaid Water in Phiri, Soweto

Soweto, an acronym for 'south western townships', is situated southwest of Johannesburg. It is the biggest complex of townships in South Africa and home to at least 1 million people. Over 120,000 Sowetan households have been targeted for prepaid meters, now considered a high priority by the city. 'Operation Gcin'amanzi' (a Zulu word for 'conserving water') is the city's name for its plan to reduce unaccounted-for water (UAW) and to deal with nonpayment of water and perceived lack of consumer awareness of the economic value of water. Anthony Still has said that it will 'make or break JW'. He also characterized it as the 'most ambitious [JW] project yet'. As a 'key mayoral strategic priority', Gcin'amanzi is a five-year intervention 'tailored to address the severe water supply problems in the city, especially Soweto'. UAW is mainly generated by physical, commercial and onsite losses in unmetered, formal, low income areas. These areas have been billed on a *deemed* consumption basis; that is, flat rate billing. Outside deemed consumption areas, the UAW is lower, at 21 per cent, and therefore in line with international standards (20–25 per cent).

Among the 'deemed' consumption areas Soweto represents by far the largest losses in terms of volumes, with a UAW ratio of 62 per cent (JW 2002a). JW reports that it is losing R158 million a year in Soweto. The council's own Contract Management Unit revealed recently that payment levels for water in Soweto were only at 15 per cent (interestingly, this is above Alexandra at 14 per cent and Ivory Park at 5 per cent, two other black townships north of Johannesburg). The current flat rate charged for deemed consumption in Soweto is R103.40 a month, one-fifth of a typical monthly old age pension, often the sole source of income for Soweto families (*Star*, 27 February 2004).

Johannesburg Water interprets the problem as an 'effect of oversupply and a lack of *ownership* of water consumption by residents' (JW 2002a) (emphasis added). Prepaid meters, which will regulate and control consumption strictly on a cash basis, are thus projected within the market discourse of ownership.

The implementation of prepaid meters started in late 2003. In May 2003, JW had placed an advertisement in newspapers calling for proposals for the supply of 'prepayment water meters and a meter management system'. It stated that 'the total number of prepayment meters that may be used over a five/six year period is of the order of 120,000' (*Star*, 15 May 2003). However, JW has assured residents that prepaid meters will not be installed against their wishes, although residents, through the Anti-Privatisation Forum (APF), argue that most people do not want prepaid water (backed by extensive survey research of close to 400 households (APF 2004; Public Citizen et al 2004)). Under the pretext of explaining to residents the benefits of these meters, JW and the city went ahead and installed prepaid meters in Phiri, one of the townships in Soweto.

Prepaid Meters in Orange Farm

Orange Farm is a sprawling, low income area, 20 km south of Johannesburg. Except where yard connections exist, water is usually obtained from water tankers. About half the Orange Farm area has no waterborne sanitation. With over 30,000 households, and very high unemployment levels, the state has designated it a 'permanent informal settlement' where 'alternate service delivery options' may be used.

The installation of prepaid meters in Orange Farm predated Soweto and was the first attempt at a technological solution for nonpayment in low income areas. Between January 2002 and January 2003 JW installed prepaid meters in about 1400 homes in Stretford Extension 4, a township in Orange Farm. JW's plan was to launch this as a pilot project and to later extend prepaid meters to Soweto and other areas if they considered it a success in Orange Farm.

In December 2001 JW signed a 'Service Agreement' with the Stretford Extension 4 community, called the 'Social Compact'. According to this agreement, all illegal street connections would be removed. JW would install the meters at its own cost, and residents would make a once-off R100 payment for the connection. In the event that meters were vandalized, the community would take responsibility for repairs. Residents would pay for water only *after* the free 6 kilolitre (kl) of water per month per household offered by the municipality was used up, and a monthly R34 sewerage charge was levied. However, the sewers would be maintained by the Social Compact (i.e. township residents) at their own cost (JW 2002b, p149).

The Social Compact became the instrument through which the project was implemented. JW and the city have stated that a targeted population was in favour of prepaid meters because it would allow them to monitor and control their own water consumption. But in an interview with Phillemon Tjega, an Orange Farm resident and community leader, a different story emerges:

> *When JW came back to say that they will be installing prepaid meters, that is when people started getting worried and the trouble started. People were afraid of what those meters could do. There is lots of unemployment here in Orange Farm. Before we did not pay for the water from the street taps* (interview, Phillemon Tjega, 12 February 2003).

After initial community resistance to the prepaid meters, meetings and workshops were organized with the assistance of the local ANC branch in order to persuade people to accept the new system and understand the benefits of prepaid meters. Tjega said, 'the ANC told those critical of the meters that they were opposed to the government and development in the area'. Quite clearly, the political boundaries were being drawn on the issue of the prepaid system.

In addition to prepaid water meters, JW has introduced community based shallow sewers. But regular maintenance of the sewer by the local community is needed. JW suggested that a 'local sanitation committee' be formed to oversee the management of the system and specify the responsibilities of the members. Unlike normal sewers, these do not require large quantities of water to flush the toilet (JW 2002b, p49).

COMMUNITY RESPONSES AND OPPOSITION TO PREPAID METERS

Over the past few years, there have been several community struggles against prepaid water meters, notably in Tembisa on the East Rand, Khutsong (near Carltonville), Orange Farm and, most recently, in Phiri. Residents sabotaged hundreds of these meters in Khutsong (DWAF 2000, p62). In Soweto, Trevor Ngwane, chairperson of the Soweto Electricity Crisis Committee and secretary of the APF, defiantly stated: 'Let Johannesburg Water come with their prepaid water meters in Soweto. We will destroy them, as we did with electricity meters' (interview, Trevor Ngwane, 12 December 2002).

Interviews conducted by the author with Soweto families in late 2003 reveal that there was much opposition to the meters. The concern is that when the lifeline supply of water is used up (i.e. the 6 kl per household per month offered as part of the ANC's national free water policy) people will be forced to use the prepaid meters. Alena Mofokeng, a Phiri resident, said: 'Cooking, cleaning and especially washing clothes uses a lot of water. I'm tired of this government. The whites were better. They never cut our water even when we did not pay for it'. Mofokeng also saw PPMs as discrimination against the poor: 'If these meters are good why did they not start with it in the rich white areas where people have lots of money? Why start in Phiri, where people are poor?' – and where unemployment rates are as high as 65 per cent.

Prepaid electricity preceded prepaid water. According to one Soweto resident: 'Many people are struggling with the electricity prepaid meters. So also having prepaid water is going to worsen the situation'. A leading member of the ANC's Women's League in Phiri stated: 'Although the government is pushing water prepaid meters, many ANC members in our branch are opposed to it. Selling water to poor people is not good. But once the politicians decide, you can do nothing. But we are trying to stop it. I cannot go against my community'.

ANC councillor for Phiri, Pat Kunene (interview, 24 September 2003), noted that city politicians and JW officials had visited Orange Farm and Kagiso (a township near Krugersdorp on the West Rand) where these meters were installed, and after speaking to people on the streets and doing house visits they believed prepaid meters would work in Soweto: 'When we went to Kagiso we could not say if these meters were good or bad but after the visit we supported it. Some councillors were first bitter about selling water to poor people but after the visit they agreed that prepaid meters would be a good thing'. Asked if JW had visited homes to explain the virtues of these meters, Kunene said they did not but 'would now be going to each home to educate people about the advantages of these meters and train them about how to use the meters'.

But according to people I have interviewed there was no consultation. One resident said: 'No, you see if there was proper consultation there would not be all this chaos' (interview, Dolly Malazi, 23 September 2003). The APF has also condemned JW for a lack of consultation:

> This is a democracy. You cannot just come into our areas and change our water system without consulting us. This is a top-down way of running government. The constitution of the country and the Water Services Act says that residents must be consulted if there are to be any changes to their water supply. Neither JW or any councillor has ever called any meeting where we were informed about 'Operation Gcin'amanzi'. We have never given any councillor any mandate to agree to the installation of prepaid water meters (APF Press Release, 2 September 2003).

Since the state's prepaid offensive began, there has been ongoing opposition. International solidarity includes organizations such as Public Citizen (USA), African Liberation Support Committee (UK), Citizens Against Privatisation (New Zealand) and Students Against Privatisation (Zimbabwe). They and others have signed an international declaration against these meters (Mothibi 2003). Many local activists opposing the installation of the meters have been arrested and face criminal charges, including malicious damage to property. A construction worker was shot after a confrontation with residents trying to stop the installations (Mothibi 2003). A pamphlet circulated by the APF captured the militancy of the protests: 'Destroy the Meter and Enjoy the Water' (APF 2003), prompting Johannesburg's most popular newspaper to say that the city's ambitious infrastructure project 'has hit a snag. The first phase known as Operation Gcin'amanzi, which is suppose to commence in Phiri, has been halted by the people' (*Sowetan*, 29 August 2003). The APF has since launched a legal challenge to have these meters declared unconstitutional and therefore illegal.

CONCLUSION

Some observers see PPMs as a responsible solution to managing the poor but criticize the way communities are being cajoled rather than consulted. For example, Mark Shepard, director of Restor Africa, argues that:

> with the restructuring of local government to include traditionally disadvantaged areas many local authorities selected prepayment as a solution to the prevailing culture of non-payment. While this appeared to be the answer, the implementation approach was wrong. Consumers were superficially and hurriedly briefed rather than consulted... As a result, prepayment has been seen as a 'punishment' for non-payment, resulting in widespread rejection by many communities (cited in Van der Merwe 2003, p31).

Furthermore, the Development Bank of Southern Africa, which finances water projects at a municipal level, states that: 'No water supply project should be implemented until the community is *fully informed* and consensus-based decisions have been taken regarding levels of service, tariff structures and credit control measures' (Water Research Commission 2003, p3).

Once installed, people may grudgingly accept prepaid meters, even though they can have very destructive consequences. But continued opposition to the meters is likely, leading to low intensity conflicts. In addition, unless they are banned outright, as they were in Britain, it will be very hard to reverse the situation, especially while many new companies with strong ANC connections continue to manufacture, punt and distribute these devices, and while municipal bureaucrats look for ways to manage the poor by remote means. At a wider level, the PPM privatizes misery in the homes of the poor, contributes to social individualization and social decay. It forms part of a new locus of the neoliberal politics of consumption.

REFERENCES

APF (Anti-Privatisation Forum) (2003) 'Destroy the Meter and Enjoy the Water', pamphlet, Johannesburg, September

APF (Anti-Privatisation Forum) (2004) 'Prepaid meters in Phiri, Soweto', Johannesburg, July

City of Johannesburg (2001) *City of Johannesburg: An African City in Change*, Zebra Press, Johannesburg

DWAF (Department of Water Affairs and Forestry) (2000) *Electronic Prepayment Metering Cost Recovery Systems*, DWAF, Pretoria

Drakeford, M. (1998) 'Water Regulation and Prepayment Meters', *Journal of Law and Society*, vol 25, no 4, pp588–602

JW (Johannesburg Water) (2002a) 'Operation Gcin'amanzi Project', November, Johannesburg Water, Johannesburg

JW (Johannesburg Water) (2002b) 'Service Agreement between Johannesburg Water and Stretford Extension 4 Social Compact', Johannesburg Water, Johannesburg

Marvin, S. and Guy, S. (1997) 'Consuming Water: Evolving Strategies of Water Management in Britain', *Journal of Urban Technology*, vol 4, no 3, pp21–46

Mothibeli, T. (2000) 'Council pins hopes on water partner', *Business Day*, 12 July

Mothibi, N. (2003) 'Soweto water battle goes global', *The Star*, 13 October

Public Citizen, Anti-Privatisation Forum and The Coalition Against Water Privatisation (2004) 'Nothing for Mahala: The Forced Installation of Prepaid Water Meters in Stretford, Extension 4, Orange Farm', Johannesburg, March

Van der Merwe, L.H. (2003) 'Metering in Demand: Uncovering Prepayment', *Water, Sewage and Effluent*, vol 23, no 5

Water Research Commission (2003) *The Institutional and Socio-Economic Review of the Use/Application of Electronic Prepaid Meter Technology in the Provision of Water Supply to Urban and Peri-Urban Areas*, Final Report vol 1, Project no k5/1206/0/1, WRC, Pretoria

Box 2 *Resolution on Prepaid Meters by South African Municipal Workers' Union (Samwu)*

Adopted at 7th National Congress of Samwu, August 2003

Increasingly both national and local government are promoting the use of prepayment meters for both water and electricity. (It has already been used for many years in electricity, but is a fairly new development for water.) There are many reasons for government to promote this – some of the reasons they have explicitly stated, and some we can assume.

The advantages of prepayment meters for municipalities:

- The council is paid before any water or electricity is consumed, which is obviously financially better for the council – they have a guaranteed source of regular income coming in before the service is actually delivered. It therefore helps them to keep their books balanced.
- The council avoids the politically charged problem of debt collection for unpaid bills.
- Once a prepayment meter has been installed, the council doesn't have the cost of sending out meter readers, of billing residents and of following up people who don't pay their accounts.
- Councils also use prepayment meters to gather in debt. For residents in debt, a certain amount of the money they pay into their card is allocated for covering arrears they have built up.

These meters, however, are very onerous for the poor. With the existing system of metering, the council sends out an account for water already consumed. In other words, the council, as an organ of state, bears the *up-front* cost of the service, while individuals pay *after* they've used the service. With prepayment meters, the individual/household must bear the cost up-front (i.e. people pay *before* they use the electricity or water). Poor individuals/households are much less able to bear this cost than the state.

In addition, prepayment meters leave no room for poor households to use credit as a means of ensuring their continued access to water. So, unless the household has ready cash when their water card runs out, they must do without water. Many poor households have to make a choice on a day-to-day basis about what they are going to spend their scarce resources on. Very often, it might be a choice between food, and buying more units on their water card. If they choose food, their lack of access to water can lead to serious health and environmental dangers, including possible loss of life. This is one of the reasons that the government in the United Kingdom has outlawed the use of prepayment meters.

In effect, these meters result in self-disconnection from services that are basic and important both for life and decent living conditions. It looks like the individual's own choice on the surface – they choose not to buy more electricity or water. But it is not a free choice. They are being forced into an unhealthy and possibly dangerous situation by poverty. Poverty, and people's inability to pay for services, is turned into individual problems with individual solutions (self-disconnection) rather than collective problems requiring social solutions. Self-disconnection might be a more politically acceptable solution for councils, in that they do not have to go out to people's homes and do the disconnecting themselves, but is unacceptable for both individuals/ households and the broader public good.

Prepayment meters also perpetuate gender inequalities. When the money runs out and households are faced with no water and no electricity, it is generally women and children (women are traditionally seen as responsible for domestic work) who must compensate by fetching water from other sources, fetching wood to make fires and so on. It increases the burden of and time spent on domestic duties for women.

Noting that:

- Many communities find prepayment meters useful ways of budgeting for their monthly expenses.
- However, prepayment meters also result in the poor self-disconnecting because they cannot afford up-front payments. This means that the council absolves itself from political responsibility for ensuring service delivery to all; and there are not even any basic procedural protections for the poor, e.g. trickler systems; timely warnings before disconnections take place; appeals and so on.
- In other countries, for example the United Kingdom, where prepayment meters have been used, self-disconnections have been shown to lead to serious health and environmental problems. For this reason they have been outlawed in the United Kingdom.
- Residents are much less able to bear the up-front cost of a service like water or electricity than the state is.
- Credit (i.e. paying *after* consumption rather than before), is an important way for poor households to ensure their continued access to water.
- Prepayment meters serve to individualize the problems of poverty and the inability of poor people to pay for services. In this way, social solutions to collective problems are undermined.
- The introduction of prepayment meters is in line with the general trend towards the commercialization of service delivery.
- Users of both water and electricity prepayment meters are generally charged more than the users of standard meters.

We therefore resolve that:

Samwu campaign for the immediate outlawing of prepayment meters because of their danger to the health and life of poor communities.

Chapter 7

Public Money, Private Failure: Testing the Limits of Market Based Solutions for Water Delivery in Nelspruit

Laïla Smith, Amanda Gillett, Shauna Mottiar and Fiona White

In 1999, the Nelspruit Local Authority contracted the British based multi-national Biwater to provide its water services for 30 years. It was claimed by the Department of Provincial and Local Government (DPLG) to be 'the largest and most sophisticated municipal public–private partnership ever concluded in South Africa'.[1] This arrangement, known as the Greater Nelspruit Water Concession, was the first contract of its kind in the South African water sector. This chapter provides a comprehensive assessment of the concession as an advanced form of privatization.

We begin by providing a background to the Nelspruit water concession to illustrate the dire need for large-scale funding to extend services to townships that, under apartheid, formed part of the homeland of KaNgane. We then highlight some of the achievements of the concession before discussing its problems – primarily those related to regulation and cost recovery.

It is worth noting at the outset that the implementation of the concession was largely driven and funded by the South African state – both local and national – and by development banks and funders. Despite claims that private capital was essential if service delivery objectives were to be met, the bulk of the capital for the concession has come from public sources and the bulk of the risk (political and financial) has been borne by the public sector; hence the title of this chapter.

It must also be noted, however, that this privatization initiative has taken place at a time of major social, political and economic change in Nelspruit – and South Africa as a whole – making service delivery and expansion difficult at the best of times. Whether the water provider in Nelspruit was public or private the challenges would be enormous. All the more reason, therefore, that South African authorities should have been much more cautious and diligent in their development and monitoring of this concession.

A Profile and Background of the Concession Area

Figure 7.1 *Location of Mpumalanga Province in South Africa*

Nelspruit is the capital of the province of Mpumalanga in South Africa (see Figure 7.1). After the democratic reorganization of local government in 1994, this historically white and affluent town became a new municipality, forming the Nelspruit Transitional Local Council (Nelspruit TLC). Overnight, Nelspruit authorities inherited the former homeland of KaNgwane and the massive service responsibilities associated with this area. During apartheid the homeland authority had been given large cash infusions by the apartheid government and with this money installed high levels of infrastructure such as waterborne sewerage and yard taps within the homeland area. Over the years, however, this level of infrastructure was severely neglected by the homeland authorities to the point where most communities relied on communal standpipes at best.

The 1994 demarcation of Nelspruit increased the population from 24,000 to 230,000 and significantly changed the profile of the communities to be serviced by local government (Kotze et al 1999, p4). Many of the newly incorporated areas had never received water and sanitation services, and the council's newly created system of infrastructure service provision was completely inadequate. For example, the number of residents per length of water pipe increased from 110 to 601, and the number of residents per length of sewer pipe from 96 to 830. It was apparent that the council would have difficulties in overcoming this shortfall with existing tariff revenues from the town of Nelspruit alone. It was also obvious that the new residents in adjoining township areas would be unable to help cover the costs for the required investment. Payment rates in the township areas were low: approximately 10 per cent of total billings, compared with 90 per cent in Old Nelspruit (interview, Frans Greyling, 25 February 2003). Although the population grew tenfold, the total income of the new municipality had only grown by 38 per cent (Kotze et al 1999, p5).

The post-apartheid demarcation also widened the Nelspruit jurisdiction to include several townships and traditional areas, including KaNyamazane, Matsulu, Tkwane, Msogwaba, and Mpakeni. These newly incorporated areas are more than 20 km from the town centre, and have left the municipality with what Maralack (1999) termed 'the national malady know as a dual town'. The core town has an unequal relationship to the surrounding poorly serviced dormitory townships. Furthermore, poverty and unemployment in the municipality are dire. According to 1996 census data, around 60 per cent of households had an income of R1000 a month or less. Almost 40 per cent of households in the concession area had incomes of R500 a month or less, well below the standard poverty line at the time of R800 a month (see Table 7.1).

Table 7.1 *Monthly household income by locality and percentage of population in the Nelspruit TLC*

Locality	R0–500	R501–1000	R1001–2500	R2501–6000	R6001–11,000	R11,001 or more
KaNyamazane	32.6	11.4	26.2	21.4	6.9	1.4
Matsulu	37.8	22.0	28.0	10.1	1.6	0.4
Luphisi	60.6	16.3	17.4	4.6	0.2	0.4
Daantjie	45.1	21.3	25.3	6.9	1.0	0.4
Mpakeni	44.2	21.5	29.5	3.6	1.2	0.0
Msogwaba	40.1	20.5	29.8	8.3	1.0	0.4
Zwelisha	51.1	22.9	20.6	4.9	0.4	0.2
Nelspruit	14.5	5.2	11.2	23.6	25.0	20.5
Nelspruit NU	50.0	21.6	11.8	8.7	5.3	2.7
All households (average)	39.63	18.35	22.64	11.60	4.95	2.80

Source: Statistics are from the South Africa Census 1996. It should be noted that the Census provides 14 categories of income but these have been amalgamated into seven categories for Table 7.1 in order to simplify the presentation of the data

As with poverty, the township areas have significantly higher unemployment rates than those in the town of Nelspruit. Table 7.2 illustrates the breakdown of unemployment by locality. Although the area suffers from serious service provision challenges and development problems, the outlook for the area is not all bad. According to some analysts, the economy of Nelspruit is on the verge of a sustained period of economic growth. In fact, Nelspruit's economy is the fastest growing in the country, with a growth rate of approximately 7 per cent (interview, Deputy Manager for Mbombela Municipality, 17 April 2003), compared with the national rate of 3 per cent (SAIRR 2003). Yet, even with the expectation that these growth rates can continue, the municipality cannot

Table 7.2 Unemployment rates by locality in the Nelspruit TLC

Locality	Unemployment rate (%)
KaNyamazane	30.9
Matsulu	36.3
Daantjie	33.2
Luphisi	31.8
Mpakeni	31.2
Msogwaba	34.5
Zwelisha	32.0
Nelspruit	3.4
Nelspruit NU	8.1
Average for concession area	25.3

Source: Gillett (2002)

supply and sustain water services from its own capital budget. Infrastructure backlogs alone were estimated to be in excess of R400 million, far greater than the capital budget available to the town council.

At the same time, the ability of the local authority to leverage additional funds for capital investments was limited by national level departments that, for example, were unwilling to provide grant funds to support public sector service extensions. As a result, the council faced a situation where none of the usual sources of finance would be sufficient to meet capital investment needs for water and sanitation. Rolfe Kotze, the CEO of the Nelspruit TLC, noted that the national Department of Finance did not allow local authorities a capital growth rate of more than 6 per cent of their entire budget. At that time, the Nelspruit budget was approximately R25 million a year, an amount far less than what was required to extend water services. Furthermore, intergovernmental transfers between 1991 and 1997 declined by 81 per cent (Finance and Fiscal Commission 1997). Nor was the Nelspruit transitional authority able to leverage loans of this magnitude on its own. It simply did not have the requisite credit rating to borrow from either the Development Bank of Southern Africa (DBSA) or commercial banks.

It must be emphasized that at this point in time national government was oriented towards fiscal austerity, part of a larger ideological shift towards market based approaches to fostering development in South Africa. The Growth, Employment and Redistribution programme (GEAR) was put in place in 1996 as a macroeconomic framework directed at stemming the growth of bureaucracy at the national, provincial and local government level, but with a platform that prioritized privatization, liberalization and deregulation. In order to show international and domestic capital that South Africa was 'open for business', significant state resources were put towards assisting local authorities to choose public–private partnerships (PPPs) as an option for addressing the crisis in service delivery. For instance, DBSA, through its Private Sector Investment (PSI) unit, was appointed to assist the Nelspruit Council to identify possible service delivery options and paid for the feasibility studies.

There was, therefore, considerable support at national levels of government in piloting a water concession in South Africa, and Nelspruit appeared to have favourable conditions for testing this service delivery alternative. In 1996, DBSA stepped in to help the local authority prepare the tender documents to invite private sector investment through a long-term concession. Once these preparations were under way, the Municipal Infrastructure Investment Unit (MIIU) also provided considerable technical support to the Nelspruit authorities in refining the concession contract. The MIIU was a USAID/South African Treasury department cofunded institution set up to promote private sector participation in municipal infrastructure, primarily through technical assistance to local authorities in preparing feasibility exercises, setting up tendering processes and designing contracts. During the 1997/2000 period the DBSA and MIIU were a formidable force within the country in providing the technical support for an ideology that purported the superiority of market based solutions to the service delivery problems facing local authorities. Together, these two institutions provided the bulk of the R4.6 million that went into the Nelspruit project preparation costs.

Interviews with key players involved in the establishment of the concession revealed that the decision for this service option was justified on three grounds. First, there was a need for significant capital investment that was deemed to necessitate the involvement of the private sector. Second, there was a desire to improve management and operational efficiency, a line of thinking that was more often implied than explicitly stated, probably owing to sensitivities relating to criticisms of the council as the former service provider. Third, most pro-concession interviewees mentioned nonpayment as an issue of concern and, while not directly linking the resolution of nonpayment to the concession, there was an assumption that the concessionaire would be better able to deal with this issue than the council, because the Greater Nelspruit Utility Company (GNUC), soon to be renamed the Greater Nelspruit Water Company (GNWC), would operate along more commercial lines. Karen Bretenbach, a programme officer with the DBSA, said that the concession arrangement in Nelspruit 'takes the politics out of water' (interview, 12 March 2001). Her view was that the GNUC is a commercial entity and therefore would address the issue of nonpayment as a matter of survival. The council, as a political entity, was deemed unable or unwilling to do this.

Despite the fact that Nelspruit authorities faced significant community and labour opposition over a four-year negotiation process, the contract for the 30-year concession with Biwater was signed in November 1999. The concessionaire is a joint venture between Nuon, a Dutch utility company, and Biwater, a British multinational water company, forming Cascal, which holds 48 per cent of shares of the GNUC. Additional ownership is by South African firms, which is discussed in more detail below.

As for the promise of private sector investment – the main rationale for bringing in a private company – the primary source of financing for this concession has actually come from public sources, primarily the DBSA through a R125 million loan over a seven-year period. For every R3 Biwater obtained from DBSA, the shareholders have contributed only R1; that is, only 25 per cent of the total investment. As of February 2003, GNUC had spent R75 million, of which R56 million had been drawn from DBSA and R19 million had been paid by shareholders, namely Biwater (interview, Harold Moeng, 17 April 2003). The concessionaire has also received a grant from the Department of Water and Forestry Affairs (DWAF) in the form of a bulk water discount of R2.28 million per annum which was scheduled to be phased out in April 2004.

Considering South Africa had so little experience in these sorts of market based partnerships, why was such a long-term concession signed? One answer could be that the magnitude of the investment required to upgrade newly amalgamated areas warranted a sufficiently long-term contract to ensure that the private sector partners could recuperate their investment. Whether the local authority had the regulatory capacity to monitor such a complicated contract seemed irrelevant at the time. The regulatory question, is, however, paramount to protecting public sector interests and is discussed in greater detail below.

SUCCESSES OF THE CONCESSION

Before discussing the problems of the Nelspruit concession it is important to acknowledge the gains that have been made. First, and most importantly, the overall level and quality of service delivery to the townships incorporated into the concession area have improved. The engineering achievements have been central to the extension and upgrading of services. A total of R40.5 million has been spent on capital works so far, with major projects including the refurbishment (ongoing) of the KaNyamazane sewage treatment plant and a new treatment plant at Matsulu. GNUC has laid 91 km of water mains in the township areas and 8 km in rural areas. It has also laid 18 km of sewer mains in township areas and 17 km in rural areas. As a result, most residents in the townships have 24-hour access to water supply and higher levels of infrastructure, namely waterborne sanitation and yard taps. Since 1999, the KaNyamanzane township has had 6000 connections installed out of a total of 8500 erven (70 per cent of the township population), 4000 of which are metered. In Matsulu, 4500 households are connected to the network out of 9000 erven (50 per cent of the population), 2250 of which are metered. In both townships households that are not metered are supplied through the standpipe system and network fed 'jojo' tanks.[2]

Second, capital works so far have resulted in 1268 temporary jobs with 47 contracts awarded to local contractors. Approximately 16 of these contracts were awarded to previously disadvantaged residents, and an additional 75 previously disadvantaged contractors were awarded subcontracts.

Third, improvements have been made with respect to the governance of water distribution. Despite the difficulties with Biwater communication strategies with township communities, the quality and frequency of communication is better than had previously existed under the Nelspruit local authority. Furthermore, the local authority, in its desperation not to see this contract fail, has cooperated with Biwater in working through the difficulties of managing the concession (interview, Nantes Kruger, 27 February 2003). One of the positive outcomes of this level of cooperation has been the development of water forums in Matsulu and KaNyamanzane, involving Biwater, the local authority, ward councillors and township residents. This is the most institutionalized vehicle to date for dealing with the communication problem between service users and the service provider. It is hoped that it will provide a space where service users can hold their political representatives accountable for problems that arise with their service provider.

Fourth, with respect to cost recovery efforts, Biwater has undergone many trials and tribulations in testing different credit control measures. In some instances, Biwater has been innovative in its application of credit control strategies, such as putting a freeze on arrears to avoid accrual of interest and removing the arrears from water bills so that households feel less overwhelmed by the amount owed. The intention of this strategy is to encourage households to develop the habit of paying their current accounts with the understanding that resolving these issues is a precondition to dealing with the more difficult issues of household debt.

PROBLEMS WITH THE CONCESSION

Despite these achievements, the concession has been plagued with a number of problems. But before addressing specific problem areas it is important to note that the Nelspruit municipality has also been undergoing dramatic political and organizational change during the period of the concession, complicating all facets of the PPP arrangement. One of the most significant of these has been the restructuring of local government boundaries.

During the demarcation process following the local elections in 2000 the Nelspruit area was once again renamed and consolidated into the Mbombela Municipality (see Figure 7.2). The redemarcation dramatically increased the population size and area of the Greater Nelspruit Area. The population more than doubled to approximately 589,460 people[3] and the area grew in size to 3451 km^2. Yet the financing for this newly enlarged area relies predominately on the tax base of the old town of Nelspruit.

Within several months of signing the contract in 1999, therefore, the concessionaire suddenly found itself responsible for only 50 per cent of the territory in the newly created Mbombela. The local authority has been eager to widen the concession area but Biwater has been hesitant to widen its contractual responsibilities given the high levels of nonpayment within the existing concession area.

The creation of Mbombela also caused a shift in the organizational structure and political landscape of the municipality. Although the municipal government remains dominated by the African National Congress (ANC), which also won the first local government elections in 1996, a number of councillors stepped down and were replaced by new councillors less familiar with the concession agreement. The Pan African Congress (PAC), which holds only one seat in the

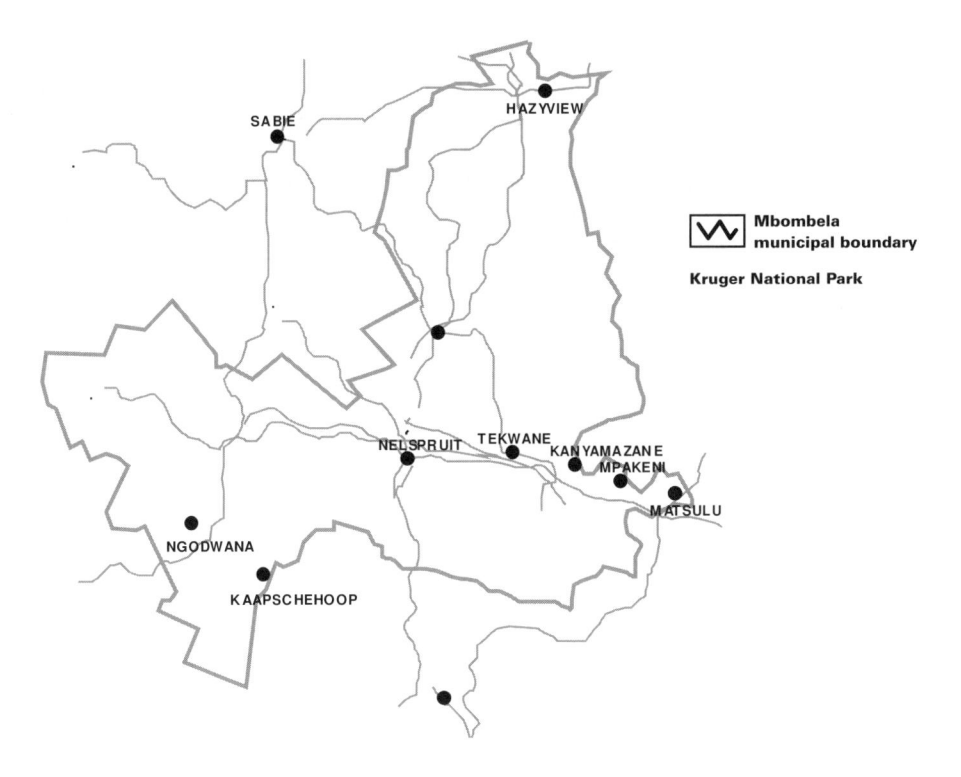

Figure 7.2 *Map of (renamed) Mbombela Municipality*

local authority but wields significant influence in the townships, did not support the concession from its inception. Mr Sipho Siwela, Provincial Secretary of the PAC for Mpumalanga and the only PAC councillor for Mbombela, claimed the concession did not have community support or the support of many ANC local councillors. ANC councillors interviewed for this research, however, generally believe that the contract has been valuable in increasing the financial capacity to provide water services to the newly integrated areas.

With this background information we now look at five specific areas of concern with the concession: regulatory frameworks; service payments; communication with the public; financial sustainability; and labour issues.

Regulatory frameworks

Strong regulatory capacity is critical when a local authority undertakes a service delivery agreement of this magnitude, yet inadequate regulation has been one of the major stumbling blocks in the implementation of the Nelspruit concession. As part of the service delivery agreement the concessionaire has been paying local authorities R1.5 million a year to regulate and monitor the contract. The local authority, perhaps due to administrative changes and other service delivery challenges in extending services beyond the concessionaire area, has not made the regulation of the water contract a priority. In theory, the ANC local councillors governing the city council have felt that the contract gave them sufficient control over the concession by retaining responsibility for setting tariffs. Since the signing of the contract, council has increased the water tariffs by 10 per cent to offset the loss of revenue arising from the state mandated 6 kilolitres (kl) of free basic water per household per month given to all GNUC customers (interview, Brian Simms, 26 February 2003).[4] Council was also supposed to steer the regulatory process through the creation of, and participation in, the Compliance Monitoring Unit (CMU) in order to oversee Biwater activities, but this critical area of involvement has been neglected.

The CMU was set up in 1999 to regulate the concession with an initial focus on the technical side such as operations and maintenance. Monthly monitoring committee meetings were held and attended by representatives from the city council administration. A technical consultant and a programme manager from the Private Sector Investments unit represented DBSA, and a consultant represented GNUC. The committee had a strong technical focus since the information that GNUC is required to provide for monthly reports is largely concerned with the operation, maintenance and status of systems and plants related to the provision of water and sanitation services, the quality of water and levels of service, the status of capital projects, and financial data including details relating to payment levels.

Over time, however, the personnel attending these monthly meetings dwindled, leaving the CMU with insufficient capacity to provide financial oversight and to examine the social side of the contract, namely customer care and the growing problems related to the nonpayment of services. One dedicated official took on the responsibility of monitoring the contract, but this was in addition to the exceedingly demanding responsibilities of being chief engineer for the entire municipality (interview, Frans Greyling, 25 February 2003). Despite the experience and technical expertise of the official involved, one person cannot monitor or regulate a concession of this size, particularly when the financial and customer care areas of expertise were not within his area of specialization. After the CMU ground to a halt, there was literally no regulation of the concession for approximately six months; it then began the process of rebuilding. Its new composition includes a project manager, a consultant from KPMG for financial advice, GNUC representatives, two city councillors and a representative from one of the water fora.

The monitoring arrangements for the concession also raise a number of concerns relating to the transparency of the Nelspruit contract, as well as the regulation of water and sanitation and PPPs more generally. First, given the importance of the Nelspruit concession as a major pilot project that could have significant impact on the direction of water and sanitation service provision nationally, it seems that its regulation is largely in-house and far from being independent. The three main parties involved (the council, the GNUC and the DBSA) have a vested interest in ensuring the success of this concession. The council, according to the people interviewed, has neither the resources nor the capacity to provide water and sanitation services to the enlarged municipality on its own and does not want to reclaim responsibility for service delivery. The GNUC, for its part, has now borrowed capital and invested heavily in the concession, and needs to make returns on this investment. The DBSA has promoted the concession as the best option for the council and is one of the lenders to the GNUC. All three parties stand to lose resources and credibility if the concession fails, particularly the DBSA (because of its heavy promotion of these kinds of arrangements) and the council (for which there would be major political fallout if the concession fails). The national government, responsible for the policy framework underpinning PPPs, would also receive a blow to its privatization policies (already under serious attack from labour and civic movements) should the Nelspruit concession not succeed.

With these vested interests comes the temptation to keep problems out of the public eye. As the contract and its monitoring was done in-house any independent assessment of the concession is difficult. It is not even possible to determine what 'success' means, as it is not known exactly what is being monitored and what the indicators of success might be. There is clearly a need for PPPs of this nature to be carefully monitored outside of the tight circles of interested parties such as councils, the DBSA, the MIIU and the private sector entities themselves.

The experience of this research also suggests that neither the national Departments of Water Affairs and Forestry (DWAF) or Provincial and Local Government (DPLG) have sufficient knowledge of the Nelspruit PPP to be able to effectively act as a watchdog. A more appropriate arrangement could be an independent regulator governed by a board that provides a mix of experience and knowledge ensuring that the interests of consumers, the private sector, labour and government are adequately represented.

Nonpayment and the implementation of 'free water'

When GNUC took over responsibility for water services in 1999 it faced a situation of massive nonpayment, particularly in township areas. Indeed, this was one of the reasons for creating a PPP: the belief that a private firm would be better at collecting revenues.

Accordingly, GNUC enforced strict credit control measures to improve payment levels, which included water cutoffs, removing meters and portions of pipes to prevent illegal reconnections, reducing 24-hour supply to intermittent hours throughout the day and night, and installing restrictors in household taps to reduce the flow of water. These measures merely resulted in increased illegal reconnections and community frustration and anger directed at Biwater workers.

Biwater has acknowledged the credit control failures and has now taken a softer approach to nonpayment through a combination of innovative debt management schemes and customer care policies (including talk show presentations, radio announcements, flyers, kombis driving through the townships with loudspeakers, and community consultations). These helped to improve payment levels but this was short-lived with the introduction of a free water policy by national government in 2001. The mandate to provide a basic lifeline of free water to all households was a service delivery challenge that Biwater was not expecting as it was not part of the contract it had signed in 1999.

The free water policy was introduced by the African National Congress in the lead-up to the 2001 local government elections. Local authorities were given two years to implement this policy and are to this day still struggling to administer it. Many local authorities have installed restrictors in households that are too poor to pay for water above the lifeline amount so that only 200 l per day trickle out of their taps. Provisional financing for this policy came from national government through the equitable share grant, a national transfer to local authorities earmarked for service delivery. As of 2003 the national treasury has provided additional resources (R822 million) to help local authorities to finance this water policy. In the Nelspruit concession, local authorities have used about 30 per cent of its equitable share grant to finance water and have transferred this to Biwater in the sum of R2.2 million a year to finance the free water initiative. Senior officials from Biwater claim, however, that the annual loss from this free water policy to the company is R8 million (interview, Harold Moeng, 18 June 2003).

Significantly, this free water policy has replaced the indigent grant that was in place in Nelspruit for low income households earning less than R800 per month, which provided up to 19 kl of free water per month. Ironically, then, the new free water policy means that the minority of poor consumers in the concession area who did claim indigence and benefited from the voucher system are worse off than they were before. They now receive two-thirds less free water and pay a higher price for the additional water they consume over 6 kl.

Reasons for nonpayment are complex. Household interviews in the two townships with the highest levels of nonpayment, Matsulu and KaNyamanzane, show that a large number of households do not pay due to grievances with the quality of service they receive from GNUC. These grievances include: water bills that were perceived as excessively high and not reflective of what households felt they consumed; complicated water bills that did not indicate what they consumed over and above the 6 free kilolitres; failure to inform households of installation of water meters; and harsh treatment of township residents by Biwater personnel.

Household incomes are another major factor. Both Matsulu and KaNyamanzane have an indigence rate of 62 per cent, with unemployment rates of 36 per cent and 30 per cent, respectively, according to the 1996 census. In many instances, people are simply too poor to pay for water. Even with the first 6 kl of water being free, many household water bills are still very high, with average monthly bills for water and sanitation of approximately R90 per month, excluding arrears. Numerous households interviewed explained that they took great efforts to use water wisely and did not understand why their bills were so high. They expressed a willingness to pay 'if their bills were reasonable'.

Politically, many residents oppose the presence of Biwater because of the draconian credit control measures being used against their communities for nonpayment, such as water cutoffs and the removal of water meters from people's property to prevent illegal reconnections. These respondents claimed that they do not pay as a form of civil protest. Others simply believed that all water should be free.

It would be false, however, to paint township residents as mere victims. While they are vulnerable to the ravages of poverty and unemployment, these households have the ability to bring the concession to a close should they decide to mobilize a long-term payment boycott. Unless the socioeconomic conditions in these areas improve, efforts to force poor people to pay for water they cannot afford may have even more volatile repercussions.

Political communication

Part of the problem underlying the free water initiative relates to how the policy was announced to the community by politicians as part of their December 2001 election campaign. Communities were not adequately informed, or perhaps chose not to hear, that anything consumed over the first 6 kl would be charged according to a three-step tariff. This translated to an increased cost to households consuming more than 20 kl a month in order to subsidize the free provision of water. The result of this poor communication is that many communities thought that *all* water was free and that they did not have to pay their service bills. This miscommunication eroded what little progress Biwater had made in increasing payment levels through customer relations. Dispelling the myth of unlimited free water proved to be a formidable task for Biwater, which has admitted that its strengths are in operations and maintenance rather than in customer relations (interview, Harold Moeng, 18 June 2003).

Politicians also admit that they have not been able to achieve community cooperation in raising payment levels. Councillors may have had difficulty in addressing these issues because they have been minimally involved in working with township residents to better understand the complexity behind the nonpayment problem. The council has not initiated any specific programmes to inform or educate members of the public about the changing nature of their services and the need for regular payment. The problems around water services have simply come under general social programmes such as the Masakhane programme,[5] a long-standing programme to improve payment levels for public services.

Financial sustainability

The nonpayment problem has led to a loss of investor confidence resulting in a moratorium on investment in the capital expenditures for extending new services within the concession area. GNUC has narrowed its focus to operations and maintenance of existing infrastructure, but even these activities are being affected by hostility towards Biwater workers by angry residents. For instance, workers are prevented from opening and closing valves in order to distribute water and are also unable to regularly read meters. The impact of this community resistance, both in terms of nonpayment and interference with workers, is having severe financial implications for the ability of GNUC to recover its costs, let alone operate water services properly.

As of January 2002, GNUC was R17 million in debt. The primary shareholder of GNUC, Cascal, has said that it will not provide more capital investments to Biwater to resume new infrastructure spending until payment levels in the two payment problem townships have reached 50 per cent. In early 2003, payment rates for Matsulu and KaNyamanzane were only at 8 per cent and 35 per cent, respectively.[6] Achieving significantly higher payment rates may be difficult (if not impossible) given the myriad of community concerns with their water services, their relationship with GNUC and the actual poverty rates of the area.

A brief glance at the price changes over a four-year period indicates why it has been so difficult to increase payment levels in areas that are indigent. Nominal price increases have been as high as 69 per cent in the second 'tariff band', the one that most affects low income households (see Table 7.3).

Table 7.3 Water tariffs in Nelspruit

	1999 Tariffs			2002 Tariffs		% increase from 1999 to 2002
Bands	Monthly consumption (kl)	Charge/kl (R)	Bands	Monthly consumption (kl)	Charge/kl (R)	
1	<6	1.26	1	<6	0	0
2	6–30	1.82	2	6–30	3.09	69
3	30–100	2.03	3	30–100	3.21	58
4	>100	2.20	4	>100	3.41	55

A pamphlet produced by Biwater indicates that at the top end of this price block (i.e. 30 kl) the average household cost is R92.70. When the basic monthly costs of R8.51 and R5.06 are added, for being in the second bandwidth of water consumption, the total monthly cost of consuming 30 kl of water – not uncommon in larger households – is R106.27.[7] This amounts to about 13 per cent of income for households with R800 per month in total earnings, well above the World Bank's suggested maximum of 5 per cent of household income being allocated to water. With the average monthly cost of sanitation, electricity and refuse collection also factored in, it is not surprising that indigent households have difficulty in affording essential services.

Biwater initially had little concern about whether township residents were able to afford their water bills, and imposed severe credit control measures. In KaNyamanzane, approximately 1100 households have had trickle meters installed out of 4500 metered connections (27.5 per cent of the total). In Matsulu, about 800 of the 2250 metered connections have had tricklers installed (35 per cent).[8] These measures have resulted in high levels of illegal reconnections and removal of tricklers, leading to high levels of unaccounted-for water (UAW) in some areas. For instance, the UAW in Nelspruit has been reduced from 25 per cent to 19 per cent while in KaNyamanzane it has deteriorated from 59 per cent to 76 per cent and in Matsulu from 68 per cent to 88 per cent. The amount of water wasted and unmeasured in these soaring UAW rates makes water delivery to these areas unsustainable for the service provider and is a significant source of financial loss to Biwater as this water is not billed. Biwater has responded to this situation by reducing water supply in certain areas like Matsulu as a form of credit control, thus jeopardizing its contractual obligations to provide 24-hour supply.

Labour

The Nelspruit concession faced serious objections and protests from labour unions in the city, which succeeded in delaying the signing of the contract. In the end, however, the city council transferred approximately 140 workers to Biwater as part of the concession agreement in 1999. Contrary to popular belief, no workers were retrenched in the transition. In fact, the workforce has increased to 225, but most new staff have been hired on a contractual basis and are nonunionized.

The labour issue is complicated by differences between the two public sector unions involved. Historically, the Independent Municipal and Allied Trade Union (Imatu) has represented white workers, has tended to have a larger membership of managers, and markets itself as an independent trade union. The South African Municipal Workers' Union (Samwu) has historically represented black labourers and is affiliated with the Congress of South African Trade Unions (Cosatu), which is a member of the tripartite alliance with the ANC (the third member being the South African Communist Party).

When the concession was first proposed, both Cosatu and Samwu were strongly opposed to it on the basis that water is a basic need, fearing that a private sector operator would try to make a profit out of water, with negative consequences for workers and low income households. Their campaigns helped to encourage community opposition to the concession. By contrast, Imatu supported the concession on the basis that it could benefit the community and was not detrimental to employees.

Samwu has raised numerous concerns about the labour implications of the concession.[9] First, Samwu workers feel they were not adequately consulted during wage negotiations and that the council's promise to involve them in wage negotiations with Biwater for the first five years after the signing of the concession contract has not been kept. Second, workers have complained that financial benefits have been unevenly distributed, such as housing subsidies being predominantly made available to white workers in management. While salaries were not reduced, workers lost benefits such as the right to deduction orders from their salaries and a tool allowance. They have also been upset that Biwater, unlike the city council, does not make loans available to its employees.

Third, workers have complained that Biwater has not kept to its contractual commitment of providing skills transfer to Biwater workers through training.

BiWater, however, claims that it listens to workers and encourages them to speak and voice their complaints. There are, for example, an Imatu and a Samwu consultant on Biwater's permanent staff, and it has set up a labour forum where workers are expected to take their grievances before approaching the unions. Both unions perceive this initiative as discouraging strong union membership and creating an environment where workers are reluctant to voice their concerns publicly.[10] For instance, no Biwater workers joined the July 2002 nationwide anti-privatization strike arranged by Cosatu despite the fact that many of them had grievances about wage negotiations.

Another concern is that the local authority has neglected its role in overseeing the regulation of the contract in terms of ensuring that labour conditions are upheld. Workers have expressed concerns about the council being uninformed of the labour situation at Biwater and failing to protect its former employees. Furthermore, the CMU, the regulatory body that oversees the concession, has failed to monitor the skills transfer that was promised as part of the negotiations.

Conclusion

Local authorities in Nelspruit have learned that a long-term contract is difficult to manage in the context of transition. Legislative changes at the national level, such as territorial demarcation, affect the local authority, which in turn affects contracts they have signed. A long contract leaves the local authority vulnerable to commercial risk because of this externally changing environment. At the same time it is unlikely, given the problems that have been experienced with the concession (such as nonpayment), that the GNUC will wish to expand its role to additional low income communities. The absence of a substantial economic base in the rest of Mbombela Council's area renders it unlikely that other potential concessionaires would find the proposition attractive either. It remains to be seen what strategies will be employed to address the service delivery requirements of these communities, but it is unlikely that the private sector will be involved unless the council, or other government authority, once again carries the risk.

In light of the difficulties the Mbombela local authority has faced with this water concession, it has admitted that it would probably not negotiate such a long-term contract again (interview, Rolf Koetzer, 28 February 2003). The local authority was initially in favour of the concession because it thought that the private investors had to take the full commercial risk. The city council is now learning that it is not immune to the failure of the concession.

These failures have contributed to a crisis in governance. The local authority has devolved its responsibilities as a service provider to GNUC and has performed poorly in the task of being a water service authority. This is primarily illustrated through its failure to take its regulatory role seriously. The local authority's neglect in regulating the concession has meant that the authority is no more capable than Biwater in dealing with the nonpayment issue. Interviews with senior officials revealed that city council has decided that should the concessionaire fail it will simply hand it over to another service provider. The attitude of abandoning the water sector expressed by the local authority during this research threatens to undermine its democratic accountability as communities have far less recourse to resolve the political problems associated with nonpayment when dealing with a contracted service provider with little understanding of the area.

It would appear that the municipality has not only lost the political will to take back the water sector but also its physical and financial capacity to do so. Furthermore, the city council claims that it cannot carry out the same level of attention to credit control issues that Biwater has done because it does not have the time, people or money to do so. The Mbombela municipality is too preoccupied with trying to get other services like roads or refuse collection working, let alone extending services to its newly acquired peri-urban and rural communities. Water services – now that it has been ringfenced, run like a business and devolved to a separate entity – is deemed the least of the Mbombela city council's concerns. As is the case in many cash-strapped municipalities across the world, the local authority wants to wash its hands of the responsibility of water services in order to focus its attention on other areas of service delivery.

The lessons learned in this process are that technical solutions do not solve the political problems of poverty. Payment for services is not simply a technical matter of getting clear bills out to service users and establishing kiosks for customer care within township areas. The payment for services is a political issue when it comes to poor people's ability to pay. The history of apartheid and the historically abysmal context of service delivery to townships matter in shaping an understanding of how to resolve the nonpayment problem. A starting point is to involve communities more widely in the service delivery process so that they can better understand how service delivery works, what it means to be a responsible customer/citizen, and how to hold their service provider accountable. These steps are part of democratizing a service delivery and must be steered more conscientiously by the local authority and its political representatives.

As a service delivery model set out to meet the needs of the poor, the logic of profit and efficiency that drives the management of concessions does not lend itself to the patience and flexibility required to deliver services to poor households. Our assessment of the Nelspruit water concession is that the privatization of water and sanitation service delivery may result in improvements in infrastructure but, in a context of high levels of poverty and major political transformation, is unlikely to result in affordable, sustainable and developmental outcomes for low income communities.

Acknowledgements

Laïla Smith, Shauna Mottiar and Fiona White were commissioned by the Ford Foundation to write an earlier version of this piece as part of a project on service delivery at the Centre for Policy Studies, Johannesburg, South Africa. Laïla Smith was commissioned by the Commonwealth Foundation to update and expand the paper for a civil society consultation with the Finance Ministers of the Commonwealth in 2003. Amanda Gillett's research contribution was part of her Master's thesis through the Graduate School of P&DM at Wits University.

Notes

1   Fax sent by DPLG to Amanda Gillett on 6 September 2001.
2   Data provided by GNUC, 16 June 2003.
3   This population increase is as of 2001 (Integrated Development Plan for Mbombela 2002).
4   It should be noted that increases in charges are primarily based on inflationary increases as set out in the formula in the concession contract.
5   Information from Councillor Bheka Mazibuko, Nelspruit Town Council, 25 February 2003.
6   Personal communication with credit control officer for Biwater, 25 February 2003.
7   This is over and above the basic connection charges of R30.25 for new users. For any household that wants to get connected to the network for the first time, the deposit fee is R438.90. The deposits are refunded only after the deduction of outstanding amounts has taken place (when the consumer leaves the concession area or terminates supply).
8   Data provided by Harold Moeng, Senior Commercial Manager for GNUC, 19 June 2003.
9   Interviews with Enos Meele, Samwu Consultant to Biwater, and Jacob Phala, Samwu shop steward for Nelspruit, 27 February 2003.
10 Interview with Dave Edge, Imatu, 24 February 2003 and Jacob Phala, Samwu, 26 February 2003.

References

Finance and Fiscal Commission (1997) 'Local Government in a System of Intergovernmental Fiscal Relations in South Africa: A Discussion Document', mimeo, Midrand

Gillett, A. (2002) 'The Impact of Water and Sanitation Service Privatisation on the Poor', report submitted to Faculty of Management, University of the Witwatersrand, South Africa

Kotze, R., Ferguson, A. and Leigland, J. (1999) 'Nelspruit and Dolphin Coast: Lessons from the First Concession Contracts', *Development Southern Africa*, vol 16, no 4

Maralack, D. (1999) 'A Profile of Nelspruit, its People and its Economy', in *The Provision of Water and Sanitation Services in Nelspruit*, www.local.gov.za/DCD/ledsummary/nelspruit/nel03.html

Mbombela Local Municipality, IDP 2002–2006, www.ledc.co.za/Docs/Mbombela%20Local@Municipality/IDP/MbombelaIDP2003.pdf

SAIRR (South African Institute of Race Relations) (2003) *Fast Facts*, SAIRR, Johannesburg, April

INTERVIEWS

Frans Greyling, Engineer for the Mbombela municipality, 25 February 2003

Office of the Deputy Manager for the Mbombela municipality, 17 April 2003

Harold Moeng, Senior Commercial Manager for GNUC, 17 April 2003, 18 and 19 June 2003

Nantes Kruger, Director of Finance for the Mbombela municipality, 27 February 2003

Brian Simms, CEO of Biwater, 26 February 2003

Enos Meele, Samwu Consultant to Biwater, 27 February 2003

Rolf Koetzer, Deputy City Manager for the Mbombela municipality and the 'grandfather' of the concession, 28 February 2003

Karen Bretenbach, Programme Officer, DBSA, 12 March 2001

Chapter 8

The Political Economy of Public–Private Contracts: Urban Water in Two Eastern Cape Towns

Greg Ruiters

The day is at hand when all municipal and state departments are going to have to become more commercial and marketing oriented (Queenstown Mayor, Johnny Johnson, *Daily Dispatch*, 31 January 1991).

This pronouncement (quoted above) by the mayor of an all-white town council in South Africa in the twilight of apartheid was prescient because privatization and other related market reforms have indeed become the key thrust of municipal reform under the post-apartheid African National Congress (ANC). But how do market rules work in actual public–private partnerships (PPPs) and what kinds of problem do municipalities face with these contracts?

This chapter examines the company–municipal interface of privatization as structured by contracts. I look at two early 1990s experiments in privatized water in the Eastern Cape to demonstrate the various ways in which water companies position themselves to make profits and some of the problems municipalities face when dealing with companies. I examine the rules of engagement and allocation of risk as dictated by water contracts, using local municipal and company records and scholarly work in the area of urban political economy. The chapter is concerned with the production of water, the nature of the water firm and how profits are made. It assumes that privatization is driven by business interests in the first instance (Lorrain 1991; Meszaros 1995; Swyngedouw et al 2002).

I start with an outline of late apartheid local privatization, then provide an outline of the key features of global water companies, since an understanding of the privatizers ought to shed light on why privatization occurs. The entrée of French multinational Suez into South Africa in the 1980s, and the basic workings and distribution of risks and hidden costs in public–private partnership (PPP) contracts as profitable ventures are outlined and appraised. Key aspects of the Queenstown and Fort Beaufort contracts are examined to show that contract design can reveal much about accumulation strategies adopted by water companies and the pitfalls for municipalities. Some of these are systemic:

asymmetry in power and information between the weak municipality and the global water corporation; high monitoring and transaction costs; 'cost creep' given the inherently incomplete nature of the contract; and unequal risk allocation. If a municipality is locked into 25 years of contractual obligations, its bargaining power weakens as the contract ages (Donahue 1989; Michael Porter cited in *Business Day*, 20 October 2003).

LATE APARTHEID MUNICIPAL PRIVATIZATION

Before the ANC government started promoting municipal privatization in the mid-1990s, the apartheid state had already begun its own privatization initiatives. In the late 1980s, despite widespread resistance from trade unions and community groups, P. W. Botha, the State President at that time, announced in February 1988 that the National Party government planned to restructure the economy by privatizing along lines similar to Margaret Thatcher's UK government (Heymans 1991, p163). The apartheid government accurately and broadly defined privatization as 'a systemic transfer of appropriate functions, activities or property from the public sector' (RSA 1987, pp8–9). Reasons for privatization were the state's fiscal crisis, labour militancy and high public sector expenditure, at that stage 38 per cent of GDP. Additional reasons cited included depoliticization of services; consumers would blame the company instead of government and this could help reduce the frequency of protests in South Africa (Heymans 1991, p171). But local level privatization did not take off extensively in the late 1980s and early 1990s. Only a few municipalities experienced privatization efforts: in Welkom the bus company was sold off; in Cape Town some of the cleaning and security services were privatized or contracted out and the orchestra and fresh markets sold; and in the Eastern Cape various services (such as building care, cleaning, security, orchestra, fresh markets, abattoirs) were put up for sale or for outsourcing (Brand 1984; Heymans 1991, p161).

The Queenstown Council was the first in South Africa to explore water privatization, starting in November 1988. Acting on a provincial government directive, this historically British frontier town appointed a committee to investigate whether the private sector could provide water services more effectively and 'cost efficiently' than the municipality. Cost comparisons had 'proved' that the private sector proposal from Aqua-Gold would be cheaper and better; therefore council signed a 25-year 'delegated management' contract with Aqua-Gold (now Suez). The contract, however, covered *only* the white and coloured areas, excluding African areas. Stutterheim, a town 50 km southward, followed suit in 1994, and Fort Beaufort in 1995. In 1995, Queenstown extended its contract to include African areas (Ezibeleni and Mlungisi).

In October 1995, with the first democratic local government elections, racially separate local authorities were amalgamated, posing new challenges for municipal managers. More than half Queenstown's 117,000 population earned less than R800 per month. Pensioners in 1998, for example, received grants of R580 per month (PDG 1999). Unemployment was well over 60 per cent.

Queenstown became a mainly administrative and services town, and the sixth biggest urban centre in the Eastern Cape Province with 15 high schools, 20 primary schools, technikons, hospitals and several private colleges (SetPlan 1999).

In the late 1980s Queenstown's black (African and coloured) townships had vigorously opposed the privatization policy (*Daily Dispatch*, 1 November 1990). It is noteworthy that a recent official study of Queenstown by the parastatal Municipal Infrastructure Investment Unit (MIIU) leaves out this fact. The MIIU report, which reads in part like an apology for apartheid, argues that:

> *The political views regarding privatization and outsourcing were positive at the time . . . it also made much sense to source the much needed expertise and capital from the private sector. . . No legislative requirements regarding community consultation and scoping existed in 1992 to oblige the Municipality to follow the processes now part and parcel of local government legislation. The Municipality and WSSA [Water Services South Africa, the name of the Suez subsidiary running the contract] nevertheless consulted with inter alia, the Queenstown Residents Association.[1] Due to the extended time lapse since 1992, WZC [the researchers contracted by MIIU to conduct the study] did not probe the nature and extent of the consultation or any record-keeping thereof that may still exist* (MIIU 2003, pp9–10).

In 1989–1990, an ad hoc organization called the 'Anti-privatization Committee' put up a strong fight against privatization in Queenstown. They demanded that:

> *[d]etained workers be paid by time spent in detention, all apartheid laws to be scrapped, one city one municipality, city council to provide land for the people, a living wage for all, stop giving land to private developers, bring back privatized services, government must conduct a social impact study of privatization and present it to the people in the process of discussions, the municipality should write to the government rejecting privatization* (Queenstown Municipality 1990a).

The Queenstown apartheid authorities responded to these demands as follows:

> *Council policy is to privatize within the framework of government policy. The council's policy on privatization is available and it should be made clear to the Anti-privatization Committee that the council favours privatization* (Queenstown Municipality 1990b, C324).

The municipal authorities complained bitterly that privatization was happening too slowly:

> *The government's privatization policy, which has been accepted as policy locally by the council, has not taken off satisfactorily as a result of a gravy train approach by the private sector as well as fear in certain staff quarters of damages to their empire-building. . . Negative reaction of overseas*

investors result[s] from boycotts, strikes and the burning down of factories (Queenstown Municipality 1990a).

The French were, however, willing to take the risk.

THE FRENCH ENTRÉE INTO EASTERN CAPE MUNICIPALITIES

It is essential that the management of the service is not influenced by the politics of the day. This can only be achieved by delegating the management of this function to the private sector, a reality proven over 100 years of international experience (WSSA 1995a, p20).

Even before the apartheid state decided to privatize, the privatizers themselves had already been knocking on the door to sell a new commodity: depoliticized public water services. In 1984, at the height of township uprisings, two top advisers to Lyonnaise des Eaux and to the French government visited South Africa for talks with 'Ministers of state and other dignitaries' (*South Africa Waterbulletin* 1984, p11). Soon after, the French–South African company Aqua-Gold (AG) signed water service contracts with homeland governments (Kwa-Zulu, Bophuthatswana and KaNgwane) and various mining companies (AG 1991). By 1989 Aqua-Gold and a large South African construction firm, Group Five, had merged. The merger increased French local knowledge and power because Group Five had built over 100 water and sewage systems in South Africa since the 1960s and was active in other sectors (roads, property development, housing and construction). Degremont (another Suez subsidiary active in South Africa) also built water plants for state-owned electricity provider Eskom and for the Umgeni Water Board (AG 1991). In addition to these mergers, Group Five later bought Everite Holdings (a pipe manufacturer) and Aqua-Gold was then moved into the Everite stable in 1992, thereby further extending vertical integration and concentration of ownership in the water sector.

Why would such a large and powerful private firm be that keen on running water systems in small Eastern Cape towns? A short answer: besides their profitability, these contracts were a low risk entrée for the French into municipal water in South Africa. It would allow them to gain local knowledge of water management problems and build a reputation necessary for winning big contracts at a later stage (see Goubert 1989; Lorrain 1991).

When the ANC won the 1994 national elections, the (by now renamed) WSSA undertook an active strategy of trying to win support from the new government:

Whilst these are early days in winning their acceptance, we now have the support of the government. We helped draw guidelines on private sector management of water and sanitation services and are now helping with a regulatory framework (Everite 1996).

Suez subsequently won a five-year contract to manage Johannesburg's water (3.5 million consumers). By 2001 the company managed water and waste collection for close to 5 million, or 12 per cent, of South Africa's population (and more than 20 per cent of the rural population). WSSA is also a shareholder in Amanz'Abantu, the programme implementing agent for rural Build, Operate, Train and Transfer (BOTT) schemes in the Eastern Cape (see Greenberg, Chapter 11, this volume).

French Water Contracts' Hidden Costs

Suez is among the world's major water companies, although water is only one of several divisions of the company (Goubert 1989). In the 1980s Suez acquired controlling stakes in the water sector in the UK, Spain and the US. Then in 1993 (one year after Ambert, the French director of operations, arrived in Queenstown) it won the Buenos Aires, Manila and Sydney water contracts (amongst the biggest in the world). By 1999, this water–media–construction giant employed close to 220,000 workers across the globe, had assets valued over US$15 billion and its water operation (Ondeo) was estimated to have over 3000 contracts in over 30 countries and employed 48,000 workers (Yaron and Rycroft 1999).

The company grew frenetically, but like its sister, Vivendi, Suez has fallen on to hard times since 2002. 'Suez has been battered by one business storm after another. First, world growth stalled, dampening demand for power. Then, certain emerging markets where Suez had placed huge bets, such as Argentina and the Philippines, slipped into an economic tailspin' (*Business Week*, 17 March 2003).

These ups and downs are crucial but may not have reversed the privatization wave. What general features characterize the urban water business? First, the company that wins a contract exercises power over a definite territory; it becomes a 'growth statesman' with a vested interest in what Logan and Molotch (1987, pp50, 74) aptly call 'urban growth machines'. Utility companies typically seek to boost their customer numbers, and the customer's consumption levels; and they promote lineal expansion of networks because all this expansion is good for business (Silva 1998), while ignoring obvious environmental costs. Once contracts are signed, firms are outside the competition. They will pay a premium for this and, thus, in the water and the construction industry corruption is widespread (Hall and Goudrian 1999). 'Capitalists can convert control over technology or location into monopoly privileges that put themselves outside of competition instead of ahead' (Harvey 1989, p136), but this adds to final municipal costs.

Second, vertical integration is another key feature of these multi-utility monopolies. Tied to allied activities like construction and spread over many hundreds of long-term contracts there are profits to be made 'downstream' as well in construction and upgrading work. Paradoxically, these huge integrated companies prefer insourcing to outsourcing. In the Ivory Coast's Abidjan contract with the private water consortium SODECI, a major problem was that 'SODECI made excessive profit on its activities as a constructor' (Kerf and Smith 1996, p13). In Harvey's words, 'powerful monopolies drag their supply chains with them' (Harvey 1989, p139).

Third, the contracts are long-term: 10 to 25 years. These contracts combine operating, maintaining and upgrading the water and sanitation systems and what the firm typically calls 'customer care'. The firm's operational responsibility includes limited capital investment in the renewal and expansion of a water and sanitation system. This outlay on capital it hopes to recoup over the life of the contract.

I will now consider the key clauses in the actual contracts in the Eastern Cape to illustrate problems and hidden costs. I start with the proposed contract guidelines, which assume 'that the operation of the present and future water and sewage facilities in the area would remain the exclusive responsibility of the operator for the duration of the contract' (WSSA 1995a, p4). Here we see several issues of concern that pertain to most contracts. The first is monopoly: the locking-in of the municipality and its loss of flexibility for the contract period. The second is the speculative or future-orientated business potential in the contract and the third is the need for contract renegotiation. The contract defines the scope of services required and the physical networks to be maintained. Strategically this is crucial since anything beyond the scope of contract goes onto the municipality's account and new network additions have to be renegotiated with the monopolist.

Many exemptions for the monopolist are granted in the contract. The company also gains by limiting its overheads and 're-municipalizing' certain of its own ancillary activities: for example, laboratory services free of charge for regular water testing; electrical and vehicle maintenance services; and staff accommodation (e.g. 'The TLC [council] shall continue to provide accommodation to certain employees at same conditions as present' (WSSA 1995a, p5)). Unlike other businesses, the firm does not pay rates and taxes for using the municipality's works and buildings attached to the water treatment works. It is liable for electricity charges but at the same internal rates at which only municipal departments are charged (WSSA 1995a, p11). These are hidden subsidies to the private firm from the municipality and hidden costs to the municipality.

Other hidden costs include the following:

- Repairs and replacement are defined in the contract to exclude some areas, despite the fact that in the past the council had helped residents with household plumbing, leaking toilets and sewer problems. Thus, the private service is a reduced service, incomparable with the old municipal service since crucial areas that affect residents' bills, such as internal leaks, are defined as outside the scope of the contract.
- The firm replaces only a specified length of pipe over the contract's life. For example, in Queenstown (from 1992 onwards), 1 km of water network piping would be replaced each year (a total of 19 per cent of the town's

network over 25 years) and 1000 domestic water meters would be renewed during the first four years (AG 1991). Fort Beaufort (as from 1994) would receive 8 km of pipe over ten years (11 per cent of its water network). The downside is that the municipality cannot be sure that pipes were replaced unless it undertakes detailed inspections and costly monitoring. Disputes, in fact, arose because the firm claimed that every pipe burst it fixed was also 'pipe replacement' (Queenstown 1993).
- Replacing old meters helped the municipality and company because old ones under-read consumption and the company charged the municipality a variable volume based rate in addition to a fixed rate (more on these rates later). Older meters and older sections of the network were, however, located in the historically white areas, which were also high consumption areas with high water pressure (and more pipe bursts), whereas black areas were unmetered with newer pipes and lower pressures. This social geography of the network is important since the contract was extended to Queenstown black townships in 1995.

DESIGN OF CONTRACTS: RISK-SHIFTING

The French 'delegated management' model shifts most risks onto the municipality (DCD 1998, p113; Water Research Commission 1995, pp7–8). Although the firm bears operational risks, escape or variation clauses soften this. For this reason, some scholars label these contracts as 'incomplete' and therefore unpredictable (Martin and Parker 1997, p10). An example of an escape clause in the Queenstown case is as follows: if the operator officially 'identifies the need for expansion or modification to part of the system, and the authority fails to act, the operator shall be absolved from any associated deficiencies in the system arising from such requirements, in so far as they affect the operation of the system' (WSSA 1995b, p12).[2]

Demand risk refers to changes in consumer usage of water and less municipal income from the lower water sales. If, for example, water consumers conserve water, then the municipality runs the risk of failing because fixed payments to the firm remain fixed. The firm only loses a portion of variable revenue (volume based). On the other hand, an influx of poor people using a lot of water but not paying also creates a problem if state subsidies decline and cross-subsidies are not encouraged.

Performance risk lies only partly with the operator because the operator is not responsible for design failures if it has informed the municipality of poor design beforehand (WSSA 1995b). Specified 'standards for quality and quantity are consistently achieved in so far as the plant is designed and is capable of performing' (WSSA 1995a, p8). Nominal sanctions apply if the operator fails to deliver within the water quality parameters; the authority payment on volume charges is reduced by 10 l of water multiplied by the number of consumer connections facing failure after 12 continuous hours of failure.

Collection risk is a municipal problem, even when a company offers to take over 'customer care'. Since the law forbids private firms from setting tariffs, and the local state fears extremities of harsh cost recovery, it bears full risk of consumer nonpayment. Persistent consumer nonpayment undermines the contract, which is premised on the assumption that better service would mean better 'customer satisfaction' and more willing payers.

Residual value risk (construction risk) refers to problems with the system at the end of the contract. In the Eastern Cape, there were no quantifiable expectations at the end of the contract. Infrastructure, it was stated, had to be in reasonable condition, but the firm has information monopoly and may hide potential or actual defects.

Operating risk means the firm can appeal for compensation for any unforeseen circumstances (such as drastic change in raw water chemistry) that raise operating costs via variation clauses. *Force majeure* clauses ensure that fixed payments continue during *force majeure* conditions. Any increased costs in such a period shall be born by the authority, says the contract. Consequently, there are fewer risks to the firm's fixed income although there are risks on volume charges (WSSA 1995a).

Force majeure is a risk shifting, profit strategy. It refers to any event beyond the operator's control: war, insurrection, martial law, nationalization, floods, an inherent design fault of the system, use or occupation by the authority or the employees of any part of the system, breakages in the system resulting in interruptions not due to the activities of the operator, disruption of essential supplies and services such as chemicals and energy or the like. 'If the operator claims relief on account of force majeure, it has 21 days after the occurrence to give notice to the authority. The authority shall continue to make payment to the operator during such a force majeure event. Any increased costs shall be born by the Authority (WSSA 1995b, p35).

Earlier the 'lock-in factor' was mentioned. Not surprisingly, municipalities rarely cancel contracts because the penalties are steep, costs of finding new operators are high and there is often massive pressure from central authorities not to do so. In the Queenstown case, the authority may cancel the contract only after the first half of the contract's life, only if it gives two years' notice of cancellation of the contract, and then it must still pay out the operator for the remaining years at a rate of 10 per cent of the global amount paid for the previous year before cancellation. Moreover, it must pay out the operator for all investments minus depreciation, plus outstanding amounts, and re-employ the entire workforce at same conditions as under the operator.

The state therefore plays an active role in supporting the monopolist. As Harvey (1989, p138) notes, because devaluation and other risks in long-term urban investments are high:

> *capitalists will not undertake long-term investments without the assurance of some stability in labour markets and without protection from excessive speculative innovation. Under such conditions monopoly control of*

technology and location appears necessary, a vital condition to guarantee long-term investment.

Fixed and Variable Costs

There are three parts to the monthly company charges payable by the municipality: fixed, volume and extras. The municipalities pay the company the fixed charge (FC); the second type of charge varies and is volume related; the third refers to the extras, or ad hoc work, such as disconnections. Fixed costs, indexed to inflation, are a form of risk-free income for the firm.

Every month the company submits statistics to the municipality showing how much potable water it produced, how much was sold to consumers and how much was lost. 'Variable', or volume charges (VC), cover the chemicals and electricity costs, set as follows: $VC = vc \times Q$ (where Q is the quantity of water metered the previous month in the town in kilolitres (kl) and vc is the unit rate charged).[3] Only water metered at the consumer's residences is charged for as volume (Q). Hence water lost between the treatment plant and residences (or bulk meters) is a loss for the company, although this is offset by the fact that bulk water (up to 50 per cent of input costs) is paid for by the municipality. Similarly, if consumers fix internal leaks, reduce water usage or if the town goes into a slump, the company loses from this demand risk.

Extras or ad hoc work done by the company have to be paid for. The company charges for disconnections of consumers and in some months these exceed reconnection. Important also is that the contract allows the company to re-outsource any of its own assigned ad hoc work (WSSA 1995b). Thus it can generate profits from smaller local firms employing ultra-cheap labour. In 2001 Queenstown disconnections were performed by a private security firm (for example, Gray Security, with 'black empowerment' connections).

The economics of the contract for the municipality depend on economies of scale, specifically the fixed/variable ratio. Queenstown's ratio of fixed to variable payments was 2.21 in 1993 because white areas were high volume users. Fixed costs made up 58 per cent of invoice before VAT. From the municipality's narrow financial view this is a good ratio. But once the low volume users were included in the ratio after the 1995 extension to African areas, the ratio was 2.36 in 1996 and then 3.03 in 2000. By 2003 the fixed charges made up 68 per cent of the total invoiced amount (MIIU 2003). In other words, the municipality spent proportionately more in fixed charges relative to declining volumes (and declining potential revenue) of water sales. It must be remembered that township homes (many with yard taps and no bathrooms) use 10 to 20 times less water than 'middle-income' areas. The general result is that the more the ratio swings in favour of fixed payments the less the contract makes economic sense for the municipality. This means that, over time, as the poor are incorporated into contracts and as volumes fall in response to higher tariffs, cutoffs and so on, the contracts become less viable for the municipality. Contracts and progressive policies do not concur.

Cost Creep

Cost creep refers to hidden costs that are not initially factored into a transaction. In the original 'bid' proposals, municipal savings were predicted based on variable and fixed payments but not on ad hoc work that can become a significant source of cost creep.

Another form of cost creep has to do with the relative weight of various payment types: fixed and variable. This, as we saw, meant fixed costs rising from 58 per cent to 68 per cent in Queenstown. But the firm anticipated higher consumption (increasing revenue for council and gains from economies of scale). As high volume users declined as a proportion of the user base (and in the Queenstown and Fort Beaufort cases there was also white population flight), and if mass water disconnections and restricted consumption for the poor are taken into account, then expansive networks that attract fixed charges would be relatively under-utilized and hence 'uneconomical'.

This is what in fact happened in Queenstown. As the local WSSA manager put it, 'today we are only pumping 9 mega-litres per day (mpd) of sewage whereas five years ago we pumped 12 mpd. But we get paid anyway' (personal interview, Andy Gerrard, 7 September 2000). The 'infrastructure trap' arises when costly infrastructures are 'overbuilt' but still need to be maintained even though underused. This problem is not unusual in South Africa where local governments now debate the level of service to be offered to the poor and insist on providing only financially sustainable levels of services such as yard taps. Poor households who had full level service in the past have been coercively or voluntarily downscaled, or 'right-sized', once they ran into debt.

In the first year the contract costs were in fact artificially reduced and the municipality did not raise tariffs, in order to buy time with public opinion. In the next two years, however, the contract price went up by over 30 per cent (MIIU 2003). Far from being a cost-effective strategy, privatized water has major problems. In Queenstown, barely a year after the contract was signed, the then white municipality wrote to Aqua-Gold asking that the pipe replacement programme be rescheduled to commence only in the 1993/94 financial year to help it lower monthly charges (Queenstown Municipality 1993a). Aqua-Gold Services' response shows what the company's strategic interests were:

> With reference to the meeting of 2/2/93 whilst we accept that we can assist the municipality by delaying the cost of replacing meters and pipelines we must stress, we have already replaced 38 meters and 238 meters of pipelines. Not replacing pipelines increases our operational burden in that more bursts will occur and this creates problems for the community. Not replacing meters causes under-reading with consequential loss to both yourselves and ourselves. It would therefore be unfair to simply deduct the costs quantified in our letter of 4th December 1992 viz., R240,000 for the pipe and R140,000 for the meters. We are of the opinion that we should replace the pipelines and half the meters as this will show the public that steps are being taken to avoid bursts and erroneous readings (AG 1993).

CONTRACTS AND LABOUR PROCESS

Private firms intensify work and reorganize both the labour process and workers' terms of employment. As the General Manager of the Sydney Water Board notes, as much as 30 per cent savings can be realized by such reorganization (Green 1994). For a South African water firm in a medium sized town labour costs may make up 60 per cent of total operating costs, and hence there are strong incentives to change working conditions and rules (WSSA 1995a). In the Eastern Cape the company committed to conditions 'no worse' than the municipality. Two things are crucial here. While normal salaries and wages remained the same as in the municipality (R841 per month for unskilled workers), over time municipal workers outside the private contract who bargained with the council were able to get bigger increases than their WSSA counterparts. WSSA bargained wages separately from other municipal workers.

The WSSA workers' packages were restructured to their detriment. All transferred workers got fewer sick days and a reduction in leave days. Managers (usually white), who used to get generous holiday leave, were reduced from 24 to 15 leave days and from 40 to 10 sick days (AG 1991).

A breakdown of the turnover and composition of the staff complement is instructive as well, and it is worth quoting the MIIU's strange formulation of this labour issue: 'as natural attrition had reduced the workforce to below required strength, WSSA started using locally based subcontractors for pipelaying and ground maintenance' (MIIU 2003, p34). What is apparent is that even with significant expansion of the pipe network and many more consumer connections, the number of workers directly employed by WSSA fell from a high of 74 in 1997 to 55 in 2002. WSSA employed 14 casuals (called contractors) and ran the operation with eight vacancies. A considerable intensification of work occurred. Over ten years WSSA has failed to create jobs. In fact, the opposite has happened. In 2002 WSSA Queenstown workers staged a militant, 19-day strike.

Another labour advantage for WSSA compared with individual municipalities lies in economies of scale and economies of contiguity (the three contracted towns are within a 150-km radius). WSSA replicates contracts and reporting formats, and highly skilled staff are moved around between the contiguous towns. Consequently, most administration, strategies, computerized analysis and complex problems are handled at the regional scale, coordinated from a single regional command centre in East London. Each town is thus merely a subpart of the larger WSSA Eastern Cape operation (which includes rural BOTTS). No strict ringfencing applies from the firm's viewpoint (an irony considering how much is made of this by supporters of corporatization (see McDonald and Ruiters, Chapter 1, this volume). Why have dedicated skilled workers for each town if the firm can rotate skilled workers across all three towns? This intensification and extensification of work provides another key to WSSA's profitability. 'In competing for the big contracts' as Marvin and Graham (1994, p51) point out, 'smaller ones may end up underwriting larger ones where more substantial cost reductions may be offered to win such large contracts'.

French models of water delivery allow companies to make their money by turning municipal entities into profitable operations.

Fort Beaufort's Terminated Contract

According to WSSA, the contracts would save the councils money: for Fort Beaufort an 8 per cent saving, for Queenstown 19 per cent. Delegated service providers would bring a stable, predictable cost structure for services, enhance the 'customer's willingness to pay' and 'help communit[ies] realise their full potential' (WSSA 1995a). Tariffs set by the municipality would have to cover the costs of the company's service. However, this was not how matters panned out.

In Fort Beaufort, in the first full contract year, the council paid R2.23 million in total water and sanitation expenses, overrunning its revenue by 6 per cent. The council was in effect subsiding WSSA by R140,000 that year.

In October 1995, the council's monthly water income of R104,358 could not cover WSSA's base rate account of R107,000 (Fort Beaufort TLC 1995). In December 1995 the council's bank overdraft stood at R1.9 million; already compulsory monthly expenditures loomed as unpayable. These payments were listed as: 'Eskom (bulk electricity) at R260,000; raw water (from DWAF) at R45,000; WSSA R200,000; salaries R280,000, wages R160,000, interest on overdraft R10,000' (Fort Beaufort TLC 1995).

Carrying the full burden of payment risks, even though WSSA had promised that payment rates would improve, the council staggered under an unpayable debt: R375,000 by early 2000 (WSSA 2000) and in late 2000 this was up to R475,000. All told, between 1995 and 2000 it faced a fourfold increase in payments to WSSA (and penalties for late payments to WSSA). Special debt rescheduling had to be negotiated but these arrangements also collapsed. The council could not catch up.

Looked at from a different angle, we see that the WSSA payments absorbed a growing proportion of the Fort Beaufort local state's budget: in 1996/97 it was 16 per cent of the council operating budget; in 1999/00 this was 20 per cent. Meanwhile consumers, by January 2000, owed the council R14 million (or 73 per cent of the operating budget). The final straw came when WSSA sued the municipality, which in turn managed to get the contract annulled on a technicality (Ruiters 2002).

Regulation of Contracts as the Answer[4]

Administratively weak municipal structures are the norm in South Africa. In the Eastern Cape municipalities discussed here very few councillors have either seen or understand the contracts (Ruiters and Bond 1999; MIIU 2003). Yet these councillors are meant to monitor and regulate outsourced contracts. To make matters worse, in the Eastern Cape contracts certain clauses, such as 'performance criteria', are vague and unenforceable – a general problem identified with outsourcing: for example, 'The Operator will be responsible for overall performance of plant such that specified standards for quality and quantity are consistently achieved in so far as the plant is designed and is capable of performing' (WSSA 1995a, p8). Nominal fines may be imposed, but to prove that a contractual offence was committed may be too expensive for the local council.

Detailed surveillance of the company will increase municipal costs and can nullify the supposed financial gains of contracting out (Donahue 1989) while repelling future bidders. Monitoring requires a bureaucracy and political will (World Bank 1994). As World Bank studies show, when business resists penalties, fines and regulation, the litigation process can be extremely disruptive and costly for communities and municipalities (Kerf and Smith 1996, pp27–28). 'When service is unsatisfactory, political and legal responsibility are more difficult to establish and enforce over private bodies than over public bodies' (Hoogland 1984, p14). The World Bank's own researchers conclude: 'Transaction costs involved in introducing private sector participation, including articulating a regulatory framework, conducting competitive bidding etc are not trivial and US studies show that they make up between 5 to 10 per cent of total project costs' (2004). It is significant then that DWAF's 'Water Law Review' (p4) strongly prefers 'reliance on a set of regulatory mechanisms that do not involve the establishment of whole new regulatory institutions (reporting, monitoring and investigative bureaucracies)'. But this merely allows the firm to get away with opportunism.

Well-known problems with contracts include the fact that private partners report selectively; they develop and maximize their own goals; take a short-term view depending on how they see their future possibilities; may deliberately offer false information; may put speed and cost ahead of efficiency and public interests; may not necessarily adopt the latest techniques and improve services given high costs; and finally, may unduly influence the principal to maximize its benefits (Donahue 1989; Patterson and Theobald 1999).

One may generalize, as Harvey (1989) does: 'the longer the [assets'] lifetime, [or the more the sunk costs] the more vulnerable such production systems become and the more state protections they need to ensure their capitalistic use in the working period'. Political clientalism, poaching influential people in high positions in local government, or civic leaders is also a common strategy (the French 'revolving door'). Sponsoring conferences, educational tours to France or Argentina and other kinds of perks (free tickets to French cultural events) help buy public support. This list does not exhaust the tricks of the trade. When all else fails corruption, graft, hiding information and providing partial information are useful tools of dissembling (Hall and Goudrian 1999).

Wolch and Dear (1989) suggest that private utilities often act as a 'shadow state'. The obverse side of the 'shadow state' is the 'hollowed-out' municipal bureaucracy, a form of 'government by contract' reduced to a web of contracts which it oversees (Stoker 1989, pp165-66). Government by contract has severe flaws. The municipality is fragmented into many contracts, and 'fragmentation of agencies has not helped local authorities to articulate a common community agenda. [They] cannot provide a coherent policy framework for sustainable development' (Patterson and Theobald 1999, p167).

The council loses its know-how and its staff to the private companies. The public–private partnership approach changes the municipalities from being active service producers to being facilitators and regulators of contracts. This is the classic neoliberal approach, espoused in South Africa's local government guiding document, the 1998 *White Paper on Local Government*. Municipal councillors striving for progressive environmental and social policies are at the weak end because they have to deal with powerful and well-connected global water companies. Privatization not only transfers services and power to private hands, it changes the service, the role of local state, and governance relationships with citizens (Lorrain and Stoker 1997; Clarke and Newman 1997; Leys 2001). Moreover, the water firms radiate their influence to the public sector as a whole where a general push for business-like behaviours soon takes root.

Prospects in Queenstown

It is significant that the Queenstown municipality (now called Lukhanji) refused to extend WSSA's contract to include 'customer management' in 1998 because it feared the further deterioration of political relations with the community. As the MIIU (2003) report points out:

> *WSSA would have preferred to be in charge of customer management and, although the contract allows for this, the Municipality is not contemplating this as an option as it fears that its debt collection and credit control policies will be more stringently applied than by the Municipality itself* (MIIU 2003).

Despite privatizing, payment levels remain precarious:

> *only 20 per cent of the consumers are restricting their water usage to 6kl per month while more than 40 per cent of the consumers using more than 6kl are not paying for the excess water used. The level of non-payment has a severely detrimental impact on municipal finances with a monthly deficit currently in the order of R400,000* (MIIU 2003).

Like other municipalities Lukhanji has adopted the use of 'tricklers' to technologically restrict the amount of water flowing to registered indigents. Moreover, 'all new low income houses will have a trickle-flow restriction device on the consumer's property' (MIIU 2003, p16).

Conclusion

It is often argued that not only can privatization work in South Africa but it *must* because the state cannot do it alone (Kasrils 2003). The key, it has been argued, is competition in bidding and effective monitoring (DCD 1997; DPLG 2000). But several problems arise: bidding may be compromised by corruption, with competitors forming consortia and agreeing to divide the spoils rather than compete (Paris, for example, is divided into a Suez controlled area and a Vivendi controlled area); secondly, too few bidders also compromise competition (Viscusi et al 1992, p408); thirdly, the bidding process is distorted in cases of asymmetrical information about the actual costs, the condition of infrastructure and local conditions; fourthly, bidding is ineffective in fixing the contract price over time due to cost creep and contract renegotiations.

Monitoring external providers is not easy and as the CEO of Dell Corporation put it recently:

> *Instead of ensuring your own employees are doing their jobs properly, you have to ensure someone else's are. You can argue with contractors and threaten to replace them, but once they have intruded themselves into your organisation and systems, that is often not easily done. You may have 'service level agreements' specifying the details of what you expect, but these are blunt instruments and deal with poor performance only after it has happened . . . companies that outsource often turn a problem they cannot manage into one they can manage even less. . . Companies need to . . . go back to the basic principle that they should never outsource what matters most* (Business Day, 20 October 2003).

In Buenos Aires, where the world's biggest contract was signed, fees were hiked *after* the consortium discovered that the system was in a worse condition than it had anticipated and the contract was changed (Cowen and Dianderas 1996). Viscusi et al (1992, p397) point to low-balling, a fifth fallacy:

> *One strategy for a prospective firm at the bidding stage is to offer a low price and then if the franchise is won to petition for a price increase on the basis that average costs were underestimated. The government agency is likely to concede the request rather than to have to incur the costs of performing another round of bidding.*

In contexts like South Africa where the social crisis of unemployment, poor health and poverty congeal most explosively at the everyday urban level, private companies do take on a high risks. They correspondingly expect high rewards.

Caught between making PPPs succeed and maintaining a degree of effective oversight, external solutions may be worse for municipalities. PPPs are not benign arrangements to promote efficiency or the better use of resources; they are accumulation strategies by capitalist firms operating as structural speculators and monopolists in the urban context. They provide vertically integrated firms with new and relatively safe business opportunities since income is guaranteed by the fixed income in the delegated management contract format.

Underscoring the fragility of water multinationals foraging in developing world water, Jamal Saghir, World Bank Energy and Water Director, concedes that their big issue now is 'how to build efficient water utilities in a post-September 11, post-Argentina crisis world where international investors are more and more reluctant to invest in emerging economies' (World Bank 2004). And, despite states' commitment to privatization, economic crises of the late 1990s and corporate scandals – alongside high-profile instances of cancelled projects – have had an unsettling effect on investors and investment. Nemat Shafik, World Bank Vice President for Infrastructure, similarly grants that: 'We are now discussing in a frank and open manner issues that weren't on the table a few years ago. We are looking at how we deal with reputational risk and high risk–high reward projects' (World Bank 2004). Yet, even if the road to privatization of water has been bumpy, commodification of water has intensified, offering easier routes to future privatization. The spectre of privatization and commodification continues.

NOTES

1 The Chairperson of the Association, Mr Hoko, subsequently became the publicity officer for WSSA.
2 This provision also appears in the Department of Water Affairs and Forestry (DWAF) Model Contract (2000, p16), drawn up by the legal firm Edward Nathan and Friedland.
3 In Fort Beaufort (January 1995) the base rate for volume of water was charged at 38 c/kl. Sewage volume charges were set at 23.8 c/kl. Any significant changes in pollution concentrations would also trigger a change in the sewage volume base rate (WSSA 1995a, p14).
4 In DWAF's Model Contract 'the Water service authority will perform inspections of the system and monitor any impact which the supply of water services may have on the environment'.

REFERENCES

AG (Aqua-Gold Services) (1991) *A Proposal for Queenstown Water and Sewage Systems, June 1991*, Municipality, Queenstown, Privatization File (MQPF), vol 1

AG (Aqua-Gold Services) (1993) 'Re: Budgetary constraint' Municipality, Queenstown, Privatization File, vol 4, 9 March, item 38

Brand, J.G. (1984) 'Privatization in Municipal Government: A Practical Viewpoint', *South African Municipal Yearbook*, 1984/5, pp47–51, Government Printer, Pretoria

Clarke, J. and Newman, J. (1997) *The Managerial State*, Sage, London

Cowen, P. and Dianderas, A. (1996) 'Infrastructure Notes', *World Bank Water,* SW-17

DCD (Department of Constitutional Development) (1997) *Guidelines on Partnerships in Municipal Service Delivery*, Government Printer, Pretoria

DCD (Department of Constitutional Development) (1998) *Regulatory Framework for Municipal Services Partnerships*, first draft, 25 August, Government Printer, Pretoria

DPLG (Department of Provincial and Local Government) (2000) 'Green Paper on Municipal Partnerships', www.local.gov.za/DCD/policydocs/gp_msp/msfor.html

Donahue, J. (1989) *The Privatization Decision*, Basic Books, New York

Dunning, J.H. (1996) *The Globalization of Business*, Routledge, London

Everite PTY Ltd (1996) *Annual Report*, Everite PTY Ltd, Johannesburg

Fort Beaufort TLC (1995) 'Overdraft and financial position', Treasurer's memo, 4 December

Goubert, J.P. (1989) *The Conquest of Water*, Princeton University Press, Princeton, New Jersey

Green, N. (1994) 'Water Industry Best Practices', *Journal of American Water Works Association*, March 1994

Hall, D. and Goudrian, J. (1999) 'Contradictions in Municipal Transformation', *Working Papers in Local Governance and Democracy*, 99/1, pp60–68

Harvey, D. (1989) *The Urban Experience*, Hopkins Press, Baltimore, Maryland

Heymans, C. (1991) 'Privatization and Municipal Reform', in M. Swilling, R. Humphries and K. Shubane (eds) *Apartheid City in Transition*, Oxford University Press, Cape Town

Hoogland De Hoog, R. (1984) *Contracting Out For Human Services*, New York University Press, Albany, New York

Kasrils, R. (2003) Address by the Minister of Water Affairs and Forestry, budget vote no. 34: Water Affairs and Forestry, 6 June, Government Printer, Pretoria

Kerf, M. and Smith, W. (1996) *Privatising Africa's Infrastructure: Promise and Challenge*, World Bank Technical Paper no 337, Washington, DC

Leys, C. (2001) *Market Driven Politics, Neoliberal Democracy and Public Interests*, Verso, London

Logan, J. and Molotch, H. (1987) *Urban Fortune*, UCLA Press, Berkeley, California

Lorrain, D. (1991) 'Public Goods and Private Operators in France', in R. Batley and G. Stoker (eds) *Local Government in Europe: Trends and Developments*, Macmillan, London

Lorrain, D. and Stoker, G. (eds) (1997) *The Privatisation of Urban Services in Europe*, Pinter, London

Martin, S. and Parker, D. (1997) *The Impact of Privatisation*, Routledge, London

Marvin, S. and Graham, S. (1994) 'Privatisation of Utilities: The Implications for Cities in the United Kingdom', *Journal of Urban Technology*, Fall

Meszaros, I. (1995) *Beyond Capital*, Monthly Review Press, New York

MIIU (Municipal Infrastructure Investment Unit) (2003) 'Evaluation Report of the Contract between Lukhanji Municipality and Water and Sanitation Services South Africa', November, MIIU, Pretoria

Patterson, A. and Theobald, K. (1999) 'Emerging Contradictions: Sustainable Development and New Local Governance', in G. Buckingham-Hatfield and S. Percy (eds) *Constructing Local Environmental Agendas*, Routledge, London

PDG (Palmer Development Group) (1999) 'Infrastructure Investment Guidelines – Queenstown Cases Study', with Development Bank of Southern Africa acting for the Dept of Constitutional Development, Pretoria

Queenstown Municipality (1990a) 'Minutes of Council, Comments on Budget Speech', July

Queenstown Municipality (1990b) 'Minutes of Town Council', 28 August–4 December

Queenstown Municipality (1993) 'Minutes of Council', 23 February
RSA (Republic of South Africa) (1987) *White Paper on Privatization and Deregulation*, Government Printer, Pretoria
Ruiters, G. (2002) 'Debt, Disconnection and Privatization: The Case of Fort Beaufort, Queenstown and Stutterheim', in D.A. McDonald and J. Pape (eds) *Cost Recovery and the Crisis of Service Delivery in South Africa*, Zed Books, London
Ruiters, G. and Bond, P. (1999) 'Contradictions in Municipal Transformation', *Working Papers in Local Governance and Democracy*, 99/1, pp69–79
SetPlan Town and Regional Planners (1999) *Queenstown IDP/LDO Draft Situation Analysis*, Queenstown Municipality, October
Silva, R. (1998) 'Environment and Infrastructure Supply in Brazil', in R. Burgess, M. Carmona and T. Kolstee (eds) *The Challenge of Sustainable Cities, Neoliberalism and Urban Strategies in Developing Countries*, Zed Books, London
South Africa Waterbulletin (1984) Water Research Commission, Pretoria
Stoker, G. (1989) 'Local Government for a Post Fordist Society', in J. Stewart and G. Stoker (eds) *The Future of Local Government*, Macmillan, Houndsmills, UK
Swyngedouw, E., Kaika, M. and Castro, E. (2002) 'Urban Water: A Political-Ecology Perspective', *Built Environment*, vol 28, no 2
Viscusi, W., Vernon, J. and Harrington, J. (1992) *The Economics of Regulation and Anti-Trust*, MIT Press, Cambridge, Massachusetts
Water Research Commission (1995) 'Preliminary Guidelines of Private Sector Involvement in Water Provision', Water Research Commission, KV 81/96, Pretoria
Wolch, J. and Dear, M. (eds) (1989) *The Power of Geography*, Unwin Hyman, Boston, Massachusetts
World Bank (1994) *World Development Report 1994: Infrastructure for Development*, World Bank, Washington, DC
World Bank (2004) 'Water Challenges Poor People Face', *World Bank News*, 24 February
WSSA (Water Services South Africa) (1995a) 'Proposal for Management, Operation and Maintenance of Fort Beaufort Water and Sanitation', Fort Beaufort Municipal Records, Queenstown, South Africa, 25 April
WSSA (Water Services South Africa) (1995b) 'Contract Agreement for Delegated Management of Water and Sanitation Services in Fort Beaufort', Fort Beaufort Municipal Records, Queenstown, South Africa, October
WSSA (Water Services South Africa) (2000) 'Monthly Report, Fort Beaufort', WSSA, Queenstown, South Africa, August
Yaron, G. and Rycroft, N. (1999) *Suez Lyonnaise Des Eaux*, Polaris Institute and Council for Canadians, Ottawa

Box 3 *Declaration of the Coalition Against Water Privatization (South Africa)*

Manifesto adopted November 2003

One of the most celebrated achievements of South Africa's transition to democracy is the Bill of Rights enshrined in the Constitution. The Bill of Rights provides that everyone has the right to have access to sufficient water. The privatization of water violates that constitutional (and human) right in every way imaginable. As the International Covenant on Economic, Social and Cultural Rights (to which the South African government is signatory) explicitly acknowledges, water is a public good fundamental for life and health, the human right to water is indispensable for leading a life of human dignity, it is prerequisite for the realization of other human rights. At all levels of life – political, social, economic and cultural – the privatization of water is anti-democratic, anti-social and anti-human.

As early as 1994, the South African government introduced its policy on water in direct violation of the Reconstruction and Development Programme (RDP) commitment to lifeline supply. This gave the water bureaucrats the authority to provide water only if there was a full cost recovery of operating, maintenance and replacement costs. The Growth, Employment and Redistribution (GEAR) policy in 1996 located the policies of water and other basic needs within a neoliberal macro-economic policy framework.

Following the neoliberal economic advice of the World Bank, the International Monetary Fund and various Western governments, the South African government drastically decreased grants and subsidies to local municipalities and city councils and supported the development of financial instruments for privatized delivery. This effectively forced local government to turn towards commercialization and privatization of basic services as a means of generating the revenue no longer provided by the national state. Many local government structures, using the enabling legislation provided by the Municipal Services Act, began to privatize public water utilities by entering into service and management 'partnerships' with multinational water corporations.

As a result of privatization, water has ceased to be a public good that is accessible and affordable to all South Africans. Instead, water and sanitation have become market commodities to be bought and sold on a for-profit basis, notwithstanding the 'free' 6000 l of water per month, per household that is not enough to cover basic needs. Households are charged more for every additional drop they use, in order to recoup the income forgone due to the first 6000 l provided. Moreover, millions of the poorest South Africans do not have access to water services and thus receive no allocation of free water.

The policy of 'cost-recovery' has seen the price of water rising, necessarily hitting poor communities the hardest. Unable to pay, poor families have been cut off from their water supplies – more than 10 million by the latest count. Additionally, over 2 million have been evicted from their homes, often as a part of the associated legal process to recover debt from poor 'customers'. Those poor communities without previous access to clean water have either suffered the same fate once infrastructure was provided or have simply had to make do with sourcing water from polluted streams and far-away boreholes.

The collective impact of water privatization on the majority of South Africans has been devastating. The desperate search for any available source of water has resulted in cholera outbreaks that have claimed the lives of hundreds. Inadequate hygiene and 'self-serve' sanitation systems have led to continuous exposure (especially for children) to various preventable diseases. There has been an increase in environmental pollution and degradation arising from uncontrolled effluent discharges and scarcity of water for food production. And, the human dignity of entire communities has been ripped apart, as the right to the most basic of human needs, water, has been turned into a restricted privilege available only to those who can afford it.

Water is a natural resource that, by its very nature, must be collectively owned and enjoyed. Privatization, by its very nature, turns water into a commodity, owned by corporate monopolies and enjoyed only on an individualized basis. Nowhere is this monopolized and individualized hijacking of the collective, human right to water more apparent than in the latest manifestation of privatized water provision, prepaid water meters. In the community of Phiri (Soweto) and in several other poor communities across South Africa, private water corporations (with the full backing of national and local government officials) are installing prepaid meters as a technological tool to enforce both 'cost-recovery' and self-disconnection. Those community members and activists resisting privatized water in Phiri and in other 'guinea pig' communities have been summarily arrested. Many have been denied bail or have been placed under apartheid-era bail conditions in order to silence their voices and to crush collective community resistance. Like the effect of the opposition from government and corporate capital to apartheid reparations, the majority of South Africans are being intimidated and/or forcibly pushed into forgoing their collective socio-economic rights, thus allowing private corporations to continue profiting from their poverty.

In light of the above, we demand that:

- the criminalization of dissent and opposition to the privatization of water be immediately stopped;
- prepaid meters be immediately outlawed and removed from all communities where they have been installed;
- the government reverse its policy of privatizing water and all other basic needs by cancelling all 'service' contracts and 'management' agreements with private water corporations;
- the government make a firm political and fiscal commitment to roll out universally accessible infrastructure;
- the government publicly affirm the human and constitutional right of all South Africans to water by ensuring full public ownership, operation and management of public utilities in order to provide free basic services for all.

Chapter 9

The Murky Waters of Second Wave Neoliberalism: Corporatization as a Service Delivery Model in Cape Town

Laïla Smith

This chapter examines the corporatization of water in the city of Cape Town, South Africa. I argue that corporatization, a service delivery alternative that is illustrative of a second wave of neoliberalism, threatens to undermine democratic accountability in the water sector by restructuring the state in ways that are invisible to the public, yet which have visibly negative outcomes for low income communities.

The first section of the chapter reviews the transition from the first wave of neoliberalism, where privatization models dominated, to a second wave of neoliberalism, where corporatization is perceived as an alternative institutional model of water delivery. I argue that a private sector ethos operates in both institutional forms but that corporatization merely internalizes the process. I then turn to a case study of how Cape Town commercialized its water sector from 1997 to 2001 and how it has ultimately come to corporatize water delivery. Of particular interest are the cost recovery measures that have been developed in this service transformation and their impact on equity under a corporatized water unit. I conclude by arguing that corporatization runs the risk of exacerbating Cape Town's water inequities due to its narrow focus on financial imperatives and its disassociation of political decision making from the day-to-day management of water systems.

FROM FIRST WAVE TO SECOND WAVE NEOLIBERALISM

From the mid-1970s, the erosion of the welfare capitalist state gave way to a first wave of neoliberal policies that were grounded in a critique of state interventionism (Brodie 1995; Jones 1998). The critique focused on a deep-seated tension between the ethic of entitlement based on individual achievement and the ethic of citizenship rights to public provision (Pickvance and Preteceille 1991, p216). During this period, local authorities faced the challenge of meeting growing demands for the delivery of cheap, good quality and widely accessible services with simultaneous cuts in fiscal transfers from state and national governments. The failure of past state-driven approaches to water supply spurred a number of shifts in the philosophy of provision in urban areas.

The transformation of the state during this early phase of neoliberalism emphasized the importance of the costs of services rather than the social benefits (Laws 1998). Key state responsibilities were decentralized and devolved to non-state actors. This form of state restructuring had distinctive effects at the local government level in countries in the South in particular. These shifts in thinking resulted in a trend towards increased private sector participation through partnerships, more decentralized management, an emphasis on demand based provision and a greater degree of cost recovery (Johnstone and Wood 2001, p7). Local authorities embarked on these partnerships by initiating a wave of privatization programmes, a step that introduced market relationships into the bureaucratic production of public services (Sclar 2000). This first wave of neoliberalism, otherwise called a 'roll-back the state' form of neoliberalism (Peck and Tickell 2001), signalled a shift from the supply of services based on need, to supply according to the ability to pay.

The growing arguments against privatization have spurred the transition to a second wave of neoliberalism. These critiques are based on widespread evidence of water privatization initiatives around the world over the last decade that have failed to ensure affordable and accessible services to the poor, such as England (Bakker 2001), Bolivia (Nickson and Vargas 2002), Argentina (Loftus and McDonald 2001), Poland (Moran 2000) and South Africa (Bakker and Hemson 2000; Ruiters 2002; Smith and Hanson 2003). These botched initiatives are symptomatic of the growing failures of service delivery alternatives that were part of the first wave, and coarser version, of neoliberalism. The negative social ramifications resulting from the difficulties facing these intensive privatization initiatives (divestiture, concessions, Build, Operate, Train and Transfer Schemes (BOTTs)) prompted widespread thinking amongst academics and practitioners on the role of the state in making markets more effective (Drache and Boyer 1995). One of the lessons drawn in reviewing this period is that marketizing essential services, without strong state regulation, undermines the public authority objectives in devolving its core responsibilities to an external provider. Rather than turning to the private sector as a panacea, state authorities are only now beginning to understand that regulating private sector activities can be far more complex than running the services themselves. Turning to the private sector is no quick fix.

These reflections, when applied to the local government level, served to catalyse a more sophisticated form of neoliberalism. In this new wave of neoliberalism, rather than *de*regulating, one option local authorities have chosen is to *re*-regulate the provision of public services through the institutional reorganization of a public service into the form of a corporation (Kelsey 2001; Robinson 2001; Bakker 2002; Swyngedouw et al 2002). The intention is to make markets work more effectively through a stronger state presence, primarily through the function of a regulator.

Peck and Tickell (2001, p4) trace the shift from the 'roll-back' form of neoliberalism to an emergent phase of active state-building and regulatory reform:

> *In the course of this shift, the agenda has gradually moved from one preoccupied with active destruction and discreditation of Keynsian-welfarist and social-collectivist institutions to one focused on the purposeful construction and consideration of neoliberalized state forms, modes of governance and regulatory relations.*

This 'roll-out' form of neoliberalism finds its genesis mainly in Western policy oriented institutions. Think tanks, universities, research centres and donor agencies have been quick to prescribe the need for greater intervention through governance regimes and increased state regulation to better protect the functioning of markets without regard to whether these new forms of re-regulation actually improve people's lives (Peet 2001). For instance, the World Bank began to aggressively promote privatization in the 1990s despite the recognition that institutional capacity is necessary and lacking. It responded to these state weaknesses with new programmes to improve governance, ranging from 'twinning arrangements', where foreign consultants are hired, to farming out public regulation to third parties (T. Kessler, Citizens Network for Essential Services, personal communication, 8 May 2003). Without much evidence to prove that the second wave of neoliberalism has improved the social and economic outcomes for those worst hit by the first wave, the benefits of the policy prescriptions of the 'roll-out the state' form of neoliberalism would appear to be simply rhetorical.

This rhetoric is well reflected in the World Bank's use of progressive policy terminology to respond to the growing criticisms of market-led forms of development (Stiglitz 2002; Ellerman 2002). The Bank outlines a 'holistic approach' to development, combining social safety nets, poverty-reduction, environmental and gender considerations with conventional neoliberal principles like increased property rights, trade liberalization and privatization (Peet 2002). The irony of this new language of development is that states must become more 'socially-interventionist' while still trying to remain 'globally competitive' in an international system that promotes deregulation (see Yaron's (2000) discussion of the GATS in the WTO).

In this new vision governments are supposed to be less politically involved in service delivery but are also supposed to ensure good governance by coordinating state, private sector and civil society stakeholders. Governments are supposed to ensure greater state regulation of economies while providing a laissez-faire economic environment for investors. Peet aptly sums up the continued contradictions of this sophisticated form of neoliberalism by describing it as 'moving to a reflexive developmentalism that incorporates its own critiques into an ever-more refined but basically unchanged version' (Peet 2001, p10). The recent arrival of corporatization on the local government restructuring scene is illustrative of this second wave of neoliberalism.

Corporatization

What is corporatization? The Queensland [Australia] *White Paper on Corporatization* defines the term as:

> *a structural reform process which changes the conditions under which Government [Owned Enterprises] operate so that they are placed, as far as practicable, on a commercial basis in a competitive environment while allowing the Government, as owner, to continue to provide broad direction by setting key financial and non-financial performance targets and community service obligations* (Government of Queensland 1992, p5).

Corporatization involves changing public institutional structures to incorporate private sector principles in the provision of services. Corporatization is a process of creating an arm's-length service entity that is fully owned and operated by the state but which is ringfenced financially and managerially from other services (Yarrow 1999; PWC 2000; PDG 2001).

The underlying private sector ethos is to recover costs in order to run a corporatized entity along commercial lines. Cost recovery is the recovery of all or most of the cost associated with providing a particular service with the objective of recovering the full cost of production. For services that can be measured, such as water, cost recovery is achieved by charging service users the full short-run marginal cost of production as well as a portion of long-term operating and maintenance costs (McDonald 2002, p18). The most frequent outcome of this cost recovery strategy is to devolve the costs from the government to the user.

An integral objective in achieving full cost recovery, particularly in a monopoly service like water, is to set up a competitive environment. The Queensland Treasury (Government of Queensland 1994, p4) notes that full cost pricing should remove advantages resulting from government ownership so that 'any edge in competition should result solely from superior management and operational factors. . . Otherwise, competition may be undermined leading to distortions in market efficiency'.

Introducing a competitive environment can involve unbundling a monopolistic sector such as water where multiple service providers compete with each other to provide quality service at cost-effective prices.[1] Another way is to remove subsidies in order to permit state-owned enterprises to compete for finance on an equal basis with private firms (Shirley 1999, p116).

The argument driving corporatization is that, by achieving higher productivity through more efficient management, local government can then leverage greater dividends for meeting equity concerns through community service agreements (PDG 2001). The aims of corporatization are therefore to provide incentive, enhance efficiency, increase economic performance and improve public accountability objectives (Government of Queensland 1997, p10).

Issues of Poor Governance

Despite these noble goals, the corporatization model holds several unresolved contradictions with the dual identities local authorities must bear in trying to be both a service provider and service enabler. Local authorities must reconcile the differing values and objectives of the public and private sectors and how their respective markets operate. The primary objective of the public sector historically has been to uphold equal and low cost services as a public good, an objective that keeps equity considerations at the forefront of the provision of public services. In contrast, the primary aim of the private sector is to make a profit for its shareholders. In order to do so, private sector methods of delivery aim to recover costs by prioritizing efficiency objectives over equity concerns.

As a governance model, corporatization purports to reconcile these differing objectives by nurturing technical managerialism at the expense of political considerations, such as upholding the value of public goods for social and individual well-being during local government debates about the distribution of services. In a separate arm's-length institution, the CEO running a newly corporatized entity can make swift decisions by having to consult a board of directors that may include only one or two political councillors. This certainly sounds more inviting to a well-trained and experienced engineer than having to move through a maze of protocols within city council. This autonomy gives engineers greater powers to ensure that a corporate entity can recover its costs through more efficient forms of management.

Corporatization is a seductive management model for engineers precisely because it promises rigid credit control mechanisms without political interference. It does this by sidestepping the councillor system through an arm's-length corporatized entity, thereby removing politicians from decision making processes in the delivery of essential services to their constituencies. This undermines councillors' ability to effectively educate and train service users to develop a sense of ownership of the service delivery process. On the surface, engineers appear as the benign agents driving this sophisticated form of state re-engineering. They are scientifically trained to make technological systems work and can be highly efficient and prized professionals in this endeavour. They are not, however, trained to consider the political problems of poverty and the social consequences of denying low income households access to essential services.

Below the surface, the manner in which corporatization transforms the state is to shift the question of how the politics of distribution is resolved from the hands of politicians to technocrats; the latter have little accountability to the public. In the move from a government to a governance model of service delivery, this quiet form of government reorganization is carried forward, often undetected by the public. The corporatization model undermines public accountability because it inherently involves a policy shift that moves away from political processes towards greater technical intervention that places a premium on efficiency at the expense of equity. This is where corporatization symbolizes a more sophisticated form of neoliberalism by virtue of how the state restructures in order to adhere to a private market logic in the provision of public services. This new form of governance is particularly dangerous in a society that is replete with inequalities and has a young track record in the democratization of service delivery, such as in South Africa.

CASE STUDY: CORPORATIZATION OF WATER IN CAPE TOWN

We now turn to an examination of the process of commercialization leading up to the corporatization of water in Cape Town, which is set for 2004.[2] The city underwent massive restructuring in the first five years following democratic elections in 1996 with the goal of integrating townships and bringing about a more equitable (re)distribution of services. Twenty-five municipal authorities were amalgamated into six municipalities in 1997,[3] which were integrated into one Unicity in 2000. I focus here on the Cape Town and Tygerberg administrations, the two most densely populated municipalities in the Cape Metropolitan Area (CMA) with 66 per cent of the total population. These two municipalities absorbed the greatest number of former Black Local Authority (BLAs) areas, otherwise known as townships, during the first amalgamation period. The amalgamation of these townships gave the Cape Town and Tygerberg municipalities the highest concentration of low income communities with service backlogs. Despite having the highest concentration of poverty within the metropolitan area, these municipalities were also the best-resourced local councils in terms of both human resources and financial capital. These were also the only two municipalities where the African National Congress (ANC) won a majority vote in the first local government elections in 1996. If corporatization was to work anywhere within the CMA, these two municipalities seemed to be the most likely areas to successfully combine both equity and efficiency objectives.

I focus on three cost recovery policies that have been central to the five-year (1997–2001) commercialization process in the water sector and assess the impact of these cost recovery policies on local government objectives for achieving equity in service delivery. I first discuss policies of pricing and water demand management in Cape Town and their role as a form of cost recovery. I then review the practice of outsourcing and its implications on workers and low income households, followed by an examination of debt management through water cutoffs. I conclude the chapter by examining the merits and limitations of corporatization as a water service delivery model.

Water demand management

The incursion of market forces into the production of water services has raised a contentious debate over the last few decades (Emel 1990; Batley 1996; Swyngedouw 1997; Bond 1999). The entry point can be traced back to the mid-1980s

World Bank-led shift from supply-side to demand-oriented approaches to service delivery. As the nature of a water service is monopolistic, government systems in the supply and delivery of water have historically been perceived as unwieldy in utilizing large-scale technologies and providing uniform distribution despite different levels of industrial, commercial and domestic demands. The move to water demand management (WDM) in the 1980s and 1990s was accompanied by an emphasis on smaller-scale technologies and more flexible forms of delivery to meet greater variability of demand (Gulyani 2001). In the context of water, the underlying approach to management was an emphasis on conservation in order to minimize the costs of future extraction. This approach also set the context for introducing private sector involvement with its offer of specialized technologies and management systems to suit the variation associated with private needs. In this context, WDM can be seen as a tool for enhancing cost recovery through pricing mechanisms that regulate supply to meet the variation of demand.

Cape Town is situated in the Western Cape, an area that is subject to the greatest water scarcity in the country. Over the course of the last century, Cape Town authorities and, since 1960 the national Department of Water Affairs and Forestry (DWAF), adapted to water scarcity through the building of dams. The cost and resource inefficiencies of this approach were shielded by the ability of the administration to secure revenues by selling high volumes of water to a wealthy minority of the city's population. Considering the water scarcity of the region, Cape Town authorities became increasingly aware of the need to make a transition from a supply-side to a demand-oriented approach in water provision. While local authorities in Cape Town have been conscious of the need for water conservation strategies for decades, the concept of WDM was only developed as a coherent policy by the 1990s.

WDM emerged as a concept at the national level through the National Water Act in 1995, a document laying the foundations for water as a national resource strategy. The concept of WDM took on new significance in Cape Town when the Cape Metropolitan Council (CMC) requested approval from DWAF to build the Skuifraam dam to avoid running out of water in ten years. DWAF replied that no new dams could be built until the concept of WDM was implemented. Cape Town's development of a WDM policy was therefore instigated by the reality of increasing water prices due to escalating costs for dam construction and constitutional obligations to make basic services accessible to all. Considering these constraints, Cape Town put forth three pillars of a WDM policy that promoted greater efficiency in the supply of water: a reduction of unaccounted-for water (UFW); an effort to reduce water consumption through public education; and a shift to market pricing that would penalize high volume users (City of Cape Town 2000).

It is this third aspect of WDM that is most crucial to our discussion here: pricing through water tariffs. The principle of 'the more you use, the more you pay' is the motivation for block water tariffs to domestic consumers. In the 1960s a three-step block tariff was introduced in Cape Town and was replaced by a five-step tariff in 1998. The latter was implemented across the six municipalities

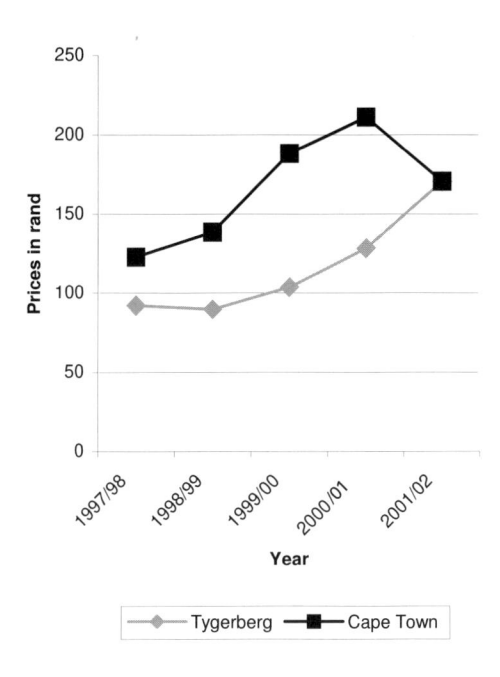

Figure 9.1 *Monthly consumption of 60 kl of water in Cape Town and Tygerberg (1997–2002)*

Source: Smith (2003)

composing the CMA, albeit with differential rates for each block. The top domestic tariff is based at the marginal cost of future resource infrastructure, such as the building of the Skuifraam dam.[4] At the lower scale, the five-step tariff policy was designed to meet the constitutional obligation of ensuring a pro-poor tariff by cross-subsidizing low end users through high rates to high level users.

Figures 9.1 and 9.2 illustrate how water demand principles were implemented in the Cape Town and Tygerberg municipalities through escalating prices for high volumes of water consumption between 1997 and 2002. These figures also reveal that households consuming 60 kilolitres (kl) of water a month (i.e. high consumption) have faced the biggest burden of price increases, particularly in the Cape Town administration since 1999, while households consuming low levels of water per month have had minimal price increases.

The implementation of the converged tariffs (see Table 9.1) was structured to balance the requirements for demand management, cost recovery and the free water policy for the first 6 kl of water.[5] The completion of meter installations in July 2001 in the iKapa area (African townships in the Cape Town municipality) initiated the transition from a flat rate tariff of R10.95 to a consumption based charge. This affected 40,000 properties, approximately 11,500 of which were billed for the first time.[6] These households now face the full cost of their consumption, yet were given little explanation of the implications of this dramatic shift on their household expenditures.

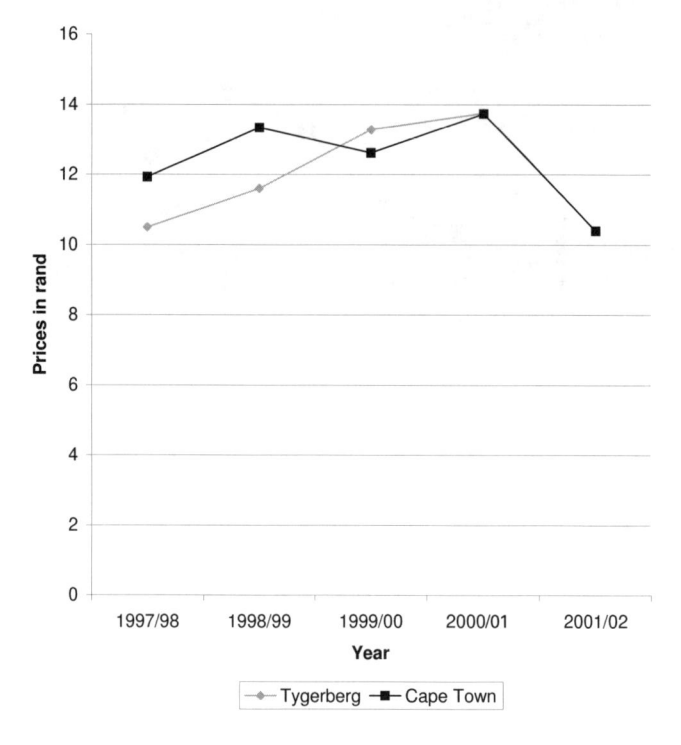

Figure 9.2 *Monthly consumption of 10 kl of water in Cape Town and Tygerberg (1997–2002)*

Source: Smith (2003)

Table 9.1 Water tariff schedule for 2002/03

Consumer category descriptions		Steps	Tariff per kl
Domestic full	Water which is used for domestic purposes and supplied through fully metered connections	Step 1 (0–6 kl)	R0.00
		Step 2 (7–20 kl)	R2.73
		Step 3 (21–40)	R4.30
		Step 4 (41–60)	R5.46
		Step 5 (61+)	R7.35
Commercial	Tariff includes a 7% cross-subsidy towards 'free water'		R3.41
Industrial			R3.41

Upon closer examination, the free water policy and five-step tariff is designed as a pro-poor policy, but it fails to take into account the location and demographics of poverty in the city. The water tariff is designed to subsidize the first 6 kl of water through price increases in the remaining steps of the five-step tariff.

Residents that consume more than 20 kl a month bear the additional costs of this new water policy. The estimation of 50 l per person per day for a household of four assumes a nuclear family structure that is more prevalent among well-off communities. This assumption excludes the notion of an extended family household structure with backyard shacks, which is the norm in many township areas. In fact, many of these low income households comprise from 15 to 30 people sharing one water source and toilet.[7] The implications of replacing flat rates with a stepped tariff to high density households receiving water could lead to a considerable increase in their monthly expenditures for an essential need. The point is that a five-step tariff policy, despite the first 6 kl of water being free, in fact increases the cost of water for the urban poor if the household size is greater than four or five people.

Water demand management has been a vital strategy for meeting the long-term water needs of a water scarce area. Environmental pressures regarding water scarcity drove local authorities to devise methods for promoting conservation and avoiding wastage. The methods employed emphasized an instrumental view of water by treating it as a commodity to be measured, metered and priced according to market demand. Local authorities have been relatively progressive in meeting both conservation needs and pro-poor policies, through the provision of free water, but at the cost of removing flat rates to historically marginalized communities. A uniform approach to the commodification of water through measurement and pricing may promote conservation, but moves away from the consideration of access to water as a basic human right, regardless of ability to pay. The implementation of WDM strategies in Cape Town has failed to consider the spatial legacy of apartheid where the highest poverty rates in the city are in high density households living in township areas with historical underinvestment in infrastructure. These households tend to consume more water by virtue of household density and also receive exorbitant bills due to water leaks in eroding infrastructure.

Outsourcing

> We [the water department] need to be compatible with companies outside in terms of costs, which the city of Cape Town is not at present. The overhead costs are just too enormous. We need to be able to do the work at the same cost as the private sector. Companies don't have the same attitude to service delivery as [city] council does. With companies we have employed over the years, they have wanted to get out and do their job, get their money and then move onto the next one as quickly as possible. Consumer satisfaction to them means absolutely nothing (Chief Water Inspector, City of Cape Town, 14 March 2001).

One of the central elements of the state commercializing service delivery and moving towards corporatization is transforming components of a public service into business units that can run autonomously in a competitive environment.

These business units can then be outsourced or insourced. The central task of local government is then to set up and monitor the appropriate regulatory frameworks and performance agreements with contractors. The growing evidence of declining service levels due to increased outsourcing that has been part of the commercialization process in Cape Town puts into question whether local government is in fact able to regulate properly and monitor these outsourced services. Interviews with shop stewards from the water sector in the South African Municipal Workers' Union (Samwu) revealed that the manner in which outsourcing has occurred has undermined the quality of service delivery to low income consumers and the conditions of labour for workers.

When the first democratically elected administration came to power in 1997 facing the task of extending services without additional financing, discussions began immediately regarding the division between core and non-core services. Non-core services such as catering, cutting of verges, road markings and auditing were outsourced. At the same time, some of the core services, such as water and refuse collection underwent a process of unbundling by contracting out aspects of the water service to small entrepreneurs. For instance, the Cape Town administration has contracted out mainlaying and water cutoffs, while the city of Tygerberg has contracted out construction work, a portion of meter installation, meter reading, water cutoffs, design for reservoirs, water network analysis (master plans), and water infrastructure maintenance such as pipe cleaning.

Interviews with numerous water managers and engineers revealed two dominant motivations for contracting out a service to a private sector provider. The first was to save on labour costs and the second was to sidestep the bureaucracy of the city council. The problem with both these motivations is that sidestepping the bureaucracy means overstepping the legislative requirements that protect workers from exploitative labour conditions as well as uphold performance standards for how services are delivered. Contract workers are often employed on a temporary or casual basis, and can be laid off when the project is complete. The guiding philosophy is to replace a set wage rate with a 'payment-by-results' system (PSI 1997, p9).

Outsourcing not only erodes the conditions of labour for workers, it also changes the way in which work is done, to the detriment of protecting the rights of service users. The guiding philosophy of the service provider in contracting out to private sector operators is to ensure profits by maximizing performance in as short a time as possible (CUPE 1998). Such an approach sometimes requires cutting corners such as standard customer relations protocol. Proponents of outsourcing treat the impacts of this approach on low income service users as a secondary consideration. This is particularly true with regard to people who are not paying for their services, such as informal settlement dwellers who use community standpipes for free.

Two problems relating to poor service agreements and their impacts on low income households are illustrated below. First, the Tygerberg administration contracted out the repairing of water mains while the Cape Town administration kept the service in-house. The protocol of a municipal worker, when repairing a burst main, is to inform residents when their water services will be shut off, particularly if it will be for more than one day. When interviewing residents from the African informal settlement of Joe Slovo, in the township of Langa (Cape Town municipality), about why their water was cut off, the majority of respondents replied that their water was cut off due to repairs and that they were notified in advance so as to be able to make alternative arrangements for accessing water. When I interviewed residents in Monwabisi Park, an African informal settlement in the township of Khayelitsha (Tygerberg administration), service users complained that they were never informed when their water was cut off for repairs, even when the duration was more than a full day. Considering the relative isolation of this community from other sources of water supply, this situation forced people living in the settlement to walk up to an hour to a nearby cemetery in an adjacent municipality to gain access to water. The brunt of the effects of contractors' efforts to cut costs by sidestepping standard customer protocols falls on the poorest in the city. If the intent of decentralizing service delivery to non-state actors is to empower local entrepreneurs, care must be taken in monitoring how accountability to the public is upheld as partnerships become disassociated from existing institutions (Newman and Verpraet 1999).

A second problem related to the unbundling of services is the inability of local authorities to properly monitor and coordinate between the different contractors of services that have been outsourced. For instance, the Cape Town approach to dealing with illegal water connections is to cut off people by removing their water meter and a portion of the pipe that is connected to it. The water cutoffs and the removal of the meter from the ground are contracted out to two separate companies. An interview with a widow living in a formal settlement within the coloured township of Mitchells Plain, who had just had her water cut off for the third time, stated that she had just gathered sufficient resources to pay the fee for the reconnection. Yet after three days of waiting she still did not have her water service reconnected. The explanation she was given by the local authorities was that the contracted company who removed the meter out of her front yard had not yet been informed by the billing department and had to first reinstall the meter before the city could reconnect the water supply. It should be noted that these outcomes are not unique to the process of corporatization, but are the result of decentralizing service delivery with cost recovery imperatives driving the initiative, rather than placing social rights to water first.

Denying a household access to water because of lack of communication between a local authority and a private contractor undermines the original intent in contracting out a service to ensure greater 'efficiencies'. Unbundling water services as part of a corporatization process to cut the cost of operations fails to take into account the city's incapacity to adequately regulate multiple service providers. Ironically, outsourcing within this weak regulatory environment does not, in fact, save financial resources by employing inexpensive labour. As one public worker explained, outsourcing in this weak regulatory environment costs the municipality more to repair the damage done by temporary workers who have been insufficiently trained to carry out their responsibilities.[8]

Debt Management and Water Cutoffs

The third cost recovery approach adopted by the City of Cape Town is water cutoffs. These cutoffs are linked to a history of poor billing practices, accumulated household debt and weak communication between local authorities and service users. The engineering departments in Cape Town and Tygerberg have been adept at addressing backlogs and delivering basic services to mushrooming township areas and upgrading collapsing infrastructure since 1996. The ability of the engineers to get services out quickly, however, exceeded the administrative capacity of the financial departments to register and bill properties receiving these services.

Cape Town has three main problems with its billing that are related to arrears, incorrect metering and discrepancies in the bills sent to households; these are largely related to the difficulties of administrative integration during the post-apartheid municipal transition to Unicities (Pieterse 2002). The combination of years of nonpayment for political reasons,[9] nonexistent customer relations, and problematic billing demonstrates the weak level of communication between local authorities and service users in African and low income, coloured areas. Township communities were penalized for these poor relations by being entrenched in accumulated debt (see Smith and Hanson (2003) for a broader discussion of this).

Local authorities developed a debt management policy in 1997 as the primary vehicle for dealing with households' soaring arrears for nonpayment. This policy calls for recovering debts owed to the local authority and includes sanctions (warning, disconnection, legal process and evictions) in the event of nonpayment of accounts (City of Cape Town 2001, p3). This debt management programme was not effective in motivating people to settle their arrears or pay their current water accounts. Local authorities had, by 1998, begun using water cutoffs as a mechanism for debt management, including households with newly metered connections in former BLA areas.

Research conducted by the author in 2001 in the Cape Town and Tygerberg administrations indicate that, between 1999 and 2001, 159,886 households had their water cut off for reasons of nonpayment. Figure 9.3 indicates that most of the 16,964 cutoffs in the Cape Town administration during that time occurred in the coloured townships. Families living in these areas have experienced generational poverty and its related social dysfunctionalities, such as gangsterism, domestic violence and alcohol abuse. Local authorities since 1996 have neglected low income, coloured townships, both in the maintenance of infrastructure and in communicating changes in service delivery to the area.[10] The fact that the highest disconnection rates are located in these low income coloured areas is a testament to local authority neglect in cultivating greater public involvement in and understanding of service delivery.

Tygerberg's cutoff policies have been far more dramatic than those of the Cape Town administration. From 1999 to 2001 Tygerberg cut off a total of 142,922 households, 77,000 of which were in 2001. Figure 9.4 shows the number of water cutoffs per 1000 bills sent to consumers and dramatically underscores

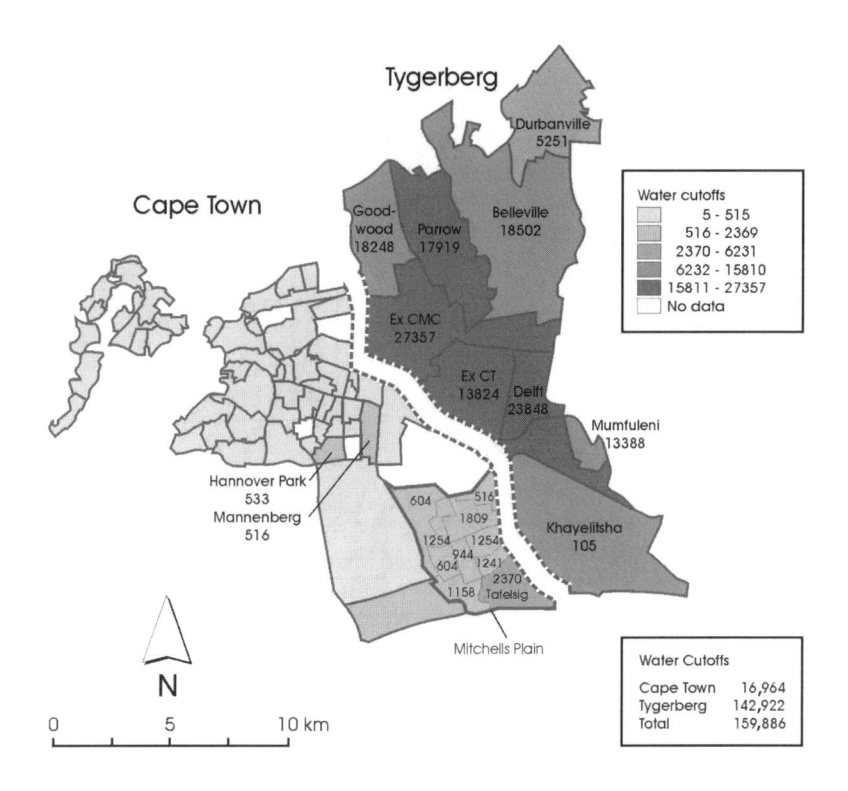

Figure 9.3 *Total water cutoffs in the Cape Town and Tygerberg administrations (1999–2001)*

Source: Smith and Hanson (2003)

the high level of water disconnections in some parts of Tygerberg (902 per 1000 customers in the African township of Mumfuleni). Overall, however, African areas have experienced lower cutoff rates than have coloured areas because when local authorities began disconnecting water to households in African areas they did so at such a high rate that it was too expensive in terms of labour and administration costs to continue. For instance, in just six months, 14,355 households had their water disconnected in the largest African township of Khayelitsha (Smith and Hanson 2003).

High cutoff rates have sparked township revolt, making these areas periodically ungovernable. Tygerberg authorities stopped cutoffs temporarily in African areas because they simply did not know how to deal with the magnitude of the nonpayment problem. After three years of increasing cutoffs and an illegal reconnection rate of 60 per cent in the Tygerberg administration alone,[11] local authorities are beginning to question whether water cutoffs are a viable cost recovery method in the townships.

On the surface, the water disconnection rates have been far higher in Tygerberg as a result of a stricter interpretation of credit control policies. For

182   CASE STUDIES IN SOUTH AFRICA

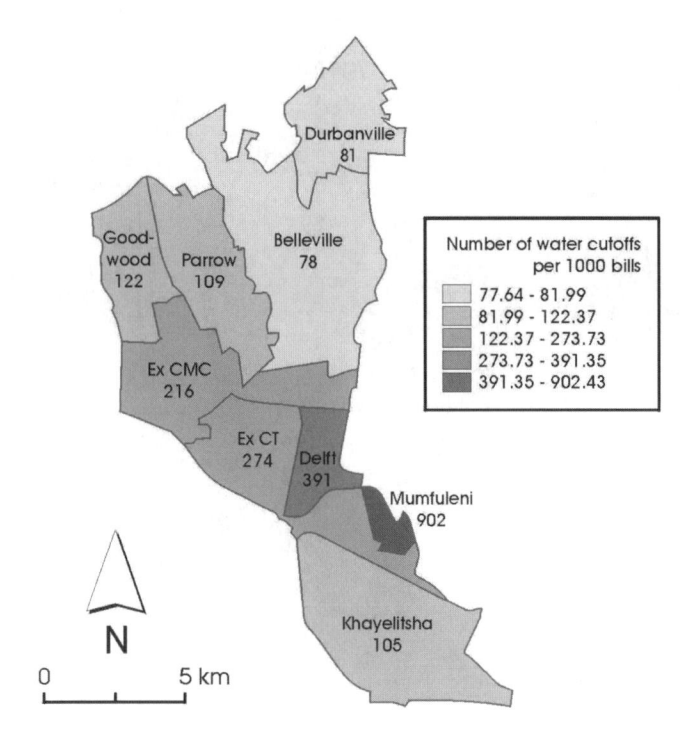

Figure 9.4 *Water cutoffs per 1000 customers billed in Tygerberg (1999–2001)*

Source: Smith and Hanson (2003)

instance, Cape Town authorities restrained household water disconnections until the entire area of iKapa had been metered and switched over to volumetric metering. A closer examination of municipal approaches to service delivery is also cause for explanation. The Cape Town approach to redistribution retained a centralized body of decision making for engineering services. This approach tried to equalize, upgrade and extend new services across the newly integrated municipality. Social services such as health, housing and community services were run along an area based management approach to align community needs within a given geographical area with a package of services that were coordinated across several departmental sectors. It is my belief that this centralized approach allowed local authorities to communicate more effectively across sectors to assess overall poverty rates. This level of attention to the poverty/ underdevelopment dimensions of low income areas may have led the city council of Cape Town to be more cautious about water disconnections. By contrast, Tygerberg developed a decentralized, area based management approach at the outset of the municipality's creation in 1996. Tygerberg was carved into nine service areas with a separate team of officials designated to address issues of redistribution within each of these areas. The level of decentralization created an administration that was effective in rolling out services but was limited in communicating service delivery problems across sectors and areas. This form of decentralization also blinded the administration from seeing the 'big picture' with regard to causes of poverty within the municipality and its outcomes in constraining household ability to pay for services.

Conclusion

The three cost recovery policies illustrated above reveal that during a time of local government organizational restructuring Cape Town authorities chose the corporatization model because it promised efficiency in service delivery. The evidence of the cost recovery method used to achieve efficiency gains has not, however, enabled the local authority to operate more efficiently and has had adverse equity impacts. The adoption of water demand management principles in the pricing of water has been critical for water conservation but has failed to take into account the locations of poverty in the city and how high density households are adversely affected. The contracting out of the components of the water sector may lower the costs of delivery but when insufficiently monitored by local government also lowers public sector standards with negative effects on low income households. Finally, the implementation of strict credit control measures through water disconnections has undermined local government's constitutional obligations to provide basic water services to all and contributed to a crisis of governance in the delivery of water.

This chapter has focused on these cost recovery examples to illustrate how the effects of the corporatization process can be just as negative as more conventional forms of privatization for low income households. Greater understanding of the logic, methods and outcomes of corporatization as a service delivery alternative can shed light on the murky waters of the second wave of neoliberalism. This new phase is attentive to the governing role local government must play as a regulator if it is to successfully monitor an external provider for the distribution of essential services. But reducing the role of local government in service delivery to a regulator is a narrow interpretation of what its service responsibilities are. This scenario leaves little scope for the local level of the state to debate and address the complexities of the politics of distribution, a political function that is exceptionally pertinent in a society that is ridden with inequalities.

Local governments in large cities in South Africa like Durban, Johannesburg and Cape Town have adopted corporatization as a service delivery alternative to deal with the problems of a historically mismanaged water sector. These problems are, however, politically based rather than technically oriented and cannot be resolved by engineers without the assistance of politicians. The role of politicians at the local level in the post-apartheid state is to mediate between the service provider (be it public or private) and the service user. This is a fundamental feature of the democratization of the South African state and is being undermined by the corporatization process and its cost recovery imperatives. In two municipalities within Cape Town, a rising level of nonpayment for water services has instigated soaring water cutoffs to approximately 160,000 households between 1999 and 2001. The spatial pattern of the bulk of these disconnections coincides with areas of the city that were historically left out of the procedures that determined how services were delivered. The growing ungovernability[12] of these township areas is due to their ongoing exclusion from the decisions that affect their day-to-day lives. Rather than concentrating power into the hands of engineers through a corporatization model, local government must broaden the decision making structures that define the process of delivery as a critical step in reducing inequality in distribution.

ACKNOWLEDGEMENTS

This chapter has been reproduced through copyright permission from Elsevier. It is an abridged version of an article published in *Geoforum*, May 2004. Much gratitude to the Municipal Services Project and the International Development Research Centre (IDRC) for having substantially financed the research for this work during my PhD at Clark University. Also many thanks to the National Research Foundation for a postdoctoral fellowship at the University of Cape Town, which allowed for the time to write this chapter.

NOTES

1 Although water is a highly monopolistic service, it consists of numerous different components that can be transformed into business units to compete with the private sector or are directly outsourced (e.g. meter reading).
2 This section presents material gathered during the author's dissertation fieldwork in 2000 and 2001. Over this nine-month period, interviews were held with approximately 100 local authority officials, politicians and civil society representatives across the Cape Metropolitan Area regarding the impact of local government restructuring on service delivery in general, and corporatization, in particular. Also, 120 household interviews were conducted in both Coloured and African townships (total of four) in both the Cape Town and Tygerberg municipalities. Each township was stratified along levels of service delivery – in-house connections, yard taps and community standpipes – in order to assess the differential equity impacts of the corporatization process.
3 These municipalities consisted of Oostenberg, Blaauwberg, South Peninsula Municipality, Helderberg, Cape Town and Tyberberg and were coordinated as municipalities within a metropolitan area by the Cape Metropolitan Council.
4 At the time of this research, the marginal cost was set at R7.00 per kl.
5 This free water policy was constitutionally legislated by the national department of DWAF to take effect in July 2001.

6   Data provided by the billings department for the City of Cape Town in June 2001.
7   Statement made on the basis of the analysis of data from the household surveys conducted by the author.
8   For instance, the labour cost for the Cape Town administration to install meters is approximately R21 per hour per worker. When this function is outsourced, the water department pays the Quality Labour Agency R18 an hour, R11 of which actually goes to the worker. The labour costs are slightly less to outsource but the public authority also provides uniforms and bus passes to the agency for the temporary workers. It is the poor quality of workmanship by a temporary worker that has not been adequately trained that costs the public authority substantially more through repairs. Public sector workers in the department know where meters are placed and as such are cautious about where to drill in the road to avoid bursting a water pipe. During an interview with Eddie Feltsman, senior meter reader in the Cape Town water department, he confessed that the department frequently had to send out a plumbing team to repair burst mains as a result of poor workmanship in areas that had been outsourced.
9   During the 1980s and early 1990s, township residents boycotted the payments for municipal services as a political protest against apartheid and the poor quality of service delivery.
10 Most of the African townships in Cape Town were spared cutoffs during this period as only 2639 of approximately 41,000 properties were billed according to volumetric consumption (personal communication with Mike Parker, Chairperson of the Convergence Process, Corporate Finance, City of Cape Town, 8 April 2001).
11 Data collected from the Tygerberg and Cape Town municipal billing departments.
12 Ungovernability here refers to deliberate and repeated acts of civil society disobedience in response to the draconian credit control measures employed by local authorities. These acts of disobedience range from nonpayment to illegal reconnections to riots, and are a form of political protest against the state's cost recovery measures.

References

Bakker, K. (2001) 'Paying for Water: Water Pricing and Equity in England and Wales', *Transactions of the Institute of British Geographers*, vol 26, pp143–64

Bakker, K. (2002) 'From State to Market: Water *mercantilización* in Spain', *Environment and Planning A*, vol 34, pp767–90

Bakker, K. and Hemson, D. (2000) 'Privatizing Water: BOTT and Hydropolitics in the New South Africa', *South African Geography Journal*, vol 1, pp3–12

Batley, R. (1996) 'Public-Private Relationships and Performance in Service Provision', *Urban Studies*, vol 33 no 4/5, pp723–51

Bond, P. (1999) 'Basic Infrastructure for Socio-Economic Development, Environmental Protection and Geographical Desegregation: South Africa's Unmet Challenge', *Geoforum*, vol 30, pp43–49

Brodie, J. (1995) 'New State Forms, New Political Spaces', in D. Drache and R. Boyer (eds) *States Against Markets*, Routledge, London

City of Cape Town (2000) 'Draft Water Services Development Plan', Department of Water and Waste Directorate, Cape Town

City of Cape Town (2001) 'Credit Control Debt Collection and Indigent Policy/Discussion Document' Credit Control Task Team, compiled for EXCO meeting, 4 September

CUPE (Canadian Union of Public Employees) (1998) 'False Savings, Hidden Costs: Calculating the Costs of Contracting Out and Privatization', Research Department, Ottawa

Drache, D. and Boyer, R. (1995) 'Introduction', in D. Drache and R. Boyer (eds) *States Against Markets*, Routledge, London

Ellerman, D. (2002) 'Russia: Thoughts on the Privatization Debates a Decade Later', World Bank Operations Evaluation Department (OED), Washington, DC

Emel, J. (1990) 'Resource Instrumentalism, Privatization and Commodification', *Urban Geography*, vol 11 no 6, pp527–47

Government of Queensland, Australia (1992) 'Corporatization in Queensland: Policy Guidelines' Government Owned Enterprises Unit, Treasury Department, Brisbane

Government of Queensland, Australia (1994) 'Corporatization in Queensland: Policy Guidelines', Government Owned Enterprises Unit, Treasury Department, Brisbane

Government of Queensland, Australia (1997) 'National Competition Policy Implementation in Queensland: Full-Cost Pricing', Government Printer, Melbourne

Gulyani, S. (2001) 'The Demand-Side Approach to Planning Water Supply', in M. Freire and R. Stren (eds) *The Challenge of Urban Government*, World Bank, Washington, DC

Johnstone, N. and Wood, L. (2001) *Private Firms and Public Water*, Edward Elgar, Northampton, Massachusetts

Jones, M. (1998) 'Restructuring the Local State: Economic Governance or Social Regulation?', *Political Geography*, vol 17 no 8, pp969–88

Kelsey, J. (2001) *Economic Fundamentalism*, Pluto Press, London

Laws, G. (1998) 'Privatization and the Local Welfare State: The Case of Toronto's Social Services', *Transactions of the British Geographers*, vol 12, pp433–48

Loftus, A. and McDonald, D.A. (2001) 'Of Liquid Dreams: A Political Ecology of Water Privatization in Buenos Aires', *Environment and Urbanization*, vol 13 no 2, pp179–99

McDonald, D.A. (2002) 'The Theory and Practice of Cost Recovery in South Africa', in D.A. McDonald and J. Pape (eds) *Cost Recovery and the Crisis of Service Delivery in South Africa*, Zed Books, London

Moran, S. (2000) 'Fluid Categories: Water System Management in Post-Communist Poland', doctoral dissertation, Geography Department, Clark University, Worcester, Massachusetts

Newman, P. and Verpraet, G. (1999) 'The Impacts of Partnership on Urban Governance: Conclusions from Recent European Research', *Regional Studies*, vol 33 no 5, pp487–92

Nickson, A. and Vargas, C. (2002) 'The Limitations of Water Regulation: The Failure of the Cochabamba Concession in Bolivia', *Bulletin of Latin American Research*, vol 21 no 1, pp99–120

PDG (Palmer Development Group) and School of Governance, University of the Western Cape (2001) *Corporatization of Municipal Water Service Providers Research Report*, Water Research Commission, Cape Town

Peck, J. and Tickell, A. (2001) 'Neoliberalizing Space: The Free Economy and the Penal State', paper presented at conference *Neoliberalism and the City*, Center for Urban Economic Development, University of Illinois at Chicago, September

Peet, R. (2001) 'Geographies of Policy Formation: Hegemony, Discourse and the Conquest of Practicality', paper presented at conference *Global Economic Change*, Clark University, Worcester, Massachusetts, 15 May

Peet, R. (2002) 'Ideology, Discourse, and the Geography of Hegemony: From Socialist to Neoliberal Development in Postapartheid South Africa', *Antipode*, vol 34 no 1, pp54–84

Pickvance, C. and Preteceille, E. (1991) *State Restructuring and Local Power*, Pinter Publisher, New York

Pieterse, E. (2002) 'From Divided to Integrated City? Critical Overview of the Emerging Metropolitan Governance System in Cape Town', *Urban Forum*, vol 13 no 1, pp3–37

PSI (Public Services International) (1997) 'The Roots of Privatization: Briefing Notes for Current Debates on Public Sector Issues', Ferney Voltaire Cedex, Public Services International, Grenoble

PWC (PriceWaterhouseCoopers) (2000) 'Feasibility Study: Water and Wastewater Utility Company', PWC, Cape Town

Robinson, C. (ed) (2001) *Regulating Utilities: New Issues, New Solutions*, Edward Elgar, Cheltenham, UK

Ruiters, G. (2002) 'Debt and Disconnection: The Case of Fort Beaufort, Queenstown and Stutterheim', in D.A. McDonald and J. Pape (eds) *Cost Recovery and the Crisis of Service Delivery in South Africa*, Zed Books, London

Sclar, E. (2000) *You Don't Always Get What You Pay For: The Economics of Privatization*, Cornell University Press, Ithaca, New York

Shirley, M. (1999) 'Bureaucrats in Business: The Roles of Privatization versus Corporatization in State-owned Enterprise Reform', *World Development*, vol 27 no 1, pp115–36

Smith, L. (2003) 'The Corporatization of Urban Water Supply: Cape Town's Institutional Transformation in Post-Apartheid South Africa', PhD thesis, Clark University, Worcester, Massachusetts

Smith, L. and Hanson, S. (2003) 'Access to Water for the Urban Poor in Cape Town: Where Equity Meets Cost Recovery', *Urban Studies*, vol 40 no 8, 1517–48

Stiglitz, J. (2002) *Globalization and Its Discontents*, WW Norton & Company, New York

Swyngedouw, E. (1997) 'Power, Nature, and the City: The Conquest of Water and the Political Ecology of Urbanization in Guayaquil, Ecuador: 1980–1990', *Environment and Planning A*, vol 29, pp311–22

Swyngedouw, E., Page, B. and Kaika, M. (2002) 'Exclusionary Governance of Water in the E.U. and the Dynamics of Commodification', paper presented at Annual Association of Geographers, Los Angeles, 5 March

Yaron, G. (2000) *The Final Frontier: A Working Paper on the Big 10 Global Water Corporations and the Privatization and Corporatization of the World's Last Public Resource*, Polaris Institute, Ottawa, pp1–88

Yarrow, G. (1999) 'A Theory of Privatization, or Why Bureaucrats are Still in Business', *World Development*, vol 27 no 1, pp157–68

Box 4 *Western Cape Anti-Eviction Co-ordinating Committee (South Africa), Press Statement*

Protest against water cutoffs: 15 March 2001
Residents and workers of Cape Town will march against evictions and water cuts on 20 March 2001. The mass march will begin at 11 a.m. at Kaisergracht and will proceed to the office of the Mayor. A memorandum will be handed over to the Mayor. The campaign is demanding that Peter Marais [Cape Town Mayor] is there to do his job by accepting the memorandum in person. Last week in Mandela Park Peter Marais escaped through the back door and refused to accept the people's memorandum.

The demands are:

- scrapping of arrears;
- an end to privatization;
- end evictions;
- an end to water cuts;
- implement the promise of free water now;
- an end to electricity disconnections;
- good quality/higher level of current of electricity in street lighting (the lights and current are dim, if they exist at all).

'The march takes place the day before Human Rights Day because we believe that free services such as housing, water and electricity are a human right that we cannot live without', said Campaign Coordinator, Faizel Brown.

In the past few weeks, the Unicity has evicted and cut the water of many residents in the city, despite the election promises that certain levels of basic services would be free. Residents from Valhalla Park, Mannenberg, Kalksteenfontien, Guguletu, Mandalay, Bishop Lavis, Ravensmead, Hanover Park, Parkwood, Khayelitsha, Delft and Tafelsig have all been left homeless and waterless over the past weeks.

Two nights ago, more than 15 houses were auctioned off in Delft immediately after the families had been evicted! In some Tafelsig homes, people are evicted but their furniture is still inside the house and they are denied access. People have been refused the right to pay off their arrears. At 16 Hangklip Road, an old lady with a paraplegic child took R400 to council offices to pay off rents arrears of R600 but she was turned away by council. Mrs Moses of 24 Hangklip Road offered to pay council R650 of the R800 she owed, but they insisted on the R800 or eviction. The committee is in possession of a cheque belonging to a man who withdrew his entire savings of R1644.46 to pay off arrears. He has been turned away by council consistently for the past two months.

There are more allegations of council abuse being reported to the Committee every day. There are reports that members of the community who get medically boarded are being instructed to sign their compensation cheques directly over to council to settle arrears. The Committee is investigating the legality of this. Some council houses cost R11,000 initially to build; the same families have been paying rent for 20 years but now suddenly owe R30,000 in arrears! The Campaign Committee wants to know how it is possible that such calculations are arrived at.

The Campaigns Committee supports the actions of the Concerned Citizens Group of Chatsworth in occupying the Durban Unicity Council offices yesterday in a protest against water cuts, and also supports the Johannesburg Anti-Privatisation Forum which is marching from Orlando Stadium on 21 March.

Chapter 10

'Free Water' as Commodity: The Paradoxes of Durban's Water Service Transformations

Alex Loftus

In September 2002, an article in the *Johannesburg Sunday Times* declared a 'torrent of praise for water man' Neil Macleod, the executive director of eThekwini Water Services (eTWS).[1] The paper went on to extol his tremendous efforts and ingenuity 'in turning around Durban's water woes' (Horner 2002). eThekwini Municipality's own publication, *METRObeat*, 'saluted' Macleod and his department for having transformed the city's crumbling water network and having ensured that 'Durban leads the way in providing one of the most basic necessities of life: water' (*METRObeat* 2002). Both articles were media responses to an award presented to Macleod by the American magazine *National Geographic*, along with the enormous praise he had received from both the South African government and other international agencies from around the world. Studies by the Water, Engineering and Development Centre (WEDC) at Loughborough University (PDG 2000), Palmer Development Group (DWAF 2001) and the World Bank (2001) have also marvelled at the municipal utility.

Praise is normally directed at the utility's vision and dynamism in responding to the needs of the urban poor while simultaneously being able to recover costs – Durban is said to be 93 per cent effective at full cost recovery (DWAF 2001) – and reduce overall demand for water. To some extent there has become something of a cult of the Durban example and the individual at its helm. Both are seen to be offering hope to other public sector providers around the world. To many, they seem to provide evidence that the state is not the unresponsive dinosaur talked of by neoliberal analysts. Instead, it can innovate, modernize and respond to consumer concerns as well as be efficient, cost-conscious and fiscally austere. To some, it has become the ideal commercialized public utility.

While accepting many of the positive gains that have taken place in Durban, this chapter goes beneath the sheen to reveal the troubled waters below. I argue, in particular, that the introduction of the free basic water policy within the city has paradoxically been a mixed blessing. While guaranteeing a minimum amount of water per month to all households, the free water policy has also resulted in a rise in the surveillance of supplies and the imposition of severe restrictions on the amount a family is able to consume. This situation has been greatly exacerbated by the structural constraints in which the municipality finds itself. On the one hand the commercialization of the city's bulk supplier (Durban buys all its supplies of water from Umgeni Water – a former water board – which subsequently has an enormous influence over the final costs of water in the city) and on the other the haunting spectre of privatization have had a profound influence on the shape and direction of eTWS's policies. Thus, twin logics – one paternalistic, the other commercial – run through all new developments within Durban's water services. As these logics intertwine and diverge they threaten to tear apart what seems on the surface to be a step towards greater equity in the shape of a free basic water policy.

This research is based on in-depth case studies in three contrasting but neighbouring areas of the city: KwaMashu, Mzinyathi and Inanda. KwaMashu is a large township constructed in the early 1960s after the eviction of families from Cato Manor. Its formal layout has been serviced with water from the time of construction. Inanda is a large informal settlement, comprising 33 distinct communities. It brims with political history and had a strong and autonomous anti-apartheid youth movement in the late 1980s which was targeted by both the Inkatha Freedom Party and the apartheid authorities (Hemson 1996). Here, water services are being introduced at differing levels of service, from standpipes to household connections. Mzinyathi lies on the banks of the Inanda dam and consists of dispersed, round mud huts. Individual ground tanks (one of the municipality's supposed innovations, discussed later) have been introduced since 2001. All three areas have extremely high levels of unemployment and poverty.

In KwaMashu, three community workshops were held over water issues in Section C of the township. These were structured as focus group interviews with participants discussing their ability to access water, how this has changed historically and how they felt it could be transformed in the future. Space was opened up for as much participation as possible and the meetings were driven by the issues highlighted by participants. All responses were summarized at the end of the workshops and they were followed up with in-depth household interviews. In Inanda, community workshops were held in Amaoti, Bhambayi and Amatikwe. Again these were followed up with in-depth household interviews. In Mzinyathi, households were randomly sampled in an area recently targeted with a large water project and in-depth interviews conducted with members of the households living there. The number of participants in the community workshops ranged from 50 in KwaMashu to ten in Bhambayi. In all five areas (including the three in Inanda), at least 20 follow-up household interviews were conducted. I also interviewed the councillors of all these areas and when possible met with the ward committees and civic organizations or development forums currently operating in the area. I also integrated some random individual sampling in each area, conducting interviews at standpipes and interviews with next-door neighbours of those who had been at the community workshops rather than the actual participants in some cases. Supplementary interviews were conducted with senior managers at eTWS and within the municipal bureaucracy.

This range of techniques gives a particularly detailed picture of what residents feel about their water services. This is in marked contrast to much of the media spin which relied on interviews with a few senior managers at eTWS. I begin, however, with the media's spin on Durban's successes to provide an outline of what are, undeniably, some of the important service delivery gains that have been made in the city.

Durban's 'Spin'

Durban Metro Water Services is widely understood to have been one of the pioneers, if not *the* pioneer of the free basic water policy in South Africa. In a press statement issued on 13 October 2000, soon after President Mbeki's announcement of the government's intention of providing free water to all households, the Minister for Water Affairs, Ronnie Kasrils, highlighted Durban as one of the best case examples, offering hope to other municipalities throughout South Africa. Kasrils stated that Durban proved the feasibility of free basic water and showed that such a radical policy could make sound financial sense (Kasrils 2000a). The development of this policy in Durban now seems to have become a part of international water folklore,[2] having been recounted in several research reports (Macleod 1997; PDG 2000; DWAF 2001; World Bank 2001). It has been told so many times to budding researchers by the main protagonists that it is difficult to detach real fact from embellished fact.

In retrospect, as Macleod and others are keen to stress, one of the key moments in the beginning of Durban's journey to a free water policy was the development of a ground tank system in informal areas. This allowed a fixed amount of water (200 l per household per day) to be delivered at a relatively low cost to shack areas in the municipality. Initially, residents were charged for the service but the municipality soon realized that the cost of charging individual households outweighed the revenue generated. It was therefore cheaper to provide the service for free.

Looking at the rest of the municipality and the costs involved in disconnecting households, it was judged on the grounds of both economic efficiency and universal fairness that the service should be extended to all consumers within the municipality (interview, Reg Bailey, 5 September 2002; interview, Dom Magubane, 9 September 2002). Thus, 6 kilolitres (kl) per household per month (200 l per day), fixed by the size of the ground tank (and based on an early estimate of the amount of water used by the average household in an informal settlement) became the fixed free water figure in Durban.[3]

Durban has been keen to innovate medium- and low-tech options for the provision of water to poorer areas of the city. It has experimented with water kiosks, water bailiffs, ground tanks, semi-pressure systems, flow limiting devices, flow restricting devices and free water standpipes. Not all of these are home-grown Durban developments; however, the large number of technological experiments attest to the dynamism of individuals within the company (many cite Macleod's vision, although Macleod himself is keen to point to the

Table 10.1 Charges in rand/kl of water consumed as of July 2003

Monthly consumption	Ground tank Low pressure	Roof tank Semi-pressure system	Domestic Full pressure	Industrial, commercial and other users
0–6 kl	nil	nil	nil	5.72
6–30 kl	n/a	3.81	5.72	5.72
>30 kl	n/a	11.45	11.45	5.72
Fixed charge	nil	nil	0–44.71	39.22–4,471.08

inventiveness of former Director, Roy Pinkerton). They are also, perhaps, a sign of the austere environment in which the utility is forced to operate. I will discuss the constraints imposed by the bulk supplier, Umgeni Water, later in this chapter, but it is worth noting here that the pressure to reduce costs, recover costs, lower demand and extend the network to outlying areas has forced eTWS to innovate.

Another technical solution to water provision has been the introduction of a more progressive block tariff on water prices. The current tariff structure (calculated over a 30-day period) is outlined in Table 10.1. Partly through such a tariff mechanism, the city has been able to reduce and stabilize demand for water at 1995 levels. It has also been able to extend the network to 100,000 new households through both the ground tank and semi-pressure tank system (Horner 2002; *METRObeat* 2002; interview, Neil Macleod, 26 March 2003). eTWS also replaced much of the decaying network in the city's townships, thereby dramatically reducing unaccounted-for water (UFW). In one section of KwaMashu, daily consumption was reduced from 25,000 kl to 17,000 kl because of the improvements to infrastructure and the targeting of illegal connections (*METRObeat* 2002).

Macleod has likened the process to a 'military operation' (Horner 2002), a metaphor that seems particularly apt when one considers some of the measures the municipality has adopted to ensure that all those who benefit from the improved service abide by its payment plans. The municipality's *METRObeat* publication referred to the operation as 'plugging the flow' – another pertinent observation for those who have had their supplies 'plugged' to a volume far lower than they were once receiving.

Interestingly, eTWS's innovative approach has also received the attention of private sector providers. From 1998, French multinational water provider Vivendi has been engaged in two phases of a trisector partnership with eTWS, originally under the Business Partners for Development KwaZulu-Natal pilot project (see Lumsden and Loftus 2003). Although Vivendi's initial hope of gaining a contract out of their dealings with the municipality was clearly one of the main motivations for the partnership, the knowledge it is gaining from working with eTWS in informal areas is also now seen as a major commercial asset in bidding for contracts in other cities in the South. There is also clearly more than a smattering of good public relations to be gained from such a 'benevolent' venture.

BENEATH THE SPIN: FROM DISCONNECTIONS TO RESTRICTIONS

Having outlined some of the progressive steps Durban has been able to make in improving water access for the urban poor, I turn now to some of the serious problems being experienced by households in the case study areas. The central theme running through this discussion is the pressure being placed on households to restrict their water supply. In spite of the free water policy, many households have amassed large water payment arrears and continue to receive large bills from the municipality. The harsh response from the municipality towards those who have consumed more than they can afford is then couched in terms of 'helping' families to regulate their own household supplies by reducing their bills. Because poor families tend to be those who have problems paying their water bills, these restrictive measures have, almost without exception, targeted the poor.

As with most other municipalities across South Africa, water disconnections have provoked some of the greatest post-apartheid resentment in the country (McDonald and Pape 2002). In Durban, the problem of disconnections came to light dramatically in a court case between the Durban Transitional Metropolitan Council and Christina Manquele. With assistance from the newly formed Concerned Citizens Forum, Manquele, a 35-year-old mother of seven from Chatsworth, argued that the council's disconnection of her water supply was a breach of her right to water as enshrined in the 1997 Water Services Act. The case went to court in 2001 and at first, with the municipality being ordered to reinstate Manquele's water supply, it looked like she would win her case. However, in its final judgement, the court argued that, because she had 'chosen' not to limit herself to the council's free water allowance and, moreover, had tried to reconnect illegally, Manquele had forgone any right to water.[4] Immediately after the case, the municipality stated that, even though it had won and thereby ensured its right to be able to disconnect, it would not disconnect supplies any more but would merely restrict individual households to the free basic allowance through the installation of flow restrictors or 'tricklers'.

The situation is now somewhat blurred. Several households visited during the course of this research (and a primary school in Inanda) *were* physically disconnected from the water supply for nonpayment at the time of the research (January to May 2003). Repeatedly, however, when I followed these cases up with either the management at eTWS or with the internal department responsible for 'account management', they argued this was impossible. The bailiffs had been instructed to insert restrictors and not disconnect.[5] To avoid undue criticism, however, I will assume these disconnections are anomalies. This will also allow me to enter into a more in-depth discussion of the effects of the 'fairer' policy of restricting supplies.

Since the development of a free water policy, eTWS has channelled much of its efforts into ensuring poor households limit their consumption to this free water allowance (and sometimes a level somewhere below this because of the unreliable methods of measurement used) or to a level that households might regard as affordable. In effect, the provision of this lifeline supply of free water has provided something of a moral justification for disconnections and restrictions and helped to fend off criticisms and reduce the likelihood of community mobilizations. It was this moral position that allowed the municipality to declare a victory in the Manquele case and deflect criticisms that it was acting in an unduly harsh manner.

Flow restrictors, or 'tricklers', are the most common way of restricting water use. They consist of a simple disc with a narrow hole in the middle, which dramatically reduces the diameter of pipes at the meter, thus restricting the flow to a daily level that approximates the free water allowance. Such a method is notoriously unreliable, however, being determined to a large extent by the ambient water pressure (which is often quite low in township areas). A prime example of this (and representative of many other cases) is shown by a household in KwaMashu C. Here, the household head had entered into an agreement with eTWS to have her water supply restricted (after having received several threatening letters from the municipality about her payment arrears). She is now receiving less than 2 kl per month, despite the fact that her tap is left open for the vast majority of the day in order to collect water. She describes the situation:

> *It takes about one hour to fill 10–15 litres. In some houses it's a little better but in others it's just as bad. I just put a big bucket under the tap and hold water in this. I flush the toilet with water from my washing. I did go to the Metro about this but they took no notice. I applied for it [the restrictor] myself but didn't know it would be like this. Other people just open it in their own way [through acts of vandalism] but I'm scared to do this myself.*

Such situations emphasize the contradictions of eTWS's current policy, whereby residents are forced to restrict their water supplies to a level that is threatening to their own personal health. Community workshops reported many similar situations. Some residents noted how they would leave the house for an hour and return to find the bucket they had left under the tap still not full. Others discussed the difficulties of dividing such a small amount of water among all household tasks. Others noted the disparities between the levels the trickler was meant to provide and the actual amount received.

In an interview with Macleod in early 2003, he confirmed that 800 to 1000 'disconnections'[6] were taking place across the municipality daily, amounting to roughly 4000–5000 per week, affecting as many as 25,000 people. Some of these households have their flow restored, but the problem of underconsumption of water due to water restrictors is clearly widespread in Durban.

'Flow limiters' offer a more advanced (but often even less reliable) alternative. These operate electronically and shut the flow off to an individual household after a certain volume has been delivered. Several of the households interviewed understood this device to be working on a timer, shutting off the supply at 9:00 in the morning for example (interviews, KwaMashu C). In fact, the limiter was restricting supplies to 200 l per day and shutting water flow off after this has been consumed. The breakdown in communication as to how the system was operating was creating its own set of problems for residents as they rushed to consume what was actually a volumetric measurement, creating an early cutoff time.

Both the flow limiters and flow restrictors are far more prevalent in formal township areas than in the informal areas or new subsidized housing developments in the city. But households in formal townships have received a piped supply of water for far longer than most others, so the anger and resentment is often more forthright. Community meetings were frequently more explosive with households in these areas, demanding answers to their questions over bills, restrictions and disconnections. The following quotes capture some of this anger and anguish:

> *They can't put me in jail . . . can't put me in jail. They told me to pay 70 something. They will think we've been playing with the water. My pension is R600 and the bill is R400. How can I pay this?*

> *I'm the only person who deals with it and I'm a pensioner. Yes, we were disconnected once for a long time and borrowed water from neighbours. I have been to the Metro in KwaMashu to discuss bills. We're just washing ourselves and flushing the toilet. Before it wasn't really an issue how much you used. Now I'm trying to think of the 1000s. I don't know what I'll do about the high bills.*

Payment problems were some of the most common at meetings. Again, this is the reason generally cited by the municipality for having to restrict supplies. It is true, from billing records, that some in KwaMashu C are consuming much more than the average throughout Durban (and as a result much more than they can afford). This is somewhat curious though, given the lack of gardens, swimming pools or cars. Much of the higher consumption can be attributed to larger household sizes. It should also be noted that census data often fails to reflect true household size because of the highly mobile populations. Thus, some families are falling into the 12–30 kl per month tariff block and others are even falling into the 30 kl and above block. As a result, they find that their bills rapidly get out of hand. One township family had amassed arrears of R30,000 and many examples of arrears of over R10,000 were encountered. The large increases in rates above 30 kl hit these residents incredibly hard, and with many lacking any income or relying on a meagre pension, the situation becomes impossible. To put this in context, 54 per cent of households in KwaMashu C have an income of less than R18,000 per year, and 12 per cent lack any income. Problems are compounded by the leaky plumbing many have within their properties. Although the municipality offers the service of a plumber to inspect for leaks for R200, this is well beyond the means of many households. The newly imposed restrictions are also creating a strange catalytic effect on the bills of others. Rather than simply creating a problem for individual households to have to deal with, households have to beg, borrow or steal water from others in order to have any access. This pushes the bills of other residents up and creates a spiral of arrears in which more and more find themselves having to manage an escalating household debt.

In an interview, Macleod argued that these problems remained ones of 'a culture of entitlement in which people don't respect the economic value of water' (interview, 26 March 2003). There is little evidence to support such claims and it is interesting to note that Macleod bases many of his views on anecdotal evidence such as the prevalence of mobile phones in townships, suggesting to him that residents can afford to pay for water but refuse to do so. More detailed, participatory research of the sort carried out for this project reveals a different picture – one in which poorer residents are painfully aware of the economic value of water but unable to cope with the rising arrears they have amassed.

For the moment, the greatest of these problems are felt by residents of formal townships. The difference in most informal areas and new, subsidized housing projects is that supplies are automatically regulated because of the mode of delivery being installed. Almost without exception, residents in these areas will get their water from a free water standpipe, a ground tank or a semi-pressure tank. Although not explicitly developed to provide a more limited quantity of water to poorer households, the semi-pressure tank has this effect by reducing the pressure of the water to households and restricting the volume that can be obtained over a certain period. The ground tank (when operating as intended) limits household consumption to a fixed 200 l per day allowance. Free water standpipes limit consumption because of the limited capacity of the human body to carry loads of water.

Relationships between eTWS and its Bulk Water Provider

People, Planet, Profit, (Umgeni Water's 'triple bottom line', Umgeni Water 2002, p1).

We turn now to look at the broader context within which eTWS operates; specifically, its relationship with its bulk water supplier, Umgeni Water. Here, I argue that the structural constraints imposed by Umgeni ensure that progressive developments for poorer residents will fail.

Since 1983, Durban has been required to buy its water supplies from the Umgeni Water Board. Ostensibly created to mediate between different users of the Umgeni River basin, this water board has acquired substantial powers in determining the tariff Durban will be required to set for end users. Much of the bulk water infrastructure managed by Umgeni Water is actually owned by the national government, which also plays an important role in selecting the members of the board. A complicated relationship has thus developed between the national and local governments with the third party mediator causing many of these problems. Most recently, Umgeni Water has appeared in the national papers owing to a series of corporate scandals and financial mismanagements, and its relationship with the two large municipalities it serves (Durban and Pietermaritzburg) has almost reached breaking point. Tariff increases passed on to the municipalities are largely seen as unjustifiable and more a result of Umgeni's attempts to commercialize than any real increases in the production costs of water.

Throughout much of the last century, the municipality, advised by its City Engineer's Department, fought the creation of a water board to supply its bulk water (see, for example, Kinmont 1959). When the Umgeni Water Board was finally created in the 1970s (with Macleod's father the head of Durban's water services at the time), the entity seemed to have much more to do with the apartheid state's need to justify its Bantustan creations than it did with sound water management. As Macleod is still keen to stress, the decision was clearly political. A third party was needed to intervene in the sale of water to KwaZulu if the future state's independence was not to be revealed as a hollow sham – a state, after all, could not be seen to be buying water from a city. The Umgeni Water Board would fulfil this third party function, in spite of the fact that Durban had built up its own bulk water works over the previous century, with its water engineers attaining local hero status. An excellent example of this is the City Engineer's Department centennial publication, gloriously titled *They Built a City* (Lynski 1982).

After long, drawn-out negotiations, the water board finally acquired all of Durban's bulk water infrastructure in 1983. The amount paid for the works was high and reflected not only the value Durban placed on its bulk water infrastructure but also the bitterness and sense of victimization it felt at the hands of a National Party government it claimed to reject. Initial government investments of the value of Durban's infrastructure put the figure at R13 million but the water board was to pay R274 million (interview, Neil Macleod, 26 March 2003). Not surprisingly, Umgeni was soon in serious debt.

As Durban's townships were then handed over to the KwaZulu administration in 1986, a bizarre system developed. The Umgeni Water Board would sell bulk water supplies to Durban, this would be reticulated through the municipality's network and then, at the newly defined border, water would be sold back to the board so that it could be sold on to the KwaZulu administration. In KwaZulu reticulation would take place through a network that, only a few years previously, had been built and operated by the local municipality.

The anomalous nature of Umgeni acquired even greater meaning as its accounting procedures and investment practices switched from being major revenue earners to huge loss generators. Essentially, the managers proved themselves to be skilled at raising finance but not so skilled at finding productive outlets for investments from the capital they had raised. Periodic crises emerged as it seemed that Umgeni might not be able to keep up its long-term debt repayments. The easiest way out of the periodic slumps it found itself in was to increase bulk water tariffs. The cost of bulk water to Durban began to soar as a result.

Post-apartheid, the 1998 Water Act has allowed water boards to set up commercial subsidiaries. Although these are required to be ringfenced, so that risk is not passed on to the parastatal, often the links are far more blurred. The losses incurred by either the public or the private part can therefore have serious effects on the partner organization. It is largely with this in mind that I refer to the commercialization of Umgeni Water, although its continued ability to access cheap finance on the private markets and its need to service debt repayments on these should be seen as a closely related problem. Thus, still searching for good areas for investment in order to keep up repayments on its long-term debt, Umgeni Water was quick to set up a commercial subsidiary, which – following Mbeki's 'African Renaissance' vision – set about expanding operations into Nigeria. Umgeni Water's stated (and rather over-ambitious, to say the least) aim is to become the 'leading water services provider in the South' (Umgeni Water 2002, p4). By 2002, it had operations planned or functioning in Algeria, Botswana, Ethiopia, Ghana, Lesotho, Malawi and Rwanda (although the vast majority of these were subsequently cancelled at a major loss to Umgeni (Umgeni Water 2003)). Water Minister Ronnie Kasrils praised Umgeni for according so closely with what he understands to be the African Renaissance (Kasrils 2000b) and Umgeni frequently cited the opportunities opened up by the New Partnership for African Development as a major driving force for its imperial ambitions (Umgeni Water 2002, p4). Under radically different national governments, Umgeni Water has thus come to be used as a tool for pursuing quite distinctive political agendas. On top of the international ventures, Umgeni Water has been a major player in the market for rural water contracts in KwaZulu-Natal. These have exacerbated its financial woes still further and provided an additional source of tension with the municipalities who are now responsible for taking over the losses incurred on Umgeni's highly inefficient projects.

With a potentially loss-making commercial venture on top of the anomalous water board, tensions with the municipality increased once again. It began to look like high tariffs at home would be financing the risky commercial ventures abroad. The Durban consumer, some argued, would be held responsible for this risk. When, in 2001, Umgeni Water tried to impose a 22 per cent price increase on bulk water supplies, Durban and Pietermaritzburg rebelled. This, they argued, would lead to a 28 per cent increase to households within their constituencies (Mhlanga 2001), something which neither municipality was able or prepared to bear. The link between Umgeni's faltering investments outside of bulk supply and the increases passed on to Durban is made explicit in the 2001/02 Annual Report for Umgeni, which stated that:

> *It is the costs relating to these rural schemes that have resulted in the 19.5% tariff increase (reduced from the initial 22.3% due to Umgeni Water cost-cutting and efficiency achievements) for the 2001/2002 year. Without the cost burden of these schemes, Umgeni Water would have been able to pass on an increase of 8%* (Umgeni Water 2002, p29).

Part of the subsequent pressure on the municipality to resist these increases came from the threat (whether real or not) that a large number of Durban's textile manufacturers would almost instantly relocate if the tariff increase was imposed (interview, Colin Butler, 17 April 2003). Links between eTWS and the Chamber of Commerce had traditionally not been confrontational and in this instance they seemed able to form an alliance against Umgeni (an alliance which appeared not for the direct benefit of the poorest of the city, it should be noted). Their position was supported by a Halcrow report prepared for eTWS, and mentioned frequently in interviews, which is said to have claimed that a 30 per cent reduction in costs could be passed on to the Durban public if the system was rationalized into a single tier (interview, Neil Macleod, 26 March 2003). The pressure worked and Umgeni was forced into a retreat, lowering the increase to 19.5 per cent and then keeping it fixed to the rate of inflation from then on. On top of this, various threats seem to suggest that its days as a separate utility could be numbered if such financial mismanagement continues. Whispers of a potential rationalization of Durban's bulk water supply into a single tier system began to spread. The ears of Vivendi pricked up once again, as it seemed that a single entity could offer a much more lucrative contract (interview, Eric Tranchent, 5 November 2002).

Nevertheless, eTWS cannot lay all of the blame for unaffordable bills in townships on its bulk water provider. Whereas average bills are undoubtedly higher because of the presence of this semi-commercial bulk water provider (and restrictions therefore more prevalent), there is still greater scope for redistributing the burden of these increases away from the least vulnerable within the municipality through cross-subsidization. The presence of Umgeni has limited the options available to the municipality, but given the acquiescence of eTWS to the demands of industry, as opposed to the needs of poorer residents, Umgeni's dissolution would be unlikely to resolve the affordability crisis of low income households in Durban.

Even though both eThekwini Municipality's city manager and Neil Macleod stated in interviews that they would be in favour of a single entity providing both bulk water and reticulation in the municipality, the fate of Umgeni Water is far from sealed. The arrival of a more conciliatory head at Umgeni, Gugu Moloi, may also mean a more collaborative approach to operations.

THE SPECTRE OF PRIVATIZATION?

Within South Africa's current neoliberal climate both Umgeni Water and eThekwini Water Services are forced to be increasingly competitive. Whereas one strategy available to Umgeni was to attempt to transform itself into a subimperial water multinational, Durban has found itself competing with separate municipalities for the location of textile production and other water intensive industries (Durban also has a large paper mill). eTWS also needs to prove itself against both Umgeni Water and other multinational water providers who are themselves keen to stress that they could do the job of providing water at a lower cost. Privatization is clearly a spectre that haunts. But how real is the threat?

Certainly, in the late 1990s it looked like a major concession contract with a large multinational was a real possibility in the city. The Business Partners for Development pilot project in Inanda and Ntuzuma, begun in 1998, looked like a clear testing of the waters in Durban by Vivendi. A wastewater recycling plant was also constructed by a Vivendi subsidiary as part of a Build, Operate, Own and Transfer (BOOT) contract signed in 1998. As late as 2002, representatives from Vivendi were still talking of the possibility of a major concession contract in Durban (interview, Eric Tranchent, 5 November 2002).

However, much of this threat now seems to have receded, both because of the insecure environment of countries in the South in which many large water multinationals realize they are now operating, and in view of the real possibility that major contracts might collapse in Buenos Aires, Jakarta and other major developing world cities. Potential profits now seem far less secure. In addition to this, senior officials in the private sector are quoted as citing apparent labour militancy in South Africa as a reason for not wishing to enter into further major concession contracts (World Bank 2001).

A final, more subtle factor is associated with the fact that many public service providers have already learnt to act like private sector providers. As a result, for some local councillors, the attraction of a multinational coming to run the water services of Durban has lost much of its shine over the last few years. Both the current city manager and representatives from the water company stated that they could see little or no reason for a major concession contract when they felt that the city's engineers could run the service better on their own (interviews, Reg Bailey, 5 September 2002, 14 February 2003; interview, Mike Sutcliffe, 19 September 2002). The stringent cost recovery measures implemented by eTWS provide ample testimony to this. Instead, corporatization seems to have become something of a sought after 'third way' for the bureaucrats at eThekwini Water Services and city council. Thus, multinationals still act as something against which eTWS appears benchmarked, but the reality of a large privatization contract with such a multinational is distant.

Conclusion

I pondered all these things, and how men fight and lose the battle, and the thing that they fought for comes about in spite of their defeat, and when it comes turns out not to be what they meant, and other men have to fight for what they meant under another name (William Morris).[7]

Durban led the way in South Africa in developing a free basic water policy. The manner in which this has been introduced and the external pressures exerted on the municipality have produced paradoxical results. For some, it has meant the ability to access a free supply of clean water for the first time in their lives. For others, it has meant the escalation of bills, a closer surveillance of the amount consumed and the restriction of supplies to a level barely enough to survive on.

Commercialization has been taking place most overtly in the city's bulk water provision. Here, Umgeni Water has entered into several risky commercial ventures and has fallen back on its bulk water sales to make up any short-term losses. The spectre of privatization and the competitive environment in which both Umgeni Water and eTWS are now having to operate has fostered a business-minded logic that provides little space for the isolated and poor household unable to pay its bill. Within the local state, the need to be both developmental and cheap – while at the same time fostering an environment conducive to industrial investment – has produced its own set of contradictions. The paradoxical effects of the free water policy can thus be seen as an outcome of this particular choreography of power relations. A right to water is thus accompanied with a clampdown on many households' access to water. To some extent, the recognition of this has helped to reconfigure the direction in which some are taking a struggle to ensure their access to water is guaranteed. This implies a shift away from a struggle that fetishizes water yet further and urges a transformation of the social relations that daily reproduce inequality in Durban.

Notes

1 eThekwini Municipality came into being following the amalgamation of former tribal land into the Durban Metropolitan Area on 5 December 2000. This is the functional name given to the entity many people still refer to as Durban. Durban Metro Water Services has thus become eThekwini Water Services.
2 At various water seminars in Oxford, I have found this to be one of the first points around which others will engage, several already having carried out research on the free water story.
3 It soon became the target for municipalities throughout South Africa. It is worth commenting at this stage on the level of the free basic water allowance. Whereas it has some bearing on an early calculation of the needs of residents in an informal settlement, it should in no way be assumed that the needs of all residents in formal townships are the same. As Arrighi (1970, p211) writes:

> *the terms 'necessities' or 'subsistence' are not to be understood in an exclusively physiological sense: people get used to what they consume and 'discretionary' consumption items can, with the mere passage of time, become necessities whose consumption is indispensable.*

Whether 6 kl per month provides sufficient water for the 'physiological' needs of many residents is itself debatable, but it certainly does not fulfil the socially defined needs of the majority of those interviewed.

4 The case is well documented in Ashwin Desai's *We Are the Poors* (2002). See also www.communitylawcentre.org.za/localgov/bulletin2001/2001_1_manquele.php
5 It should be noted that senior managers still consistently referred to 'disconnections'. This could either be a sign of the relatively recent shift in policy or a recognition that the outcome is qualitatively similar.
6 Presumably, he meant by this that tricklers are being put in place.
7 William Morris, from *A Dream of John Ball*, first published in 1887.

REFERENCES

Arrighi, G. (1970) 'Labour Supplies in Historical Perspective: A Study of the Proletarianization of the African Peasantry in Rhodesia', *The Journal of Development Studies*, vol 6, no 3

Desai, A. (2002) *We Are The Poors*, Monthly Review Press, New York

DWAF (Department for Water Affairs and Forestry) (2001) *Free Basic Water Implementation Strategy*, case study, Durban Unicity

Hemson, D. (1996) "For Sure You are Going to Die!' Political Participation and the Comrade Movement in Inanda, KwaZulu-Natal', *Social Dynamics*, vol 22, no 2

Horner, B. (2002) 'Torrent of Praise for Water Man', *Sunday Times*, 22 September

Kasrils, R. (2000a) 'Delivery of free water to the poor', media statement by Ronnie Kasrils, MP, Minister of Water Affairs and Forestry, 13 October

Kasrils, R. (2000b) 'Draft Speech for use by Mr Ronnie Kasrils, MP, Minister of Water Affairs and Forestry for the launch of the commercial sector of Umgeni Water', speech presented at the International Convention Centre, Durban, 10 November

Kinmont, A. (1959) *Report on the Water Supply of Durban*, City Engineers Department, Durban

Lumsden, F. and Loftus, A. (2003) *Inanda's Struggle for Water through Pipes and Tunnels: Exploring State-Civil Society Relations in a Post Apartheid Informal Settlement*, Research Report no 6, University of Natal Centre for Civil Society, Durban

Lynski, R. (1982) *They Built a City – Durban City Engineer's Department 1882–1982*, Concept Communications, Durban

McDonald, D.A. and Pape, J. (2002) *Cost Recovery and the Crisis of Service Delivery in South Africa*, Zed Books, London

Macleod, N.A. (1997) 'Water and Sanitation For All: Partnerships and Innovations – The Durban Water Tank System', paper presented at *23rd WEDC Conference*, Durban, South Africa, September

METRObeat (2002) 'Interview with Neil Macleod' (eThekwini Municipality), September

Mhlanga, E. (2001) 'Durban hit by 28% rise in price of water', *The Mercury*, 29 May

PDG (Palmer Development Group) (2000) *PPP and the Poor in Water and Sanitation. Interim Findings. Case Study: Durban South Africa*, Water, Engineering and Development Centre, Loughborough, UK

Umgeni Water (2002) *Annual Report 2002*, Umgeni Water, Pietermaritzburg

Umgeni Water (2003) *Annual Report 2002/2003*, www.umgeni.co.za/reports/annual/report2003/index.htm

World Bank (2001) *Durban Metro Water: Private Sector Partnerships to Help the Poor. A Case Study*, Water and Sanitation Programme, www.wsp.org/publications/af_durban.pdf

INTERVIEWS

Reg Bailey, Acting Manager, Research and Development, eThekwini Water Services, 5 September 2002, 29 November 2002, 14 February 2003
Dom Magubane, Community Liaison Officer, eThekwini Water Services, 9 September 2002
Neil Macleod, Executive Director, eThekwini Water Services, 26 March 2003
Colin Butler, Durban Chamber of Commerce, 17 April 2003
Eric Tranchent, Project Manger, Vivendi, 5 November 2002 (conducted by Fiona Lumsden)
Michael Sutcliffe, City Manager, eThekwini Municipality, 19 September 2002

COMMUNITY WORKSHOPS

Amaoti, 16 January 2003
Amatikwe, 26 January 2003
Bhambayi, 6 March 2003
KwaMashu Section C, 3 March, 10 March, 20 May 2003

HOUSEHOLD INTERVIEWS

Conducted throughout Amaoti, Amatikwe, Bhambayi, KwaMashu C and Mzinyathi over the period January to May 2003.

Box 5 *The Phiri Water Wars of 2003*
Trevor Ngwane, Anti-Privatisation Forum

The Anti-Privatisation Forum (APF), a coalition of several dozen groups on the Witwatersrand, South Africa, grew out of campaigns to resist the City of Johannesburg's attempts to privatize and corporatize services and a general shift of public bodies towards harsh commodified service delivery. The APF came together in July 2000 when many different organizations – the Anti-iGoli 2002 Committee, the South African Municipal Workers' Union, education workers, NGOs, students and the South African Communist Party – felt that privatization (broadly understood as intensified capitalism) was creating intolerable conditions for the poor and working class. Protestors held parallel meetings alongside a big international conference on 'Urban Futures' and resolved that: 'Everyone here has decided that privatization is bad, and wants to do something to fight it.'

The main campaigns fought by the APF have been around water, electricity, evictions and solidarity with striking workers. With a central office in downtown Johannesburg, the APF is linked to affiliated groups in different communities. In the Vaal, to the south, for instance, there is the Bophelong Community Forum, the Working-Class Community Coordinating Committee and three others. In the east, the Kathorus Concerned Residents and the Vosloorus and Daveyton Peace Committee Civic have engaged Ekurhuleni Metro Council. The Johannesburg cluster includes Soweto and Orange Farm, the Thembelihle Committee and two affiliates in Alexandra, while three new affiliates come from the North West Province. The APF also sees its role as trying to organize regional solidarity committees so that people can come out to support each other when they hear of an eviction or a water cutoff.

The disparate struggles against water privatization in Johannesburg and other areas of the country then took on a broader scope with the formation of the 'Coalition against Water Privatisation' in 2003. The Coalition has a particular focus: to oppose a certain type of water marketization, prepaid meters.

The Phiri struggle

In the early morning of 22 August 2003, braving the Soweto cold, a group of residents of Matilili Street, Phiri, gathered in the street to share their concerns. They were all at a loss about what to do about the imminent installation of prepaid water meters in their community. New pipes were laid under the streets and over the following weeks water would be diverted from the old leaky system to the new circuit: the cash nexus, the prepaid meter, would confront residents. But many people struggle to make ends meet in this part of Soweto. Many households depend on a senior citizen's government pension to keep body and soul together. Someone suggested that they contact the Soweto Electricity Crisis Committee for help.

A delegation arrived at the Johannesburg offices and soon a comrade was promptly on his way to Phiri; his mission was to help residents organize a mass meeting to find a way forward. In the social movements in South Africa it is standard to call a mass meeting, an assembly of local people to share ideas and experiences to find a common way forward. The meeting resolved to resist the prepaid meters with a protest planned for the following day at the piping trenches in Phiri. Police and private security forces arrived to enforce the testing of Johannesburg Water's prepaid meters experiment on the poor (see Harvey, Chapter 6, this volume). By the end of day one of this encounter at least ten people had been arrested.

The first meeting of the full Coalition, a month later, discussed these events and resolved to do everything possible to support the struggle in Phiri because water is a right and everyone should have enough of it; secondly, if the project succeeded in Phiri it would be installed in the whole of Soweto (over 180,000 households) and elsewhere in the country.

One of the Coalition's activities was to conduct research into prepaid meters; large surveys were conducted in Orange Farm and Phiri, demonstrating widespread resistance to, and dissatisfaction with, the prepaid meter system.

Mass mobilization also remains a key and the Coalition's approach is based on the view that the struggle cannot be won in Phiri alone, or on the issue of water alone. There is a constant exploration for new allies on issues being addressed by the Coalition as it builds the campaign to support the Soweto Water Warriors and all peoples facing water deprivation. On 21 March 2004, Human Rights Day, the Coalition organized a protest to coincide with the opening of the new Constitutional Court, the supposed ultimate institutional guarantor of human rights in South Africa. The Coalition wanted to point out the hypocrisy of a country with a constitution which, unprecedented amongst the world's nations, guarantees socioeconomic rights to its citizens but which denies many people their right to clean water, the most basic resource to sustain life. The Coalition also wanted to highlight the increasingly intolerant attitude of authorities to criticism and dissent as exemplified by Johannesburg Water's paid advertisements branding those who resist prepaid meters as criminals and opposed to development.

Chapter 11

The Rise and Fall of Water Privatization in Rural South Africa: A Critical Evaluation of the ANC's First Term of Office, 1994–1999

Stephen Greenberg

On coming to power in 1994, the first democratically elected government in South Africa was faced with a daunting task of developing and implementing a systematic programme of rural water delivery almost from scratch. Apartheid had created distorted rural settlement patterns, with scattered rural settlements in areas far from resources. A large number of Africans in rural areas had no formal water supply. In 1993 it was estimated that some 8 million rural residents lacked an adequate water supply and some 14 million did not have access to adequate sanitation (SAIRR 1994, pp253–54). Figures from 1990 indicate that as little as 25 per cent of the population had access to formal water supply in KwaZulu-Natal and the Transkei (SAIRR 1994, p354).

Just under half of the current South African population is categorized as rural. Figures from the mid-1990s show that 15 per cent of the rural population lived in rural towns, approximately 25–30 per cent lived on white-owned commercial farms and the remaining 55 per cent lived in the former homelands. In the latter group, the majority lived in dense settlements that were in effect rural ghettos (see DBSA 1994; Rural Development Task Team/Department of Land Affairs 1997). Since that time, some urbanization has taken place, but there is also a trickle of return migration of retrenched workers especially from the mines. The population around small towns living in informal settlements has swelled as farm workers are retrenched or evicted.

More than 70 per cent of the rural population live in poverty (Rural Development Task Team/Department of Land Affairs 1997, p18) and incomes are largely derived from dwindling remittances from wage earners working in urban areas, and from government grants and subsidies (May 1996). In the former homelands, artificial economies were created on the back of government bureaucracies. But the gradual dismantling of these bureaucracies in the post-apartheid era has meant the decline of homeland economies and a resultant population movement out of these areas.

Water supply to rural areas is differentiated according to the type of settlement. Rural ghettos in the former homelands, informal settlements on the edges of rural towns, commercial farms and scattered villages in the deep rural areas all require different types of water supply and different technologies to bring clean water to the population. Rural water supply was one of the key programmes of the new government's Reconstruction and Development Programme (RDP). The need for a visible, fast and large-scale delivery meant that many of what became the RDP Phase I Presidential Lead Projects were based on projects the apartheid government was already considering prior to 1994: 'Plans that had been shelved by apartheid-era consultants were dusted off and resurrected' (interview, Martin Rall, 19 February 2001). In the second and third years of the RDP programme, a more systematic approach drawing on provincial and district level structures arose.

This chapter provides a critical perspective on the African National Congress's (ANC) first term of office (1994–1999) and its experiences with water service delivery and extension in the rural areas. The first section of the chapter looks at the official statistics on water delivery in this period and deconstructs what would appear on the surface to be a highly successful roll-out programme. I then look at the policies of commercialization and privatization that accompanied this first-stage roll-out of services, with a particular focus on the Build, Operate, Train and Transfer (BOTT) system that was employed as well as the underlying policies of cost recovery. These policies have served to undermine both the depth and the quality of water service extension to rural areas and raise troubling questions about the sustainability of a commercialized approach to water delivery in rural areas in particular and South Africa more generally.

DECONSTRUCTING OFFICIAL STATISTICS

By November 2000, the official tally of rural people receiving water from *new* government sponsored schemes stood at almost 6.5 million (DWAF 2000b). Water supply to rural areas was seen as one of the most successful development achievements of the new government. Yet there was considerable unease just below the surface as questions about the accuracy of the figures were raised. Despite a multibillion rand programme, and after six years of implementation, there was no systematic monitoring and evaluation of programmes in place.

The official numbers need careful consideration. First, where do they come from? Second, what exactly do they reflect?

The first question is about the way that the totals are reached. Methodologically, calculations of beneficiary populations were likely to be inaccurate. For the first water supply projects at least, the estimated beneficiaries were based on inaccurate apartheid census figures. Once a project was completed, the full number of people in the area was simply added to the total of beneficiaries receiving a water supply, regardless of whether all the people were actually getting water from the system, or whether the population figures were accurate (Hemson 2000, p49). In this way, the number of beneficiaries leapt by tens or hundreds of thousands each time a new bulk supply project was completed.

A simple example will show how problematic this can be. The Vulindlela Presidential Lead Project in KwaZulu-Natal aimed to supply water to 250,000 people. In 1999, the Department of Water Affairs and Forestry (DWAF) claimed that the project was already serving 200,000 of these people, based on the infrastructure already in place. Yet only 2700 of the 4500 households that had paid had actually been connected (Sirenya 1999). Using an average of eight people per household, just over one-tenth of the total planned beneficiaries were actually receiving any water from the scheme. The figures are therefore inaccurate if 'beneficiaries served' means the actual number of people getting water. In addition, the consultants tasked with carrying out the projects, rather than community members, provided DWAF with the figures. This opened up the distinct possibility of artificial inflation, according to Dr Charles Reeve, Project Officer with the European Union's Water and Sanitation Delegation in South Africa and member of DWAF's Monitoring and Evaluation Unit (interview, 12 February 2001).

The second question is about what is being measured. The numbers could reflect the potential number of people being reached by the water supply projects, or the *actual* number. The supply could refer to a standpipe a kilometre from a person's home, or it could be a tap in the house. Beneficiaries might be satisfied with their levels of service or dissatisfied. The figures make no distinction between these variations. DWAF's totals reflected the number of people for whom infrastructure had been built. Whether people were actually getting water, how much and how regularly was ignored (interview, Charles Reeve, 12 February 2001). In short, the state has claimed to have 'supplied water' where only bulk infrastructure has been supplied, reservoirs and dams have been built, and where reticulation to houses or standpipes was yet to be built.

At the start of 2001, the claims that 6.5 million people had access to Reconstruction and Development Programme (RDP) levels of service included well over 500,000 people provided *only* with bulk infrastructure. This was especially so in the Northern Province. Moreover, at least 1.5 million people who were being served by El Niño drought relief measures at *below* RDP minimum levels were also added into the total (interview, Charles Reeve, 12 February 2001).

At the start of 2000, when the official number of beneficiaries stood at 4.88 million people, Ronnie Kasrils, the Minister of Water Affairs and Forestry, had given a breakdown of rural people served since 1994. He said that 1.65 million people were receiving lower than RDP short-term levels, 2.63 million people were receiving service at RDP short-term levels, and that 600,000 people had access to bulk infrastructure but no reticulation as yet (Kasrils 2000a). Hence, only 46 per cent of the supposed beneficiaries, even according to official totals, had access to infrastructure that *potentially* could provide them with RDP minimum or better levels of service. Even where people were actually getting water from the system the figures also assume that 100 per cent of people in newly supplied areas were receiving 100 per cent of their water from the schemes. But this is not the case, further reducing the totals.

Other official sources reveal a different picture from DWAF's. These sources measure *actual* access to water rather than *potential* access. The annual October

Table 11.1 *Number and percentage of non-urban African households with selected water supply, 1996–1999*

Main source of water	1996 '000s	1996 %	1997 '000s	1997 %	1998 '000s	1998 %	1999 '000s	1999 %
Reticulated onsite	702	20.9	800	23.4	897	25.7	1080	27.2
Reticulated public tap (communal standpipe)	1149	34.3	1060	31.0	1045	30.0	1243	31.4
Borehole onsite	105	3.10	89	2.6	73	2.1	83	2.1
Borehole communal	243	7.20	284	8.3	250	7.2	260	6.6
Water carrier/rainwater tank	105	3.10	94	2.7	128	3.7	107	2.6
Natural sources*	1041	31.0	1044	30.5	1030	29.6	1108	28.0
Total households**	3354	100.0	3424	100.0	3484	100	3961	100.0

Source: October Household Surveys, Statistics South Africa
*Natural sources are flowing water/stream, dam, pool, well or spring
**Includes 'other' or 'unspecified'

Household Survey (conducted by the government's statistical service) provides a richer overview of rural water delivery since 1996. Table 11.1 shows a slow increase in reticulated onsite supply, and an almost constant one-third of rural households relying on water sources other than reticulated water or water from boreholes. The percentage of households relying on alternative supplies showed only a very slow decline from 1996 to 1999, taking into account population increase.

THE RISE OF WATER PRIVATIZATION IN RURAL AREAS

In 1997, DWAF was concerned that at the rate water provision was going it would take 30 years to meet the basic water supply backlog. A 'rapid delivery infrastructure programme' in line with the wider government approach to public–private partnerships (PPPs) saw DWAF bring in the private sector to carry out the rural water supply programme (DWAF 1997, p1). The contractual framework for this was the BOTT programme. The programme was designed around the private sector, with companies organizing themselves into consortia to bid for provincial contracts. Thus Amanz'abantu Services in the Eastern Cape, AquaAmanzi in KwaZulu-Natal, the Consultburo Consortium in Mpumalanga and Metsico in Northern Province signed BOTT contracts in July 1997 (*Business Day*, 14 July 1997). These consortia gained a monopoly over rural water supply programmes in these provinces, controlling 300 out of a total of 357 projects.

Before 1997, the private sector had done construction work, but was kept out of operation or management of water services. Then-Minister of Water Affairs and Forestry, Kader Asmal, said the BOTT contracts showed that 'the technical capacity of the private sector can be tapped in a variety of ways without jeopardising public ownership or social infrastructure' (*Business Day*, 14 July 1997).

BOTT was initiated from the top, without community input, raising fears that communities would resist working with the appointed consultants (RSS 1997, p23). While the BOTT process was being set up, all other initiatives were halted, making matters worse. Existing projects then had to be reorganized to fit into the BOTT framework (DWAF 1998a, p15). DWAF Head Office designed the BOTT programme without regional stakeholder inputs; regions were kept in the dark about how BOTT would operate or be implemented. Misunderstandings and distrust arose from the outset (DWAF 1998a, p4). DWAF also failed to create systems for monitoring the contracts before signing them. The impression was that 'BOTT was created in a vacuum and then dropped into a void' (DWAF 1998a, p27). Numerous studies and evaluations concluded that BOTT fell short of 'rapid delivery' expectations (see, for example, Mvula Trust 1997a,b,c; DWAF 1998a; ERT 1998; Hemson and Bakker 1999).

For critics of the programme, BOTT was deemed more expensive than publicly provided services and was blamed for skewing development priorities by introducing a profit motive (Hemson 1999). In KwaZulu-Natal, DWAF's regional office raised concerns that the unit cost per borehole was significantly higher than would have been the case if the regional office or traditional implementing agents had managed construction. More generally, it pointed out that: 'It is a given that projects executed using the BOTT process will cost more than had the non-BOTT process been used' (DWAF 1998a, p8). Cost overruns on the Nqutu Phase I, Ndatshana and Emanjokwane BOTT projects, for example, reached 154 per cent, 55 per cent and 337 per cent, respectively, at a combined value of over R10,856,000 (DWAF 1998a, p30).

An external evaluation team suggested that the reduced throughput meant 'the process had become more expensive raising issues of value for money' (ERT 1998, p36). According to Martin Rall, Managing Director of Mvula Trust (a nongovernmental agency involved in water delivery in rural areas): 'The cost per capita of BOTT projects stood at around R1600 compared to Mvula costs for similar projects of R400 per capita' (interview, Martin Rall, 19 February 2001). Rall suggested that the reasons for this included built-in clauses on inflation and preliminary and general (P&G) costs.[1] 'DWAF created a vehicle to spend a lot of money quickly, but it hasn't been fed and thus lots of money has been spent just to keep the vehicle going', said Charles Reeve, referring to the P&G costs. 'BOTT became a pull on other resources when the budget was cut back in 1998' (interview, Charles Reeve, 12 February 2001).

The external evaluation of BOTT, by a team including World Bank staff, pointed to the potential for 'cost-padding', stating that 'the absence of competition after the PIA [project implementing agency] has been selected may serve to increase costs' (ERT 1998, p43). Secondly, the schemes allowed involvement of the private sector at highly inflated rates. The private companies carried very little risk, and did not commit their own capital (Hemson and Bakker 1999, p10).[2] 'The private sector tends to prefer management contracts with a guaranteed income, like the BOTT programme, because there is a low chance of profiting from water supply if it is based on the risk of cost recovery from local users in rural areas. But why not just build capacity in councils to manage the supply?' asked Martin Rall. Rall argued that 'BOTT was designed to be in favour of the contractors. It was not a valuable experiment, except in what not to do. It was expensive and skewed against government' (interview, Martin Rall, 19 February 2001).

A scathing internal evaluation of the KwaZulu-Natal BOTT consortium pointed to the poor grasp of institutional and social development issues, the fragmented operation of the team (with companies acting separately and in their own interests), and the lack of effective reporting. The evaluation stated: 'In terms of the BOTT objectives, the process has failed in KwaZulu-Natal' (DWAF 1998a, piv). Some, however, felt that BOTT at least allowed the state to spend money (avoiding the problem of rolling over state funds). 'It certainly increased DWAF's capacity to spend', said Charles Reeve. 'The reviews that questioned BOTT were looking at the process rather than the impacts of BOTT' (interview, 12 February 2001).

The role of the private sector in small towns and rural areas grew further when, in March 1999, the state granted a 30-year concession to Siza, a subsidiary of French company Société d'Aménagement Urbain et Rural (SAUR), and partly owned by South African conglomerate Metropolitan Life, to manage and supply water to the town of Dolphin Coast in Northern KwaZulu-Natal. The concession, worth over R500 million in new investments, with half being raised by SAUR and half by South African banks, drew early criticisms. The contracts were signed on terms very favourable to the private sector, leading Charles Reeve to argue that, although there may be advantages in his mind to involving the private sector, 'they mustn't be given too much latitude, as was the case in these concessions. We need to build the ability in local government to sign contracts that are to their advantage' (interview, 12 February 2001). Yet another concession was signed a month later between Nelspruit town council and the Greater Nelspruit Utility Company, which has as its majority shareholders British firm Biwater and local black empowerment group Sivukile Investments. Investments worth R140 million were expected (Hemson and Bakker 1999; see also Smith et al, Chapter 7, this volume).

In 2001, Siza in Dolphin Coast failed to make a scheduled payment to the KwaDukuza municipality, and suggested a hike in water tariffs of 15 per cent because there were too few consumers in the area to recover their costs. Siza general manager Thiery Chatry said: 'The pipes are in place, but the customers aren't there. We need scale to pay the costs of all (our) obligations' (quoted in Simon 2001). Residents of the Dolphin Coast area faced hikes of more than 45 per cent in one year as the cost of bulk water also increased.

Local Government and Water Management in Rural Areas

Alongside more private sector participation in project management and delivery, political oversight was being transferred from DWAF to local government. The Constitution made water services the responsibility of local government.

These functions had to be transferred to elected local councils. But in many rural areas local government had to be built from scratch. With this in mind, targeted capacity building support to local government was included in DWAF's Community Water Supply and Sanitation (CWSS) programme. Local government would take operational responsibility for new water supply schemes together with the community (DWAF 1996, p6). In KwaZulu-Natal, for example, Umgeni Water, a regional water board, sought to transfer responsibilities to local government as soon as this was feasible, with the board returning to a bulk water supply function (see Loftus, Chapter 10, this volume).

Within this context, the actual implementation of the BOTT programme provoked major tensions between local government and the private sector. The uThukela and uMzinyathi Regional Councils in KwaZulu-Natal, for example, claimed they were inadequately consulted about the BOTT process and only received notice about it after the contract was awarded. The councils believe they were forced to provide projects to the BOTT consortium even though they had the capacity to carry them out themselves (DWAF 1998a, p22). The councils reported being dissatisfied with the performance of the consortium, and regarded tariff proposals 'as too high and not conducive to promoting and achieving cost recovery' (DWAF 1998a, pv).

The BOTT contracts required the building of local government capacity, but this was not adequately defined. The overall results of capacity building, according to a DWAF review conducted in 1998, were 'mixed at best and highly disappointing at worst, with poor value for money being obvious in too many cases' (DWAF 1999, p47).

Generally, councils seemed reluctant to accept transfer of existing schemes (DWAF 2000b, p10). An evaluation of the Eastern Cape programme found that 'councils lacking capacity would still need substantial practical support from external sources to meet their obligations to community WS [water and sanitation] schemes' (Pelpola and Reeve 2000, p11). A lot of the infrastructure was in disrepair, yet the local authority was expected to immediately pay full costs for water, even if there were leakages. The result was that 'local government is facing the prospects of inheriting "white elephants" with high price tags' (Breslin 1999, p22). In these circumstances, local government simply refused to take sole responsibility for the schemes (DWAF 1999, p33). The result was that limited transfers actually took place in the provinces of Mpumalanga, North West, KwaZulu-Natal and the Northern Province. There was slightly greater success in the Free State, Eastern Cape and Western Cape (DWAF 2000a). There were no pilots in Gauteng or the Northern Cape provinces.

COST RECOVERY: WHO SHOULD PAY FOR WATER PROVISION?

Financial sustainability relates to the way capital costs and operating and management (O&M) costs are covered. Infrastructure must also be upgraded and renewed over time, and someone must pay for this. This became one of the key questions in water supply: who pays the costs of pipes and taps, maintenance and repairs? Under apartheid, capital costs and O&M were mainly carried by the state via the homeland governments in an effort to legitimize the system. Attempts at cost recovery were half-hearted and universally unsuccessful. Generally, people had to pay an initial fee to get connected, but after that the supply was free or heavily subsidized (McDonald and Pape 2002). Costs were covered in full with central government providing coupons for free diesel, paying for borehole equipment and supplies, pump operators' salaries and equipment repair (Blaxall et al 1996, p9).

DWAF saw this explicit and implicit subsidization as unviable in the long term and adopted a two-pronged cost recovery strategy. The first prong was an attempt to phase out subsidies inherited from former homeland schemes and to transfer responsibility for them to local government. This proved difficult to implement, and despite aiming to make users pay for water supplies, cost recovery remained at extremely low levels, less than 1 per cent of O&M costs for the first phases of the national government's RDP (Kasrils 2000b, p5).

In 1994 the RDP proposed 'a tariff that covers operating and maintenance costs of services for rural areas' (RDP section 2.6.10.3). It also mentioned a lifeline tariff 'to ensure that all South Africans are able to afford water services sufficient for health and hygiene requirements' (RDP section 2.6.10.1), but this was not clearly defined and soon became synonymous with O&M costs. Local users were therefore expected to cover these costs, and infrastructure and water supply was to be limited to what was locally affordable. The 1994 RDP I Business Plan stated that projects would be selected based on acceptance by the recipients that tariffs would cover O&M costs at least (DWAF 1994, p2). It defined financial sustainability as the ability of water supply systems to generate enough income to cover their costs with no financial support from the state (DWAF 1994, p2).

In 1999, revenue from water services stood at just R6.6 million, a fraction of the R690 million costs incurred (DWAF 2000b, p52). The Medium Term Expenditure Framework (MTEF), which indicates government's budgetary plans for the following three years, showed that government would continue augmenting the Water Trading Account in 2002/03 to the tune of R784 million (Department of Finance 2000, p293). This suggested that government was expecting to continue subsidizing a large number of completed projects. To help ease the transfer of refurbished schemes DWAF introduced a schedule of decreasing subsidies to local government over a period of five years, rather than stopping them immediately (ERT 1998, px).

Parallel to this, the Division of Revenue Act made existing subsidies part of the income local councils received from national government. The local council could choose whether to continue subsidizing water, or reduce (or eliminate) the subsidy and use the money for other purposes. In the words of DWAF Director General Mike Muller: 'We are trying to build a culture of choosing between priorities' (comments at Human Sciences Research Council seminar, Pretoria, 13 February 2001). This raised fears that water services, and in particular sanitation, might not be seen as a priority (Makhetha Development Consultants 1999, p7).

The second part of the strategy was to rely on local recovery of some of the capital costs and all of the O&M costs of new projects, so that DWAF would avoid subsidizing any additional schemes. National government would cover the full costs of constructing the basic infrastructure (capital costs) for a communal standpipe. However, this was a once-off grant, with longer-term replacement costs included in the tariff structure. If people wanted a higher level of service, like a yard tap, they had to raise the money themselves. Theoretically, schemes were designed to allow for upgrading. Individuals who wanted higher levels of service such as the RDP's medium-term aim of onsite supply (yard connections or taps in houses) would have to pay for it by taking a loan or by including these costs in the tariff. DWAF saw higher tariffs as an indication of 'a desire [by communities] to improve their basic needs and reach long term goals of the RDP by themselves' (DWAF 1994, p6).

ATTEMPTS TO IMPLEMENT A 'USER PAYS' POLICY

A number of problems cropped up as government implemented its 'user pays' policy. In particular, there were obvious inequities between communities that had to pay on a cost recovery basis for water from new systems and those that received a subsidized supply from former homeland schemes. For example, cost recovery was hampered in the Khunwana water project in North West Province because neighbouring villages were paying less (Mvula Trust 1999a, p13). Insufficient consultation with communities before the start of the projects and recipients being unaware of their responsibility for O&M costs compounded problems (RSS 2000, p18).

A 1998 survey of RDP schemes indicated that for six completed schemes in Mpumalanga there was no cost recovery. In the Eastern Cape, out of 15 completed schemes, only four schemes indicated some cost recovery (ERT 1998, p52). Table 11.2 reveals that more than 80 per cent of rural households still defaulted on water payments after five years of delivery efforts.

In the Izingolweni water project in KwaZulu-Natal prepaid meters were installed but the community was unable to pay. As a result, only 323 of the estimated 7583 households involved in the scheme were actually drawing water

Table 11.2 *Percentage of African non-urban households paying for water, 1995–1999*

Does the household pay for water?	% of total non-urban African households*				
	1995	1996	1997	1998	1999**
Yes	12.9	13.2	15.0	12.5	18.2
Sometimes	4.9	4.5	2.7	3.3	–
No	82.2	87.1	81.4	83.0	81.3

Source: October Household Surveys, Statistics South Africa
* Figures may not total 100% because 'unspecified' has been left out
** 'Yes' and 'Sometimes' responses were merged in the 1999 survey

from the prepaid system. The rest had returned to unprotected sources (Mvula Trust 1999a, p11).

While some people agreed in principle with water tariffs they anticipated periods where they would be unable to pay (RSS 1997, p28). At the KwaDlamini water project west of Estcourt in KwaZulu-Natal, for example, payment levels declined steeply in the months when schools were opening (Mvula Trust 1999b, p32), suggesting that people used money to pay school fees first. In other cases, although people indicated their willingness to pay for water, concerns were raised over a unit price that was higher than initially agreed upon (Mvula Trust 1997c, piv).

Willingness to pay may be linked to knowledge of the O&M requirements of water supply systems. In those projects where people were well informed and prepared, levels of payment were much higher (see, for example, DWAF 1998b). Evidence suggested that communities with no history of paying for water often responded positively to requests for payments without fully understanding the long-term ramifications (ERT 1998, p55). In the Gong Gong water project in the Northern Cape service payments dropped from almost 40 per cent at the start of the project in August 1998, to 18 per cent just a few months later and then no payments by the start of 1999. In many areas, local people argued that it was the government's responsibility to pay for water (DWAF 1998b, p10). In a survey of Kgobokwane, 78 per cent of respondents said they would not be responsible for payment for water delivered by the project, and 87 per cent indicated they were unwilling to pay for yard connections (Mvula Trust 1997b, p12).

LEVELS OF CONSUMPTION, STANDARDS OF SERVICE AND WALKING DISTANCES

The primary aim of the rural water supply programme was to provide basic water supply to RDP short-term standards (25 l per person per day, no more than 200 m from their household) with the ability to upgrade to 60 l per capita per day (lcd). Table 11.3 shows the distance non-urban Africans had to go to fetch water, according to statistics from October Household Surveys between 1996 and 2000. The data indicates a surprisingly slow improvement in access to water measured by distance to the supply. In 1999, about 64 per cent of households had access to water within the RDP short-term distance of 200 m. This is up only slightly from 58 per cent in 1996. Less than a third of African rural households had water in their yards or dwellings by 1999. If one considers that these figures include peri-urban areas, the situation for the deep rural population is likely to be skewed further towards longer distances. (It should be noted that some of the unevenness of data in Table 11.3 could be the result of changing methodologies used by Statistics South Africa (SSA) in gathering information.)

A survey in the Eastern Cape indicated that a majority of respondents felt it was easier to get water in 1999 than before 1995. At the same time, however, many people continued to use the pre-1995 sources of water in conjunction with government supplies, rather than changing completely, with less than 30 per

Table 11.3 *Distance non-urban African household residents have to go to fetch water, 1996–1999*

Distance	% of total non-urban African households			
	1996	1997	1998	1999
In dwelling/yard	25.0	27.9	28.8	30.4
Less than 200 m	32.9	35.9	31.3	33.5
200 m – 1 km	29.0	27.9	29.2	25.4
Over 1 km	13.1	8.4	10.4	10.2

Source: October Household Surveys 1997–2000, Statistics South Africa

cent getting all their water from a government scheme (RSS 2000, p29). These studies once again bring into question the official figures of the number of beneficiaries of water projects, based as they were on the assumption that 100 per cent of people in areas where there are completed projects were actually getting water from them.

Table 11.4 shows findings from research on water supply projects around the country. In many cases, beneficiaries of projects were receiving less than the RDP minimum of 25 l per person per day. Various blockages to access resulted in people choosing to limit their use of water from the schemes mainly to cook, drink and wash hands and faces, relying on other sources for washing clothes and bodies (interview, Charles Reeve, 12 February 2001). Under-utilization of the schemes increased the unit cost of water for those still using them, leading to further declines in use (Rall 2000). Mike Muller, Director General of DWAF, transferred the responsibility for failed schemes to communities, saying:

> *Where schemes are not delivering water because communities have decided not to pay for diesel for pumps, this is their decision. We believe that on reflection, they will reconsider. Supply interruptions may be an essential part of establishing working arrangements and do not necessarily mean that a project has failed* (quoted in Wellman 1999).

In some cases, residents consider the free river water they were using before to be more acceptable than paying for water from the project, especially when there is no improvement in quality. In the Sandile Regional Water Supply Scheme in the Eastern Cape water was unavailable in many parts of the area and was contaminated where it was available. People were unwilling to pay for a system of such poor quality. In one survey, water was contaminated by the time it reached the user in eight out of ten evaluated projects (Mvula Trust 1999a, pp6, 17, 34). Related to this is the issue of poor workmanship by consultants building infrastructure. As an Mvula Trust evaluation put it, 'now that the projects are completed, enormous problems are emerging in some project sites in relation to project design and construction. Materials are shoddy, corners were clearly cut, and communities now have questionable infrastructure' (Mvula Trust 1999a, p36).

Table 11.4 *Per capita consumption on various water supply projects*

Project	Water consumption (litres/capita/day)	Reasons for low consumption	Source
Various Eastern Cape RDP projects	13.5		RSS 1997, p29
George Moshesh (Transkei Presidential Lead Project)	10–15	Availability of other (free) sources of water	DWAF 1998b, p10
Shemula (KZN Presidential Lead Project)	3.5	Cost and distance	Mvula Trust 1997c, ppiv and ix
Various Northern Province projects	As low as 12	Installation of meters	ERT 1998, p53
Various Eastern Cape projects	Less than RDP minimum of 25	Non-operation of schemes, lack of water in the system and restricted access to the system. Problems included lack of money for diesel, regular pump breakdowns, and nobody to fix the pumps.	RSS 2000, pp29–33

Table 11.5 shows the results of a number of independent evaluations conducted on a sample of RDP projects in 1998 and 1999 that revealed problems with keeping the systems operational.

Table 11.5 *Non-functioning schemes*

Project area	Extent of functioning	Source
Eastern Cape	26% of 19 completed RDP schemes working in 1998.	Mvula Trust evaluation, cited in RSS 2000, p19
Eastern Cape	34 of 71 villages receiving water. In 32 villages the schemes were either not working or only partially working, while the remaining five were incomplete.	RSS 1997, p4
Kgobokwane	'The whole system is out of operation for a large portion of time, [and] it is clear that the operating arrangements have been a failure'.	Mvula Trust 1997b, p17
Mvula Trust schemes in KZN and Mpumalanga	Two out of 13 evaluated projects had water flowing for more than 70% of the time in 1999.	see Mvula Trust 1999b, c, d*

* It must be noted that projects known to have sustainability problems were specifically chosen so these figures cannot be generalized (see Breslin 1999, p2)

Sources inside the Department of Water Affairs and Forestry were reported to have said that water connections to as many as 2 million people were no longer functioning by 1999 (Ronnie 1999). A Danida report in 1999 noted evidence of a marked deterioration of RDP schemes (Buhl-Nielsen and Pitso 1999, p17; see also Rall 2000). A general experience of participants at the Appropriate Practice Conference in 1999 was that, 'in terms of the numbers of projects completed as well as numbers of communities served, an unacceptably high number of projects were collapsing almost as soon as the external support was withdrawn' (Makhetha Development Consultants 1999, p4). A DWAF evaluation revealed that: 'Communities too frequently end up being littered with parts of schemes that leave pipelines empty and unconnected to pump stations and standpipes. This might be an attempt to provide "some for all" but it sometimes provides "nothing for most"' (DWAF 1999, p45).

MACHIAVELLIAN PLANNING AND COMMUNITY REFUSAL TO PAY

Standards of service are closely linked to willingness to pay. Where schemes had collapsed, households are less willing to pay. 'Decent services have not been provided to rural communities', said Charles Reeve. 'So you can't expect cost recovery' (interview, 12 February 2001). Many people feel that payment for services is only justified if a higher level of service is provided, in particular, yard connections. In the absence of this, many households have stopped payments (Water Research Commission cited in RSS 2000, p19).

The link between standards of services and payment can be shown in a number of cases across South Africa. A survey carried out by DWAF in Tonga, Mpumalanga, indicated that respondents were unwilling to pay 10 cents per 25 l for the RDP basic level of service. This would represent 25 per cent of estimated average monthly disposable income of R60 in the village (cited in ERT 1998, p53). In the Kgobokwane project, 'people clearly want yard connections and are dissatisfied with the public standpipe system provided' (Mvula Trust 1997b, p11). In the Mvula-constructed Ephangweni scheme in KwaZulu-Natal, community groups and the water committee agreed on yard connections to address nonpayment of services (Mvula Trust 1999b, p9). At Arekwaneng village in Mpumalanga some felt the government should pay for services and others said they were only prepared to pay for yard connections (Mvula Trust 1999c, p6). A Danida project to develop cost recovery systems reported that 'unhappiness with basic service levels and service quality . . . and an overall sense that flat rate tariff systems are unfair have proven to be major obstacles in improving cost recovery' (Buhl-Nielsen and Pitso 1999, pp16–17).

In Setlagole in the North West, people refused to pay for water from standpipes at an average distance of 500 m, insisting that they wanted RDP levels of service before they were willing to pay. The Moretele Presidential Lead project had cost recovery rates of only 4 per cent because of strong dissatisfaction with the level of service, consisting of communal taps (DWAF 1999, pp20–23). Communal taps also undermine the health benefits of improved water supply, since 'the sheer physical effort of getting water to the house will hamper efforts to increase water consumption' (Holden 2000).

As payment became one of the central imperatives for successful schemes, services standards became more uneven and planning took on a more Machiavellian dimension. Mvula Trust (1997b, pxi) recommended locating pipes 'in a manner that allows non-paying wards to be cut off from their water supply'. Thus, the economic imperative for cost recovery began to overshadow efficient services to the intended beneficiaries. Communal standpipes were increasingly being built with prepayment meters to ensure payment up front. At the same time, the 200 m criterion was relaxed, with standpipes further apart to limit the cost of installing the prepayment meters (Bond et al 1999, p12). In the Kgobokwane project, for example, the business plan indicated that only 60 per cent of people would get a water supply within 200 m of their dwellings. The remainder would have to walk further because of financial constraints (Mvula Trust 1997b, p13). In Ramokokastad in North West Province, taps were 500 m from most households but people had to pay four times more than they were previously paying for a similar level of service (Mvula Trust 1999a, p15).

There were some attempts by government to recover costs using strong-arm tactics. DWAF explicitly argued the case for this: 'In general the harsher the measures the better the cost recovery. No amount of adversity must be allowed to sway officials. In this regard the support of councillors/local authorities is essential' (DWAF 1998b, p21).

In practice, this meant confrontation with communities that sometimes turned violent. For example, in Douglas in the Northern Cape, police in armoured vehicles accompanied municipal workers to insert flow restrictors so defaulters could only access a limited monthly supply (Hemson and Bakker 1999, p7). A suggestion was made by DWAF that the most effective way of making people pay, while not acting unconstitutionally, is to 'restrict the flow of water to a most inconvenient trickle of 25 litres per person spread over 24 hours' (DWAF 1998b, pp12, 22). In some cases, other members of the community were paid piece-rates to reduce pipe flow diameter to defaulting households (DWAF 1998b, pp14, 17). These attempts by DWAF to pilot cost recovery mechanisms at local level met with resistance from communities, and ultimately led DWAF to label them an 'abject failure' (DWAF 1999, p25). More recently, prepaid meters have become the target of opposition to 'user-pays' policies in places like Phiri in Soweto and Mpumalanga Township in KwaZulu-Natal.

The real import and effect of the cost recovery policy lies in the way it has increasingly dictated the design choices of water supply programmes, rather than in actual attempts to recover costs from the rural poor. As Mike Muller of DWAF has said:

> *In urban . . . formerly white areas, we engineer our schemes for the way we expect that people will actually behave. . . In our rural schemes, on the other hand, we engineer for how we* want *people to behave, how we think they should behave. We want them to take only 25 litres per day, so we design a system that can only provide that much. But then if people want to fit a flush toilet and septic tank, or to water a few cabbages beyond our per capita*

allowance, the system breaks down. The pipes at the end run dry (Muller 1999, p5; emphasis added).

CONCLUSION

While there is some cause for celebration in the extension of water supplies to rural areas in South Africa since the end of apartheid, these successes have been neither as far-reaching nor as unproblematic as government statistics would have us believe. This review of the first five years of service delivery shows that the commercialization of water services (through the use of private sector providers, primarily in the form of BOTTs) and the introduction of private sector operating principles (including, most importantly, full cost recovery measures) have served to slow down both the width and depth of service extension, leaving millions of predominantly poor, rural South Africans with little or no water access.

There has been some recognition by DWAF of the failures of these market initiatives – as indicated in the quotes provided above – and there has been a formalization of a 'free water' policy in the form of 6 kilolitres of water per household per month being provided at no cost since December 2000, but delivery of this free water policy has been uneven, and tariff rates after the free amount have often nullified the gains of the free supply (see McDonald and Pape 2002 and Loftus, Chapter 10, this volume).

The fundamental policy of cost recovery remains central to government's water delivery plans, as does the principle of public–private partnerships, bringing into question the successes of rural water delivery since 2000. Government's aims of providing access to potable water to all South Africans by 2008 must therefore address the twin questions of sustainability and affordability if the errors of the 1990s are to be adequately addressed.

NOTES

1 Preliminary and general costs were consortium charges paid by DWAF to set up and maintain offices and administrative systems at regional level. There was much criticism of these, since it was felt that these public resources could better be spent on building the administrative capacity in district and local councils (see Hemson 1999).
2 The criticism of private companies being allowed to make profit without carrying risk was levelled at consultants more broadly too. In the Winterveldt Presidential Lead Project, for example, 'most of the financial risks are borne by the government . . . [and] it is evident that the consultants are operating in a substantially risk free situation with payment on a time and cost basis with no ceiling or limit set' (Mvula Trust 1997a, p29).

REFERENCES

Blaxall, J., Morgan, P. and Schultzberg, G. (1996) *External Evaluation of Mvula Trust – Volume 1: Main Report*, Evaluation Management Team, Johannesburg

Bond, P., Dor, G. and Ruiters, G. (1999) 'Paying for Water', draft discussion paper for the Rural Development Services Network, RDSN, Johannesburg

Breslin, E. (1999) 'Lessons from the Field: Rethinking Community Management for Sustainability', paper presented to *Appropriate Practice Conference*, East London, 14–17 March

Buhl-Nielsen, E. and Pitso, R. (1999) 'Danida Support to CWSS: North West Province: Project Completion Report', www-dwaf.pwv.gov.za/directorate/waterservices/pds/danida

Department of Finance (2000) *National Expenditure Survey*, Department of Finance, Pretoria

DBSA (Development Bank of Southern Africa) (1994) *South Africa's Nine Provinces: A Human Development Profile*, DBSA, Halfway House, Johannesburg

DWAF (Department of Water Affairs and Forestry) (1994) 'Reconstruction and Development Water Programme Presidential Projects: National Business Plan', www-dwaf.pwv.gov.za/directorate/waterservices/pds/

DWAF (Department of Water Affairs and Forestry) (1996) 'Reconstruction and Development Water Supply and Sanitation Programme 1996/97: Revision 1', www-dwaf.pwv.gov.za/directorate/waterservices/pds/

DWAF (Department of Water Affairs and Forestry) (1997) 'RDP 4 Business Plan', www-dwaf.pwv.gov.za/directorate/waterservices/pds/

DWAF (Department of Water Affairs and Forestry) (1998a) 'The Review of the National BOTT Programme W 6018B – KwaZulu Natal: Draft Report', DWAF, Pretoria

DWAF (Department of Water Affairs and Forestry) (1998b) *12 Successful Cost Recovery Case Studies for Water Services in South Africa*, Water Services Chief Directorate, DWAF, Pretoria

DWAF (Department of Water Affairs and Forestry) (1999) 'Danida Support to CWSS: North West Province – Pilot Project Descriptions, Resources and Lessons', www-dwaf.pwv.gov.za/directorate/waterservices/pds/danida

DWAF (Department of Water Affairs and Forestry) (2000a) 'Water Services Progress Reports', www-dwaf.pwv.gov.za/WSDocs/Me/SA/MonthlyReport/

DWAF (Department of Water Affairs and Forestry) (2000b) *Progress Report: Allocation for Poverty Alleviation, Infrastructure and Job Summit Projects*, DWAF, Pretoria

ERT (External Review Team) (1998) *External Review of the Build Operate Train and Transfer (BOTT) Programme*, DWAF, Pretoria

Hemson, D. (1999) 'Beyond BOTT? Policy Perspectives in Water Delivery', preliminary report to Rural Development Services Network, RDSN, Johannesburg

Hemson, D. (2000) 'Policy and Practice in Water and Sanitation', *Indicator SA*, vol 17, no 4, pp48–53

Hemson, D. and Bakker, K. (1999) 'Privatising Water: BOTT and Hydropolitics in the New South Africa', paper presented to the SA Sociological Association, Saldanha Bay, 6–9 July

Holden, R. (2000) 'Further thoughts on cost recovery', letter to *Maru A Pula*, no 17, July, p8

Kasrils, R (2000a) 'Parliamentary Media Briefing', input for cluster press briefing, 10 February

Kasrils, R. (2000b) 'African Elephant of Delivery', address by Ronnie Kasrils, MP, Minister of Water Affairs and Forestry, National Assembly Budget Debate, 9 June

Makhetha Development Consultants (1999) 'Research Needs and Requirements', synthesis report from *Appropriate Practice Conference*, East London, 14–17 March, prepared for Water Research Commission

May, J. (1996) 'Assets, Income and Livelihoods in Rural KwaZulu-Natal', in M. Lipton, F. Ellis and M. Lipton (eds) *Land, Labour and Livelihoods in Rural South Africa. Vol 2: KwaZulu-Natal and Northern Province*, Indicator Press, Durban

McDonald, D. A. and Pape, J. (eds) (2002) *Cost Recovery and the Crisis of Service Delivery in South Africa*, Zed Books, London

Muller, M. (1999) 'Appropriate Practice for Rural and Peri-Urban Water Supply', paper presented to Appropriate Practice Conference, East London, 14–17 March (mimeo)

Mvula Trust (1997a) 'Evaluation of Winterveldt Water Supply Scheme', synthesis report (final draft), commissioned by DWAF

Mvula Trust (1997b) 'Evaluation of Kgobokwane Water Supply Scheme', synthesis report (final draft), commissioned by DWAF

Mvula Trust (1997c) 'Evaluation of Shemula Water Supply Scheme', synthesis report (final draft), commissioned by DWAF

Mvula Trust (1999a) 'Report Number 2 on "DWAF Revisiting of Water Service Projects – Sustainability Processes" Evaluation Outcomes', submission to DWAF Task Team Meeting 2, 19 February

Mvula Trust (1999b) 'Community Water Supply and Environmental Sanitation: Strengthening Sustainability Initiative (AusAID3) – KwaZulu Natal – Durban Evaluations', Mvula, Durban

Pelpola, K. and Reeve, C. (2000) 'M&E Challenges in SA RDP: Community Water Supply and Sanitation Programme', DWAF, Pretoria

Rall, M. (2000) 'Creating White Elephants', letter to *Maru A Pula*, no 17, July, p7

Ronnie, R. (1999) 'Govt must supply affordable water', *Business Day*, 17 March

RSS (Rural Support Services) (1997) *Evaluation of the CWSS Projects in the Eastern Cape*, RSS, East London

RSS (Rural Support Services) (2000) 'A Study of Current Water Policy in Relation to Rural People's Experiences and its Implementation: Case Studies from the Eastern Cape', final draft report, RSS, East London

Rural Development Task Team/Department of Land Affairs (1997) *Rural Development Framework*, Department of Land Affairs, Pretoria

SAIRR (South African Institute of Race Relations) (1994) *Race Relations Survey, 1993/1994*, SAIRR, Johannesburg

Simon, B. (2001) 'Municipal Partnership Pioneer in a Squeeze', *Business Day*, 6 June

Sirenya, M. (1999) 'Operational and Cost Recovery Challenges at Vulindlela', input presented to Session 5, Appropriate Practice Conference, East London, 14–17 March

Wellman, P. (1999) 'Sustainability of SA's "water miracle" questioned', *Sunday World*, 9 May

INTERVIEWS

Martin Rall, Managing Director, Mvula Trust, 19 February 2001

Charles Reeve, Project Officer, European Union's Water and Sanitation Delegation in South Africa, 12 February 2001

Part 3

Case Studies in the Region

Chapter 12

Stillborn in Harare: Attempts to Privatize Water in a City in Crisis

Rekopantswe Mate

Although water privatization was seriously considered in the City of Harare, Zimbabwe, in the late 1990s it was effectively stillborn due to the political and economic crises that have plagued the city since 1997. Recommendations in 1996 by a German firm of water engineering consultants, GKW, funded by the African Development Bank (ADB), laid out a plan for corporatizing the city's water and sanitation services and recommended a major expansion of the city's water supply through the construction of a new dam (Kunzwi) to deal with what was argued to be looming water shortages in Harare. Water multinational Biwater jumped at this opportunity and proposed a far-reaching Build, Own, Operate and Transfer (BOOT) scheme, but the proposal – and the debates around it – were kept largely secret and only collapsed when the city was plunged into deeper political crisis in 1998. Efforts since that time by the European Investment Bank (EIB) to resuscitate the GKW proposals have been unsuccessful as well, as the city stumbles from one crisis to another.

This chapter provides an overview of these privatization initiatives and the technocratic, knee-jerk obsession of bureaucrats, consultants and private service providers with dam building as the only solution to Harare's water shortages. I begin with a look at the politico-economic context of privatization in Zimbabwe to better situate the water debate in Harare in the broader ideological transitions in the country. This is followed by an overview of the demographics and social hydrology of Harare and a review of the political crises that the city has faced.

GKW's initial recommendations are then examined, along with Biwater's bid to introduce a BOOT scheme, followed by a review of the EIB proposals for financing water reforms. Significantly, the EIB proposals read like a list of World Bank conditionalities, including the introduction of commercial operating principles as laid out in the initial GKW report. I conclude with a discussion of the ongoing (and apparently fruitless) efforts to fund the dam construction amidst Harare's deepening financial and managerial woes.

Data for the chapter is derived from media sources, interviews with key informants (including city employees) and council documents. The most important of the latter are what I have termed the 'Kunzwi project files', containing internal memos, letters and minutes of meetings of the 'Kunzwi steering committee' from 1997 to 2003, with references to events going back to 1990. This is the first time these files have been reviewed in any detail. Only distilled versions of this information have been reported by local media in the past.

The Kunzwi files could not be taken out of Town House (the seat of Harare City Council (HCC)), however, and there was no photocopier for me to copy their contents. Consequently, information from the files – access to which took considerable negotiation, cajoling and pleading – was summarized through handwritten notes over two intensive days of review. The handwritten notes were later transcribed into electronic format in chronological order to get a better sense of the flow of events, and who played what role, when. Efforts to get official clarification on issues that were not clear in the files have proved futile. I therefore take responsibility for this interpretation of events.

Privatization in Zimbabwe

Privatization entered public debate in Zimbabwe in the 1990s as part of a series of neoliberal economic reform packages, namely, the Economic Structural Adjustment Program (ESAP) in 1990–1995 and its sequel, the Zimbabwe Program for Economic Transformation (ZIMPREST) in 1995–2000. Although the government claims to have abandoned neoliberalism, privatizations and other reforms still linger.

Donor countries and their agencies, multilateral donors like the World Bank, business people and some individuals saw privatization as a panacea for the mounting economic challenges that the government of Zimbabwe faced and the related decline in the quality of service in many sectors (Bond and Manyanya 2002). Although the World Bank would have preferred the privatization of more parastatals in all sectors (agriculture, water, electricity, telecommunications, transport and so on), the government has proceeded rather slowly. For instance, the Privatization Authority of Zimbabwe (PAZ) was only formed belatedly in 1999 as an advisory body to the Cabinet and a facilitator for privatization. Its mandate does not include the privatization of municipal services, however. It focuses solely on state-owned enterprises.

The year that PAZ was formed it produced a privatization manual which read much like a World Bank brochure: it sought to reduce government expenditure in subsidies to poorly performing enterprises; ensure efficiency and competition in the economy by doing away with monopolies; empower indigenous [read black] Zimbabweans to participate in the economy; and to raise revenue for treasury. Now PAZ says that it does not just privatize state-owned enterprises but seeks to 'restructure' them by changing management styles and shareholding through 'strategic partnerships' with corporate bodies or individuals that have either money or technical expertise (interview, Priscilla Mapuranga, Public Relations and Communications Executive, PAZ, 11 March 2004). This enables government to make more money from the sale or to earn a higher dividend where it remains a shareholder. Under this programme, the national steel company, the national telecommunications company and the electricity authority are set for 'restructuring' and/or privatization.

Asked about the implications of the international isolation of Zimbabwe and its impact on finding potential business partners, the PAZ Public Relations Executive argues that:

> *Business is business. It is not politics. People look for business opportunities everywhere in the world regardless of the politics of the day as long as they are sure they can make their money. The political climate is not a deterrent; the challenge is to put in place viable management systems and to adhere to international business practices* (interview, Priscilla Mapuranga, 11 March 2004).

For local government services, the World Bank recommended that subsidies be removed to cut government expenses. The argument was that local governments had to be able to earn or attract their own resources through cost recovery and by running themselves as for-profit entities (Bond and Manyanya 2002). This, along with a generic administrative malaise in local government, led to legislative changes in the Urban Councils Act of 1996 (*Hansard* 1995). Many local authorities in Zimbabwe began to look at commercialization and privatization of municipal services as a way of raising income by playing the role of facilitator/regulator of services rather than providing the services directly. In Harare, a number of municipal services were subsequently privatized, including refuse collection and liquor sales (both of which have been widely criticized as failures).

HARARE'S WATER CHALLENGE

Harare is the capital city of Zimbabwe. It has grown dramatically since independence in 1980 from a surface area of 559 km^2 to its current size of approximately 900 km^2 (CSO 1994), and from approximately 650,000 people in 1982 to close to 2 million today. Hitherto, colonial era restrictions on black mobility into urban areas rendered cities places of employment only and not places of permanent residence (Barnes 1992). Blacks could visit only when they had proven business such as employment or visiting a bona fide employee for a specified time. After independence these restrictions were relaxed and people came into the city unchecked for a variety of reasons. Urban migration intensifies whenever there are political and economic shocks, such as during droughts.

The city has a total of 106,945 houses in low income areas generally referred to as high-density (HD) suburbs. These houses are home to the majority of Harareans. Most residents are lodgers, however, estimated to outnumber house owners by five to one (*Hansard* 1995). In a study done by GKW (1996), it was noted that in older, low income residential areas densities were as high as 284 people per km^2 and were projected to rise to 300 people per km^2.

Table 12.1 *Harare's sources of water and their net capacities*

Water body	Net capacity (usable water) in million m³	Percentage of fullness in March 2004
Lake Chivero	247,181	94.1
Lake Manyame	480,236	65.3
Seke Dam	3,380	32.0
Harava Dam	9,060	30.8

Source: The Zimbabwe National Water Authority (ZINWA)'s Research and Data Department in Harare, March 2004

Harare currently draws water from four water bodies with a combined net capacity of 739,857 m³ (see Table 12.1). They are all in the same catchment area, the Manyame catchment, which is heavily polluted because of its proximity to the industrial sites of Harare, Ruwa and Chitungwiza. Lake Chivero is the largest and also the most heavily polluted (Moyo 1996). Heavy pollution means that more chemicals are required in water purification, many of which are imported, putting strain on Zimbabwe's extremely limited foreign exchange reserves and increasingly threatening to shut down the city's water system (so serious is the problem that USAID provided a US$200,000 grant to the HCC for the purchase of water treatment chemicals in early 2004) (*Herald*, 16 February 2004). These dams are rarely filled to their limits, however, because of the frequency of droughts or below normal rainfall, bringing into question the need for additional dam capacity.

Besides inadequate and low quality raw water, there are additional technological challenges that the Municipality of Harare has to contend with which further compromise water services. A review of internal correspondence in the Kunzwi files shows that the city has the capacity to process 640 megalitres (Ml) of water a day but because its plant and equipment is not fully functional it produces on average only 560 Ml a day. The average daily demand, meanwhile, stands at 750 Ml, creating a shortfall of 190 Ml a day.

Due to the age of Harare's 3000 km water reticulation system and lack of water pressure control devices, the city also incurs an estimated 30–40 per cent loss of processed water due to underground leakages (GKW 1996), significantly higher than the international average of 20–25 per cent. The city copes best in the winter when demand is relatively low; shortages and erratic supplies become a problem in the hot season (October–December), which also marks the onset of rains. During this time of the year, water levels (net capacities) in dams are also likely to be at their lowest, meaning that less water is being extracted for processing. This exacerbates pressure levels within the water reticulation system making it harder for elevated water reservoirs such as the Letombo reservoir to the east of Harare to be filled with water. In turn, people in the eastern parts of Harare, including low and high income residential areas and the local board of Ruwa, are now routinely the worst affected by water shortages.

Much of the plant and equipment in the water and sewerage system is also past its 'use by date'. For instance, the sewerage system that caters to houses on smaller plots (mostly owned by low and middle income earners) is beset with problems of inadequate pressure, which causes frequent bursts and backups. Since independence there has been no major public works to expand or rehabilitate the water and sanitation infrastructure in the city (GKW 1996).

A City in Crisis

In 1998 a team of foreign and local contractors repaired Warren Control Pump Booster Station, exposing the ineptitude and brazen mismanagement of Harare City Council (the local contractor, incidentally, was an engineering company owned by the president's nephew). Contractors were not paid at agreed times, leading to media reports of their pending confrontation with HCC. This confrontation came in October 1998, the time of year when the weather is hottest and water demand is highest. The contractors stopped work, demanding payments as a condition to continue. It emerged that the city was simply unable to pay the bills. The HCC had no money and had already run up enormous overdrafts with its banks. This set alarm bells ringing. Central government ended up giving the city a Z$78 million loan to pay the contractors so that repair and maintenance could proceed and took over supervision of the project (*Herald* 1998). This was a clear vote of no confidence in the HCC leaders. But, as if in retaliation, city councillors immediately gave their executive mayor and his administration a formal vote of confidence in council (*Thompson Report* 1999). Nonetheless the crisis opened a Pandora's box, putting the HCC in the spotlight in ways it was unaccustomed to.

As if that was not enough, the HCC could not pay its own employees at the end of October 1998, confirming that the city was in deep financial crisis. Workers went on a wildcat strike in which council property worth millions of Zimbabwe dollars (cars in particular) was destroyed by angry employees. Investigations showed that workers' fringe benefits such as medical insurance, social security and pension were deducted but not forwarded to relevant authorities, and had become a slush fund for the city's runaway budget (*Thompson Report* 1999).

The city seemed to live from hand to mouth and fumble from one crisis to the next and companies became wary of doing business with HCC because of nonpayment for goods and services rendered (ZIANA 1998b). Amongst other complaints was the increase in potholes, satirically called 'King Solomon's mines' in reference to the Executive Mayor, Solomon Tawengwa. Revenue collection was lax as well, as advertising companies erected billboards willy-nilly on streets without paying the city any fees (ZIANA 1998a). New office blocks, including government buildings such as the Reserve Bank, operated without being rated because the city had no property valuators. In early 1999, Harare also had a cholera outbreak.

While all of this was taking place there was ongoing construction of the mayoral mansion, first projected to cost Z$5 million, ballooning to Z$55 million, at ratepayers' expense. In addition, the mayor had a council-approved

Mercedes Benz and a 4x4 vehicle, yet the city had been reduced to four running ambulances down from 20 because no resources were allocated for their repairs. This at a time when HIV and AIDS were taking their toll on the health care system and demand for emergency services was on the increase.

Financial record keeping was also a problem; the City of Harare was disqualified from a World Bank housing scheme assistance programme in 2001 because its books were not balanced (*Herald* 2001). Audited statements for the 1997/98 financial year were only produced in 2001. This also weakened Harare's credit rating, making it impossible for the city to borrow money independently.

There was also heated media debate about the quality and safety of Harare's drinking water after tonnes of fish in Lake Chivero were mysteriously found dead. When scientists from the Department of Biological Sciences at the University of Zimbabwe studied the lake and concluded that it was heavily polluted, the media savvy Tawengwa protested, claiming the city's laboratory and scientists' findings contradicted the university team's findings. He accused university scientists of hidden agendas to oust him. GKW (1996) had noted, however, that the city's laboratory sorely needed an upgrade. It lacked modern equipment and its employees were not well supervised. Nonetheless, the mayor and HCC employees stoically maintained that Harare water was safe to drink, with the mayor making a point of publicly drinking tap water. Rumours that he had installed a water filter at his home did not help matters.

Tawengwa had also presided over the privatization of refuse collection which saw considerable rates increases for the service yet a decline in quality according to most media accounts. As a result, there were many organizations, with people of various political, ideological and economic backgrounds, who called for the mayor's resignation, including people of his own party. People did not trust his judgement or his ability to manage the city and control resources.

The Minister of Local Government, National Housing and Public Works (MLGNH&PW) threatened the council with dissolution. However, before the minister took action he demanded a full report of circumstances leading to the shortage of water and the nonpayment of contractors and workers and set up an independent committee to do the work, headed by Malcolm J. Thompson, a former Public Service Commissioner. The committee, now commonly referred to as the Thompson Commission, was expected to investigate gross financial mismanagement and poor administration, which were affecting the day-to-day running of the council. It worked with accounting firm Deloitte & Touche as auditors.

The tall shadows of political heavyweights

Political patronage was in evidence in the investigations. For instance, then-Director of Works, Christopher Zvobgo, brother of a long-time official and legal adviser to the ruling party, Dr Eddison Zvobgo, ran the Department of Works as an independent private entity and made use of council plant and equipment without council permission. In the process he made decisions that were ecologically harmful, in direct contradiction of the regulations of his department. For instance, he allegedly used council equipment for the extraction of pit and river sand for the construction industry without council's permission (*Sunday Mail* 1998). The mayor, too, was considered President Robert Mugabe's 'blue-eyed boy' (*Financial Gazette* 1998). *The Financial Gazette* of 29 October 1998 wondered whether Tawengwa was 'protected by the powers that be'. Apparently, prior to Tawengwa's election in intra-party primaries, eight or nine other candidates were presented as party candidates but no one other than Tawengwa received presidential approval. On the street some people say that this was posthumous payback to Tawengwa's father who, on the eve of independence, hosted, gratis, returning nationalist leaders at the family hotel in Highfield, Harare.

Meanwhile, people aired their complaints anonymously. Provincial governors speaking to the press complained that when local authority officials in other parts of the country messed up they were suspended immediately, yet Tawengwa and the HCC were being treated with 'kid gloves' (*Financial Gazette* 1998). The fact that Tawengwa had made a much-publicized visit to State House to meet the president in the middle of Harare's crisis increased speculation that he was a presidential protégé and therefore untouchable. No details of the visit were divulged, with Tawengwa saying it was a 'private visit'. It is possible that other heads of departments and senior employees also had other patrons, albeit less powerful.

Nevertheless, the *Thompson Report* confirmed that Harare was in a mess administratively, financially and technologically. It also confirmed that there was gross mismanagement of funds with monies being diverted from budgeted projects to unbudgeted projects with no consultation. Plants and equipment were also in disrepair.

Consequently, Tawengwa, together with 42 elected councillors, was dismissed by the MLGNH&PW in February 1999, much to the relief of most residents in Harare. The minister was empowered by the Urban Councils Act of 1996 to dismiss a wayward council and create a 'Commission' to run a municipality in the absence of elected officials, pending elections. Although this move was unprecedented, the minister argued that the whole council was responsible for the mess.

Subsequent to the dismissal of councillors and the mayor, some heads of departments were dismissed as well, including the Director of Works, Christopher Zvobgo, and Elias Mudzuri, then a senior member of staff in the Department of Works. Mudzuri later emerged, however, as the first opposition party executive mayor, giving credence to the saying, 'Forsaken by the ruling party, embraced by the opposition'.

The minister duly seconded a Commission headed by Elijah Chanakira (hereafter referred to as the Chanakira Commission) to run Harare for six months. Perhaps due to factionalism within the ruling party it seems there was no agreement on the ideal mayoral candidate to put forward for subsequent elections. This led to the extension of the term of the Chanakira Commission for two years, fomenting perceptions of a governance crisis in the city despite the fact that the Commission was initially welcomed by Harareans as a better option than the Tawengwa regime. According to the Urban Councils Act of 1996 (Section 80.3.a), a Commission stays in office at the 'pleasure of the minister', pending council elections. The extension was therefore technically legal, if not politically wise.

In was in the midst of this crisis that Harare toyed with the idea of privatizing its water and sanitation services.

BUILDING AN ADDITIONAL SOURCE OF WATER FOR HARARE: BIWATER'S FOOT-IN-THE-DOOR

A site for additional dam capacity for Harare had been identified for years (Kunzwi, situated 100 km east of Harare) but discussions around bids and modalities for its construction took place first only during the Tawengwa mayorship. Initial discussions involved two potential funders: the large multinational water provider, Biwater, and a consortium comprising the African Development Bank (ADB), the European Investment Bank (EIB) and the French Development Agency (AFD). Discussions with the two funders proceeded simultaneously even though the EIB-led consortium (so named by the author because of the lead role taken by the EIB) seems to have had a head start. Some informants suspect Biwater must have greased the palms of some top officials in HCC to have been included in the discussions.

According to entries in 'Kunzwi files', Kunzwi dam was one of ten priority dams which were supposed to be built in the mid-1990s using donor funds. It was in this context that, at an investment conference held in London in March 1997 to woo British investors, representatives of the Ministry of Rural Resources and Water Development (MRR&WD) apparently 'invited' Biwater to Zimbabwe to participate in water development in the country. Biwater's interest in the dam project seems to be in dispute though. Entries in the 'Kunzwi files' say that Biwater was interested in 'water supply' and not dam construction, but subsequently Biwater indicated a desire to fund construction of the dam as well.

In an undated file copy of a 'letter of intent', Biwater International said it would make a 'US$200 million investment' in the Kunzwi scheme (reconstructions of the files show the letter to have been written in May 1998). The value of the investment was later halved to US$100 million for reasons that are unclear. In any event, Biwater intended to 'evaluate' the economic viability of the scheme using 'private sector finance', for which government guarantees would not be necessary. Based on this letter of intent Biwater would provide the following information in anticipation of signing an agreement:

- economic viability study of the project;
- financing plan including suggestions for a joint venture company structure;
- separate project development plans, timetables and key milestones; and
- an indicative tariff range and 'lifetime economic model'.

A signed agreement would allow Biwater to go ahead with the project. If Kunzwi was built according to Biwater's plans and sourced finances, the City of Harare would have to refund Biwater for all expenses incurred on completion of the project (a classic BOOT scheme). Construction was expected to take three years.

In a letter written on 6 August 1999, the Biwater Corporate Director for Africa (by this time Biwater had offices in Harare) made reference to the undated letter of intent and included a formal BOOT proposal, indicating that there were 'a lot of decisions' still to be made. It seems Biwater was using foot-in-the-door sales tactics whereby you interest a client by revealing product information incrementally, with the tricky bits coming last. Solomon Tawengwa, as Executive Mayor of Harare, signed the original letter of intent on 31 August 1998, ostensibly with the BOOT proposal in mind. In his letter to MLGNH&PW dated 1 September 1998, the mayor summarized Biwater's plans noting that the company would do a feasibility study for free with no strings attached. He noted, however, that within HCC there were concerns about water pricing, pointing to worries that prices would escalate if HCC agreed to Biwater's plans. A month later Harare was plunged into the political crisis described above, leading to Tawenga's dismissal and endangering the Biwater agreement.

Entries in the Kunzwi files made during the Chanakira Commission reveal that the mayor signed the letter 'against professional advice'. For instance, it is alleged that the Finance and Environment committees had not reviewed Biwater's proposal. Some informants claim that this demonstrates that bribery was taking place. But it could also be argued that Biwater was going to do a free feasibility study, providing an alternative source of information and a basis for weighing options, and that the mayor was well within his rights to do something about the Biwater proposal lest he was accused of inaction.

The Chanakira Commission later summarized Biwater's proposal in confidential office correspondence as follows:

- A special purpose company (SPC) would be established and registered in Zimbabwe with all shares belonging to Biwater and its subsidiaries. *'Unconditional acceptance'* [emphasis in the original] of this aspect was expected if the contract was signed.
- The SPC would 'award a fixed price contract to Biwater International for the design, procurement, construction and commissioning of Kunzwi Project without going to tender. The SPC will [sic] award a long-term contract to Biwater International to operate and maintain the scheme for the 20 year operating period'.
- The HCC would have no control over bulk water tariffs. According to a proposal made in January 1999 bulk water from Kunzwi would be charged at Z$24.65 per m^3 with a 25 per cent mark-up for the HCC, meaning it would cost Z$30.81 per m^3 at the time.
- Biwater wanted 'institutional strengthening', for which the HCC was expected to plug all leaks in the water infrastructure (noting that this would take three years to complete).

The summary further noted that Biwater's letter of intent was proposing that the City of Harare refund Biwater for all expenses incurred after project completion. The Chanakira Commission noted that there was nothing in the documents about the currency or exchange rates to be used. Biwater had indicated neither the calibre of its personnel nor their qualifications.

Although the Chanakira Commission had been bound by the signed letter of intent to continue talking to Biwater, it summarily revoked the letter in August 1999 saying it was signed for the wrong reasons and that Biwater 'did not' have money. Amongst other things it was noted that Biwater is a 'water supply company', not a dam builder, so it was too early to work with the company. The Commission summary goes on to note that 'the BOOT proposal pre-empts the tender procedure and transparency'.

Biwater had been gunning to have a signed agreement by October 1999 but when informed of the Chanakira Commission's decision to end negotiations that was the end of Biwater's interests in Harare's water woes. As a result, Biwater did not walk out on a deal in Harare as stated by Bond and Manyanya (2002); it had the carpet pulled out from under it by the HCC. The bad publicity of the Tawengwa council meant that all its decisions were subjected to more critical scrutiny in the running of the city's affairs. It is also speculated that since Biwater's competitors had worked for a longer time with the City of Harare they could have passed information to the parent ministry alerting it of suspected 'misconduct'.

With Biwater out, there was only one contender left: the EIB-led consortium.

THE EIB CONSORTIUM AND ITS STRINGENT CONDITIONALITIES

With the EIB consortium, recommendations made by GKW's 1996 feasibility study were adopted and turned into strict conditionalities. GKW (1996) lamented the technological and expertise weaknesses that beset the city's Department of Works. It noted that its personnel did not have the expertise to supervise the construction of Kunzwi or to manage the waterworks that would be constructed afterwards. It also pointed out that the water account was in shambles and recommended that it be ringfenced into a stand-alone, 'publicly owned company' which would be called the Harare Water and Sewerage Authority (HWASA), run on a 'commercial basis' and staffed by professionals. In addition it recommended that the water reticulation system needed a serious overhaul but top priority was to rehabilitate the Morton Jaffray waterworks and Firle sewerage works, plug underground water leaks and redesign the pipe networks. Plugging leaks was deemed particularly important before Kunzwi water was introduced into the network because the 30–40 per cent loss was considered too high to be economically worthwhile. EIB was willing to fund the project and the money would be sourced from EIB (€25 million), ADB (€21 million), AFD (€10 million) and the Government of Zimbabwe (€7 million), disbursed according to the conditions detailed below.

In a summary made by the Chanakira Commission it was noted that the EIB camp turned GKW recommendations into 'conditionalities' for funding Kunzwi. There are indications in the form of inter-office correspondence throughout 1998, however, that the national government and the City of Harare were confident that Kunzwi would be built by the EIB camp (making one wonder what the Biwater negotiations were all about). Perhaps it was this confidence that made the EIB camp impose such stringent demands, knowing that the City of Harare had no other options. The demands were as follows:

Milestones:

- formal letter of request for funds for Institutional Strengthening and Priority Rehabilitation (ISPR);
- commitments from GoZ [Government of Zimbabwe] and HCC that HWASA would be created as a 'publicly owned company' to provide 'cost effective' water and sewerage services;
- commitment that no capital investment deals would be entered into which would compromise the economic viability of HWASA; and
- lender access to auditors' report and audited statements for the 1997/98 fiscal year.

Before signing for the loan:

- GoZ commits to completing Warren Pumpstation;
- GoZ and HCC commit to implement 'supplementary tariff rises to keep pace with inflation', and thereafter 'to maintain increases of 10 per cent above CPI inflation in 2000'; and
- GoZ gives full proof of separate bank accounts for HWASA.

Before first disbursement:

- create a Project Implementation Unit (PIU) in the MLGNH&PW which would oversee the implementation of funder conditionalities;
- appoint head and staff of PIU who are acceptable (professionally) to lenders;
- GoZ will direct HCC to appoint international auditors acceptable to lenders;
- prepare terms of reference for the institutional strengthening process acceptable to lenders; and
- GoZ will prepare and present to lenders acceptable draft policy proposals for HWASA.

Before second disbursement:

- HWASA working to the satisfaction of lenders; and
- tariff structure implemented to the satisfaction of lenders.

Summary of projects envisaged:

- PIU to ensure the establishment of HWASA in the shortest possible time; and
- institutional strengthening (IS) to ensure capacity to support, guide, supervise and control the priority rehabilitation (PR) projects.

It seems that the donors were not interested in the niceties of local government autonomy. They wanted assurances that the city would keep its end of the deal, and if central government whipped the city into line through imposing new councils, that was fine. It is also clear that EIB et al were not sure about Biwater's interactions with the City of Harare and wanted an assurance that no agreement would be signed with Biwater or other contenders.

Because so much time has lapsed and there have been so many staff changes in the MLGNH&PW, it is not possible to say what central government's reaction to these conditionalities was. For the City of Harare, after the dismissal of the Tawengwa Council, the Chanakira Commission's motto seems to have been 'proceed with extreme caution'. The Commission raised more questions than answers, especially about the feasibility of a lot of the proposals and demands, particularly in regard to the establishment of HWASA and implications for other City of Harare activities. The water account, despite being in a state of some chaos, was still one of the city's cash cows. Ringfencing would have put its funds out of reach of the city for possible redistributive purposes. The Chanakira Commission felt that a feasibility study was necessary to assess this and other recommendations made by the EIB group.

The City of Harare under the Chanakira Commission had limited capacity to conduct feasibility studies, however, due in part to limited funds. Besides, part of its mandate was to put things in order before making major decisions. In view of the fact that there were no audited statements this became one of the major administrative priorities.

There are no minutes of meetings held with the EIB-led consortium during the Chanakira Commission so it is impossible to know how the EIB group reacted to the Commission's misgivings. It is also not clear what central government's position was at this time. Perhaps everyone was too preoccupied with dealing with the 'mess' at Town House. In any event, the Chanakira Commission's unanswered questions could be said to have translated into a stalemate, which in turn translated to no action on Kunzwi.

CHASING ELUSIVE LOCAL INVESTORS

In the first quarter of 2000, the EIB offer was still on the table with its conditionalities. There are indications that communication between EIB, government and the City of Harare was still ongoing. EIB sent its representative from Brussels to visit HCC although details of these discussions were not filed. By October 2000, the steering committee on Kunzwi indicated that there were no funders for the project and that the EIB proposal had been shelved. In July 2001, the City of

Harare wanted to go it alone, proposing that US$75 million be budgeted in 2002 as capital development to build Kunzwi. It is not clear where this money was supposed to come from bearing in mind that bookkeeping lagged behind by four years and no one knew for sure what was in the city accounts.

A year later, in July 2002, the steering committee on Kunzwi noted with regret that the City of Harare could not manage building Kunzwi alone. At that meeting a representative of the Department of Water Development (DWD) suggested that the city could use the Biri-Manyame Dam (with a net capacity of 172,463 million m^3) already built by government and within a 100 km radius northwest of the city (although the city would have to invest in waterworks to transport it). This offer has not been followed up on, however, and it is not clear whether the Biri-Manyame Dam might be an option if funding for Kunzwi is not found.

In August 2002, it was suggested that Kunzwi would be built using local financial resources. But the cost of construction had escalated to Z$21 billion from Z$77 million in 1997 and from Z$360 million in 2000. This increase was due largely to runaway inflation, which at the end of 2003 was pegged at around 700 per cent per annum.

Nevertheless, government called for local financiers' bids for funding Kunzwi under a BOOT arrangement, advertising in local newspapers in early 2003. Details of who the bidders are, and to whom (if anyone) a tender has been awarded, remain confidential.

Even if local financing can be found, high local interest rates could more than double the cost of bulk water. A memorandum dated 3 September 2002, from the City Treasurer to the Director of Works at the HCC, is noted that a Z$21 billion loan would cost the city Z$8.4 billion a year at inflated local interest rates of about 40 per cent, plus 'capital repayments' of Z$840 million a year for 25 years, driving the cost of water production from Z$34.00 to Z$87.00 per kilolitre immediately. It also noted that: 'Managing a debt and cashflow of this magnitude is a mammoth task, which requires a lot of professionalism and good debt collection systems', neither of which the HCC has in abundance.

Conclusion

In closing, it is worth highlighting the HCC's preoccupation with dam construction and its techno-economic orientation to development – a knee-jerk response to water shortages that suggests the only way to increase water supply is to develop untapped water (re)sources that require massive capital investments (on these points more generally see Petrella 2001; Louw and Kaisser 2002). Consequently, water resource development is seen as a business venture, an 'economic' matter like any other business development.

This is not unique to Harare. Robinson (2002) notes that the City of Bulawayo (Zimbabwe's second largest city) had Mtshabezi Dam built to augment its water supply, but to this day there are no pipelines linking the dam with the city's waterworks and it lies idle. Bulawayo's residents are now clamouring for the much-publicized Zambezi Water Project which, if implemented, would bring tap water by pipeline from the Zambezi River some 400 km away! Marondera town also asked the government for an additional water source after the 1991/92 drought. Its wish was granted in the form of Wenimbi Dam but to this day the dam lies unused.

Another interesting case of expensive fixes is that of the Pungwe pipeline built for the City of Mutare to augment its water supply. Mukheli et al (2002) note that Mutare had three options to choose from: it could build a 30 km pipeline to an existing dam, Osborne, at a cost of US$37 million; it could build another dam; or it could build a 46 km pipeline to the relatively pristine Pungwe River at a cost of US$100 million. It chose the third option amid considerable protest. Mukheli et al (2002) argue that this choice was made with the collusion of donors, politicians and international engineering firms, against the will of residents. Now that the Pungwe Pipeline is up and running water availability has improved, but in low income areas of Mutare relations with the city authorities have become tense, as cost recovery measures – designed to pay back the costs of the capital project – have driven up the costs of water.

In all of this discussion better water demand management (WDM) has been largely ignored as a solution to water shortages. WDM requires the reduction of water losses, better maintenance of water facilities, reduced over-consumption of water and more equitable distribution of water (Mwendera et al 2003). If Harare could reduce its current 30–40 per cent loss of processed water to international norms of 20 per cent (or lower) this would reduce pressure for a new dam. In fact, Mwendera et al (2003) argue that without WDM strategies, most water shortage claims in Zimbabwe are false, giving credence to the argument by Louw and Kaisser (2002) that: 'The cheapest water in future may well be the water which was wasted in the past.'

The fixation with dam building in Harare continues to hold up any effective water service reforms in the city and maintains a focus on large capital investments – capital which is unlikely to be forthcoming from local sources, suggesting that Harare will continue to be faced with harsh, commercially oriented conditionalities from donors or from profit-oriented multinational water firms. Whether either of these external sources of funds is even still interested in Harare's water problems, given its political and economic turmoil, is unclear.

REFERENCES

Barnes, T. (1992) 'The Fight for Control of African Women's Mobility in Colonial Zimbabwe, 1900–1939', *Signs*, vol 17, no 3

Bond, P. and Manyanya, M. (2002) *Zimbabwe's Plunge: Exhausted Nationalism, Neoliberalism and the Search for Social Justice*, University of Natal Press, Durban

CSO (Central Statistical Office) (1994) *Harare 1992 Census Report*, Central Statistical Office, Harare

Financial Gazette (1998) 'Tawengwa hangs on despite calls for his head', 29 October

GKW (1996) 'Harare Water Supply Study Stage II, HWS 1993: Intakes, Transmission, and Treatment and Supply', GKW Consultants, mimeo

Hansard (1995) 5 December, Government Printer, Harare
The Herald (1998) 'Nkomo to decide Tawengwa's fate', *The Herald*, 27 October
The Herald (2001) 'Municipality produces 97/98 audited accounts', 1 August
The Herald (2004) 'Water Problems Persist in Harare's Eastern Suburbs', 16 February
Louw, D.B. and Kassier, W. E. (2002) 'The Costs and Benefits of Water Demand Management', IUCN report, Centre for Agriculture Marketing (South Africa), Johannesburg
Moyo, N.A.G. (ed) (1996) *Lake Chivero: A Polluted Lake*, University of Zimbabwe Publications, Harare
Mukheli, A., Musopye, G. and Swatuk, L. (2002) 'Is the Pungwe Water Supply Project a Solution to Water Accessibility and Sanitation Problems for the Households of Sakubva (Mutare), Zimbabwe?' *Physics and Chemistry of the Earth*, vol 27, pp723–32
Mwendera, E.J., Hazelton, D., Nkhuwa, D., Robinson, P., Tijenda, K. and Chavula, G. (2003) 'Overcoming Constraints to the Implementation of Water Demand Management in Southern Africa', *Physics and Chemistry of the Earth*, vol 28, pp761–78
Petrella, R. (2001) *The Water Manifesto: Arguments for a World Water Contract*, Zed Books, London
Robinson, P. (2002) 'Overcoming Constraints to the Implementation of Water Demand Management in Southern Africa: Zimbabwe Country Report', IUCN, Harare
Sunday Mail (1998) 'Council takes Director to task', 27 December
The Thompson Report (1999) Government Printer, Harare
ZIANA (Zimbabwe National Water Authority) (1998a) 'Council pulling down illegally erected billboards', ZIANA, Harare, 11 December
ZIANA (Zimbabwe National Water Authority) (1998b)'City struggles to feed herd of cattle', ZIANA, Harare, 27 December

INTERVIEWS

Priscilla Mapuranga, Public Relations and Communications Executive, PAZ, 11 March 2004

Chapter 13

'There is *Still* No Alternative': The Beginnings of Water Privatization in Lusaka

Karen Cocq

This chapter examines water services in Lusaka, the capital of Zambia. I begin by tracing the political economy of structural adjustment in the country, from the early 1980s until today, and discuss the ways in which market reforms have strengthened the national elite. I then turn specifically to the water sector to analyse the legislative and institutional reforms that began in 1993. Ongoing efforts to open water services in Lusaka to private sector participation (an initiative supported by the state, the World Bank, donors and private water companies) exemplify how neoliberal ideology has penetrated the policy-making arena to the degree that privatization is still considered a sound policy measure, despite domestic and international evidence to the contrary, and how any possibility of public alternatives has been foreclosed.

The core of this research was undertaken in 2001–2002. Interviews were conducted with local government officials, resident World Bank officials, union representatives, staff from the national regulator and staff from various development NGOs working in the water sector. Information was also obtained through participation and observation in various local and national level meetings with 'stakeholders' involved in the drafting of the water chapter of the Poverty Reduction Strategy Paper (PRSP), as well as from government and NGO documents. I also interviewed a delegation of experts from Severn-Trent International Plc, based in the UK, who conducted a private sector participation options study in Lusaka (with World Bank funding) and obtained information from documents relevant to their investigation. Severn-Trent's research was considered confidential at the time and to the best of my knowledge the outcomes and recommendations of the study have not yet been made public.

THE POLITICAL ECONOMY OF STRUCTURAL ADJUSTMENT IN ZAMBIA

After independence from the British in 1964, the Zambian government under Kenneth Kaunda undertook a programme of 'African democratic socialism' under the leadership of the United National Independence Party (UNIP). The programme included expansion of the civil service and increased spending on social programmes to promote health and education. Between 1968 and 1972 the state began a programme of partial nationalization of major enterprises, most importantly in the mining sector on which the economy depended for an average of 40–45 per cent of GDP (Burdette 1988, pp68–80). These nationalizations were ostensibly aimed at transferring economic control into Zambian hands.

But during this same period there began to surface increased conflict between factions of UNIP and other newly created parties. This led to the creation of a 'one-party participatory democracy' in December 1972, banning all parties except UNIP (Burdette 1988, p62). These conflicts were evidence of an 'incipient class politics' (Burdette 1988, pp71–73). The nationalization programme, coupled with the economic crisis of the 1970s that decimated small enterprise, had promoted the concentration and consolidation of indigenous capital while the one-party state structure facilitated the movement of politicians into business and vice versa. The development of this 'bureaucratic bourgeoisie' (Boone 1998, p139) would foreshadow the influence of this class leading up to the early 1990s, when this group would situate itself at the forefront of the opposition and pro-democracy movement (Bartlett 2000).

Structural adjustment under UNIP: 1983–1991

From 1973 to 1984, terms of trade fell 77 per cent, copper prices collapsed and interest rates soared, leaving the Zambian government with an external debt of 400 per cent of GDP by 1986 (Young and Loxley 1990, pp5–7). The situation eventually led President Kaunda to enter into a structural adjustment agreement with the International Monetary Fund (IMF) in 1983, which included currency devaluation, wage control, and the lifting of price controls on commodities and inputs. This was followed by a more comprehensive package in 1985 focused on liberalizing foreign exchange rates. The resultant increases in the cost of living and skyrocketing prices for essential commodities, such as the staple maize meal, spurred riots in late 1986.

This popular pressure in addition to pressure from labour, manufacturers and UNIP leaders caused Kaunda to cancel the agreement on 1 May 1987 (Simutanyi 1996, pp826–27). In its place he introduced the New Economic Recovery Programme (NERP) intended to promote growth from Zambia's 'own resources' and which undid many of the policy measures of the structural adjustment facility. NERP's initial success (6.2 per cent growth in real GDP in 1988) waned as the international financial institutions (IFIs) and the donor community began denying financial assistance in response to the country's increasing non-compliance. A worsening crisis forced the government to reopen negotiations with the IMF in June 1989, requiring the lifting of subsidies and price controls once more. A more than 100 per cent increase in the price of maize meal by June 1990 resulted in more riots that caused 27 deaths (Simutanyi 1996, p828).

Structural adjustment under MMD: 1991–2002

Growing political opposition to the one-party state played a significant role in the development of structural adjustment policies in Zambia. The concentration of policy decisions in the hands of the president increasingly became the focus of public discontent, and various groups began viewing political reform as a prerequisite for public debate on structural adjustment (Bartlett 2000, p431). Local business interests had suffered under UNIP's statist policies and sought to break the monopoly on decision making in order to push for a move to a free market economy (Simutanyi 1996, p831). It was under these circumstances of increasing pressure for political reform that the Movement for Multiparty Democracy (MMD) was born. This coalition of interest groups would lead the charge for a liberal democratic transition under the leadership of Frederick Chiluba, a high-ranking trade union bureaucrat from the Zambia Congress of Trade Unions (ZCTU).

Once in office, the MMD proceeded with a more rigorous implementation of the 1989 adjustment agreement signed with the IMF. The party took advantage of the early euphoria of its victory to push through fast-paced reforms in order to minimize the level of opposition. Bartlett (2000, p433) notes that the movement for change that led to the defeat of UNIP in the 1991 elections was actually not a movement at all. The push for democratization was dominated by the business elite, the churches and bureaucratic right-wing union leadership such as Chiluba, to the exclusion of other groups. Positioning itself at the forefront of opposition as the only legitimate political force, the MMD was able to unite disparate political positions, both for and against structural adjustment, under the banner of democratization and rally extensive support for its political objectives while its economic platform, though entirely neoliberal in orientation, remained vague.

Furthermore, although labour had given the MMD its organizational strength and its popular legitimacy, the business elite was the party's driving political and economic force while the leadership had a strong neoliberal agenda (see Chiluba 1995). Following elections, labour became increasingly marginalized within and outside the party, and was consequently reduced to opposing merely the pace and sequence of structural adjustment reforms rather than the reforms themselves (Simutanyi 1996, pp836–38).

PRIVATIZATION THEN AND NOW

In the earliest days, privatization in Zambia was taken up with great enthusiasm and with much support from the World Bank and the major donors, and hailed as an essential feature of Zambia's economic recovery. But over the course of the 1990s the much-lauded benefits of privatization did not materialize, evidence of corruption and nepotism grew, and increasing domination of the economy by foreign capital sat poorly with many Zambians. By the end of the decade criticism of Zambia's privatization experience abounded.

Although the World Bank has claimed that Zambia's privatization programme was 'the most successful in Africa' (Campbell White and Bhatia 1998, p4), Craig has argued that the privatization process in Zambia was, instead, of a dual nature; it simultaneously created the conditions for recolonization of the economy by foreign capital while concentrating local capital accumulation and political power (Craig 2000, p363). Mechanisms for broadening ownership, by breaking up large entities into smaller share packages, for example, remained impossibly out of reach of the general population; and members of government used their political influence, and in some cases ill-gotten funds, to favour their acquisition of assets (Craig 2000, pp361–63). Even the World Bank has since conceded that Zambian citizens account for only 5 per cent of the privatization sales (*Mmegi* 2004).

In response to these critiques – and to high profile privatization failures such as the pullout of Anglo-American at the Konkola Copper Mines (KCM) in 2002 – the government has become more cautious of wholesale privatization, stressing instead the role of 'private sector participation' and 'partnerships', a language that has infiltrated virtually every aspect of economic and development policymaking. President Mwanawasa has used this new approach to distinguish himself from the old MMD, though the flavour of his economic policies remains the same (*Times of Zambia* 2002a). Amongst donors and the IFIs, privatization is still the order of the day (IMF 2000; *Times of Zambia* 2002b).

Critical opposition to privatization and liberalization policies does exist, albeit from a rather disparate collection of interests. Several official opposition parties and politicians, many of whom have been recycling through various parties and brands of politics since the early post-independence era, have been critical of the government's perceived enslavement to the international financial institutions and have questioned their control over national decision making (*Post* 2004).

The labour movement is divided on the issue of privatization. The ZCTU called a massive strike by civil servants in late February 2004 to protest about tax increases and wage freezes as part of a new IMF agreement, and yet has also come out vocally supporting the commercialization of the electricity utility ZESCO (*Times of Zambia* 2003b). The Federation of Free Trade Unions Zambia (FFTUZ), on the other hand, strongly opposes privatization and has openly condemned any further pursuit of such policies and the role of the IMF and World Bank (UNI 2002).

Several indigenous NGOs have been critical of privatization as well, to varying degrees. Again, some have rejected the very concept of privatization, linking it to the global economy and to debt relief, while others have pointed to problems of mere process. It is primarily these latter NGOs that took part in the 'civil society' consultations for the PRSP, restricting their critique to tinkering with the policy prescriptions, while the underlying framework of neoliberalism remained unchallenged.

Thus, the debate around privatization has largely been restricted to questions of *who* gets to dictate private sector-led development (the government or the World Bank), rather than *whether* private sector-led development is the correct policy option. The mantra of 'privatization' (and its synonyms) has survived remarkably turbulent times and continues to wield considerable policy influence and ideological hegemony.

WATER PRIVATIZATION IN ZAMBIA

Zambia is one of the most urbanized countries in the region; approximately 40 per cent of its 10.3 million people live in cities (World Bank 2003a). Approximately 80 per cent of the population lives in poverty (on less than US$1 per day), and 56 per cent of urban residents are considered poor (CSO 1998). The capital city Lusaka has a population of approximately 1.3 million, about 800,000 of whom live in informal settlements (World Bank 2001a), also known as 'peri-urban areas' or 'compounds'.

An estimated 82 per cent of urban households in Zambia have access to clean water: 6 per cent from boreholes and protected wells, 47 per cent from individual taps, and 29 per cent from public standpipes (MLGH 2000, p2). In peri-urban areas – where the majority of the urban poor live in extremely difficult conditions – water supply and sanitation services, if available, are inadequate and unreliable. At least 56 per cent of peri-urban residents do not have access to safe water and as many as 90 per cent lack access to adequate sanitation facilities (MFNP 2001, p3). Services in these areas vary widely from one settlement to another, but water is received mainly through public standpipes, unprotected wells prone to contamination, and occasionally from small private vendors at inflated prices (MLGH 2000).

Water sector reforms: 1993–2002

By the early 1990s the water supply and sanitation sector in Zambia had severe institutional, legislative and financial problems. Municipal companies managed very poor revenue collection from inadequate billing and extensive water losses through the leaky infrastructure system. Years of dwindling federal transfers, accelerated by drastic cutbacks under decentralization policies of the 1990s, severely limited infrastructure maintenance and development. The result has been very poor quality service delivery, particularly to peri-urban areas, and a heavy reliance on NGOs and donors to meet the water and sanitation needs of the poor (Bull 2000). It was these practical problems that, in part, precipitated the launching in March 1993 of what has been called the most comprehensive water sector reform process in the Southern African region (Phiri 2000, p32).

Yet the catalyst for reform came with the rise of the MMD and its sweeping privatization programme. The water sector reforms were linked to other major reforms of the time: the Public Sector Reform Programme (PSRP), which focused on downsizing the civil service and encouraging decentralization, and structural adjustment measures adopted under the auspices of the World Bank (Phiri 2000, p11). It is also said that the commercialization of water services was 'inevitable if Zambia was to retain any hope of further assistance from the main donors' (Phiri 2000, p32). Indeed, these donors – the governments of Germany, Norway and Ireland – financed the reforms, with additional support from the World Bank and the African Development Bank (see, for example, World Bank 1995).

The new government and the donor community considered the crisis in the water sector to be a result of 'deep-seated institutional weaknesses' (PCU 1993): mismanagement, poor coordination of activities and corruption; lack of capital and investment, from insufficient central government transfers, poor revenue generation and bloated bureaucracy; and weak technical capacity, exacerbated by overstaffing. The neoliberal development agenda of both the government and the donor community dictated that private sector solutions were the best, and only, option and required the creation of an 'enabling environment' for private capital. The nine-year reform process that began in 1993 therefore resulted in several important legislative, institutional and financing changes in Zambia's water sector, outlined below.

Legislative changes

National Water Policy

The National Water Policy was adopted in 1994 and stipulated seven principles that would guide the reform process and the management of the sector into the future (NWP 1994, p28):

1 separation of water resources functions between water supply and sanitation;
2 separation of regulatory and executive functions within the water supply and sanitation sector;
3 devolution of authority to local authorities and private enterprises;
4 achievement of full cost recovery for water supply and sanitation services (capital recovery, operation and maintenance) through user charges in the long run;
5 human resources development leading to more effective institutions;
6 technology appropriate to local conditions; and
7 increased government spending in the water sector.

The most significant changes introduced through this policy are the recognition of water as an economic good rather than a public good, the adoption of full cost recovery, and the commercialization of all water utilities in the country. The policy states that the financial crisis in the water sector is caused by inadequate investment and poor cost recovery, resulting from a 'perception of water as a cost-free social good rather than as an economic one', and, as such, tariffs must 'reflect both the cost and *true economic value of a commodity*' in order to 'provide the right signals' to consumers and bring adequate returns to the supplier (NWP 1994, emphasis added).

The devolution of functions associated with water services places increased responsibility on city councils that are already in financial crisis,[1] leaving few options for improved service delivery within the public sector and beyond cost recovery. Although the policy commits government to increased spending in the sector, a review of the reforms undertaken in 2000 concluded that all seven principles had been followed with the exception of this last one (Phiri 2000, p13).

Water Supply and Sanitation Act

The Water Supply and Sanitation Act No 28 of 1997 establishes the creation of a national regulator, the National Water Supply and Sanitation Council (NWASCO), and allows a local authority to establish utility companies in collaboration with private capital provided the local authority holds at least 51 per cent of the shares.

Peri-Urban Water Supply and Sanitation Strategy

The Peri-Urban Water Supply and Sanitation Strategy was passed in 2000 in order to complement the National Water Policy and the Water Supply and Sanitation Act where they fail to address peri-urban issues (MLGH 2000). It specifies that 'communities to be assisted with improved services shall be on the basis of expressed demand for better services and demonstrable willingness to make contributions (in cash or in kind) . . . to ensure that only facilities they want, are willing to pay for, and are committed to manage are put up' (MLGH 2000, pp14–15). Communities should therefore contribute at least 10 per cent of the capital costs of a scheme, as well as all operation, maintenance, repair and replacement costs, and government should provide appropriate grants so that tariffs do not exceed 10 per cent of household income (MLGH 2000).

Institutional changes

National Water Supply and Sanitation Council (NWASCO)

NWASCO is responsible for developing guidelines for service provision, tariff setting, and for the establishment, licensing and monitoring of commercial utilities. NWASCO is also required to establish and manage a Devolution Trust Fund (DTF) that will provide grants to support utilities with commercialization.

Advisory responsibilities within NWASCO are held by representatives from the relevant government ministries, the Chamber of Commerce and Industry, the Environmental Council, the Consumer Protective Agency, the Competition Commission, members of the private sector and from the public, all of whom are appointed by the Minister of Local Government or NWASCO itself. NWASCO has begun to establish community based and voluntary Water Watch Groups to represent consumer interests and monitor service provision (NWASCO 2002).

Concerns have been raised about NWASCO's capacity to enforce service extension to peri-urban areas because its financial viability is largely dependent on the capacity of commercial utilities to pay their licensing fees (Phiri 2000). This may mean that both the service provider and the regulator will prioritize revenue generating neighbourhoods at the expense of poor areas. Despite recommendations for government assistance for NWASCO, and a capacity-building grant from the World Bank's Public–Private Infrastructure Advisory Facility (PPIAF) for US$319,000 in March 2001 (World Bank 2001b), NWASCO's regulatory strength remains uncertain.

Lusaka Water and Sewerage Company (LWSC)

Water services in Lusaka were operated as a department of the city council until 1990, when the Lusaka Water and Sewerage Company (LWSC) began operations as a 'limited private company' whose assets are wholly owned by Lusaka City Council.

Water loss is high at over 50 per cent caused by dilapidated infrastructure and leaky pipes, a high incidence of illegal connections, low billing and low collection (LWSC 2002a; Severn-Trent 2002). LWSC has 33,000 registered customers (including communal taps), 40 per cent of whom are metered. The remainder are charged on an estimated 'assessed consumption' flat rate basis. Continuity of service in many areas is highly erratic, far less than 12 hours per day in many cases, and often discontinued for several days during the week. Collection efficiency is low; revenue is collected for only 22–25 per cent of water produced (Severn-Trent 2002, Section 4, p16). Various government ministries owe LWSC an estimated 18 billion kwacha (US$4.1 million) in unpaid bills (LWSC 2002b). LWSC recorded losses of 8 billion kwacha in 2001 alone, registered a deficit of 20.6 per cent of gross operating income, and bad debts have averaged about 27 per cent of the budget since 1997 (Severn-Trent 2002).

LWSC is the only commercial utility in Zambia that has a peri-urban policy and a corresponding department that handles service delivery to these areas. LWSC is currently active in all 13 peri-urban areas ('compounds') of Lusaka and has calculated a total served population of approximately 506,000 people (LWSC 2002c).[2] LWSC is a corporatized unit; it is still publicly owned and operated but has been financially ringfenced from other sectors in order to isolate its costs and revenues, and is being managed increasingly on private sector principles that ultimately make it more profitable and saleable (see McDonald and Ruiters, Chapter 1, this volume, for a more detailed discussion of the impacts of ringfencing).

The approximately 1000 workers in the Water Department of City Council were transferred to LWSC upon formation. The company's poor financial situation has prevented it from properly retrenching many workers. In interviews with the union, representatives believed that many dismissals during the reforms were unfounded but used to streamline staff without compensation. Current staff levels are over 500 and LWSC would like to further streamline this number. Government officials claim that an estimated US$5 or 6 million is required to finance retrenchments, and the vast majority of this is expected to come from funds released through debt relief.

Financing changes

Tariffs

Under the former UNIP government, three tariff rates existed: the lowest rates for high-density (theoretically low income) areas, and the highest rates for low density (theoretically high income) areas. In the 1960s and early 1970s, when existing infrastructure was built, free water was provided to many poor areas. In later years, lack of investment in the sector resulted in deteriorating service and an inability, and unwillingness, to enforce payment (World Bank 2001c). Volumetric consumption was not measured.

The newly revised tariff structure developed by NWASCO in 2001 is aimed at full cost recovery and its stated intention is to promote equitable distribution and access, improvement of public health, conservation and environmental protection. The guidelines stipulate that the basic requirement for domestic consumption of 30 l per person per day, or approximately 6 kilolitres (kl) per family (six or seven people) per month, should be provided at a 'social price oriented at the purchasing power of the poor'. The recommended structure is a rising block tariff, represented by the lower line in Figure 13.1. In such a scenario, the first 6 kl are provided at a subsidized cost of 700 kwacha per cubic metre (dependent on tariff levels set by LWSC and NWASCO). The social tariff is calculated to be 50–70 per cent of the average tariff per cubic metre. All consumption over this amount is billed at the average cost per cubic metre of water (NWASCO 2001). The upper line in Figure 13.1 represents price points under a simple three-block tariff structure where price increases would jump as consumption passes from one block to another, a model not advised by NWASCO.

Access for the poor is largely provided through communal standpipes operated through supervised kiosks, a method popular with LWSC, NGOs and donors, where water is sold on a per bucket basis at the social tariff price. In areas where communal standpipes do not exist, households will often spend more than half their monthly income on purchasing water from private vendors (MLGH 2000).

LWSC increased tariffs in late 2002, their first increase since 1996. The 15 per cent increase raised the official social tariff from K3000 (US$0.68) to K3500 (US$0.80) per month for communal standpipes, and from K14,000 (US$3.19) to K14,500 (US$3.31) for individual taps.[3] According to NWASCO there are still significant variations in tariffs charged within and between different compounds, often by as much as 20 per cent or more, and the principle of cross-subsidization from higher blocks to the social tariff block is not always applied.

No comprehensive study of the impact of cost recovery has been done, but it is said that recovery from peri-urban settlements has increased significantly, rising to 25 per cent in 1997 from less than 1 per cent in 1990 (Nyumbu 1998). This is probably due to the fact that little, if anything, was charged for water in many of these areas prior to the reforms. The LWSC and ministry officials argue that the social tariff is primarily aimed at increasing access rather than recovering costs, and many consumers are still not charged for water due to limited

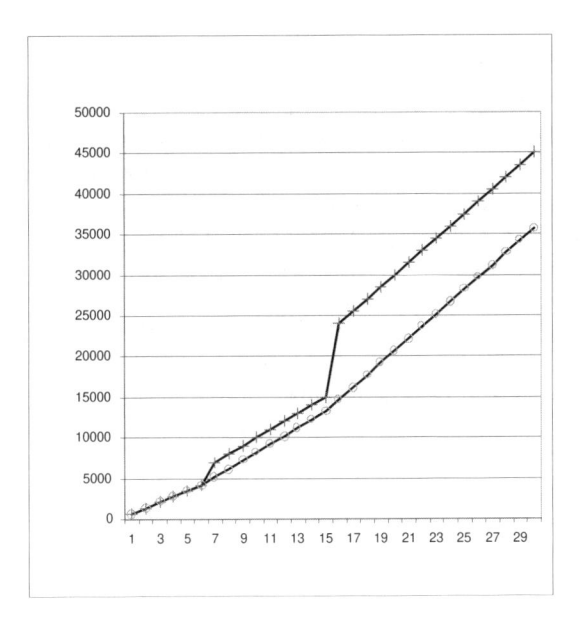

Figure 13.1 *Water bills for different consumption levels under NWASCO tariff structure*

capacity to collect revenue, but it is generally acknowledged that the introduction of tariffs in areas that once received water for free will limit access for low income households.

The Devolution Trust Fund

During the reforms, a Devolution Trust Fund (DTF) was established within NWASCO to provide an incentive for commercial utilities to extend coverage to peri-urban areas. But the exact purpose of the DTF is unclear. The Statutory Instrument No 65 of 2001, which defines the modalities of the DTF, clearly states that the objective of the Fund is to assist utilities in the commercialization process but says nothing about service extension to peri-urban areas as an objective, intended result, or even a condition of accessing the Fund. The DTF is currently being conceived as a grant facility, but it is also unclear whether it will become a loan fund in the future, or whether it is supposed to be temporary or permanent. Capital for the DTF is in part expected to come from funds released through debt relief (about US$20 million), with other funds coming directly from central government. The lack of legislative (and institutional) clarity around the nature and purpose of the Fund may pose the risk that priorities other than accessibility and affordability (such as re-capitalization and retrenchment funds for commercial utilities) will hijack these monies.

Poverty Reduction Strategy Paper

The Water Sector chapter of the PRSP was drafted in consultation with a handful of government representatives and a few NGOs who were tasked with the job of completing the final text (in a mere six weeks). Representation for the poor in this process rested solely on the input of the few (mostly international) NGOs present (Anon 2002). Abiding by World Bank and IMF criteria for a successful PRSP, the water services section of the chapter devotes the majority of its attention, and its budgetary allocation, to furthering commercialization while service extension to the urban poor is left largely in the hands of NGOs. A total of US$30 million of debt relief funds has been allocated for recapitalization of commercial utilities and retrenchments, compared with a total of only US$22 million to increase national water and sanitation coverage, particularly for the poor, by 50 per cent (MFNP 2002, p8).

The priorities of the water chapter demonstrate how the PRSP process as a whole operates within the constraints and expectations set by the World Bank and the IMF, so that this supposedly 'nationally owned' strategy for spending debt relief funds differs little from the prescriptions of the now despised structural adjustment programmes.

WATER PRIVATIZATION IN LUSAKA

In February 2002, Severn-Trent Water International Plc, based in the UK, began a private sector participation (PSP) options study for Lusaka, funded by the Public–Private Infrastructure Advisory Facility (PPIAF) of the World Bank. The study was conducted under the supervision of a steering committee comprising representatives from the Ministry of Local Government and Housing, Ministry of Finance and National Planning, Ministry of Trade, Zambia Privatisation Authority, Lusaka City Council, NWASCO and the LWSC. The final report prepared by Severn-Trent contained recommendations upon which the World Bank would make the final decision, in consultation with the Government of Zambia. Upon completion, the report was presented for 'broader consultation' at a Stakeholders Workshop in July 2002 that was attended by 45 people. Invitees included the steering committee and affiliated agencies, as well as two nongovernmental organizations (NGOs). This workshop composed the bulk of the consultation conducted during the study, and there was no publicity of the study or public access to any information. I obtained a leaked copy of the draft report that was completed in May 2002, and present an analysis of its recommendations below.

Severn-Trent's recommendations

The draft report states that Zambia's privatization programme has 'progressed well' but that infrastructure, water, power and telecommunications were undertaken last because they were considered politically sensitive and, for the water sector specifically, a series of major reforms had to be completed in order for private sector participation to be properly implemented (Severn-Trent 2002, Section 3, p5).

Amongst the country's investment incentives the report highlights political stability, the abolition of controls (price, interest rate, exchange rate, and free repatriation of earnings and payments), a 30 per cent corporate tax rate for firms listed on the stock exchange (lower than the standard 35 per cent) and no capital gains tax (Severn-Trent 2002, Section 3, p3). Other perks include the possibility of a full divestment of LWSC's assets (contrary to the stipulations of the Water and Sanitation Act limiting private ownership of utilities to 49 per cent) and the availability of donor funding for service extension to currently unserviced areas (Severn-Trent 2002, Section 4, p6).

The report raises particular concern about LWSC's financial situation and low tariff levels, and the outcomes of a 'demand assessment' of the 'willingness and ability to pay' of Lusaka's residents (or 'consumers', to use the report's preferred terminology). According to Severn-Trent, the very low 'willingness to pay' is the result of both a legacy of poor quality service and a legacy of free water residual from UNIP days. The report acknowledges that the ability of residents in peri-urban areas to pay for water may be constrained by high levels of poverty and that reasonable tariffs from a commercial perspective would exceed the World Bank's recommended 5 per cent threshold of household income spent on water (Severn-Trent 2002, Section 8, p8).

An independent survey undertaken in one of Lusaka's low income areas in 2001 (Turton 2002) showed that 42 per cent of respondents did not feel their monthly water charge of K3000 was fair because their supply was not regular and meters were not installed or not properly functioning, causing some to complain about 'paying for air' (faulty meters sometimes measured consumption even if taps did not produce water when turned on). People also felt they deserved individual house connections. This same survey showed that 45 per cent of respondents did not feel price mechanisms were an appropriate control on demand because they did not feel wealthy consumers would be deterred from wasting water, and that poor consumers deserved to have access regardless of their ability to pay. This study is not included in Severn-Trent's report.

In light of these concerns, Severn-Trent has recommended a ten-year lease contract as the preferred option for private sector participation in Lusaka. This would mean that the private operator would lease facilities from the municipality and take over responsibility for operation, maintenance and management of the system, as well as billing and collection. The city would be left with the responsibility for new capital investments (Severn-Trent 2002, Section 14, p3). According to the report, this arrangement is the most viable given the legal and regulatory framework, the financial risk assessments, and the corresponding interest expressed by its 'market testing' in which several international water companies surveyed expressed a preference for a lease given the risk factors (Severn-Trent 2002, Section 7, p1). Severn-Trent also recommends a new tariff structure, including an increase of at least 35 per cent initially and a simplified 'rising banded' structure, outlined in Table 13.1.

Table 13.1 Severn-Trent's recommended 'rising banded tariff'

Domestic	
Band 1	Basic human needs (6 kl per month per household) set at operating cost (excluding depreciation)
Band 2	Normal consumption (7 to 30 kl per month) set at full cost recovery
Band 3	Discretionary use (in excess of 30 kl per month) set at full cost recovery multiplied by a factor of 1.5, for example
Non-Domestic	single band set at full cost recovery

Source: Severn-Trent 2002, Section 4, 22

The report recommends fitting prepaid meters to all 'bad payers' in order to improve collection rates, though it acknowledges that this strategy could be prone to vandalism (Severn-Trent 2002, Section 4, p1). Prepaid meters are already being introduced in Lusaka by the electricity provider, ZESCO, with plans to extend their use across the country (*Times of Zambia* 2003–2004). According to ZESCO's public relations department, because Zambians 'lack discipline' the meters have been 'a hit' and will improve the company's cost recovery (*Times of Zambia* 2003a). Prepaid meters are popular because they act as a self-disconnection mechanism for poor people and thus shift the burden of public discontent away from the service provider (see Harvey, Chapter 6, this volume).

Severn-Trent also recommends that current cross-subsidies between sectors, from non-domestic to domestic and from commercial/industrial to government, should be eliminated so as not to 'deter the economic growth of the country' and to establish the 'principle of equity of treatment between all users'. The report concludes that LWSC's primary objectives of achieving commercial sustainability and extending services to un(der)serviced areas are at odds (Severn-Trent 2002, Section 4, p25). It therefore recommends that donor funding be used as investment capital for service expansion and improvement, especially in poor areas, because this will help make the 'investment climate' more attractive to a private operator (Severn-Trent 2002, Section 11, p5). On this point, the report acknowledges that 'although many forms of PSP [private sector participation] do not involve the private sector investing large sums of private finance, the involvement of PSP acts as a catalyst to attract donor financing' (Severn-Trent 2002, Section 5, p2).

The leasing of LWSC is expected to provide a model for private service delivery for the entire country under a national PSP in water that is currently being developed by the World Bank. Although I have been unable to confirm whether the recommendation of the lease contract has been approved by the World Bank, this appears to be the case as the PPIAF of the World Bank approved a grant of US$204,000 in December 2002 for 'consensus building and knowledge sharing on the process of implementation of the private sector participation Option Study' and to establish 'an effective local champion for PSP' (World Bank 2003b, p3). A loan of US$35 million is also being prepared by the World Bank to support the start-up of the lease contract and other PSPs in Zambia. This loan, scheduled to be approved in mid-2004, will focus on commercialization, decreasing government support to sectors with 'subsidies' and full cost recovery (World Bank 2003b, p3). Approximately US$26 million of this proposed loan will be devoted to rehabilitation and network extension, working capital for operating costs in the start-up phase of lease contracts and support for transaction costs for selected PSP options (World Bank 2003b, p4).

This kind of support by the Bank for private sector participation in water services in Zambia is not only reminiscent of its efforts in Ghana with the focus there on 'consensus building' (see Amenga-Etego and Grusky, Chapter 15, this volume), but also clearly illustrates the degree to which Bank financing subsidizes (to use a word they so despise) the privatization of water services. The Zambian example reveals the 'carrot-and-stick' approach that the World Bank uses to force the state's retreat from service delivery through loan conditionality and ideological commitment, on the one hand, and entice private sector involvement through subsidies on the other.

Possible implications of the lease recommendations

Severn-Trent's recommendations raise some major concerns regarding service extension to the poor, job security and corruption. Each of these concerns is outlined briefly below.

Service extension to the poor

Financing for service extension to peri-urban areas has not been figured into Severn-Trent's draft capital plan for Lusaka. The head of the Severn-Trent research mission in Zambia stated in an interview that investment in service extension to the poor 'can't be justified in financial terms, so [we] will still look to the public sector and donors to provide for these areas' (interview, Peter Boyce, 22 April 2002). Despite the fact that service extension is included in the licensing conditions of LWSC, NWASCO has been unable to enforce this and thus the likelihood of forcing a large foreign private operator to comply is even less likely. Moreover, Severn-Trent's approach to servicing the poor may allow the 'cherry-picking' of financially viable service areas to be written into a contract.

Labour

Severn-Trent has recommended that current staff numbers at LWSC (approximately 500) be trimmed to around 300. Exactly how this is done will be left to the discretion of the service provider that wins the contract. Given LWSC's poor financial state, the funding source for proper retrenchments remains in question. Again, Severn-Trent believes such funding would have to be secured from the public sector (through debt relief) and from donors, thereby permitting a private operator to enhance profitability while using public money (whether from debt relief or other sources) to mitigate the consequences.

Drawing on past experiences in Zambia, union representatives were concerned with the tendency for privatization to incur massive job losses, stagnate wages (despite high rates of inflation) and weaken commitment to local development. As one union member said, 'private companies can close up fast. Directors can fly off overnight with all their money and you are left in the cold' (interview, Zulawu representative, 19 April 2002).[4]

In May 2002, LWSC employees announced that they would be resigning from the Zambia United Local Authorities Workers Union (Zulawu) in order to form their own national water and sanitation employees union for all the utility companies being commercialized in the country (*Monitor* 2002a). In interviews with Zulawu representatives it does not appear that the union has a policy or position on privatization, and it is unclear whether the new union will either. Until being interviewed for this research, the union was completely unaware of the purpose of Severn-Trent's visit to Lusaka or of the possibility of privatization, and the company had not approached them at any time during the course of its study or presented the union with a copy of the draft report. All this suggests that a union in this case, especially one that has been newly formed, will not be an effective counterweight to private interests.

Corruption

There have been allegations of corruption against the Managing Director of LWSC, Mr Charles Chipulu. In the 26–29 April 2002 issue of *The Monitor*, an article reported that he had allegedly offered the eight members of the company's board of directors, and all 67 of Lusaka's city councillors, free water for six years (amounting to a total of K15 million (US$3420) in lost revenues per month) in return for a renewal of his employment contract.

Workers at LWSC have claimed that this is not the first time Chipulu has orchestrated such deals, having written off water bills for key government officials in 2001 amounting to K8 million (US$1824) (*Monitor* 2002b). Interestingly, no reference of this case has been made by Severn-Trent, the World Bank or by LWSC during or after the PSP study, raising the possibility that such practices will persist or even be exacerbated under a private sector arrangement in which greater flows of capital will be passing through the company.

CONCLUSION

Development policy in the South continues to be overwhelmingly dominated by neoliberal mantras of privatization and cost recovery, and the case of Zambia is no exception. The degree to which the World Bank and the IMF control domestic policymaking in the country is evidenced not only by direct influence through debt relief strategies and loan conditionalities, but also through the ideological hegemony of neoliberal 'truths' in state and donor circles. MMD governments since 1991 have served as the local champions of privatization that the World Bank so highly values (and so desperately needs), with the result that the legislative, regulatory, economic and policy environment in Zambia allows privatization to move forwards despite past failures. Economic crisis has become a political opportunity for the penetration of private interests, while space for political debate is constrained within a narrow and hegemonic neoliberal logic.

Unfortunately, there is little cause for optimism. Given the political and ideological situation in the country and the class consolidation facilitated by privatization in Zambia, there is little reason to believe that the coming privatization of water services in Lusaka (or anywhere else in the country) will be stopped. Despite a certain amount of resistance from civil society groups, from some of the political opposition and from sections of organized labour, critiques of privatization (and neoliberalism more generally) are fractured, heterogeneous and largely superficial. Perhaps the only hope for resistance lies in the possibility for mobilization once privatization begins to reveal what it has done in other parts of the world and once Zambians realize who really wins and who really loses.

NOTES

1 As a case in point, in 2001 and 2002 several municipal councils in Zambia were crippled by massive strikes of council staff demanding salaries that had not been paid for months (*Times of Zambia* 2002b).
2 Peri-urban populations can be quite transient and the impact of HIV/AIDS has made household sizes extremely variable. Because of unreliable population counts, insufficient records of LWSC's activities, and the presence of alternative NGO schemes, it is extremely difficult to assess the number of peri-urban residents LWSC serves. The reform review of 2000 noted that the sustainability and effectiveness of commercialized utilities could not yet be proven, and questioned whether any real incentives yet existed for LWSC to expand service delivery to the poor.
3 Annual inflation in 2002 was 21.5 per cent and 17.4 per cent as of January 2004 (CSO 2004).
4 For reasons of confidentiality, the name of this representative from the Zulawu local has been withheld.

REFERENCES

Anon (2002) *Minutes of PRSP Consultative Meeting*, Lusaka, 29 January
Bartlett, D. (2000) 'Civil Society and Democracy: a Zambian Case Study', *Journal of Southern African Studies*, vol 26, no 3
Boone, C. (1998) '"Empirical Statehood" and Reconfigurations of Political Order', in L. Villalon and P. Huxtable (eds) *The African State at a Critical Juncture: Between Disintegration and Reconfiguration*, Lynne Reiner Publishers, Boulder, Colorado
Bull, M. (2000) *Water Sector Reforms: Community Participation, Gender and Sustainability*, University of Zambia, Lusaka

Burdette, M. (1988) *Zambia: Between Two Worlds*, Westview Press, Boulder, Colorado
Campbell White, O. and Bhatia, A. (1998) *Privatisation in Africa*, World Bank, Washington DC
Chiluba, F.J.T. (1995) *Democracy: The Challenge of Change*, Multimedia Publishers, Lusaka
Craig, J. (2000) 'Evaluating Privatisation in Zambia: The Tale of Two Processes', *Review of African Political Economy*, no 85, pp357–66
CSO (Central Statistical Office) (1998) *Living Conditions in Zambia*, Government of Zambia, Lusaka
CSO (Central Statistical Office) (2004) 'Inflation Statistics', www.zamstats.gov.zm/cpi/cpi.asp
IMF (International Monetary Fund) (2000) 'Decision Point Document for the Enhanced Highly Indebted Poor Countries Initiative', www.worldbank.org/hipc/country-cases/zambia/Zambia_DP_Revised.pdf
LWSC (Lusaka Water and Sewerage Company) (2002a) *Tariff Adjustment Application – Appendix C, Table 4.1*, LWSC, Lusaka
LWSC (Lusaka Water and Sewerage Company) (2002b) *Tariff Adjustment Application – Appendix C, Table 3.1*, LWSC, Lusaka
LWSC (Lusaka Water and Sewerage Company) (2002c) *Tariff Adjustment Application – Form 7a and b*, LWSC, Lusaka
MFNP (Ministry of Finance and National Planning) (2001) *Economic Report*, MFNP, Lusaka
MFNP (Ministry of Finance and National Planning) (2002) *Poverty Reduction Strategy Paper*, MFNP, Lusaka
MLGH (Ministry of Local Government and Housing) (2000) *Peri-Urban Water Supply and Sanitation Strategy*, MLGH, Lusaka
Mmegi (2004) 'Zambians grappling with Privatization', 19 January
The Monitor (2002a) 'LWSC employees resign from ZULAWU', no 234, 28–30 May
The Monitor (2002b) 'Councillors bribed with free water', no 225, 26–29 April
NWASCO (National Water and Sanitation Council) (2001) *Guidelines on Tariffs*, NWASCO, Lusaka
NWASCO (National Water and Sanitation Council) (2002) *Draft Guidelines for Water Watch Groups*, NWASCO, Lusaka
NWP (1994) *National Water Policy of 1994*, Government of Zambia, Lusaka
Nyumbu, I. (1998) *Strengthening Capacity of Water Utilities to Provide Water and Sanitation Services, Environment and Hygiene Education in Low-Income Communities: Case Study of Lusaka Water and Sewerage Company*, Water Utility Partnership, London
Phiri, Z. (2000) *Reorganisation of the Water Sector: Review of German, Irish, and Norwegian Support to the Water Sector in Zambia*, Water Sector Reform Support Unit, Government of Zambia, Lusaka
PCU (Programme Coordination Unit) (1993) 'Water Supply and Sanitation Sector Problems', www.zambia-water.org.zm/sector_reforms.htm
The Post (2004) 'Sata asks gov't. to reveal its deals with IMF', 27 February
Severn-Trent Plc (2002) 'PSP Options for Water Services in the City of Lusaka, Zambia', Draft Report, Severn-Trent Plc, Lusaka
Simutanyi, N. (1996) 'The Politics of Structural Adjustment in Zambia', *Third World Quarterly*, vol 17, no 4, pp825–39
Times of Zambia (2002a) 'Wholesale privatization out', 5–12 December
Times of Zambia (2002b) 'ZNCB sale bid on course – IMF', 14–23 December
Times of Zambia (2003a) 'ZESCO pre-paid scheme a hit', 10–21 April

Times of Zambia (2003b) 'ZCTU supports ZESCO commercialisation', 16–24 June

Times of Zambia (2003–2004) 'ZESCO pre-paid tariff project', 22 December 2003–21 January 2004

Turton, A. (2002) *'Water Demand Management', 'Natural Resource Reconstruction', and 'Adaptive Capacity': Establishing the Linkage between Variables*, report for the Water Research Fund for Southern Africa (WARFSA), African Water Issues Research Unit, University of Pretoria, www.up.ac.za/academic/libarts/polsci/awiru/_warfsa_final_report/warfsa_final_report_appendix_d7.pdf

UNI (Union Network International) (2002) 'Thousands protest against privatization', 16 December, www.union-network.org/uniflashes.nsf/58f61ccf5875fe90c12567bb 005642f9/2024f9c49e911415c1256c9100523df0?OpenDocument

World Bank (1995) 'Urban Restructuring and Water Supply Project: Staff Appraisal' Report, www-wds.worldbank.org/servlet/WDS_IBank_Servlet?pcont=details& eid=000009265_3961019101817

World Bank (2001a) 'Upgrade of Low Income Settlements, Country Assessment Report: Zambia', www.worldbank.org/urban/upgrading/zambia.html

World Bank (2001b) 'Zambia: Institutional Capacity Building for NWASCO', http:// wbln0018.worldbank.org/ppiaf/activity.nsf/6d5570c1ad89c83b85256b6600721d33/ 3e597ee6b0a4b11b852569c3002ccec5?OpenDocument

World Bank (2001c) 'Zambia: Public Expenditure Review', December, www-wds.world bank.org/servlet/WDSContentServer/WDSP/IB/2002/01/18/ 000094946_020109 04014560/Rendered/PDF/multi0page.pdf

World Bank (2003a) 'Zambia data profile', *World Development Indicators Database*, http:/ /devdata.worldbank.org/external/CPProfile.asp?SelectedCountry=ZMB& CCODE=ZMB&CNAME=Zambia&PTYPE=CP

World Bank (2003b) *Support to Water Reform*, Project Information Document, www-wds.worldbank.org/servlet/WDS_IBank_Servlet?pcont=details&eid=000104 615_20031106091213

Young, R. and Loxley, J. (1990) *Zambia: An Assessment of Zambia's Structural Adjustment Experience*, North-South Institute, Ottawa

Zambia United Local Authority Worker's Union (Zulawu) (1999) 'Collective Agreement on Conditions of Service for Unionised Employees for the Period 1 January 2000 to 31 December 2001', Zulawu, Lusaka

INTERVIEWS

Peter Boyce, Head of Severn-Trent mission at LWSC, 22 April 2002

Zulawu representative, 19 April 2002

Chapter 14

Water Privatization in Namibia: Creating a New Apartheid?

Labour Resource and Research Institute (LaRRI)

> We cannot afford to provide water free of charge. Manna has only fallen from heaven once. It does not fall every month (Nickey Iyambo, former Minister of Regional, Local Government and Housing; *Namibian* 2000b).

The commercialization of water services in Namibia since the early 1990s has dramatically altered the social, political and economic landscape of this public service. This chapter seeks to explain the origin and development of these shifts in government water policy, with specific reference to the harmful effects of cost recovery on low income households. The chapter outlines the kind of community resistance that is emerging as a result of these commercialization/ privatization initiatives and concludes with suggestions for water policy reform.

BACKGROUND TO WATER SERVICES IN NAMIBIA

In precolonial Namibia all water was obtained from natural springs, shallow wells in the beds of ephemeral rivers and surface water resources. When water resources dried up, populations migrated or, occasionally, perished in the severe droughts that periodically affect the country. Under German colonial rule, Namibia experienced the growth of towns and large-scale agriculture requiring more reliable sources of water. Wells were deepened and shallow boreholes were drilled.

A civil engineer, Dr T. Rehbock, was commissioned in 1896 to investigate the occurrence, availability and utilization of water resources in the territory. In February 1909 the foundation for an organization to investigate and develop the water resources in Namibia was laid by a decision taken at an agricultural conference in Berlin, Germany. Professor F. Jaeger, a German geographer, compiled the first water register in 1913, by which time assistance from the German government had enabled many farmers to construct a substantial number of boreholes and farm dams in the territory (Heyns 1991, pp20–27). The introduction of geohydrology and the expansionist plans of the German colonialists were interrupted by the outbreak of the First World War. In July

1915, South Africa occupied the territory. During this period of military rule engineers facilitated drilling work and dam construction (with a remarkable degree of cooperation between the Germans and South Africans).

After the declaration of Namibia as a Class C Mandate by the League of Nations under the control of the Union of South Africa, the South West Africa (SWA) Administration was put in place. An irrigation department was formed which in many ways is the predecessor of the modern Department of Water Affairs (DWA). In 1948 a commission recommended a long-term policy for agricultural development and the setting up of a Soil Conservation Board. The board planned and financed water supply works and the construction of farm dams and boreholes (Heyns1991, pp20–25). Attention was paid to the enactment of water legislation through the implementation of a series of legal measures.

In 1969 the Water Affairs Department was integrated into the Department of Water Affairs of South Africa and this increased the resources available for local water service schemes. By 1974 a Master Water Plan was adopted and several large dams and groundwater supply projects were completed. The DWA became a separate organ in the Government Service of SWA in 1980, divorced from its mother body in South Africa. Between 1980 and 1990 the DWA extended its investigations and research activities and established a number of additional supply schemes, including the 260 km Grootfontein Omatako canal and massive dams such as the Omatako (1983), Otjivero (1986) and Oanob (1990). Other major hydrological work included the Omaruru groundwater recharge enhancement investigation, the quantification of surplus water available from state dams for irrigation as well as the integrated system analysis for the Eastern National Water Carrier.

Before the drive towards privatization and commercialization, the DWA supplied water in bulk to regional authorities, who in turn supplied stock farms and settlements. These water services were heavily subsidized (particularly for white Namibians).

THE SHIFTING ROLE OF THE STATE IN WATER PROVISION

After independence in 1990, the new government formed the Ministry of Agriculture, Water and Rural Development (MAWRD), which absorbed the DWA. Almost immediately there was discussion of running water services on market principles. As early as 1991, P. Heyns, then Permanent Secretary of the MAWRD, argued for the commercialization of bulk water (Heyns 1991):

> [S]erious consideration should be given to transform a certain portion of the Department into a rationalised corporation. The design and construction of planned water schemes can be privatized, as well as the operation and maintenance of viable bulk water supply schemes. By creating a more

> *business-like organization to manage the establishment and running of water schemes, a longer term financial strategy . . . can be pursued, better manpower development can be achieved and a better service provided to the community without neglecting the social obligations of the government.*

In August 1994 the feasibility of commercializing bulk water supply was investigated and a Water and Sanitation Committee (WASCO) was established to coordinate the implementation of the Water Supply and Sanitation Policy (WASP) guidelines. These guidelines were later endorsed by the state. In October 1997 the government promulgated the Namwater Act, creating a stand-alone, corporatized bulk water provider – the Namwater Corporation – duly registered as a state-owned company in December of that year (for more details on the definition of 'corporatization' and its relationship to other forms of privatization see McDonald and Ruiters, Chapter 1, this volume).

According to Namwater its primary function is to provide bulk water 'to customers in sufficient quantities, of a quality suitable for the customers' purposes and by cost-effective, environmentally sound and sustainable means'. The first performance contract for Namwater set out five-year financial targets and granted Namwater the power to 'determine and levy, in consultation with the minister, tariffs on a full cost recovery basis for water supplied' (MAWRD 2000a, p4).

The reference to full cost recovery reinforced government's increasing emphasis on water's economic aspects rather than its being a public good and essential human right. Helmut Angula, then Minister of Agriculture, Water and Rural Development, underscored these financial objectives in his comments at the opening of Namwater in April 1998: 'Namwater's commercialization means that the financial burden on Government to subsidise the cost of supplying water to all its citizens has now been somewhat eased' (*Namibian* 1998).

In other words, national government has offloaded the financial costs of bulk water supply by creating a ringfenced business unit responsible for recovering its own costs, that is, by charging consumers the full price of the water consumed. The minister suggested that the commercialization of water services brought government one step closer to the goal of contracting out certain public services in an effort to cut down on expenditures and reduce the size of the public service.

The Namibia Water Resources Management Review (NWRMR) is revealing in this respect. Written in 2000, the NWRMR is an extensive study of the country's natural water sources, carried out as a joint research project by the Ministry of Water, Agriculture and Rural Development, the World Bank and the German aid agency Deutsche Gesellschaft für Technische Zusammenarbeit (GTZ).

In the NWRMR, government is seen as a 'facilitator' and 'regulator' of services, rather than a provider:

> *The role for government in the water sector is a purely regulatory role with the actual supply portions open for operation by the private sector as either a privatized entity or as an operator under public sector ownership... This role would include the removal of significant barriers to entry, the de-politicisation of water as a commodity and the reduction in the potential risks borne by private sector that may arise therefrom* (MAWRD 2000b, p91).

The report goes on to argue for a more thorough market transformation of the country's bulk water provider (MAWRD 2000b, p83):

> Profit Motive – *At present Namwater is a non-profit organization and as such there are few incentives to compete for the right to operate, or to improve efficiency. Economic theory dictates that profit maximisation is a fundamental incentive to efficiency improvements . . . the profit motive is an essential driver of static and dynamic productive efficiency.*
> Competition for the Water Market – *Policy should be oriented towards ensuring contestability is not unnecessarily restricted, i.e. that entry into the water market is not restricted. The extent to which other private sector operators might find bulk water supply in Namibia attractive would need to be investigated.*

Great importance has been attached to the NWRMR in government circles; the Minister of Agriculture, Water and Rural Development, Helmut Angula, announced soon after its release that the recommendations of the review were helping government to reform the water sector (*New Era* 2000).

It did not take long for government to make further moves in this direction. In June 2002, national government began drafting a new law granting powers to the State-Owned Enterprises Governance Council (SOEGC) and the Central Governance Agency (CGA) to privatize parastatals such as Namwater. The chairman of the SOEGC, Dr Abraham Iyambo, said at the time that these consultations would further formalize the process of 'divestiture' of state assets (*Namibian* 2002f). The IMF, in its annual country performance evaluation that year, 'welcomed the newly established Cabinet committee on public enterprise reform and urged the authorities to formulate a time-bound privatization plan'.[1]

As of March 2004 the Bill had not yet been tabled in parliament, but it is clear that government is committed to the further commercialization of water in the country, and possibly to the outright privatization of water services, having already established several public–private partnerships (PPPs) with multinational water companies, as discussed below.

WINDHOEK'S MANAGEMENT CONTRACT

In 1997, the City of Windhoek signed a cooperation agreement with Berliner Wasser Betriebe (BWB) of Germany (BWB serves about 3.5 million people worldwide and is one of the largest municipal water supplier companies in Western Europe with 6300 employees).[2] This cooperation agreement includes advice about new technologies, training and technical support.

In July 2001, BWB, along with water giants Vivendi (from France) and VA Tech WABAG (from Austria), signed a 20-year management contract to provide drinking water to Windhoek via a water reclamation plant near the Goreangab Dam. The plant remains the property of the city but the management is in the hands of the Windhoek Goreangab Operating Company (WINGOC),[3] which is owned by the three multinationals. In December 2002, WINGOC recruited a German CEO to head the operations for the first three years. The management contract can only be terminated if the private company does not meet its contractual obligations. Otherwise the city will have to pay compensation equivalent to three years' profits. The private consortium may, however, terminate the contract if conditions change: for example, in case of excessive pollution of the Goreangab Dam or groundwater sources.

The Windhoek plant is capable of supplying 21,000 m^3 of water per day, accounting for approximately 50 per cent of the city's water demand. It recycles sewerage water pumped from the older sewage plants into the 'already heavily polluted' Goreangab Dam and purifies this wastewater through a 'multi-barrier process' into potable water.[4] Windhoek is currently the only city in the world where this technology is being used to reclaim sewerage water for drinking purposes, prompting President Sam Nujoma to state at the inauguration of the plant that 'the stakeholders [private companies] intend to market and export this technology to countries in the SADC region and the world at large. I believe that countries with similar climatic conditions like ours will greatly benefit from the services of similar equipment' (*Namibian* 2002g).

Some critics (Wellmer 2004) have argued that the PPP was forced on the city by the European Investment Bank (see Mate, Chapter 12, this volume, who raises similar concerns about the EIB in Zimbabwe) and was unnecessary due to the fact that Windhoek already had highly qualified staff with the technical and managerial capacity to run the plant effectively.

IMPACTS OF COST RECOVERY

We turn now to a look at the impacts of Namwater's cost recovery mandate, and the effects this has had on municipalities (who must buy their bulk water from Namwater) and low income households (who must buy their water, in turn, from municipal authorities).

At a national level, Namwater's water tariffs are calculated on a schematic basis within four zones, each of which are structured to fully recover costs and do not allow for cross-subsidization between regions. Namwater has also opted for a purely volumetric tariff rate, with capital costs (infrastructural and financial) included in the volumetric component. The tariffs are reviewed annually and subject to approval by the board of directors. The proposed tariff schedule is issued to government as a *secret Cabinet submission*. The process is nonparticipatory and is not open to public scrutiny. Once approved, the tariff schedule for the more than 200 water-points serviced by Namwater is published in the *Government Gazette*.

Namwater signalled its commitment to cost recovery early on when, in April 1999, shortly after its formation, it reduced supplies to the town of Rehoboth by 50 per cent in order to recover outstanding water debts.[5] In April 2000, Namwater increased tariffs by 20 per cent in Windhoek, the capital city, while increases across the country averaged 17 per cent (*Namibian* 2000a).

This spate of annual price increases continued into 2003, with Namwater threatening 'a reduction of water supply to Namwater defaulters' in July of that year, arguing that it was owed more than N$90 million. The company then secured backing from Cabinet before going ahead with enforcement measures (*Namibian* 2003e). Ironically, the ministries of Land and of Local Government – which are represented, along with all other ministries, on the board of directors of Namwater – were also in arrears. All quickly made partial payments (*Namibian* 2003g).

Measures taken to enforce cost recovery have included the reduction of water pressure to towns and villages. In the town of Usakos the supply pressure was reduced by 50 per cent for more than a month in 2003, effectively cutting off water to certain areas. In this case the lower lying (traditionally white) residential and business areas were not affected, but the (black) townships in the higher areas lost all water pressure for more than a month. People had to travel for up to 12 km to adjacent farms to buy water, sparking community resistance.

In another case, the Tsumeb municipality suspended water services to all government schools for more than a week when the Ministry of Basic Education failed to settle its debt. This incident was by no means unique. The Gustav Kandkii Junior Secondary school in Otjinene, for example, had its water supply cut by Namwater in January 2004 due to the nonpayment of water bills by the Ministry of Regional, Local Government and Housing. Pupils at Mayuni Senior Secondary School in the Caprivi, also stranded without water in October 2003, were forced to walk up to 6 km to the Kwando River to collect water. They complained about the stench from toilets and staged a stay-away protest. 'The health hazard is obvious. The learners cannot wash themselves properly and the kitchen cannot keep the hygienic standards required by a hostel kitchen. We are dealing with a time bomb and the losers are the learners – the future of Namibia', said Anne Marie Melgaard of the Support Environmental Education in Namibia project (*Namibian* 2004a,b).

In July 2003 several other towns had their bulk water supply reduced for failing to pay debts (*Namibian* 2003h). Hardest hit were Rundu, Opuwo, Usakos, Katima Mulilo and Kalkrand (*Namibian* 2003f). At Katima Mulilo water supply was completely cut off. In Okakarara, the water supply was reduced. At Opuwo even the hospital had been left without water. The response of Erastus Negonga, the Permanent Secretary in the Ministry of Regional, Local Government and Housing, to all of this: 'We are not in a position to bail them out. We hope that they will work very hard to pay their accounts' (*Namibian* 2003i).

The predicament of the local government authorities

Local authorities in Namibia have responded to Namwater's cost recovery measures in a number of ways, including:

- the periodic adjustment of tariffs to correspond to Namwater's commercialized cost and pricing structure;
- subsidization and cross-subsidization of services within municipal zones;
- the installation of prepaid water meters (primarily in low income areas);
- outsourcing of water supply and sanitation functions; and
- staff retrenchments.

Prior to the corporatization of Namwater, national government had spent between N$200 and N$300 million each year on a subsidy scheme to 36 municipalities and 21 proclaimed villages and settlements. The provision of services in Windhoek City, for example, was annually subsidized by N$20 million (*Namibian* 2001). Now that deficit is recovered from the consumer.

The effect on small towns and villages has been particularly hard. Ondangwa's Town Council, for example, relied on central government to pay 80 per cent of its water bill. 'The delivery of services will be affected . . . [and] capacity has been undermined to a large extent' remarked the Town Clerk, Funneka Shigwedha. 'The withdrawal of subsidies means that Council will have to use its funds for operational activities and that means there will be no further capital development – or extension of infrastructure' (*Namibian* 2001).

At Katima Mulilo, the council ran out of money to administer the town's affairs and was unable to pay its staff by late 2003. Municipal workers had to go without their salaries for long periods; investment schemes could not be paid and workers were in danger of losing their pension funds as the town's financial state deteriorated. There were outstanding telephone bills that could not be paid and in some instances the municipal telephone lines were cut.

The town's prepaid meter water system was expected to relieve fiscal constraints by bringing in fresh cash, but this system collapsed, with mechanical problems leading to unmetered water supply. Meanwhile, the town still lived with a rationed water supply from Namwater of about six hours a day. Not surprisingly, the officials at Katima were reluctant to enter into a service agreement with Namwater for fear that they would lose control of the setting of tariffs, a very political question affecting the balance of power and support within the local authorities. The Katima Mulilo Council subsequently announced its decision to cut its staff by over 40 per cent (*Namibian* 2003k). The Auditor General's report for the year 2000–2001, tabled in parliament in March 2003, showed that local authorities were in deep financial trouble, but Namwater continued to impose its rates hikes.

The following examples are symptomatic of a more general trend:

- Karasburg had N$942,685 in loan repayment arrears by June 2001. It moved to outsource some of its services as a result, contracting Southern Electricity

Company (SELCo) of South Africa to manage its electricity supply for 15 years (SELCo was also given the option of taking over the water distribution function at its earliest convenience).
- Okahandja's deficit was N$4.5 million by June 2001, apparently mainly due to nonpayment of debts by residents of the Nau-Aib township.
- Luderitz's debts amounted to N$6 million by June 2001, up from N$1.5 million in 2000.
- Omaruru Council claimed it was owed more than N$600,000 and had a bank balance of only N$1000.
- Gobabis had a cash flow problem and advances to the tune of N$6.5 million had to be made to finance operations during 2001 (*Namibian* 2003b).

Effects on the poor

In a few of the wealthier municipalities, such as Walvis Bay, councils could afford to pay their bulk water bills and even absorb some of the cost increases by keeping rate hikes below those of Namwater (*Namibian* 2003c). But this is an exception to the rule, largely because Walvis Bay has a range of alternative income sources related to the harbour activities, mining and industry which it can use to cross-subsidize water but which are not available to most of the smaller and more remote towns and villages in the country.

When Namwater increased tariffs by 20 per cent on 1 April 2000, the City of Windhoek raised its prices from N$2.65 per cubic metre to N$3.11. Previously, the city's Tariff Stabilisation Fund had been used to counter the effects of rising water prices but by June 1998 the fund was already in debt by N$10.3 million.

Some members of Windhoek City Council objected to the price increases, with the Mayor of Windhoek, Matthew Shikongo, commenting that: 'Past studies done on the affordability level of the poorest sector of our community have shown that water is already unaffordable to this sector' (remarkably, the CEO of the city served on the Namwater board that decides on tariffs) (*Namibian* 2000a). By mid-2002, the City Council was, however, defending its decision to again implement the annual tariff increase and average water prices went up by a further 13 per cent – price hikes were approved by the City Council on 12 June (Namibian 2002b).

For smaller towns it proved even harder to subsidize household water consumption. In Henties Bay, for example, bulk water price increases forced retail costs up to N$3.25 per cubic metre, as compared with Walvis Bay at N$2.50 and Swakopmund at N$2.70. The Mayor of Uis, a small town with little or no industry and a very poor working class community, reported that his municipality was now charging water at N$4.11 per cubic metre (*Namibian* 2003a).

Water cutoffs

The most common way for municipalities to deal with payment arrears is suspending water supply to defaulting households, a function that has also been contracted out in many cases. The municipality of Windhoek, for example, employs a private contractor to cut water supplies in Katutura and Khomasdal.

This private contractor said that his team cuts off water to more than 100 houses per day (confidential interview, 17 October 2003). With an average household size of six people – even larger in low income households – this means that at least 600 people per day and 3000 a week have been having their water cut in these two areas alone in Windhoek as a result of Namwater's cost recovery mandate. When people resist these cutoffs by breaking the locks on the taps, municipal workers are sent to cut the underground pipes that lead to the house.

Revealing the political sensitivity of water cuts, one official interviewed pointed out that prior to the elections of 1998 their office in Okuryungava was contacted by the mayor's office and told to stop the cutoffs for the time being 'because we are busy with an election'. After the elections the official could continue cutting off supplies. The official also admitted that staff members were not sure of the legality of the measures to enforce cost recovery. They appealed to members of the community to take the council to court over the issue, as they themselves were convinced that the cutoffs were illegal. Even municipal officials often could not afford to pay their own water accounts.[6]

'The price of water skyrocketed beyond the capabilities of a good number of residents', according to one Oshakati resident, when the suspension of water services was announced in September 2002 (*Namibian* 2002d). Residents who had their water cut because they could not pay their bills faced a serious health risk as they were forced to resort to the dirty water from flood pans (oshanas). Many residents took water from broken pipes in town. Gardens withered and toilets could not be used. Some residents had been without water for months, even years, because they could not pay their bills. Karina Amupunda said that her water had been cut for a year, but she still received regular water bills.

In Otjinene, one school had to be shut down when students walked out as they and the staff could no longer bear the stench and accumulated filth after Namwater had cut the water supply to their school. The bill had not been paid by the Ministry of Regional and Local Government – the very same ministry that was part of approving the increased water tariffs!

Auctioning of houses

The repossession and confiscation of movable property has become an increasingly familiar phenomenon to many people, particularly in poorer townships. The daily rounds of the Messenger of the Court has become a feared and hated phenomenon. One of the main functions of this office is to seize the property of those who failed to pay their municipal debts (*Namibian* 2003j). The officers of the court often lock people out of their homes, particularly if their houses have been sold to collect debts.

At Goreangab, where several thousand working class families live in small brick houses and self-constructed shacks not far from the Goreangab Dam, a movement has emerged to challenge this. Having had enough, people from

Goreangab eventually marched to the Windhoek mayor's office to demand the reconnection of water supply and an end to the confiscation of poor people's erven (*Namibian* 2004c).

Of the many people evicted from their homes over the past few years, two examples serve to illustrate the effects of this policy. In late 2003 a 24-year-old woman in Katutura was given notice that her home would be sold by auction in order to recover outstanding water bills. Anna Gretha had inherited the house, and municipal debts, when her mother passed away. She has three dependants, including her younger sister who is at school. She is unemployed and is HIV-positive. However, on the day of the auction in mid-December 2003 many members of the community gathered outside the Katutura Court to defend her and the sheriff eventually cancelled the auction when the community grew irate.

Another resident in Katutura was not so fortunate. Mrs Nanus, a pensioner with six dependants and a N$250 monthly allowance, was evicted by the sheriff after her house was sold by the Windhoek municipality to recover outstanding water bills. At first, members of the community and her neighbours resisted the eviction and carried her furniture back in to the house. However, the Messenger of the Court returned with a group of armed Special Field Force members, a division of the Namibian Defence Force, and ejected the woman and her children from the house by force.[7]

Prepaid water and the 'new apartheid'

In the Democratic Resettlement Community (DRC), an informal settlement on the outskirts of Swakopmund, the town council decided to introduce prepaid water meters as a way to recover debts on outstanding arrears from residents. According to the Town Clerk of Swakopmund, Eckart Demasius: 'Council wants to create a payment culture. When people move to a town they must learn to abide by the rules of the town' (*Namibian* 2002c).

Problems were reported with the functioning of the cards early on, and meters were damaged by residents trying to get water or not understanding how they worked. The system was then replaced by new, 'tamper-proof' prepaid meters, which the company claimed were inviolable (*New Era* 2003). Realizing this, some people decided it was easier to simply bypass the prepaid system by cutting the water pipe beneath the ground and filling their canisters from there. The meters continue to fail and many people have been left with no water supply at all.

The prepaid meters also cause great inconvenience. It is a long distance to the municipal offices in Mondesa to buy credits for the meters in DRC (approximately 3.5 km by foot each way; N$4 by taxi) and it is not possible to buy water credits after 5:00 p.m. or on weekends, making it extremely inconvenient and dangerous for families that run out of water at those times. On several occasions shack fires have burned out of control because there was insufficient water in prepaid meters in people's homes.

Poor communities have said that the policy of prepaid meters is the 'new apartheid' of Namibia, in part because the meters have been installed in black townships and shanty towns, not in rich suburbs or in the industrial areas where vast amounts of water are consumed. The result is that those who can afford to pay are able to use as much as they please on 'credit' meters while those without the means are often left without water and have to pay in advance.

Prepaid meters are now being marketed by the national government as the solution to bad debts and water conservation across the country: 'One needs to ensure a direct correlation between payment for services and consumption', argued Nickey Iyambo, former Minister of Local Government (*Namibian* 2002a). Nossob River Systems, the company that installed the meters in the DRC, has since won a N$35 million contract to install prepaid water meters in about 20 other towns and villages in Namibia (*New Era* 2004).

In 2003, the town of Arandis became the first municipality in the world to be completely dependent on prepaid water meters. 'We hope the prepaid system will bring an end to bad debts', said the Arandis Town Clerk, Florida Cloete (*Namibian* 2002a). It was also reported that Nossob was working on a prepaid water trough for animals, to be introduced in communal farming areas.

In Rundu, the mayor formally appealed to the residents of informal settlements to use the new prepaid water meters and threatened to have the water pipes closed to areas where the meters were vandalized. The council had installed over 700 meters at lower income houses in the town and in the so-called informal settlements (*Namibian* 2003d).

In a bizarre twist of events in the town of Rehoboth, the South West Africa People's Organization (SWAPO) MP Alfred Stefanus Dax led a march of 50 people to the municipal offices, with people actually demanding prepaid water meters. The MP and his followers insisted that the council sign the contract for the installation of 1315 prepaid meters. The crowd vented their anger by throwing buckets of human excrement into the municipal offices (*Namibian* 2002e).[8] It is possible, however, that this was the work of political agitators promoting prepaid technology given that most other communities who had experienced the prepaid system resented and resisted it.

Constitutional implications

The Preamble of the Constitution states that no person may be discriminated against on the grounds of race, sex or socioeconomic standing. Article 95 obliges the government to promote and maintain the welfare of the people, through policies, amongst others, aimed at maintaining 'an acceptable level of nutrition and standard of living of the Namibian people and to improve public health'.

The Namibian government is also a signatory to international laws such as The Convention on the Elimination of all Forms of Discrimination against Women (1979) and the Convention on the Rights of the Child (1989), and international law is recognized as part of Namibian law by virtue of Article 144 (*LAC News* 2003).[9]

Furthermore, the Local Authorities Act of 1992, section 30(1), stipulates that a municipality must: (a) supply water to the residents in its area for household, business or industrial purposes, and (b) provide, maintain and carry on a system of sewerage and drainage, for the benefit of the residents in its area. The Act is directly enforceable in a court of law and the obligation of the local authorities to provide services (including water services) 'to the benefit of its residents' is actionable in court if they fail to do so. Whether legal action will be undertaken, as has begun in some parts of South Africa on water cutoffs and household evictions, remains to be seen. In the UK, prepaid meters have already been outlawed. The UK's 1998 Water Act declared prepayment meters to represent a threat to public health and water cutoffs to be an unacceptable method of recovering outstanding debt (see also Flynn and Chirwa, Chapter 3, this volume).

Conclusion

The withdrawal of state subsidies on water services and the application of cost recovery measures has affected the entire country and thrown local government authorities into a financial and political crisis. It has also precipitated a crisis for many poor households. The withdrawal of subsidies for household water provision illustrates government's attempts to redefine its 'core functions' and its reluctance to provide basic services by subjecting these services to the dictates of the market. The provision of water has become a purely economic matter with private firms and market oriented public managers seeking maximum profits/surplus in their operations.

The extensive water cutoffs being enforced throughout the country undermine public health, increase the cost of providing health services, expose the poor to preventable diseases, amplify the possibility of epidemic outbreaks and erode working class life. The eviction of working class families and pensioners due to unpaid (or unpayable) water bills effectively undercuts government's housing policy as well, and in many cases has forced people to move into shacks. This policy has in many instances been perceived as a continuation of colonial practices of land dispossession. The policy of water cutoffs and evictions over water bills is an unacceptable method of recovering debt. It is reversing some of the social progress made in Namibia since independence. The aggressive cost recovery policy represents an attack on the welfare gains made by the oppressed people in their struggle for decent living conditions.

In this context the following recommendations for water reform in Namibia arise:

- Access to water should be regarded as a fundamental and inalienable right of every human being, regardless of socioeconomic status, and should be protected by legislative and institutional guarantees.
- A thorough assessment should be undertaken to establish the correlation between the commercialization of water services and disease prevalence in Namibia.

- The provision of basic water services, including urban and rural water supply should be reincorporated into the public sector as a core function of government, operated on a nonprofit and transparent basis.
- A free minimum lifeline of household water supply (commensurate with the requirements of health, hygiene and culture) should be implemented to safeguard the interests of indigent families, children and pensioners.
- A publicly accountable institution tasked with the regulation and determination of water quality, quantity and tariffs should be established. A transparent system of community participation in the determination of water tariffs should be implemented to safeguard the people and their resources from excessive exploitation.
- Subsidies for the provision of basic water services to the poor should be prioritized.
- The policy of water cutoffs and the system of prepayment for water services (self-disconnection) should be withdrawn and declared illegal.

The emergence of community movements, alongside labour organizations, fighting against the privatization and commercialization of water, and against the withdrawal of basic services, are essential forces in the struggle for decent social and public health policies and practices in Namibia. Such struggles are themselves increasingly being globalized as community and labour movements throughout the world are connecting in solidarity to begin to challenge the destructive logic of the market.

Acknowledgements

This chapter is based on a study carried out by Jade McClune for the Labour Resource and Research Institute (LaRRI) in Namibia. The full study is entitled 'Water Privatization in Namibia: Creating a New Apartheid' and can be accessed on LaRRI's website at www.larri.com.na.

Notes

1 *IMF Concludes Article IV Consultations with Namibia*, 22 February 2002, www.imf.org
2 BWB also operates in Albania, Azerbaijan, China, Croatia, Hungary, Poland, Russia, Thailand, Turkey, and holds consulting contracts with governments in many more countries involved in the privatization of water and waste services. See www.berlinwasser.net/e_data/e_refer.htm
3 Media reports suggested that WINGOC would only operate the plant until 2010, but Berlinwasser's website states that the contract is valid for 20 years; www.berlinwasser.net/e_data/e_refer.htm
4 VA Tech WABAG's website: www.wabag.com
5 Namwater claimed that it was owed N$5.5 million.

6 This exchange took place in late November 2003, during a confrontation between the officials at Okuryungava and Ada/Gui (the Pensioners' and Destitute Children's Association) over the lack of water supply to poorer households.
7 It was reported in an interview with Mr Johannes Hendricks from the Pensioners' and Destitute Children's Association, Ada/Gui, that in January 2004 he had seen Mrs Nanus wandering the streets of Katutura aimlessly, speaking to herself and strewing flowers. He could not even talk to her as she was not sensible to anyone who tried. He said that she suffered much when she lost her home and was psychologically disturbed by the ordeal.
8 Chairperson of the Council's Management Committee, Jakobus Louw, said the delay in signing the contract was caused by the fact that Nossob River System wanted to install 4000 more prepaid meters. This would cost the already financially stretched council N$13 million. The council was struggling to pay off a N$6 million 'historic' water debt to Namwater.
9 International treaties signed by Namibia (i.e. the president) and ratified by parliament immediately become part of Namibian law.

References

Heyns, P. (1991) *Perspective on Water Affairs*, MAWRD, Department of Water Affairs, Windhoek
LAC News (2003) Issue 13, November
MAWRD (2000a) *Namibia Water Resources Management Review, Theme Report; Financial and Socio-economic Issues*, MAWRD, Windhoek
MAWRD (2000b) *Namibia Water Resources Management Review, Theme Report; Legislative and Regulatory Framework*, MAWRD, Windhoek
The Namibian (1998) 'Namwater aims to recover costs', 17 April
The Namibian (2000a) 'Council 'rejects' water increase', 28 April
The Namibian (2000b) 'Govt urges Namwater to tighten taps on costs', 17 October
The Namibian (2001) 'Govt subsidy withdrawal hits poorer municipalities', 11 May
The Namibian (2002a) 'Arandis on the map with a water first', 12 June
The Namibian (2002b) 'City defends rate hikes', 28 June
The Namibian (2002c) 'Water woes worsen for DRC residents', 7 August
The Namibian (2002d) 'Water defaulters face risks', 18 September
The Namibian (2002e) 'Rehobothers cause stink in prepaid protest', 19 September
The Namibian (2002f) 'Govt drafts new law to formalise privatization', 16 October
The Namibian (2002g) 'Windhoek Municipality launches N$100m water reclamation plant', 3 December
The Namibian (2003a) 'Henties pounds the drum on cost of water', 17 February
The Namibian (2003b) 'Local councils in dire straits', 4 March
The Namibian (2003c) '10% water increase at Walvis', 26 June
The Namibian (2003d) 'Rundu residents urged to use water meter system', 9 July
The Namibian (2003e) 'Namwater to get serious with debtors', 17 July
The Namibian (2003f) 'Namwater halves Katima and Opuwo water supply', 23 July
The Namibian (2003g) 'Namwater warns of further action against debtors', 29 July
The Namibian (2003h) 'Water squeeze hurting towns', 30 July

The Namibian (2003i) 'Water rage at Rundu', 4 September
The Namibian (2003j) 'Don't shoot the messenger. It's all in a days work', 30 October
The Namibian (2003k) 'Katima Council runs out of money', 25 November
The Namibian (2004a)'Bad smell shuts school at Otjinene', 6 February
The Namibian (2004b) 'No Solution in sight for "Smelly School"', 18 February
The Namibian (2004c) 'Enough is enough', 12 March
New Era (2000) '50% of Rural People have Access to Potable Water', 26–29 March
New Era (2003) 'Prepaid water system fails at Katima', 17–20 November
New Era (2004) 'Accusations fly in water quarrel', 2–5 February
Wellmer, G. (2004) *Vulamanzi! Beteiligung privater Unternehmen an oeffentlichen Wasserwerken und die Rechte armer Verbraucher*, KOSA, Bielefeld, Germany

Box 6 *Draft Manifesto Against Water Privatization in Namibia*

The Ada /Gui Senior Citizens and Destitute Children's Association, Windhoek, Namibia. Adopted April 2004

Ada/Gui is a community organization comprising workers, youth, unemployed people, pensioners and activists fighting for social justice in Windhoek, Namibia. The name 'Ada /Gui' means 'Let us Unite.' Ada /Gui has been campaigning since 1996 around issues such as the right to housing and the right of pensioners, single mothers, the unemployed and poorer families to have access to water and basic services.

It is on the basis of this minimum programme in defence of the interests of the working class that the Ada /Gui will send its candidates into council. Any councillor from the Ada /Gui that does not carry out the tasks entrusted to him or her by the community, will be removed from office within six months. Ada /Gui will not sit for five years with councillors that do not do their work, but will within six months remove any candidates who do not show progress in carrying forward the programme of the people as outlined in this Manifesto. Every successful candidate from Ada /Gui that enters into council will be required to use a portion of their income from council to open a councillor's office in the area in which they live, within two months of being elected to office.

A vote for Ada /Gui is a vote against water and electricity cutoffs. It is a vote against the eviction of poor people from their homes. A vote for Ada /Gui is a vote against privatization, against corruption, against the exploitation of the poor and downtrodden. A vote for Ada /Gui will give power to the people, it will give voice to the needs of the aged, of the unemployed, the workers, the youth, the destitute children and all those people whose voices are never heard within the city council. A vote for Ada /Gui is a vote for a healthy and powerful community. Now is the time to defeat the political parties who have betrayed the interests of the people time and again. Now is the time to seize our own power. Now is the time to stand up for our rights and to defend what is ours.

During and after these elections Ada /Gui will campaign for:

- an immediate end to the policy of total water cutoffs;
- taps that provide water, even to the poor, should be opened;
- the implementation of a basic free minimum lifeline of water to every individual and household;
- water to be subsidised and made affordable to all;
- basic infrastructure for water and sewerage services to be extended to the poor;
- water services to be based on the needs of the community not on profit-making motives.

Ada /Gui calls for:

- the cancellation of the outstanding municipal arrears – scrap the old debts!
- the cancellation of the bank-related interest added on to municipal arrears;
- the cancellation of the lawyers' fees being levied over and above the debts and arrears;

- the implementation of a flat rate of N$20 for basic services provided to pensioners and destitute people;
- the implementation of a minimum quota of free electricity for pensioners, poor and destitute people;
- consideration and humanity on the part of municipal officials when dealing with the problems of poverty and deprivation with the community.

Ada /Gui demands:

- an immediate end to the confiscation of poor people's homes and erven over municipal debts;
- an immediate end to the arbitrary and illegal eviction of destitute and poor people from their homes;
- a programme of public works to create employment and extend infrastructure for basic services.

Our communities urgently need:

- municipal offices in our areas where people can buy electricity;
- the extension of electricity to our homes and erven;
- toilets and drainage systems to protect the environment and health of the people;
- streetlights to make our neighbourhoods safer;
- more buses at affordable rates for workers and students;
- clinics in our areas;
- recreational facilities for school children and also senior citizens.

Ada /Gui rejects:

- those councillors and officials that ignore the needs and situation of the community;
- the system of prepaid water meters; we need taps to live decent healthy lives;
- the policy of water privatization as a betrayal of the buxom interest of the nation;
- the policy of water cutoffs as a crime against humanity;
- the eviction of poor people from their homes and erven as a violation of basic human rights.

Down with water cutoffs!
Down with evictions!
Down with privatization!
Scrap the municipal arrears!
Scrap the bank-related interest!
Scrap the lawyers' fees!
Forward to the free basic lifeline of water!
Forward to human rights and social justice!
Forward to a new city council!

(Note: This is an abbreviated version of this Draft Manifesto)

Chapter 15

The New Face of Conditionalities: The World Bank and Water Privatization in Ghana

Rudolf Nsorwine Amenga-Etego and Sara Grusky

In 2001, against tremendous odds, civil society organizations in Ghana opposed a World Bank-backed project to contract the urban water system to large multinational water corporations. The Ghana National Coalition Against the Privatization of Water (National CAP of Water) successfully interrupted 'business as usual' in the world of multinational corporate takeovers of public assets, setting back the timetable for completing the privatization deal for three years running. The water privatization project continues to encounter numerous obstacles, not the least of which is the groundswell of resistance from Ghanaian civil society. Some Ghanaian government officials would like to suspend the privatization scheme and the major corporate water companies have reassessed the terms of their bid proposals. Yet, the World Bank is determined to push the project forward.

This chapter dissects and analyses the World Bank's water sector reform proposal, and the strategies and mechanisms of the World Bank's influence on Ghanaian government and civil society. The opposition movement organized by the National CAP of Water is also analysed with a focus on the impact of the opposition movement on the strategies and decision making of the World Bank, the government of Ghana and the large multinational water companies. The opposition in Ghana is alive and ongoing. The final outcome of the struggle is yet to be determined and, as of this writing, the World Bank has unleashed yet another public relations campaign to sell the privatization scheme.

HISTORICAL CONTEXT: A HISTORY OF RESISTANCE

Ghana plays an important historic and symbolic role on the African continent as the first country to challenge the colonial order and gain independence in 1957 from British rule. Kwame Nkrumah, Ghana's postcolonial leader, then launched a campaign for the complete independence of the African continent. This anti-colonial history undoubtedly influenced World Bank and International

Monetary Fund (IMF) officials to give special attention to courting Ghana and later trying to promote the country as the West African neoliberal 'success story'. However, the governments and people of Ghana have been at least as creative and successful at resisting as they have been at implementing IMF and World Bank structural adjustment policies (SAPs).

Nkrumah rejected IMF loan conditionalities that would have interrupted his massive public-ownership development policies that built railroads, dams, harbours, industry, medical and educational facilities (Frimpong-Ansah 1991). Yet, most of the military and civilian governments that followed accepted IMF and World Bank loan packages requiring the usual array of government budget cutbacks, public sector retrenchment, import liberalization, removal of price controls and subsidies, privatization of public enterprises and currency devaluation. In 1971, following the implementation of the second round of IMF economic policies, currency devaluation caused prices of basic food items like sugar, rice and milk to rise sharply and the military used the popular discontent as a pretext to overthrow the elected government (Boafo-Arthur 1999). The repeated and widespread domestic opposition to IMF and World Bank policies made it clear to political leaders in the post-Nkrumah era that, while bringing resources and foreign investment, imposing neoliberal policies could have a very high political cost.

During the 1970s and 1980s, many critics argued that IMF and World Bank officials cared little whether governments were military or civilian, dictatorial, authoritarian human rights abusers.[1] In fact, many analysts have argued that successful Bank and Fund style reform required autocratic, centralized governments (no checks and balances) and some amount of repression or 'political immobilization' (Bello et al 1982; Callaghy 1990, pp9–10). This was certainly the model of Flight Lt Rawlings who took power in a successful military coup in 1981, won popular elections in 1992 and 1996, and ruled for almost two decades using 'an array of non-democratic and authoritarian political practices in combination with neo-corporatist arrangements to gird its rule' (Gyimah-Boadi 1990, p133). Rawlings used anticolonial and socialist rhetoric when it was politically expedient, especially in the early years, but was quick to negotiate with the IMF and World Bank in 1983 when this strategy appeared most likely to consolidate his long-term power by providing an immediate and reliable source of finance.

Over the next two decades, the Rawlings government negotiated a steady succession of IMF and World Bank loan packages. The tough medicine of structural adjustment was initially justified as necessary to pull Ghana out of debt, yet by the late 1980s Ghana's debt had risen to over US$2 billion and by 2000, after two decades of IMF and World Bank advice, it reached over US$6 billion (Iddi 2003, p2). With this overwhelming debt load, Ghana became eligible for the IMF and World Bank 'Heavily Indebted Poor Country Initiative' (HIPC) and was rewarded for its faithful following of IMF and World Bank policies by a new debt relief package and even more loans, all conditioned on the very same failed policy prescriptions. It has been a dangerous quagmire that, 20 years later, has left Ghana with the same dependence on a few primary export commodities (cocoa and gold) and lack of domestic industrial capacity that had thwarted its development two decades earlier.

Government elites along with IMF and World Bank officials alternately gloated and scowled about economic growth rates, inflation rates and privatization proceeds over the two-decade period. But generally Ghana's role on the international stage was to pose as a good performer and a neoliberal success story. The 'macroeconomic indicators' obscured the real social and environmental impacts of SAPs that included massive cuts in the government budget and new fees for basic human services such as health and education. The imposition of user fees for education led to reduced enrolment rates and primary school dropout rates as high as 40 per cent (SAPRI 1998). In 1990, 80.5 per cent of children were reaching fifth grade, but by 2000 the number had shrunk to 66.3 per cent (UN 2002). There was also a rise in the tuition costs for secondary and tertiary education. Total enrolment at tertiary level stands at 50,000 in a population of nearly 20 million. New fees for health care reduced outpatient attendance by as much as 33 per cent, particularly in rural areas (SAPRIN 2001).

SAPs promoted export agriculture over food production for the domestic market reducing land and resources devoted to the cultivation of basic food crops. IMF and World Bank policies included the removal of agricultural subsidies causing a rise in input prices and trade liberalization measures resulting in a flood of cheap imports. All of these policies harmed local food producers. Subsistence farmers, who constitute most of the 80 per cent of the poor who live in rural areas, have been the hardest hit by these policies.

The rush towards privatization also had severe social and environmental impacts. The state-owned gold mines were privatized in the mid-1980s; the new foreign investors paid little in taxes, challenged traditional community land rights in order to stake their claims to the mineral wealth, and imposed lax and exploitative labour, health and environmental standards. The IMF and World Bank pushed an expansive privatization agenda during the 1990s focusing on privatization of banks, railroads, ports, the oil refinery, agricultural marketing boards, public transportation, telecommunications, gold mines and other state-owned industries (IMF 2000, pp85–98).

A number of Ghanaian scholars, authors and activists have argued that Rawlings's success in implementing IMF and World Bank structural adjustment programmes was not unrelated to his ruthless and autocratic style of governance (Gyimah-Boadi 1990; Boafo-Arthur 1999). Opposition was intimidated and silenced through laws such as the Preventive Custody Law under which any person could be arrested and detained 'in the interest of national security' and laws that prescribed death by firing squad to political offenders (Boafo-Arthur 1999). Even under such repressive circumstances, and especially as the Rawlings government experienced pressures to democratize in the 1990s, opposition to SAPs was a steady undercurrent that burst forth in moments of great societal tension. For example, in 1995, the government had to withdraw the proposal for a 17.5 per cent value-added tax (VAT) after large popular protests turned violent and five people were killed (Kofi 1997). The VAT is an infamous IMF and

World Bank invention, a regressive tax measure designed to increase government revenues by burdening everyday consumers with a new sales tax.

Given this history it is not at all surprising that, especially after Rawlings's party was voted out in 2000 and President Kufuor came to power with promises of greater political freedoms, pressures to resist IMF and World Bank policies and efforts to explore alternative approaches to development grew stronger. In this context, the World Bank-backed proposal to contract the urban water system in Accra to large foreign multinationals was met with tremendous anger and scepticism from Ghanaian civil society.

THE GOVERNMENT OF GHANA, THE WORLD BANK AND THE GLOBAL WATER COMPANIES

It is not unusual that large World Bank-backed privatization schemes contain a dose of scandal, corruption and bribery. The first attempt to privatize the water system in Ghana, in 1999, had just such an infamous beginning. Ghana's Ministry of Housing and Works selected the Enron subsidiary, Azurix, over the two other bidders (Suez and Vivendi). The two losing companies claimed unfair bidding practices. As the deal started to fall apart allegations were made that Azurix gave US$5 million in kickbacks to key Ghanaian politicians. Peter Harrold, World Bank representative in Ghana at the time, acknowledged 'suspicions of corruption' and a draft schedule of payments by Azurix showed a US$5 million upfront payment (*Financial Times* 2002). Azurix officials denied committing bribery. But, due to public protest, the contract offer was withdrawn. The World Bank backed out on its loan and the whole water privatization project was forced to start all over again.

The real beginning of the water privatization project in Ghana started a number of years before the Azurix scandal, however. The so-called 'reform' of Ghana's water sector was shaped by two interrelated World Bank policies on **decentralization** and **unbundling**.

The intent of decentralization was to devolve certain fiscal, administrative and development responsibilities from the central government to district assemblies. The district assemblies prepare a five-year plan and receive an annual allocation from central government. While decentralization can increase local participation, and improve the accountability and transparency of government, many critics of the approach claim it is primarily driven by fiscal concerns – that is, the desire to reduce central government expenditures and increase the revenue generation responsibilities at the district assembly level. Reducing central government's budget deficit has always been a central World Bank and IMF concern, one that has increased as Ghana's debt load has grown. Decentralization set the stage not only for devolving the provision of water and sanitation services to the district level, but also placed new fiscal burdens on the mostly impoverished rural population.

Decentralization was accompanied by a phenomenon called unbundling or ringfencing by the World Bank (but often referred to as cherry-picking by trade unions and civil society groups). Bluntly stated, the unbundling process is one whereby the profitable and the unprofitable sectors of the production process of a good or service are separated. The unprofitable sectors remain in the public sector and the profitable sectors are transferred to the private sector. The details of the unbundling process in Ghana had two dimensions (World Bank 1998). First, it required the separation of the profitable urban water sector from the unprofitable rural water sector. Prior to the unbundling process, the wealthier urban areas subsidized water in the poorer rural areas. With unbundling, two separate government agencies, one for rural water and one for urban water, were created and the cross-subsidy was effectively ended. Second, the unprofitable rural sewerage services were removed from the jurisdiction of the water company.

When essential human services are provided by the state, the unique taxing powers of governments provide them with the capacity to redistribute income and implement cross-subsidies with the intent of increasing social equity and the well-being of the entire population. This redistributive capacity is often lost when essential services are unbundled and privatized.

Below are the five steps that the decentralization and unbundling processes have taken in Ghana's water sector. These changes set the stage for the privatization of Ghana's urban water sector:

1 Dissolution of the GWSC. The Ghana Water and Sewerage Corporation (GWSC), which was responsible for the provision, distribution and conservation of both the rural and urban supply of water, was dissolved in early 1999. It was replaced by two new institutions, the Ghana Water Company, Ltd (GWCL) and the Community Water and Sanitation Agency (CWSA).
2 Devolution of responsibility for rural water. The water supply systems in 110 rural communities and small towns were transferred to local level government known as district assemblies. Thus, the responsibility of rural water service was removed from the GWSC.
3 Creation of the CWSA. The government created the Community Water and Sanitation Agency (CWSA) in 1999 to facilitate the provision of safe water and sanitation services to rural communities and to provide technical assistance to the district assemblies.
4 Creation of the GWCL. The Ghana Water Company, Ltd (GWCL), created in 1999, is authorized to provide, distribute and conserve the water supply for public, domestic and industrial purposes. It has responsibility for approximately 101 urban water systems which include approximately 216,700 connections. These are the water systems to be transferred to the private companies.
5 Devolution of responsibility for urban sewerage. The responsibility for sewerage treatment in Accra was removed from the GWCL and transferred to the Metropolitan Authority.

More Reform in the Water Sector: The Regulatory Structure

To prepare for privatization, the government of Ghana formed the constitutionally mandated Public Utility Regulatory Commission (PURC) in 1997 to ensure appropriate regulation in the water and electricity sectors (PURC 1997). The tasks of the PURC include setting utility rates, protecting the interests of consumers, monitoring services and promoting fair competition. Unfortunately the PURC has been subjected to pressures from the IMF and World Bank to move rapidly towards full cost recovery and what is called an 'automatic tariff adjustment mechanism'.

The IMF decided that the PURC's implementation of a plan for full cost recovery and automatic tariff adjustment mechanisms should be a condition for the completion of the fifth review of Ghana's Poverty Reduction and Growth Facility loan (IMF 2002, p56). An automatic tariff adjustment mechanism would impose some formula whereby water tariff rates would fluctuate automatically with the shift of the Ghanaian currency on the international market. This would help protect large multinationals from exchange losses in the wake of currency depreciation. Since the Ghanaian currency has generally depreciated rather than appreciated on the international market this mechanism, along with the commitment to full cost recovery, virtually guaranteed a continued upward trend for consumer water fees.

The fact that the IMF attempted to use its influence as a lending institution to pressure the PURC to implement automatic tariff adjustments is a major example of institutional overreach. While the PURC has attempted to address affordability issues, non-compliance on the part of the PURC with IMF's loan conditions can threaten access to funding for the government of Ghana. In effect, the IMF interfered with the decision making of an independent Ghanaian regulatory body. Yet the IMF claims the loan condition is necessary to 'safeguard macroeconomic stability'.

The decision of the IMF to interfere in Ghanaian regulatory affairs sets a troubling precedent and raises serious concerns about the difficulties PURC will face in maintaining its independence from large water and electricity multinationals who are less inclined to be concerned about political process and even more focused on the bottom line. Given that the World Bank and IMF promote strengthening domestic legal and regulatory structures as a mechanism to ensure that privatization meets social equity goals, it is especially ironic that institutions appear to be intervening (on behalf of multinational corporate interests) in the independent policymaking of these regulatory bodies.

Civil Society Says 'No' to Water Privatization

In May 2001 a broad cross-section of Ghanaian civil society, including women's groups, religious organizations, trade unions, public health workers, environmental groups, organizations of the physically challenged and students, gathered together under the banner of the Ghana National Coalition Against the Privatization of Water (National CAP of Water) to organize opposition to the World Bank-backed proposal to privatize the urban water supply. They recognized that it would be no small task to oppose a project backed by the World Bank, large multinational corporations and the government of Ghana. In fact, the major corporate bidders interested in Ghana include some of the largest water multinationals in the world: Suez, Vivendi, SAUR and Biwater. The formation of the National CAP of Water expressed the deep and widespread concern that the privatization of water would have serious negative impacts on public health, women's work, access to safe, affordable water, national sovereignty, local control and accountability. The groups vowed to defend water as a public good and a human right, to build public awareness of the water privatization proposal, and to mobilize a broad cross-section of society to oppose the privatization of water.

The response to the public launching of the National CAP of Water was immediate as people reacted with indignation upon learning about the water privatization proposal. There was furious debate in public meetings, newspapers and on live radio talk shows. Government officials and the World Bank claimed they were not proposing water privatization but rather 'private sector participation' or PSP as they chose to call it. Regardless of the name, the idea of private sector involvement in water delivery and treatment appeared to be widely unpopular. The National CAP of Water demanded from the government a proper consultation with civil society on the proposal, full transparency of all bidding and consulting documents so that the public would be aware of the content of the proposal, and a commitment to examining a wide range of alternative solutions. Communities around the country organized themselves into Local Action Committees (LACs) and circulated petitions and statements rejecting privatization, demanded resources and re-engineering for the public water company, and universal access to clean and affordable water.

The water privatization proposal was unpopular, in part, because the preparation for privatization had already driven up consumer water prices. In 2001 IMF and World Bank loan conditions mandated a 95 per cent hike in consumer water rates and ongoing price hikes have been implemented (see Box 15.1 for a chronology of World Bank and IMF conditionalities). The free market policies of these institutions include full cost recovery. This means that consumers must pay the full cost of the operation and maintenance of the water utility. Government subsidies are reduced or cut entirely and consumer fees for water are increased. The increased revenue flows make the water utility more lucrative on the international market. Yet, the majority of the population in Ghana cannot afford to pay the market price for water. More than 50 per cent of the population earns less than US$1 a day and approximately 40 per cent fall below the national poverty line (IMF 2003). Currently, about 35 per cent of the Ghanaian population lack access to safe water and 68 per cent lack sanitation services (WSRS 2002a). A recent survey by the Ghana-based Integrated Social Development Center (ISODEC) demonstrates that poor households in five

Box 15.1 *Water sector reform conditions in IMF and World Bank loans to Ghana*

World Bank, Ghana Water Sector Restructuring Project. This US$100 million loan provides for the renovation and rehabilitation of urban water infrastructure in Ghana. The loan was originally scheduled for board approval in 2000, but has now been rescheduled three times. World Bank officials have stated that the loan will not be approved until the Government of Ghana (GOG) concludes contract negotiations with a private sector company.

International Monetary Fund, Poverty Reduction and Growth Facility Loan, fifth tranche (February 2002). This loan includes conditions requiring the 'early implementation of the Public Utilities Regulatory Commission's plan for full cost recovery in the public utilities, with automatic tariff adjustment formulae for electricity and water'.

World Bank, Third Economic Reform Support Operation Credit for Ghana (July 2001). This loan included a wide range of actions that the GOG was expected to complete prior to the approval of the loan. These actions included 'increasing electricity and water tariffs by 96 per cent and 95 per cent, respectively, to cover operating costs, effective May 2001'.

International Monetary Fund, Poverty Reduction and Growth Facility loan, fourth tranche (June 2001). This loan includes a long list of 'structural benchmarks'. Structural benchmarks are policy actions that will negatively influence the approval of future loans if the GOG does not comply with them. One of the many structural benchmarks requires 'publication by the Public Utility Regulatory Commission (PURC) of its strategy for achieving full cost recovery in the public utilities and implementation of automatic tariff adjustment formulae[2] for electricity and water'.

World Bank, Country Assistance Strategy (CAS) (June 2000). The World Bank's Country Assistance Strategy (CAS) describes the loans the Bank plans to extend to the GOG over the next two to three years. The 29 June 2000 CAS for Ghana proposes loans ranging between US$285 million and US$640 million. If the GOG adequately complies with conditions known as 'triggers' it will be eligible for more loans (closer to the US$640 million limit). If the government does not comply adequately with the triggers, it will be eligible for fewer loans (closer to the US$285 million). The triggers in Ghana's CAS require that the GOG expand private sector participation in infrastructure including power, urban water, rail and ports.

IMF and World Bank, Interim Poverty Reduction Strategy Paper (IPRSP) Policy Matrix (June 2000). The Poverty Reduction Strategy Paper (PRSP) is, in theory, a borrowing government document that provides the 'policy framework' for IMF and World Bank lending. In reality, borrowing governments know the spectrum of policies that the lending institutions find acceptable. However, it serves the political interests of the IMF and the World Bank to make their own policy conditionalities appear as if they are generated by the borrowing government. In practice, the Policy Matrix attached to the PRSP is often written by the IMF or the World Bank, rather than the borrowing government. The Policy Matrix for Ghana includes, under the policy area titled 'Urban Water', the following statement: 'Divest urban water systems to private sector operators: issue invitation for bids'.

> **Second Community Water and Sanitation Project (August 1999).** Performance triggers are the criteria or conditions used to evaluate an individual project and determine eligibility for subsequent loan instalments or loans for the project. One of the performance triggers for the Second Community Water and Sanitation Project includes achieving increased rates of cost recovery from rural communities.
>
> *Sources:* IMF and World Bank loan documents. Many are available at www.imf.org and www.worldbank.org

communities in Accra – Madina, Sukura, Mamobi, Nima and Ashaiman – spend between 18 and 25 per cent of their income on water alone (Amenga-Etego 2003).

During the last two decades rapid urban population increases and expansions in urban areas, particularly Accra, have contributed to a decrease in the percentage of urban households supplied with piped water. At a time when rapid urban growth necessitated greater public investment in the expansion of the water and sanitation infrastructure, government deficits and IMF and World Bank policies requiring budget cutbacks resulted in cutbacks in funding for the public water system. The result has been a major crisis in access to potable water. According to the Water Sector Restructuring Secretariat in Ghana, 53 per cent of the total population, and 78 per cent of the poor, have no piped water.

Households without access to piped water rely on a variety of less reliable and less hygienic sources, including mobile vendors (such as water tankers) and fixed vendors, shallow wells and deep wells, boreholes, springs, and/or commercially bottled or bagged water. A study of one urban area, Kumasi, found that 15–30 per cent of the population relies on hand-dug wells (ISODEC 2001). Supplies from untreated sources such as shallow wells, streams and rivers represent the greatest threat to public health because of the high exposure to contamination from improperly disposed sewage and refuse, as found in gutters and dumps, and industrial pollutants. According to UNICEF (2003), inadequate water and sanitation contributes to 70 per cent of diseases in Ghana.

The World Bank has used this crisis in the provision of water and sanitation services to argue that privatization or 'private sector participation' is the only reasonable solution to the problem and to label public institutions as inefficient, wasteful and corrupt. The National CAP of Water recognizes the urgent need to reform the public institutions responsible for providing water services but has responded with a campaign rooted in the conviction that reform of the water sector must first and foremost achieve protection of the rights of all to potable water by working towards universal access to water and sanitation services. The Accra Declaration, issued during the founding conference of the National CAP of Water, stated the following common principles, beliefs and values:

- That water is a fundamental human right, essential to human life to which every person, rich or poor, man or woman, child or adult is entitled.

- That water is not and should not be a common commodity to be bought and sold in the marketplace as an economic good.
- That water is a natural resource that is part of our common heritage to be used judiciously and preserved for the common good of our societies and the natural environment today and in the future.
- That water is an increasingly scarce natural resource, and as a result crucial to the securities of our societies and sovereignty of our country. For this reason alone, its ownership, control and delivery and management belong in the public domain today and tomorrow.

While the World Bank claims that the crisis can be solved by contracting operations to private multinational water companies, the National CAP of Water believes the public water system can be effectively reformed:

> We also recognize that even as the public is critical about the performance of our public institutions, many recognize the valiant efforts of thousands of workers, managers and engineers who provide services amidst neglect and difficult financial constraints. It is these efforts that convince us that under the right circumstances, Ghanaian workers, management and technical expertise, private businesses, artisans, community leaders, etc. can effectively reform the institution (ISODEC, undated).

Reform efforts would also need to strengthen local expertise and build the capacity of local management:

> We believe that any reform must be aimed at achieving FULL protection of the right of all to potable water. This necessarily entails primary reliance on local expertise, enterprises and institutions. To this end it must seek to strengthen rather than weaken public institutions. It must recognize and strengthen, rather than punish the efforts of workers and local management. In principle it should be locally driven rather than foreign-interest driven (ISODEC, undated).

The Ghana National CAP of Water has been highly successful in mobilizing a broad cross-section of Ghanaian society and building a forceful opposition to the privatization proposal. Key to the success has been the strong alliance built among communities, NGOs, trade unions, religious organizations and professionals. Ghana's trade union confederation, the Trade Union Congress (TUC), plays an important political role in Ghana and the TUC's outspoken opposition to the water privatization proposal was an important influence in the popular debate. In addition, 20 years of controversial IMF and World Bank policies have created profound scepticism towards privatization and trade liberalization as a solution to the country's problems, particularly when large foreign multinationals are involved.

In addition to building a broad-based campaign in Ghana, the National CAP of Water has effectively built linkages with a growing international network of organizations working to stop privatization of water resources. Members of the National CAP of Water toured internationally to speak about the issue. NGOs, journalists, academics, filmmakers and others travelled to Ghana to learn about the water privatization proposal. The National CAP of Water organized an international fact-finding mission to bring human rights lawyers, public health experts, trade unionists, environmentalists and others to analyse the World Bank's water privatization proposal. As opposition grew, both domestically and internationally, the World Bank, the government of Ghana, and the multinational water companies began reassessing their positions.

ELITE CONSULTATION: MANUFACTURING CONSENT

The decision to place Ghana's urban water system on the auction block and open it to bids from foreign multinational firms was hardly the outcome of an open, transparent and democratic decision making process. As noted above, external pressure on the government came primarily from multilateral creditors such as the World Bank and IMF. Yet the level of resistance to the water privatization scheme led the Ghanaian government and the World Bank to create an elaborate pretext of consultation and various public relations and communications strategies. While real consultation with the citizens of Ghana never took place, the World Bank and other bilateral donors funded numerous foreign consultants to produce studies favourable to privatization and even funded a special secretariat within the Ghanaian government to push forward the privatization scheme.

The Water Sector Restructuring Secretariat (WSRS), funded by the World Bank, and situated as a special elite body within the Ghanaian Ministry of Housing and Works, was charged with, amongst other things, rationalizing the privatization project to Ghanaian civil society. The WSRS claimed that there had been numerous workshops, consultations and participatory approaches. As opposition to the water privatization solidified, the WSRS became more vehement in defending its position. For example, in a document dated 8 March 2002, it stated:

> *Consultation with Ghanaians on the PSP (private sector participation) started in 1994 when a study of PSP options was commissioned. The study culminated in a three-day review workshop on 6–8 February 1995. At this workshop there were 60 participants from the Ministry of Works and Housing, Ministry of Local Government and Rural Department, Ministry of Transport and Communication, Members of Parliament, State Enterprises Commission, Public Services Commission, Office of Chief of Staff, Ghana Water and Sewerage Corporation, Water Resources Research Institute, GIMPA, World Vision Int. and individual consumers. Since then this participatory approach has been used in implementing the process* (WSRS 2002b).

Unfortunately, the water reform options presented at this workshop were restricted to different possible privatization schemes. Options for public sector reform were not included. In addition, the consultations identified above were primarily directed towards winning over various governmental bodies rather than involving a broad representation of civil society, with very few 'individual consumers' in attendance.

The WSRS also identified their 'public awareness campaign' as evidence of consultation and the participation of civil society. According to the WSRS the objective of the programme was to 'educate and inform the public on the benefits of the PSP to ensure that civil society adequately understands and appreciates the needs for the programme' (WSRS 2002b, Attachment 1). The pedantic tone of this approach attracted the ire of those who opposed the water privatization project, arguing that a more genuine consultation process would have been to listen to the viewpoints of consumer groups and citizens rather than trying to convince them of a predetermined position.

For all practical purposes the consultation was undertaken with foreign consultancy firms, rather than with the people of Ghana. Six major foreign consultancy firms were commissioned by the Ghanaian government, funded largely by loans from the World Bank and the British Department for International Development (DFID), to assess the reforms needed in Ghana's water sector. The consultant firms, two US firms and four UK firms, were all ideologically favourable to privatization and several had a history of working with the major multinational water companies. They all concluded that privatization was the best way forward and advised the government on tariff structure, institutional and regulatory structures, investment priorities and the 'business framework' for the privatization contract (see Box 15.2 for a list of these firms and their consultancy reports).

Temporary Victory

The persistent organizing of the National CAP of Water, and the groundswell of resistance that developed, led the government of Ghana, in early 2003, to issue an official statement suspending the privatization project. A number of obstacles had developed in the negotiation process and the major multinational water companies initially interested in bidding on the deal were reconsidering the terms they were willing to offer. They also saw increased political risks in the face of resistance. The World Bank had originally convinced the government of Ghana of the benefits of the privatization scheme by claiming that the private sector would bring significant investment capital to the project. However, the World Bank had to backtrack on this claim. Originally the private sector bidders agreed to bring a total of US$140 million of their own money to the project, but this was scaled back to US$60 million and then to zero in the current round of negotiations.

The reluctance of the major multinational water companies to invest capital in the Ghana project had a number of dimensions. Local resistance in Ghana

> **Box 15.2** *Major consultant firms commissioned on Ghana water privatization*
>
> **Louis Berger, USA:** *Republic of Ghana – Increased Private Sector Participation in the Urban Water Sector*, Final Business Framework Report for the Ministry of Works and Housing, September 1998.
>
> **London Economics and John Young & Associates, UK:** *Ghana Urban Water Supply: Demand Assessment and Willingness to Pay Study*, Progress Report, 12 February 1999.
>
> **Sir William Halcrow & Partners, Ltd, UK:** *Consultancy Services for the Restructuring of the Water Sector – Final Report – For the Republic of Ghana*, Ministry of Housing and Works, 1995.
>
> **Stone & Webster Consultants, USA:** *Information Memorandum, Republic of Ghana. Enhanced Leases for the Operation, Maintenance, and Management of Urban Water Supply Systems in Ghana*, March 2001.
>
> **The Adam Smith Institute, UK:** *Social Survey Workshop. Research Amongst Residential Households: The Research Process and Key Findings*, 21 March 2002.
>
> **WS Atkins International, Ltd, UK:** *Urban Water Sector Restructuring Project: Review of Investment Priorities*, Final Report, 17 April 2001.

combined with the financial collapse of two of the largest showcase water privatizations in the world (in Manila, Philippines, and Buenos Aires, Argentina) led Suez and other water multinationals to reassess their strategies. Key to this reassessment was the decision to reduce their exposure in developing countries. They were particularly concerned about the impact of developing country currency fluctuations on their profit margins. Rather than investing capital in developing countries Suez and the other major water companies are seeking shorter-term operation, service and management contracts. All of a sudden the World Bank was left holding a half empty bag of tricks. The government of Ghana stated that it was considering cancelling the privatization project altogether.

WORLD BANK LAUNCHES NEW PUBLIC RELATIONS CAMPAIGN

The main actors in the privatization negotiation – the government of Ghana, the World Bank and the bidding multinational corporations – were unprepared for the level of opposition encountered in Ghana. The multinational water companies grew more concerned about potential risks, were less interested in making a deal and proposed less attractive terms. The less attractive terms and the growing domestic opposition caused a number of sectors within the Ghanaian government to grow increasingly uneasy about the water privatization project. Only the World Bank remained adamant about pushing the water privatization project forward.

Unfortunately, because of the dependency on external loan resources, the World Bank holds significant influence over domestic policymaking in Ghana. Arguably, the Bank was concerned that dropping the privatization project altogether would appear to be admitting defeat, threatening the overall prestige and credibility of the World Bank programme in Ghana. Backing down on the water privatization project could also impact negatively on other pending privatization deals in the country. The World Bank views the water privatization project as pivotal for its overall privatization campaign in Ghana (major bank and electricity privatizations are in the works as well). In addition, Ghana is viewed as an important showcase for World Bank policy in all of West Africa and its water project in Ghana is seen as part of its overarching commitment to implementing the Millennium Development Goals of improving access to water and sanitation services.

For all of these reasons, the World Bank was unwilling to drop the water privatization scheme. Its answer to the stalemate was to launch a renewed public relations campaign to sell the programme. The first step in this programme was to remake the World Bank's Ghana country team. A new high-ranking country director for Ghana was hired: Matts Karlssen, a previous World Bank vice-president for public affairs. The Bank also hired a new water and sanitation specialist for West Africa and a new 'civil society specialist' for Ghana. The second step was to remake the image of the privatization project itself. The Bank is now claiming that in response to the concerns of civil society it has a new proposal. The new proposal is to offer the interested bidding water multinationals a three-year service management contract (as opposed to the previous ten-year lease contract). The government of Ghana has yet to approve the alternative proposal.

The National CAP of Water is concerned that a service management contract could be worse than a lease. With a lease arrangement, the private sector's reward is tied to performance and it faces the risk of lost invested capital and profits if it fails to perform. With the new service management contract now being proposed the government of Ghana will bear all the risks while the private company enjoys guaranteed payments. In addition, it is possible that the three-year contract is simply a manoeuvre to get a foot in the door. The three-year contract could contain a clause that offers the global water companies a ten-year lease or management contract after the three years are up.

The National CAP of Water argues that it is not fooled by the World Bank's new public relations scheme. The resistance to the privatization of water will continue and the National CAP of Water states that the ultimate objective remains clear: We must ensure that water remains in public hands and that access to potable water is available to all and guaranteed as a human right.

Notes

1 The World Bank discourse on 'governance' began in the 1990s and carefully overlooks the role that the institution's own policies have played in propping up authoritarian and corrupt governments.
2 Automatic tariff adjustment formulae require that tariffs reflect shifts in the international exchange rate of the cedi (Ghana's currency). In other words, consumer rates go up when the value of the cedi depreciates in international markets. This is a common requirement of multinational corporations who want to be shielded from the effects of shifts in soft currency exchange rates when they invest in developing countries.

References

Amenga-Etego, R. (2003) *Water Privatization in Ghana: Stillborn or Born Deformed?*, Integrated Social Development Centre, Accra
Bello, W., Kinley D. and Ellinson, E. (1982) *Development Debacle: The World Bank in the Philippines*, Institute for Food and Development Policy, San Francisco
Boafo-Arthur, K. (1999) 'Structural Adjustment Programs (SAPS) in Ghana: Interrogating PNDC's Implementation', *West Africa Review*, vol 1, no 1
Callaghy, T.M. (1990) 'Lost between State and Market: The Politics of Economic Adjustment in Ghana, Zambia and Nigeria', in J. Nelson (ed) *Economic Policy and Policy Choice*, Princeton University Press, Princeton, New Jersey
Financial Times (2002) 'The Enron collapse: Enron – over there and overpaying – two faces former chief', 12 February
Frimpong-Ansah, J. A. (1991) *The Vampire State in Africa: The Political Economy of Decline in Ghana*, James Currey, London
Gyimah-Boadi, E. (1990) 'Economic Recovery and Politics in PNDC's Ghana', *The Journal of Commonwealth and Comparative Politics*, vol 28, no 3
Iddi, A. (2003) *Ghana's Indebtedness: A Case of the Devil and the Deep Blue Sea?* Norfolk Education and Action for Development, Norfolk
ISODEC (Integrated Social Development Centre) (2001) 'Protecting the Rights of the Poor in Urban Water Reforms: A Social Mapping Exercise in Support of the Kumasi Water Improvement Project', Box 19452, Accra-North, Ghana
ISODEC (Integrated Social Development Centre) (undated) 'Why Water Privatization in Ghana Must be Stopped. In the interest of two transnational corporations, vested interests in Ghana, foreign governments and the World Bank conspire to violate our Rights to Water', ISODEC, Accra
IMF (International Monetary Fund) (2000) *Ghana: Selected Issues*, IMF Staff Country Report no 2
IMF (International Monetary Fund) (2002) 'Ghana – Fourth Review Under the Poverty Reduction and Growth Facility', Washington, DC, 1 February
IMF (International Monetary Fund) (2003) *Ghana: Poverty Reduction Strategy Paper*, IMF Country Report no 03/56
Kofi, A. (1997) 'Ghana-World Bank: Star Pupil has Second Thoughts on Reform', *InterPress Service*, 17 February
PURC (Public Utility Regulatory Commission) (1997) Establishment and Functions of Public Utility Regulatory Commission, Act 538, Accra, Ghana

SAPRI (Structural Adjustment Policy Review Initiative) (1998) *Ghana Opening National SAPRI Forum*, 'Civil Society Perspectives on Structural Adjustment Policies', 10–12 November
SAPRIN (Structural Adjustment Policy Review Initiative Network) (2001) *Impact of SAP on Availability and Access to Health Care*, Ghana Country Report, April
UNICEF (2003) 'Water Environment and Sanitation (WES) Country Profiles: Ghana', www.unicef.org/programme/wes/water_day/cases/ghana.htm
United Nations (2002) 'World Development Indicators: Ghana Country Profile', April
World Bank (1998) 'Ghana Water Sector Restructuring Project', Project Information Document, World Bank, Washington, DC
WSRS (Water Sector Restructuring Secretariat) (2002a) 'PSP in the Urban Water Sector in Ghana', Presentation, Ghana Ministry of Housing and Works, Accra, 5 February
WSRS (Water Sector Restructuring Secretariat) (2002b) 'Response to Christian AID/ ISODEC Anti-PSP Campaign', Ministry of Works and Housing, Accra, Ghana, 8 March

Box 7 *The Accra Declaration on the Right to Water*

Adopted 19 May 2001 by the Ghana National Coalition Against the Privatization of Water

At the end of four days of debate during the National Forum on Water Privatization in Accra, Ghana, which took place on 16–19 May, we declare as follows:

- We are a diverse group of individuals and organizations drawn from various parts of the country, and from other parts of Africa, Europe and the United States; [we are] involved in the private, public and voluntary sectors and working at varying levels of society.
- We are united by the following common principles, beliefs and values:
    - That water is a fundamental human right, essential to human life to which every person, rich or poor, man or woman, child or adult is entitled.
    - That water is not and should not be a common commodity to be bought and sold in the market place as an economic good.
    - Water is a natural resource that is part of our common heritage to be used judiciously and preserved for the common good of our societies and the natural environment today and in the future.
    - Water is an increasingly scarce natural resource, and as a result crucial to the securities of our societies and sovereignty of our country. For this reason alone, its ownership, control, delivery and management belong in the public domain today and tomorrow.
    - The public sector is legally and constitutionally mandated and designed to represent the public interest. The essential purpose of the private sector on the other hand is to make profit, not to promote the public good. Any public benefits arising from the private sector's activities are incidental, not designed. As a result, the private sector cannot be trusted with the public interest.
    - Citizens have the right to effectively participate (as distinguished from being informed) in the shaping of public policies which fundamentally affect their lives such as the control of water, and that government has a responsibility to enforce this right.
    - Community participation in the management of water systems is valid/legitimate, essential and beneficial to the overall effectiveness in affordable and sustainable water delivery.
    - Water management policies should be designed to ensure social equity such as gender equity, public health and environmental equity.

Guided by the above stated principles, we commit to:

- Forming and promoting a Ghana National Coalition Against the Privatization of Water herein called 'The Ghana National CAP of Water' which will be a broad coalition of individuals and organizations committed to the above principles and to the following objectives:

    - To conduct a broad-based campaign to ensure that all Ghanaians have access to adequate and affordable portable water by the year 2010.
    - To ensure that the right to water is explicitly guaranteed under the Constitution of the Republic of Ghana.

- To ensure that the ownership, control and management of water services remain in public hands.
- To promote public awareness and debate about the privatization process.
- To promote alternative solutions to the problems militating against universal access to water including problems of public management efficiency.

We recognize:

- The important role that the local private business sector can play, and should play, in partnership with communities, Ghanaian artisans and experts and local government in ensuring efficient and effective supply of water services.
- The inability of the Ghana Water Company Ltd (formerly Ghana Water and Sewerage Corporation) over the years to provide efficient and effective services resulting in public frustrations and some loss of faith in the company. However these perceived and real failures can only be appropriately understood within the context of the broader failure of governance and democracy over the years encompassing a wide range of institutions including the security services, the judiciary and many more. It is unlikely that the acceptable solution for the failures of these institutions will be to privatize them.
- The severe shortage of investment in the water sector required to deliver adequate and affordable water to all. Whilst the severity of this resource problem is itself debatable, it has nevertheless led to solutions resulting in heavy dependency on foreign creditors (especially the World Bank) which has in turn compelled the country to accept rigid conditionalities that have limited our options for financing and reforming the water sector.
- We recognize the close link between access to water and improved public health in view of the fact that nearly 70 per cent of all diseases in Ghana are currently water related.

We reject:

- The view that privatization (the participation of foreign transnational corporations) is the appropriate solution to the problems bedevilling our water sector.
- The view that 'to be private is to be efficient, and to be public is to be inefficient'.
- The view that the public sector, in this case the GWC Ltd, is incapable of being reformed to deliver water services efficiently and effectively to all.
- The view that the participation of communities in the management of urban water supply is not feasible and cannot be efficient.
- The commodification of water.
- Efficiency solutions which result in the violation of social and environmental rights and justice such as the rights of workers, women, children and the preservation of the natural environment.
- The World Bank imposed policy of charging rural and small town communities an upfront contribution to capital cost. This policy discriminates against rural and small town dwellers as it does not apply to those who reside in large cities. The policy has also resulted in excluding poor communities incapable of paying from enjoying their right to consume potable water.

(Note: This is an abbreviated version of the CAP Declaration. For the full text see www.isodec.org.gh/Papers/accradeclaration.PDF)

Index

NOTE: All acronyms and abbreviations are indexed under their full names only. See List of Acronyms and Abbreviations, page xii.

Accra, 278, 279n5, 283, 291–292
Ada/Gui Senior Citizens and Destitute Children's Association, 6, 271nn6 & 7, 273–274
African Development Bank (ADB), 225, 232, 234, 245
African National Congress (ANC), 5, 25–26, 35, 36, 109, 173; and municipal government in Nelspruit, 136–137, 138, 140, 143; and municipal reform in Eastern Cape, 148, 149, 151; and prepaid meters in Johannesburg, 120, 124, 125, 127; in rural South Africa, 206–220
agriculture, 7, 25, 44–50, 78, 93, 94, 118, 226, 258–261, 277
AIDS (HIV), 230, 255n2, 267
Alternative Information and Development Centre (AIDC), 36
Angola, 28, 35, 44, 46, 49, 50
Anti-Eviction Campaign, 6, 35, 188
Anti-Privatisation Forum (APF), 6, 16, 35, 36, 123, 125, 126, 188, 204–205
anti-privatization groups. *See* privatization: opposition to. *See also under names of individual groups*
apartheid, 9, 25, 32, 45, 46, 54, 55, 65–66, 130–131, 145, 148–150, 151, 167, 177, 185, 197, 206–207, 213, 220; anti-apartheid, 190, 198, 206; 'new apartheid', 267–270; post-apartheid, 4, 25, 48, 132, 148, 180, 183, 193
Argentina, 1, 152, 160, 163, 169, 287. *See also* Buenos Aires
Asmal, Kader, 209

Bantustans, 197
Berliner Wasser Betriebe (BWB), 261–262, 270nn2 & 3
Bill of Rights, South African, 59–73, 166
billing, of water, 6, 16, 37, 68, 70, 71, 99, 121, 123, 128; in Cape Town, 175, 177, 179–180, 182, 185; in Durban, 193, 195–196, 199–201; in Namibia, 263–267, 269; in Nelspruit, 131, 136, 140–145; in Zambia, 241, 254. *See also* pricing, of water; rates; tariffs, water
Biwater, 28, 106, 135–146
Black Local Authority (BLA), 173, 180
Botswana, 35, 44, 45, 47, 49, 50, 52, 54, 55, 198
bribery. *See* corruption
Britain. *See* United Kingdom
Buenos Aires, 31, 152, 162, 200, 287. *See also* Argentina
Build, Operate, Train and Transfer (BOTT), 5, 118, 152, 158, 169, 207, 209–212, 220

Build, Own, Operate and Transfer (BOOT), 16–17, 28, 200, 225, 233–234, 237
bulk water. *See* water: bulk
Buxton, Andrew, 86

Camdessus, Michel, 105
Canada, 33–34, 36, 91–92
Canadian International Development Agency (CIDA), 33–34
Canadian Union of Public Employees (CUPE), 36
Cape Metropolitan Area (CMA), 173, 175, 184
Cape Metropolitan Council (CMC), 174
Cape Town, City of, 5, 18, 19, 28, 32, 34, 38n8, 111, 112, 149, 168–184, 184nn2 & 3, 185nn8 & 10, 188
capital, accumulation of, 21, 30, 31
capitalism, 3, 13, 14, 19, 21–23, 31, 152, 155, 160, 162, 168, 204
community based organizations. *See* community groups
Central African Power Corporation (CAPC), 50
Central Governance Agency (CGA), 261
Chanakira Commission, 231, 233–236
cherry-picking. *See* ringfencing
children, 6, 68, 129, 167, 267, 270, 271nn6 & 7, 273–274, 277, 292
China, 1, 270
Chipulu, Charles, 254
cholera, 8, 46, 72, 167, 229
Citizen Utility Board (CUB), 65
civil society organizations, 6, 53, 83, 85, 170, 184, 185n12, 243, 255, 275, 278–281, 283–285, 286, 288
class, working, 73, 204, 265, 266, 269, 273
Coalition Against Water Privatization. *See* South African Coalition Against Water Privatization
Coates, Barry, 86

colonialism, 9, 43–46, 48, 227, 259, 269, 275
commercialization: and outsourcing, 177–179; in Cape Town, 168, 173, 177, 178; in Durban, 189–190, 197, 198, 201; in Namibia, 259–262, 264, 269, 270; in Pretoria, 99–115; in rural South Africa 207, 220; in urban South Africa, 59–73, 81, 94, 120, 129, 166; in Zambia, 243–255, 255n2; in Zimbabwe, 227; of water, theories of, 3–9, 13, 17–37
Committee on Economic, Social and Cultural Rights (CESCR), 60, 62, 67
commodification, 3, 5, 6, 9, 13, 19–24, 31, 118, 163, 177, 204, 292
community groups, 2, 5, 15, 17, 27, 29, 35, 36, 80, 92, 149, 218, 246, 273
Community Water and Sanitation Agency (CWSA), 279nn1 & 3
Community Water Supply and Sanitation (CWSS), 212
competitiveness, 16–18, 21–22, 30, 47, 107, 108, 118, 170, 171, 177, 184, 199, 201, 210, 226, 234, 261, 280; and GATS, 82, 83, 87, 90; in Eastern Cape, 152, 158, 160, 162
Compliance Monitoring Unit (CMU), 138
conditionalities. *See* privatization: conditionalities of
Congo, Democratic Republic of the (DRC), 35, 44, 48, 50, 51
Congress of South African Trade Unions (Cosatu), 26, 36, 143, 144
Constitution, of South Africa, 4, 59–73, 87, 166, 205, 211, 291
constitutional issues, 4, 24, 59–73, 99, 107, 118, 126, 166–167, 174, 175, 183, 184n5, 219, 268–269, 280, 291
consultants, 8, 32, 33, 84, 109, 138, 144, 170, 207, 208, 210, 216, 220n2, 225, 285, 286–287

consumption, water, 9, 20, 26, 48, 67, 73, 129, 142, 238; in Cape Town, 174–176, 185; in Durban, 192, 194–196; in Eastern Cape, 152, 154, 157; in Johannesburg, 120, 123, 124, 127; in Namibia, 265, 268; in rural South Africa, 215–219; in Tshwane, 101, 102–104, 108, 110, 112, 115; in Zambia, 247–252
Corporate Europe Observatory (CEO), 86
corporatization, 3–6, 14, 17–18, 19, 23–25, 28–29, 34, 38, 59, 63–64, 65, 76, 204; in Cape Town, 168–184, 184n2; in Durban, 200; in Eastern Cape, 158; in Johannesburg, 120, 122; in Namibia, 260, 264; in Tshwane, 99–115; in Zambia, 247; in Zimbabwe, 225
corruption, 1, 4, 21, 152, 160, 162, 233, 242, 245, 253, 254, 273, 278, 283, 288n1
cost analysis, 3, 17, 30
cost recovery, 3, 8, 14, 17–18, 23, 25–26, 28–29, 34, 46, 55–56, 59, 65–67, 83, 99, 109–110, 112–115, 130, 136, 155, 166–167; in Cape Town, 168, 169, 171, 173–183, 185n12; in Durban, 189, 200; in Ghana, 280–283; in Namibia, 258–269; in rural South Africa, 207, 210, 212–220; in Zambia, 245–246, 248, 252–254; in Zimbabwe, 227, 238
Council of Tshwane Metropolitan Municipality (CTMM), 99–131
country assistance strategy (CAS), 282
credit meters, 114, 121, 268
cross-subsidization, 17–19, 66, 89, 100, 108–110, 113, 154, 175, 176, 199, 252, 262, 264–265, 279
cutoffs, water, 4–5, 14, 28, 37, 38n6, 67–71, 118, 187, 204, 273–274; in Cape Town, 173, 178–185; in Durban, 193–196; in Eastern Cape, 156; in Johannesburg, 121, 122; in Namibia, 265–266, 269, 270; in Nelspruit, 139, 140; in Tshwane, 99, 101, 108, 111–113

dams, 7, 16, 30, 49, 50, 79, 174–175, 190, 208, 209, 225, 228, 232–234, 236–237, 238, 259, 262, 266, 276. *See also* Kunzwi Dam
debt collection, 3, 38, 68, 70, 113, 121, 128, 161, 237
decentralization, 34, 169, 179, 182–183, 244, 278–279
Democratic Republic of the Congo. *See* Congo, Democratic Republic of the
Democratic Resettlement Community (DRC), 267, 268
Department for International Development (DFID), 33, 286
Department of Provincial and Local Government (DPLG), 26, 71, 130, 139
Department of Trade and Industry (DTI), 65, 87–88, 91, 92, 95nn5 & 6
Department of Water Affairs and Forestry (DWAF), 25, 27, 34, 38, 46, 51, 54, 90, 91, 99, 109, 135, 139, 159, 160, 163nn2 & 4, 174, 184n5; and rural South Africa, 208–220
Department of Water Development (DWD), 237
Development Bank of South Africa (DBSA), 32, 133–135, 138–139, 225, 232, 245
development banks, 6, 32, 37, 130, 225, 232, 245
Devolution Trust Fund (DTF), 246, 249
disconnections. *See* cutoffs, water.
district councils (DC), 47
divestiture, 2, 3, 14–16, 26, 28, 169, 251, 261, 282
Doha, 27, 88, 118

Doha Development Agenda (DDA), 88
Dolphin Coast, 28, 31, 211
drip valves. *See* trickle meters
Durban, 5, 18, 28, 29, 35, 106, 183, 188, 189–202

Eastern Cape, 5, 28, 38n6, 73, 148–163, 209, 212, 214–217
economic growth, 53, 132, 252, 277
Economic Structural Adjustment Program (ESAP), 226
electricity, 2, 24, 29, 34, 37, 50, 56, 64, 68–70, 78–79, 128–129, 188, 204, 273–274; in Eastern Cape, 151, 153, 157, 159; in Ghana, 280, 282, 288; in Johannesburg, 125; in Namibia, 264, 265; in Nelspruit, 142; in Tshwane, 99, 100, 105, 112, 114; in Zambia, 243, 252; in Zimbabwe, 226, 227
England. *See* United Kingdom
Environmentally Sound Management of Inland Waters (Eminwa), 50
Erwin, Alec, 88, 95n6
Eskom, 29, 30, 48, 54, 118, 151, 159
eThekwini Water Services (eTWS), 189–202
European Investment Bank (EIB), 32, 225, 233–236, 262
European Services Forum (ESF), 84, 85, 86
European Union (EU), 79, 84–87, 88, 90, 92–93, 95n2, 208
eviction, 5, 6, 35, 37, 113, 118, 166, 180, 189, 191, 204, 206, 267, 269, 273–274

Federation of Free Trade Unions Zambia (FFTUZ), 243
Fort Beaufort, 5, 148–149, 154, 157, 159, 163n3
France, 2, 19, 32, 38n8, 92, 122, 148, 150–153, 154, 159, 160, 192, 211, 232, 262

free basic water, 4–5, 7, 26, 37, 47, 55, 59, 62, 66, 67, 71–73, 82, 89, 95, 118, 166, 188, 220; in Cape Town, 175–177, 184n5; in Durban, 189–202; in Johannesburg, 124, 125; in Nelspruit, 139, 140, 141; in Tshwane, 99, 101, 105, 108, 110, 112, 113, 115; in Zambia, 248, 251, 254
French Development Agency (AFD), 232, 234
Friends of the Earth International (FOEI), 84

gender, 44, 129, 170, 291
General Agreement on Tariffs and Trade (GATT), 77
General Agreement on Trade and Services (GATS), 4, 27, 32, 77–95, 118, 170
Germany, 33, 225, 245, 258–259, 260–262
Gesellschaft für Technische Zusammenarbeit (GTZ), 33, 260
Ghana, 6–7, 29, 32–33, 35–36, 199, 253, 275–289, 291–292
Ghana National CAP of Water, 6–7, 35, 36, 275, 281, 283–286, 288, 291–292
Ghana Water and Sewerage Corporation (GWSC), 279
Ghana Water Company, Ltd (GWCL), 279
GKU Consultants, 225, 227, 230, 234–235
Global Water Partnership (GWP), 34
governance, 33, 53, 77, 135, 144, 161, 170, 172–173, 183, 231, 261, 277, 288n1, 292
government, local, 17, 25, 26, 32, 34, 64, 66, 91, 92, 93, 128, 166–167, 292; in Cape Town, 169–170, 171, 172, 173, 177, 183, 184n2; in Durban, 196; in Eastern Cape, 149, 150, 157, 160, 161; in Johannesburg, 121, 126; in

INDEX   297

Namibia, 264–265, 269; in Nelspruit, 131, 133, 136, 140; in rural South Africa, 211, 212, 213; in Tshwane, 99, 108; in Zimbabwe, 227, 230, 236
Greater Nelspruit Utility Company (GNUC), 130, 134–135, 139, 140–145
groundwater. *See* water: groundwater
Growth, Employment and Redistribution (GEAR), 118, 133, 166

Harare, 6, 45, 46, 225–238. *See also* Zimbabwe
Harare Water and Sewerage Authority (HWASA), 234–236
health care, 2, 8, 14, 24, 31, 60, 77, 92, 93, 230, 277
Heavily Indebted Poor Country Initiative (HIPC), 276
HIV. *See* AIDS (HIV)
housing, 7, 24, 60, 63, 114, 143, 151, 182, 188, 195, 196, 230, 250, 263, 269, 273, 278, 285. *See also* settlements, informal

iGoli 2002, 122, 204
Inanda, 190, 193, 200
Independent Municipal and Allied Trade Union (Imatu), 143, 144
indigent policies, 99–100, 108, 113–115, 160
industry, 30, 38, 45–48, 84, 89, 154, 199, 231, 246, 265, 276; service industry, 83–86
inflation, 146n4, 156, 199, 208, 210, 235, 237, 254, 255n3, 277
informal settlements. *See* settlements, informal
infrastructure, 7–9, 14, 26, 28, 30, 31, 33, 46, 61, 65, 66, 72, 118, 166–167, 273–274; in Cape Town, 175, 177, 178, 180; in Durban, 192, 196, 197; in Eastern Cape,

155, 157, 162, 163; in Ghana, 282, 283; in Johannesburg, 126; in Nelspruit, 131, 133, 134, 135, 141, 142, 145; in Namibia, 264; in rural South Africa, 208–209, 212, 213, 214, 216; in Tshwane, 100, 105, 107, 110, 113; in Zambia, 244, 247, 248, 250; in Zimbabwe, 229, 233
institutional strengthening (IS), 233, 235–236
Institutional Strengthening and Priority Rehabilitation (ISPR), 235
Integrated Social Development Centre (ISODEC), 281
integrated water resource management (IWRM), 51, 52, 55
Interim Poverty Reduction Strategy Paper (IPRSP), 282
International Consortium of Investigative Journalists (ICIJ), 36
international financial institutions (IFIs), 25, 32, 113, 241, 243
International Monetary Fund (IMF), 33, 37, 105, 118, 241–243, 250, 254, 261, 276–285

Japan Services Network (JSN), 84–85
Johannesburg, 5, 27, 28, 29, 31, 33, 34, 36, 37n2, 45, 106, 152, 183, 188, 204–205; compared with Cape Town and Tshwane, 111, 112; prepaid meters in, 120–127
Johannesburg Bylaws, 69–70
Johannesburg Water (JW), 71, 73, 120–127, 204–205

KaNyamanzane, 135, 136, 140, 142, 143
Kasrils, Ronnie, 28, 29, 191, 198, 208
Kaunda, Kenneth, 240, 241
Khor, Martin, 88
Konkola Copper Mines (KCM), 243
Kotze, Rolf, 133

Kunzwi Dam, 225, 232–237
Kunzwi files, 225–226, 228, 232–233
KwaMashu, 190, 192, 194, 195
KwaZulu-Natal, 66, 72, 192, 197–198, 206, 208, 209, 210–212, 214–215, 218–219

labour groups, 4-6, 26, 29, 35, 80, 91, 92, 94, 139, 143–144, 242, 243, 253–255, 270. *See also under names of individual unions*
lakes, 52, 228, 230
legislative issues, 4, 13, 15, 24–27, 29, 34, 60–63, 65, 68, 71–73, 86, 144, 150, 166, 178, 227; in Namibia, 259, 269; in Zambia, 240, 244, 245–246, 249, 255
Lesotho, 35, 44, 45, 48, 49, 54, 198
Liberalization of Trade in Services (LOTIS), 86, 95n4
local action committees (LACs), 281
Lochner, Andre, 110
Lusaka, 6, 50, 240–255. *See also* Zambia
Lusaka Water and Sewerage Company (LWSC), 247–248, 250–254, 255n2

Macleod, Neil, 189, 191, 193, 194, 196, 197, 199
Malawi, 35, 44, 45, 49, 50, 52, 54, 56, 198
Mamdouh, Hamid, 94
Mandela, Nelson, 34, 35, 69
Manila, 31, 152, 287. *See also* Phillipines
marginal cost, 65, 171, 175, 184
marketization, 13, 21, 24, 29, 31, 34, 169, 204
Marx, Karl, 21
Matsulu, 132–133, 135–136, 140, 142–143
Mbeki, Thabo, 26, 88, 191, 198
Mbombela Municipality, 136–137, 144, 145

Medium Term Expenditure Framework (MTEF), 213
meter reading, 3, 14, 18, 23, 28, 121, 178, 184
Ministry of Agriculture, Water and Rural Development (MAWRD), 159
Ministry of Local Government, National Housing and Public Works (MLGNH&PW), 230–236
Ministry of Rural Resources and Water Development (MRR&WD), 232
Moeng, Harold, 135, 140, 141
Moore, Michael, 88
Mouton, Frans, 106, 107
Mozambique, 6, 24, 28, 32, 35, 44, 46, 49, 50, 54, 56
Muller, Mike, 27, 91, 213, 216, 219
Multilateral Agreement on Investment (MAI), 93
multinationals, 5, 15, 24, 28–31, 94, 122, 148, 163, 166; in Durban, 192, 199–200; in Ghana, 275–289; in Namibia, 261, 262; in Zimbabwe, 225, 232, 238
Municipal Infrastructure Investment Unit (MIIU), 8, 33, 134, 139, 150, 158, 161
Municipal Systems Act (South Africa), 25, 26, 65–66, 69, 107, 113
Mvula Trust, 29, 34, 210, 216–219
Mzinyathi, 190

Namibia, 6, 24, 28, 32–33, 35, 36, 44–45, 49–50, 52, 54, 258–271, 273
Namibia Water Resources Management Review (NWRMR), 260–261
Namwater Corporation, 260–266, 270n5, 271n8
National Coalition Against the Privatization of Water. *See* Ghana National CAP of Water
National Water Policy (Zambia), 245, 246

National Water Supply and Sanitation Council (NWASCO), 246–250, 253
Ncalo, Themba, 99, 112, 115n5
Nelspruit, 5, 28, 33, 106, 130–146, 211
neoliberalism, 2, 6–7, 9, 15, 20, 29, 36, 37, 52, 56, 109, 110, 122, 127, 161, 166, 189, 199, 226, 276, 277; ideology of, in Zambia, 240, 242, 243, 245, 254, 255; 'second wave', 168–185
New Economic Recovery Programme (NERP), 241
New Partnership for Africa's Development (Nepad), 29, 118
Nigeria, 29
Nkrumah, Kwame, 275, 276
nongovernmental organizations (NGOs), 2, 4, 15, 17, 18, 20, 27, 29, 31, 33, 34, 35, 36, 43, 45, 50, 51, 52, 80, 86, 91, 94, 96; in Ghana, 284, 285; in rural South Africa, 204, 210; in Tshwane, 102, 107, 110; in Zambia, 240, 243, 244, 248, 250, 255n2
nonpayment, of services, 31, 37, 67–69; in Cape Town, 180, 181, 183, 185; in Durban, 193; in Eastern Cape, 155; in Johannesburg, 122, 123, 124, 126; in Namibia, 263, 265; in Nelspruit, 134, 136, 138, 139–141, 144–145; in rural South Africa, 218; in Tshwane, 100, 112, 113; in Zimbabwe, 229–230
Northern Cape, 212, 215, 219
Northern Pretoria Municipal Sub-Structure (NPMSS), 103, 104

operating and management (O&M), 212–215
Orange Farm, 120, 124–125, 204–205
Organization for Economic Cooperation and Development (OECD), 91, 94
outsourcing, 3, 18, 23, 27–29, 264; in Cape Town, 173, 177–180, 184n1, 185n8; in Eastern Cape, 149–150, 152, 156, 159–160, 162; in Tshwane, 101, 108, 113–114

Palast, Gregory, 86, 95n3
Palmer Development Group (PDG), 189
Pan African Congress (PAC), 136–137
Panitchapakdi, Supachai, 85
participatory budgeting, 8
peri-urban areas, 46, 115n4, 145, 215, 244, 246–249, 251, 253, 255n2
Philippines, 1, 152, 287. *See also* Manila
Phiri, 123, 125, 126, 167, 204–205, 219
policymakers, 2–4, 6, 25, 29, 32, 38n8, 47, 48, 53, 55, 90, 122, 240, 243, 254, 280, 288
post-apartheid. *See* apartheid: post-apartheid
poverty, 45, 101, 104, 128–129, 162, 167, 190, 206; in Cape Town, 170, 172, 173, 176, 177, 180, 182, 183; in Ghana, 274, 281; in Nelspruit, 132, 141, 142, 145; in Zambia, 244, 250, 251
Poverty Reduction Strategy Paper (PRSP), 244
prepaid meters (PPM), 4–7, 14, 23, 34, 93, 128–129, 167, 204–205, 252; constitutional implications of, 59, 66, 68, 70–71; in Johannesburg, 120–127; in Namibia, 264, 267–271; in rural South Africa, 214, 219; in Tshwane, 112, 118
Pretoria, 4, 28, 66, 99–115. *See also* Tshwane
PriceWaterhouseCoopers (PWC), 32, 84–86
pricing, of water, 1, 6, 55–56, 59, 64–67, 73, 166, 215; in Cape Town, 171, 173–177, 183; in Durban, 192, 198; in Eastern Cape, 157, 162; in Ghana, 281; in Namibia, 260, 263–266; in

Nelspruit, 140, 142; in Tshwane, 106, 113, 114; in Zambia, 248, 251; in Zimbabwe, 233, 234. *See also* billing, of water; rates; tariffs, water
priority rehabilitation (PR), 236
Private Sector Investment (PSI), 18, 24, 33, 133–134, 138–139, 252
private sector participation (PSP), 2, 15, 17, 134, 250, 252–253, 254, 281, 285–286
private sector partnerships (PSPs), 14, 29, 135
privatization: alternatives to, 7–9; conditionalities of, 4, 6, 8, 30, 32, 33, 56, 225, 234–236, 238, 253, 254; definition of, 2–4, 13–17; opposition to, 1–9, 13, 23, 35–37, 243
Privatization Authority of Zimbabwe (PAZ), 226–227
Project Implementation Unit (PIU), 235–236
Public-Private Infrastructure Advisory Facility (PPIAF), 247, 250, 252
public–private partnerships (PPPs), 2–3, 5, 8, 13–15, 23, 26, 27, 29, 32–34, 43, 56, 101, 118; in Eastern Cape, 148, 162; in Namibia, 261, 262; in Nelspruit, 133, 136, 138–139; in rural South Africa, 209, 220
public–public partnerships (PUPs), 8, 56
Public Sector Reform Programme (PSRP), 240, 243, 250, 282
Public Services International (PSI), 36
Public Utility Regulatory Commission (PURC), 280, 282
push button taps, 112–113

Queenstown, 5, 148–163

race, 44, 104, 268

Rall, Martin, 207, 210, 211
Rand Water, 29, 101, 112, 115n4
rates, 1, 65, 66, 99–100, 107, 113, 143, 153–154, 175, 177, 195, 220, 230, 248, 264, 280–281; boycotts of rates, 113, 141, 185; ratepayers, 65, 229. *See also* billing, of water; pricing, of water; tariffs, water
Rawlings, Flight Lt., 276–278
Reconstruction and Development Programme (RDP), 166, 207–208, 213–218
redistribution, of wealth, 9, 67, 108, 133, 179
Reeve, Charles, 208, 210, 211, 216, 218
ringfencing, 3, 8, 17–18, 25, 29, 66, 100, 105–106, 158, 171, 198, 234, 236, 247, 260, 278–279
rivers, 34, 47–51, 54–56, 101, 196, 216, 238, 258, 263, 268, 271, 283
rural areas, 5, 22, 31, 44, 46, 47, 50, 66, 72, 135, 145, 152, 158, 206–220, 280, 277–279, 279nn1, 2 & 3, 283, 292

sanitation, 1, 14–17, 23–26, 33, 34, 38, 44, 46, 70, 77, 82, 166–167; in Eastern Cape, 151, 153, 159; in Ghana, 278, 279, 281, 283, 288; in Johannesburg, 120, 122, 124; in Namibia, 260, 264; in Nelspruit, 131, 133, 135, 139, 141, 143, 146; in rural South Africa, 206, 208, 212, 213; in Tshwane, 99, 100, 110, 114, 115, 115n1; in Zambia, 250, 251, 254; in Zimbabwe, 225, 229, 232, 234–236
settlements, informal, 15, 17, 31, 45, 72, 124, 178–179, 190–191, 201, 206–207, 244, 259, 264, 267–268
Severn-Trent International Plc, 240, 250–254
sewerage. *See* toilets; waste management
Siwela, Sipho, 137

social movements, 9, 37, 83, 204
South Africa, 1, 3–6, 8, 24–38, 44, 56, 95nn5 & 7, 259, 265, 269. *See also* Cape Town; Constitution, of South Africa; Durban; GATS; Johannesburg; Nelspruit; Pretoria; rural areas
South African Coalition Against Water Privatization, 6, 35, 166–167
South African Municipal Workers' Union (Samwu), 6, 35–36, 73, 128–129, 143–144, 178
South African Water Caucus, 6, 35, 118–119
South West Africa (SWA), 259
Southern African Development Community (SADC), 4–6, 24, 25, 27, 33, 34, 36, 43–56, 262
Southern African Power Pool (SAPP), 48
Southern and Eastern African Trade, Information and Negotiations Institute (SEATINI), 36
Southern Electricity Company (SELCo), 265
Soweto, 73, 120, 123–125, 167, 204–205, 219
special purpose company (SPC), 233
State-Owned Enterprises Governance Council (SOEGC), 261
structural adjustment policies (SAPs), 242, 276–277
structural adjustment programmes, 6, 53, 56, 118, 250, 277
Suez, 14, 15, 28, 31, 85, 87, 93, 106, 122, 148–152, 162, 278, 281, 287
Swaziland, 24, 35, 44, 45, 49, 50, 54
Swedish International Development Agency (SIDA), 55

Tanzania, 28, 35, 44, 49, 50, 54, 56
tariffs, water, 5, 6, 16, 26, 55, 65–67, 72, 89, 127; in Cape Town, 174–177; in Durban, 192, 195–199; in Eastern Cape, 155–159; in Ghana, 280, 282, 286, 289n2; in Namibia, 260–266, 270; in Nelspruit, 131, 138, 142; in rural South Africa, 211–220; in Zambia, 245–252; in Zimbabwe, 232, 233, 235; in Tshwane, 99–115; lifeline, 55, 66, 213. *See also* billing, of water; pricing, of water; rates
Tawengwa, Solomon, 229, 230–234, 236
Thompson Report, 229–231
toilets, 72, 125, 153, 177, 194, 195, 219, 263, 266, 274
townships, 5, 72, 73, 219; in Cape Town, 173–185; in Durban, 190–201; in Eastern Cape, 150, 151, 154, 156; in Johannesburg, 120–125; in Namibia, 263, 265–266, 268; in Nelspruit, 130–145; in Tshwane, 99–101
Trade Union Congress (TUC), 284
Transnational Local Council (TLC), 131–133, 153
trickle meters, 14, 67, 72, 122, 129, 142, 143, 161, 193–194, 202n6, 219
Tshwane, 4–5, 28, 99–115, 115nn4 & 5. *See also* Pretoria
Tygerberg, 173, 175–182, 184n2

Umgeni Water, 29, 151, 190–201, 212
unaccounted-for water (UAW), 123, 143, 174, 192
unbundling, of services, 171, 178–179, 278–279. *See also* ringfencing
unemployment, 45, 124, 125, 132, 133, 140, 141, 149, 162, 190, 167, 273
United Kingdom, 1, 2, 14, 15, 22, 28, 33, 65, 68, 71, 73, 111, 128–129, 149, 151, 169, 211, 232, 240, 250, 269; and GATS, 85, 86, 92, 95n3; and prepaid meters, 120, 122, 126; and Ghana, 275, 286, 287

United National Independence Party (UNIP), 241, 242, 248, 251
United Nations (UN), 1, 14, 33, 34, 50, 51, 60, 78
United Nations Conference on Environment and Development (UNCED), 51
United Nations Development Program (UNDP), 14, 33, 34
United Nations Educational Scientific and Cultural Organization (UNESCO), 34
United Nations Environment Program (UNEP), 50
United States, 15, 25, 30–32, 36, 64, 66, 69, 70, 84–85, 86, 88, 152, 160, 286, 287, 291; USAID, 8, 33, 134, 228

Vivendi Universal, 14, 15, 28, 30, 84–85, 87, 93, 152, 162, 192, 199–200, 262, 278, 281

waste management, 2, 6, 8, 18, 24, 93
water: bulk, 6, 15, 29, 46, 115n4, 135, 156, 196–199, 201, 211, 212, 233, 237, 259–263–265; credits, 6, 267; groundwater, 46, 52, 112, 259, 262; quality of, 47, 51, 56, 66, 79, 138, 154, 160, 216, 228, 230, 260, 270; quantity of, 47, 51, 66, 67, 154, 156, 160, 196, 270; production of, 3, 9, 20, 22, 23, 48, 50, 99, 148, 173, 197, 237; restrictions, 5, 14, 67–71, 101, 108, 113, 161, 190, 193–196, 199; scarcity of, 9, 43, 44, 52, 167, 174, 177; tankers, 102, 124, 283; tanks, 135, 190–192, 196, 209; treatment of, 16, 153, 228. *See also* billing, of water; consumption, water; cutoffs, water; dams; free basic water; lakes; pricing, of water; push button taps; tariffs, water; toilets; trickle meters; unaccounted-for water; yard taps

Water and Sanitation Committee (WASCO), 260
water demand management (WDM), 55, 173–174, 177, 183, 238
Water, Engineering and Development Centre (WEDC), 189
Water Environment and Sanitation (WES)
Water Resources Management Strategy (WRMS)
Water Sector Restructuring Secretariat (WSRS), 285–286
Water Services Development Plan (WSDP), 106–107
Water Services South Africa (WSSA), 150, 151–152, 157–159, 161, 163n1
Water Supply and Sanitation Collaborative Council (WSSCC), 14, 34, 114
Water Supply and Sanitation Policy (WSSP), 260
Wesselius, Eric, 86, 95n3
Windhoek, 45, 49, 261–267, 270n3, 273
Witwatersrand, 45, 204
women, 17, 125, 129, 268, 280, 281, 292
World Bank, 1, 6, 14, 30, 32–34, 37, 37n1, 112, 118, 142, 160, 163, 170, 174, 189, 210, 260; programmes of, in Zimbabwe, 225–227, 230; support from, in Zambia, 240, 242–245, 247, 250–254; and Ghana, 275–289, 292. *See also* privatization: conditionalities of
World Conservation Union (IUCN), 34
World Health Organization, 14, 46, 73
World Summit on Sustainable Development (WSSD), 27
World Trade Organization (WTO), 4, 77–81, 83–88, 91, 92–94, 95nn3, 5 & 6, 118–119, 170
World Water Council (WWC), 34–35

yard taps, 101, 102, 115n2, 131, 135, 156, 157, 184, 214

Zambezi River Action Plan (Zacplan), 50–51
Zambezi River Authority (ZRA), 34, 50
Zambia, 6, 24, 28, 33, 35, 36, 44, 45, 50, 54, 240–255. *See also* Lusaka
Zambia Congress of Trade Unions (ZCTU), 242–243
Zambia United Local Authorities Workers Union (Zulawu), 154, 155n4
Zimbabwe, 6, 24, 28–29, 35, 36, 44–45, 47, 49–52, 54, 55, 126, 225–238, 262. *See also* Harare
Zimbabwe National Water Authority (ZINWA)
Zimbabwe Program for Economic Transformation (ZIMPREST), 226